Pennant Hopes Dashed by the
Homer in the Gloamin'

ALSO BY RONALD T. WALDO AND FROM MCFARLAND

Hazen "Kiki" Cuyler: A Baseball Biography (2012)

*The Battling Bucs of 1925: How the Pittsburgh Pirates
Pulled Off the Greatest Comeback in World Series History* (2012)

*Fred Clarke: A Biography of the Baseball
Hall of Fame Player-Manager* (2011)

Pennant Hopes Dashed by the Homer in the Gloamin'

The Story of How the 1938 Pittsburgh Pirates Blew the National League Pennant

Ronald T. Waldo

McFarland & Company, Inc., Publishers
Jefferson, North Carolina, and London

LIBRARY OF CONGRESS CATALOGUING-IN-PUBLICATION DATA

Waldo, Ronald T.
 Pennant hopes dashed by the homer in the gloamin' : the story of how the 1938 Pittsburgh Pirates blew the National League pennant / Ronald T. Waldo.
  p. cm.
 Includes bibliographical references and index.

 ISBN 978-0-7864-7202-4
 softcover : acid free paper ∞

 1. Pittsburgh Pirates (Baseball team)—History—20th century. 2. National League of Professional Baseball Clubs—History. I. Title.
 GV875.P5W36 2013
 796.357'6409043—dc23   2013020695

BRITISH LIBRARY CATALOGUING DATA ARE AVAILABLE

© 2013 Ronald T. Waldo. All rights reserved

No part of this book may be reproduced or transmitted in any form or by any means, electronic or mechanical, including photocopying or recording, or by any information storage and retrieval system, without permission in writing from the publisher.

On the cover: The infield of the 1938 Pittsburgh Pirates. From left to right, third baseman Jeep Handley, shortstop Arky Vaughan, second baseman Pep Young and first baseman Gus Suhr (National Baseball Hall of Fame Library, Cooperstown, New York)

Manufactured in the United States of America

McFarland & Company, Inc., Publishers
 Box 611, Jefferson, North Carolina 28640
 www.mcfarlandpub.com

Table of Contents

Acknowledgments vi
Preface 1

1. Murderers' Row and the Waner Brothers 5
2. Bill Benswanger and Arky Vaughan Arrive on the Scene 25
3. New Blood Offers Hope to Pirates Fans for 1938 Season 40
4. Bad Luck During Spring Training in San Bernardino 53
5. Bucs Bust Out of the Gate Due to Arky Vaughan's Heroics 69
6. Paul Waner's Slump and Talk of Rebuilding for Next Year 88
7. Pirates Regroup as Benswanger and
   Traynor Nix Deal with New York Giants 107
8. Johnny Rizzo Shines as Pirates Climb into First Place 126
9. Pittsburgh Feels the Pressure and
   Starts to Wilt in the Summer Heat 146
10. Traynor's Boys Attempt to Hang on While Chicago Surges .. 166
11. Pittsburgh's Final Collapse and the Homer in the Gloamin' .. 186
12. Disastrous Season and a Second-Division Finish in 1939 207
13. The End of an Era 222

Appendix A: 1938 Pittsburgh Pirates Roster 232
Appendix B: 1938 Statistics 234
Chapter Notes 236
Bibliography 257
Index 259

Acknowledgments

I wish to extend my gratitude to a few people whose efforts and assistance allowed this book about the 1938 Pittsburgh Pirates to become a reality. While the story of any player or team cannot be told without months of extensive research, enhancements to the narrative such as photographs and direct quotations from people who were connected to that era of baseball history were made possible thanks to three individuals.

There are two people whom I wish to thank for granting me permission to use quotable material that helped to breathe life into the story about the 1938 Pittsburgh Pirates. I appreciate all of the help and assistance I received from Linda Parker, Administrative Assistant to the Editors for Newsroom Permissions at the *Pittsburgh Post-Gazette*, and Shawn Schrager, Director of Commerce and Product Development at *The Sporting News*. I am deeply indebted to Linda and Shawn for allowing me to use direct quotes from articles in *The Pittsburgh Press, Pittsburgh Post-Gazette* and *The Sporting News*. Thank you for your help on the book about the 1938 Pittsburgh Pirates as well as my previous two projects.

I would also like to extend a hearty thank you to Jenny Ambrose, Assistant Photo Archivist at the Baseball Hall of Fame. Even though Jenny was extremely busy working on other things, she was able to give me excellent photo options as usual for my latest book project. I appreciate all of Jenny's assistance providing me with faces to go along with the names that are mentioned throughout this book. I am grateful for all of your keen assistance and for additional help from the Baseball Hall of Fame on this project and my previous works on Fred Clarke, the 1925 Pittsburgh Pirates and Kiki Cuyler. To Jenny Ambrose, Linda Parker and Shawn Schrager, I salute your truly professional demeanor.

Preface

One of major league baseball's distinguishing traits is that its combatants battle through a protracted season to determine a champion. Players, managers, coaches and owners connected to the rival teams wage a six-month fight that sometimes does not produce a winner until the season's final days. Throughout the game's history, there have been numerous exciting pennant races, while on other occasions teams have seized an immediate lead and thoroughly dominated the competition. In a few instances, teams that have claimed a pennant and slipped into the World Series at the last moment were able to utilize their late-season momentum in order to capture a championship.

Some of the greatest teams in baseball history are still remembered today due to the total supremacy they exhibited while claiming a title. In 1927, the New York Yankees occupied first place for the entire regular season, recorded 110 victories, and then swept the Pittsburgh Pirates in that year's World Series. Sparky Anderson's 1984 Detroit Tigers also led the American League race from start to finish before they defeated the San Diego Padres in the World Series. In 1998, the Yankees dominated the American League as they went 114–48 and were victorious during the Fall Classic. Even though the 1906 Chicago Cubs were upset by the cross-town White Sox in that year's World Series, they earned a place in National League history by posting a record of 116–36 and finishing twenty games in front of the second-place New York Giants.

Yet it's the rags-to-riches story of a team that has come from out of nowhere to claim a pennant that has especially tugged at the hearts of fans. In 1914, the Boston Braves were mired in last place on July 4 with a record of 26–40. From that point forward, the Braves began an improbable run that reached its climax when they won the National League pennant and then swept the heavily favored Philadelphia Athletics in the World Series.

The 1951 New York Giants roared back from being thirteen-and-a-half games down on August 11 to tie Brooklyn for the pennant and force a three-game playoff. New York claimed this series, two games to one, when Bobby Thomson hit his famous game-winning home run off Brooklyn's Ralph Branca on October 3, 1951, at the Polo Grounds. During the 1908 season, baseball fans were treated to exciting pennant races in both leagues. In 1964, the St. Louis Cardinals claimed the National League title over Cincinnati on the season's final day.

While fans that cheered for the 1964 Cardinals and the 1914 Braves experienced the joy of claiming victory after an exciting pennant race, rooters in other cities were disappointed when their favorite team was unable to secure the heralded crown. For every exciting tale of a baseball team making a great late-season run, there was also the depressing saga of a team that had blown the pennant. Boston's storybook finish in 1914 could not have been possible if the New York Giants had not suffered a total collapse during the season's final months. In 1964, St. Louis would not have gotten the opportunity to defeat the New York Yankees in the World Series if Gene Mauch's Philadelphia Phillies had not blown the six-and-a-half game lead they held on September 14.

In 1938, the Chicago Cubs joined the fraternity of baseball teams that claimed a pennant in dramatic fashion as they went 21–5 in September and secured the National League flag during that season's final week. What made this comeback even more exhilarating for Cubs rooters was that it was done after longtime Chicago manager Charley Grimm was replaced by veteran catcher Gabby Hartnett in July. As joy and happiness prevailed in the Windy City, sadness and depression was the common theme in the Steel City as Pie Traynor's Pittsburgh Pirates were the victims of Chicago's late-season surge. After leading the National League race for more than two months, Pittsburgh was unable to hold back the charging Cubs as they grabbed the flag that had seemed destined to fly at Forbes Field.

By 1938, Pirates fans were used to disappointing results from their team. Many of those rooters still remembered the 1921 season, when Pittsburgh suffered similar heartbreak when the Pirates blew the National League pennant after having held a seven-and-a-half game lead over the New York Giants on August 23. The tumble that occurred in 1938 was much worse than in 1921 because it happened in such a catastrophic manner. This book examines that 1938 Pittsburgh Pirates season and the players who were involved in one of most monumental collapses in team history. While most of my efforts in this book concentrate on the fateful 1938 season, I also pay special attention to events that shaped that squad and look at the aftermath of the blown pennant.

Two key questions must be asked before the 1938 Pittsburgh Pirates are examined. Were they the best team in the league, only to wilt under the pressure of a long season and choke in the end? Or were they a group of overachievers who almost parlayed a combined record of 40–14 in June and July to an improbable National League pennant? These questions, along with a host of other circumstances such as bad luck and not playing a full schedule, are thoroughly dissected in this work. In the process, my aim is to shed new light on the star-crossed season of a Pittsburgh Pirates squad that too often is overlooked when great teams in the franchise's history are discussed.

Many baseball fans and historians will recognize the names of Hall of Famers Paul Waner, Lloyd Waner, Arky Vaughan and Pie Traynor, all of whom were associated with the 1938 squad. However, even devoted followers of Pirates baseball history may not have heard of players like Jeep Handley, Bob Klinger, Mace Brown, Pep Young and the great Johnny Rizzo who dominated baseball that season. Most trivia buffs probably would be surprised to find that Rizzo was the man whose franchise record Ralph Kiner tied when he smacked 23 home runs in 1946. This team took on the character that it did due to the pep of players like Young and Handley, Rizzo's powerful hitting, and the sheer guts that pitcher Bob Klinger exhibited. These little-known players were just as important to the success of the 1938 Pirates as were the four future Hall of Famers.

Although the 1938 season was viewed as a major disappointment by Pirates fans at the time, the accomplishments of this squad rightfully stand alongside their successful counterparts during the franchise's storied history. There is no shame in ordaining the 1938 Pirates as one of the top squads in Pittsburgh baseball history in spite of the fact that their failure during the season's final week was one of the worst choke jobs ever experienced in the game. When all is said and done, this failing should not obscure the fact that the 1938 Pittsburgh Pirates squad battled until the very end.

1

Murderers' Row and the Waner Brothers

Early twentieth-century baseball supplied a welcome diversion for devoted fans across America, who were able to forget their troubles each afternoon while rooting for their favorite team. Youngsters and adults alike who pulled for Christy Mathewson, Honus Wagner, Cy Young or Ty Cobb always could use baseball as a positive outlet even if they faced personal hardships. As the years went by, new players appeared on the scene who became the objects of hero worship in cities across America. The old guard of star performers were replaced by men like Babe Ruth, Rogers Hornsby, Mel Ott and Lou Gehrig during the 1920s. By 1937, a new wave of players such as Joe DiMaggio, Ducky Medwick, Hank Greenberg and Lefty Gomez were being given the royal treatment by loyal and passionate baseball fans.

Times were extremely difficult for a large portion of the American population in 1937 as the unemployment rate hovered over 14 percent for most of the year. Families struggled to get by as the Great Depression continued to cripple the efforts of many who battled desperately to get back on their feet. While America tried to pull itself out of its economic mire, countries like Germany and Japan flexed their imperialistic muscles in an effort to expand influence across the globe. Such behavior was condemned vociferously by the United States. President Franklin Delano Roosevelt gave a bristling speech on October 5, 1937, that criticized Germany and Italy for their involvement in Spain's Civil War. Mr. Roosevelt also chastised Japan for its misguided conflict with China. President Roosevelt suggested that these aggressor nations should be "quarantined" by the use of heavy sanctions. "When an epidemic of physical disease starts to spread," Roosevelt explained, "the community approves and joins in a quarantine of the patients in order to protect the health of the community against the spread of the disease."¹

A spokesman for Japan's Foreign Office wasted little time responding to President Roosevelt's terse remarks by defending his country's involvement in China, while at the same time chiding the United States for seeking to deny the people of crowded Japan the right to take control of its great territories. "We hear lately heated arguments on the unequal distribution of resources between the 'have' and the 'have not' countries," said the spokesman. "If the 'haves' refuse to concede the rightful demands of the 'have nots,' peace will be very difficult to maintain. But Japan does not make demands on this point as her right. Japan's only demand is that her people be permitted to enjoy freedom of movement and happiness which is rightfully hers."²

While President Roosevelt and his counterparts from the Japanese government continued to engage in international diplomacy, baseball fans across the country prepared to forget issues both foreign and domestic for a few days during the 1937 World Series. On October 6, the same day that Japan responded to President Roosevelt's criticism, the New York Yankees were busy taking down the New York Giants at Yankee Stadium in Game One by a score of 8–1. Rooters who were hoping for a long World Series soon realized that a seven-game affair was not in the cards. Joe McCarthy's Yankees duplicated their first-game effort by claiming Game Two by the same score; then on October 8, Yankees pitcher Monte Pearson throttled the Giants at the Polo Grounds, 5–1. Screwball pitcher Carl Hubbell kept the hopes of Giants fans alive on October 9 as he tossed a complete-game 7–3 victory over the Yankees.

Any further suspense regarding the 1937 World Series was brought to an abrupt end one day later when star hurler Lefty Gomez claimed his second victory of the five-game set, 4–2, and brought the Yankees their second consecutive world championship and sixth baseball title during the past two decades. For the second season in row, manager Bill Terry's Giants had fallen victim to their American League brethren from New York. A new Yankee dynasty was emerging as players such as Lou Gehrig, Frankie Crosetti, Joe DiMaggio and Bill Dickey seemed determined to surpass the number of championships team owner Jacob Ruppert had collected in the 1920s.

New York's success in 1936 and 1937 prompted comparisons to be made to those teams from the past, which had been spearheaded by Babe Ruth. A few weeks after the World Series ended, former third baseman Joe Dugan offered some insight by revealing Ruppert's opinion about the 1927 New York Yankees. Dugan, a tavern owner in uptown Manhattan since retiring from baseball, met with the Colonel after Ruppert had called out his former player for not selling his beer in the bar.[3]

"You know, the Colonel is a remarkable fellow," said Dugan. "Imagine a busy man like him knowing I didn't carry his product—and getting disturbed about it! I guess I talked with him for an hour and the longer I sat in his office, the more amazed I became. Do you know, he keeps intimate tab on most of his players—not only the current ones, but all the old-timers? For instance, he knows the whereabouts of all of the 1927-team and just what they are doing. That's his favorite team—the 1927ers. He said to me the other day: 'They were a great bunch, Dugans,'—he always called me Dugans—'yes, they were really great. They would have beaten even my 1937 team. That's how great they were.' There has been much debate on this subject. This is the first expression that has come from the owner of the Yankees. His testimony can hardly be dismissed as inconsequential, and he says that roistering, swashbuckling crew of 1927 was tops. I rather think so myself."[4]

In late October, Jacob Ruppert returned to the city where some of this 1927 World Series glory had been achieved when he attended the United States Brewers Association convention in Pittsburgh. While in the Steel City, Ruppert also attended an American Legion function with Pittsburgh Pirates manager Pie Traynor, team president Bill Benswanger and team vice-president Sam Watters. Within an hour of stepping off his train, Ruppert was ribbing his hosts about ancient history and joking about a possible matchup between the two squads in the 1938 World Series. "Well, it's just ten years ago this month since I last set foot in this great city and fine baseball center," said Ruppert. "Perhaps some of you will recall that we knocked off your Pirates four times in a row in 1927. Now, I would like nothing better than to see Pie Traynor lead his club to a flag next summer, and I promise that we shall strive to repeat the dose next October, except that we may do a more thorough job."[5]

Baseball fans in Pittsburgh certainly remembered the four-game sweep at the hands of Ruppert's Yankees in the 1927 World Series a decade earlier. Pittsburgh had not tasted the thrill of competing in the Fall Classic since Ruth, Gehrig and company thwarted the Pirates' effort to claim their second championship during a three-year span. The Pirates, under the stewardship of manager Bill McKechnie, had won the 1925 World Series by rallying from a 3–1 deficit against the Washington Senators. Pittsburgh claimed victory in dramatic fashion when they won an exciting Game Seven against Senators star hurler Walter Johnson at Forbes Field.

It looked as if Dreyfuss might get an opportunity to claim another championship in 1926 until team dissension tore the team apart while he was on a summer vacation in Europe. The Pirates ended up placing third in the National League pennant race after leading the league for a short time. Veteran players Babe Adams, Carson Bigbee and Max Carey were sent packing after they initiated an insurrection by trying to have team vice-president Fred Clarke removed from the bench. When the 1926 season ended, Bill McKechnie was handed his release as manager of the team. Former Detroit Tigers shortstop Donie Bush was named as his replacement.

Bush did a fine job leading Pittsburgh back to the Promised Land during a hectic pennant race with New York and St. Louis in the summer of 1927. The Pirates clinched the National League title on October 1 when they defeated Cincinnati by a score of 9–6. Pittsburgh finished the campaign with a 94–60 record, while St. Louis finished one-and-a-half games back at 92–61 and New York placed third with a record of 92–62. Pittsburgh's gift for winning the National League pennant was a date against Miller Huggins' New York Yankees in the 1927 Fall Classic. Dubbed "Murderers' Row" by sports writers because of the long ball proficiency of players like Babe Ruth and Lou Gehrig, the Yankees rolled through a tired Pittsburgh squad as New York pulled off a four-game sweep in the World Series.

In spite of the fact that Pittsburgh failed to win a contest during the 1927 World Series, they played New York tough throughout the four games. The Yankees hit .279 during the Series, while Ruth accounted for his team's only two home runs against Donie Bush's troops. Psychological factors seemed to play a greater role than physical ones. Worn out from the long National League pennant race, Pittsburgh's players seemed to lose faith in their ability to compete with the Yankees as the Series progressed. Pittsburgh outhit New York in Game One at Forbes Field on October 5, but still lost the game, 5–4. The Yankees played horrible baseball, and they knew it. They were able to claim victory because the breaks went their way.[6]

After the game, sportswriter Ford Frick shared a taxicab back to the Yankees hotel with Babe Ruth, Tony Lazzeri and Dutch Ruether. The prevailing consensus among these three ballplayers, and the whole Yankee squad for that matter, was that the Series basically was over after only one game. Babe Ruth offered this straight-to-the-point assessment: "If these fellows couldn't beat us today, they never will. We played terrible baseball and still won. This looks like a four-game series."[7]

Ford Frick continued to drive this point home as he commended the decision of New York manager Miller Huggins to pitch youngster George Pipgras against the Pirates in Game Two of the Series on October 6. Frick believed this choice pierced the very soul of Pittsburgh's players. Huggins basically was sending a message to the Pirates that he feared them so little that the Yankees were willing to use a rookie pitcher while veterans such as Herb Pennock, Urban Shocker, Dutch Ruether and Bob Shawkey were available.[8] Huggins' strategy proved brilliant as Pipgras was sensational and New York defeated Pittsburgh, 6–2. When the game ended, New York Giants manager John McGraw turned to former Pirate great Honus Wagner in the press box and declared: "This series is as good as over now. Huggins has got them whipped. Sending that kid against them is the final blow."[9]

Huggins continued to remain at the top of his game as a baseball strategist in Game Three at Yankee Stadium on October 7 by handing the starting assignment to southpaw Herb Pennock even though the Pirates had brutalized left-handed pitchers over the past few seasons. All Pennock did was carry a no-hitter into the eighth inning and reward Huggins' faith in him by defeating Pittsburgh, 8–1. The Yankees manager again remained cool and collected in Game Four on October 8. With the scored tied 3–3 in the ninth inning, New York loaded the bases with nobody out against Pirates relief pitcher Johnny Miljus. Pittsburgh's hurler temporarily staved off a Yankees victory by striking out Lou Gehrig. Miljus then got two quick strikes on Bob Meusel. This prompted one of Huggins' players to implore him to try pushing the winning run home with some daring strategy.[10]

"Let's try the squeeze, Hug," clamored Joe Dugan. "We've got to get Combs home."

"Listen," Huggins said with a grin on his face. "If we don't get a hit we'll win this game on a wild pitch. That fellow is trying too hard. He's putting too much on the ball. He'll wild pitch, sure as fate."[11]

Shortly after Huggins made his comment, Miljus recorded the inning's second out by striking out Meusel. Tony Lazzeri stepped to the plate and blasted a long foul ball into the bleachers.

Lazzeri never got a chance to take a swing at a second pitch. Huggins sat quietly in the Yankees dugout and watched his prophecy come true as Miljus' next pitch skipped past catcher Johnny Gooch and allowed

Earle Combs to cross home plate with the deciding tally of the Series.[12] It seemed that Huggins had pushed all of the right buttons as New York claimed its second world championship of the decade. Pittsburgh owner Barney Dreyfuss was heartbroken over the fact his team had been swept and was not in a congratulatory mood after Game Four. "No team that is good enough to win the championship of a major league should lose four straight games to the pennant winner of the rival league," he said with bitter scorn.[13]

Dreyfuss, who had owned the Pirates since 1900, was embarrassed over the fact that his squad had become only the second team in World Series history to be swept by its opponent. His anger may also have been the result of rumors that a prodigious display of batting-practice power by Huggins' players on the day prior to Game One had demoralized the Pirates before an inning of baseball was played. After the Pirates squad held their morning workout at Forbes Field on that day, some of the players hung around to watch the Yankees take batting practice. Miller Huggins, realizing that a huge psychological advantage could be gained, gave pitchers Herb Pennock and Bob Shawkey specific instructions. "Groove everything," Huggins said. "We'll show these chaps some hitting. Let them see a few go over the fence. It won't do them any good."[14]

Once Huggins' batting practice hurlers started tossing alley balls to their teammates, his stable of solid hitters showed the Pittsburgh players why they were known as "Murderers' Row." Earle Combs, first batter up, drilled the first baseball thrown his way into the left field bleachers. Shortstop Mark Koenig took his turn and smacked a ball that hit the wall in dead center field. Ruth, in three successive powerful swings rocketed as many long drives into the right-field stands. Lou Gehrig launched two more into the same area and Bob Meusel hit a drive over the left-field wall that left the stadium. Even backup outfielder Ben Paschal kept pace with his more famous teammates by drilling a few pitches over the fence.[15] When Ruth was finished taking his turn, he gave his seal of approval while going back to the dugout. "That's easy," muttered baseball's premier slugger. "They can leave the stand right where it is, as it is just right."[16] While the Yankees players were putting on this blistering hitting show, Pittsburgh third baseman Pie Traynor turned to pitcher Lee Meadows and gave his evaluation of the events unfolding before them. "The papers have been right," said Traynor. "These fellows can hit."[17]

These events have become part of baseball legend and have led some to conclude that the 1927 World Series was essentially over before it began. Perhaps Dreyfuss was one of them, but it seems unlikely. There can be little doubt that Traynor, a fearless ballplayer who was never rattled on a baseball diamond, was making a valid point to his teammate rather than throwing in the proverbial towel. Other Pittsburgh players such as Lloyd and Paul Waner maintained that New York's explosive batting practice display did not deflate the team's confidence one bit. The rumor-mongers had claimed that Lloyd had turned to brother Paul during the practice session and commented about how big the New York players were. However, further probing showed that this was not true since Lloyd had left the park immediately after Pittsburgh's practice session. Lloyd did not know whether Paul had watched New York's workout, but he did not think it mattered since nothing on a baseball field scared his brother.[18]

It turned out that Paul Waner had indeed watched the Yankees' batting display but he most certainly was not intimidated. Paul knew that New York used "souped up" baseballs at times in hitting practice. Paul had even managed to get a few swings in using those special baseballs and had blasted four out of the park.[19] This was not the type of power one expected from a man who stood five foot eight inches tall, weighed 153 pounds and was labeled as a disciplined batter who liked to smoke drives into gaps in the outfield. Knowing all this, it seems unlikely that Dreyfuss could have concluded that his players had been intimidated.

Moreover, once he had had time to recover from his disappointment, there was every reason for Dreyfuss to be optimistic about the future. Pie Traynor, Paul Waner and Lloyd Waner all were warriors who never gave an inch of ground on a baseball diamond and never felt intimidated by opponents. These three players were a big reason why Pittsburgh had claimed the National League pennant in 1927. Dreyfuss and Pirates manager Donie Bush had every reason to expect Traynor and the Waner Brothers to lead the squad to another National League championship in 1928.

Harold "Pie" Traynor was considered the grizzled veteran among this great trio even though he was only 28 years old. Traynor was born on November 11, 1898, in Framingham, Massachusetts. Traynor's baseball career got off on the wrong foot in 1920 when he was chased from the field by Boston Braves manager George Stallings after a Braves scout failed to inform the manager that he had asked the youngster to join the team for a workout. Traynor eventually hooked up with Portsmouth of the Virginia League and played shortstop for that team during the summer of 1920.[20] In September of that year, Barney Dreyfuss paid $10,000 to acquire Traynor. He played 17 games for the Pirates late in the year and batted .212. Traynor was farmed out to Birmingham of the Southern Association for the 1921 season. After appearing in 131 games for the Barons and hitting a blistering .336, Pittsburgh manager George Gibson recalled the youngster for good at the end of August.[21]

Dreyfuss and Gibson decided to name Traynor as the Pirates' starting third baseman for the 1922 campaign even though the youngster had played shortstop exclusively during his two years of minor league baseball. Playing shortstop for Pittsburgh was not a practical option since veteran Rabbit Maranville was a fixture at that position. Traynor rewarded Pittsburgh management's faith in him by batting .282 in his rookie season, while he also gobbled up grounders and speared line drives at the hot corner with relative ease.

Pie followed up his strong rookie showing with an even better effort in 1923 as the rising star batted .338, led the National League in triples with 19 and drove home 101 runs. One month after the season ended, former Detroit Tigers manager Hughie Jennings declared that Traynor was definitely the best third sacker in the National League and possibly the greatest in either league. Jennings opined that Joe Dugan of the Yankees was great, but he considered Pie superior after only two seasons of playing major league baseball.[22]

Barney Dreyfuss and the Pirates made a move following the 1923 campaign that was aimed at giving Traynor a new partner on the infield's left side. Dreyfuss handed over $40,000 to owners of the American Association's Kansas City Blues to acquire star shortstop Glenn Wright.[23] The arrival of Wright on the scene for the 1924 season seemed to spell the end for Rabbit Maranville in Pittsburgh. Maranville's irresponsible off-field activities had angered Dreyfuss and made life difficult for manager George Gibson and his successor, Bill McKechnie. Maranville was the subject of numerous trade rumors during the winter, but Traynor was adamant that Maranville was desperately needed on the team.

"It certainly is my hope that there is nothing to the talk that the Rabbit is to go to Philadelphia for Jimmy Ring," said Traynor, "or that he will go to the Giants by way of the Braves. Of course, the Pirates need another pitcher, one who can take his turn regularly, but no team gets very far toward winning a pennant unless it has a strong man at shortstop. I have heard talk that Glenn Wright, the Kansas City recruit, would replace Maranville if the latter were traded. This would mean two youngsters on the left side of the diamond, for although I am considered a regular I am not a veteran by any means. With the Rabbit gone I would consider our chances of winning a pennant hurt considerable, no matter how good a pitcher we might get in return. Games would be lost in our infield that ordinarily would be won."[24]

As it turned out, Traynor's fears were unfounded. He and Wright bonded and formed a cohesive, air-tight unit on the left side of Pittsburgh's infield. Meanwhile Maranville moved to second base, where he played steady ball until being traded to the Chicago Cubs in October of 1924. Wright batted .287 during his rookie campaign and led the team with 111 RBIs. Traynor saw a minor drop-off in his batting average in 1924 as an early-season slump limited him to a .294 mark for the year. Pittsburgh's third baseman was the center of attention after the season ended due to the latest chapter in a long-running feud between Barney Dreyfuss and New York Giants manager John McGraw.

After Commissioner Kenesaw Landis banned Giants outfielder Jimmy O'Connell and coach Cozy Dolan for offering a bribe to Philadelphia's Heinie Sand during a late-season game against Philadelphia, Dreyfuss took the opportunity to insinuate that McGraw was behind this act. Dreyfuss also believed Dolan had been acting on the orders of McGraw when the Giants coach approached Traynor one year earlier and advised the Pirate player to hold out for $15,000 in 1924. Traynor immediately informed Dreyfuss of what had happened and Giants management was warned not to tamper with players from opposing clubs. Dreyfuss felt that Landis should investigate the bribery case further and even call off the World Series if necessary.[25] McGraw, whose team represented the league against Washington as scheduled in the 1924 Fall Classic, wasted little time responding to Dreyfuss' accusations.

"That Traynor case is a joke," said McGraw. "Dreyfuss took it to Judge Landis a year ago and the judge threw it out. It seems that Cozy Dolan met Traynor under the stands at Pittsburgh last year, complimented him on his fine year, and told him that he ought to get a good salary out of Dreyfuss for this season. Pie asked him how much he thought he ought to ask for and Cozy said he thought Pie should ask for $15,000. That's the long and short of it. Judge Landis reviewed the whole thing and said it seemed a rather natural conversation between ball players. There was nothing wrong in it. Now when baseball is getting a black eye for this O'Connell case, Dreyfuss pops up and throws this other thing into the ring. Does he think that is helping baseball?"[26]

Dreyfuss ended up having the last laugh in this case as New York lost to Washington in seven games in the 1924 World Series and were then kept out of the big event one year later when his Pirates won the National League pennant and were crowned champions of the baseball world. Traynor was one of Pittsburgh's top performers in 1925 as he batted .320, scored 114 runs and recorded 106 RBIs. Pie followed up his stellar regular season with a scintillating performance against Washington in the World Series. Traynor was brilliant in the field and batted .346 against the Senators. Before the first game, former Pirate great Honus Wagner stated in the syndicated column he was writing during the Series that he expected Traynor to be the star of baseball's biggest event. After Pittsburgh claimed victory over Washington, Wagner continued to heap praise on the Pirates brilliant third baseman.[27]

"I picked Pie Traynor before the Series opened as likely to star," said Wagner, "and I was pleased at the way he came through. He is one of the greatest youngsters in the business. I always loved baseball, and would have played it whether I was paid or not. I think Pie is much the same way. The game is his life, and he wasn't flustered or off his stride in a single game. In fact, he was the one player on the two teams who played his normal game every day."[28]

Traynor's career continued to rise, with his popularity in Pittsburgh increasing each time he made a spectacular play at third base or banged out a clutch hit. Traynor took his role as a fan favorite very seriously and did his best to represent the Pirates organization in an honorable fashion. During Pittsburgh's spring training trip to Paso Robles in 1926, Traynor did his part in community relations efforts in the California town. On March 6, Traynor joined manager Bill McKechnie at Paso Robles High School to address the students there. After these two members of Pittsburgh's organization spoke to the attentive pupils, they ended the assembly by showing photos from the 1925 World Series.[29]

Opposite: Third baseman Pie Traynor was one of the stars of Pittsburgh's pennant-winning team in 1927 when he batted .342 and drove home 106 runs. Even though Traynor only hit .200 during the World Series against New York, Yankees first baseman Lou Gehrig proclaimed him one of the greatest third basemen in baseball history after the four-game series (National Baseball Hall of Fame Library, Cooperstown, New York).

1. Murderers' Row and the Waner Brothers

Traynor was not deterred one bit during Pittsburgh's disappointing 1926 season as he maintained his status as one of the game's brightest stars by hitting .317 and playing his usual cerebral game at third base. Pie continued his hitting barrage at the plate during the Pirates' pennant-winning season in 1927 with a .342 average and 106 RBIs. Even though Traynor only hit .200 during the four-game World Series sweep by New York, numerous Yankees players were impressed with his play during the championship. Lou Gehrig heaped praise upon Traynor after Game Three when he commended Pittsburgh's third baseman for playing a brilliant game. In spite of not having seen much of Traynor prior to the Fall Classic, Gehrig already regarded him as a first-rate third baseman. After watching him actually play in person, Gehrig became convinced that Traynor was one of the greatest third basemen of all time.[30]

When the 1927 World Series ended, Yankees manager Miller Huggins immediately tipped his hat to opposing skipper Donie Bush and his players, singling out Pie Traynor, Glenn Wright, Paul Waner and Lloyd Waner as stars of the first order.[31] The Waner Brothers certainly had nothing to be ashamed about in their first World Series as their performances compared favorably to those of Babe Ruth and Lou Gehrig. In their much-anticipated head-to-head battle, Paul Waner (.333) and Lloyd Waner (.400) barely outclassed Gehrig (.308) and Ruth (.400) at the plate. This solid World Series performance by the Waner Brothers came on the heels of a phenomenal campaign during the 1927 National League pennant race. Paul Waner had an exceptional sophomore season, leading the league in hitting with a .380 average and in runs batted in with 131. Younger brother Lloyd posted a .355 batting average, one of the highest by a rookie in baseball history.

The Waner brothers, separated by three years in age, were natives of Harrah, Oklahoma. Their father, Ora Lee Waner, had starred for the Oklahoma City baseball team from 1896 to 1900 before the Western League came into existence. Ora gave up his baseball career when he got married. In 1915, when Paul was 12 years old and Lloyd nine, the two youngsters and a third brother, Ralph, started honing their baseball skills by smacking dried-out corn cobs with broomsticks on the family farm. Ora scolded his sons for cluttering up his barnyard, but numerous reprimands did no good. After the elder Waner watched his sons on a few occasions as they swatted the jiggling, darting corn cobs, he realized a baseball career could be in Paul and Lloyd's future since they were better natural batters than their father.[32]

Paul Waner started his professional baseball career at the age of 20 for the San Francisco Seals of the Pacific Coast League. Brought out to the coast as a pitcher, Paul injured his arm during the team's spring practice session in 1923. Fearing that he would be cut loose from the squad, Paul shagged flies for teammates and threw the baseball back to the infield underhanded even though it caused him excruciating pain. After doing this for a few days, Paul finally got a chance to take some turns at the plate and consistently bashed baseballs all over the ballpark. Seals manager Dots Miller eventually converted Waner into an outfielder and a great baseball career was born.[33] Paul put up big numbers by batting .369 (1923), .356 (1924) and .401 (1925) during his three seasons with San Francisco. On October 13, 1925, Waner and teammate Hal Rhyne were purchased by the Pittsburgh Pirates in a conditional deal.

Paul Waner quickly became a favorite of the rooting populace in Pittsburgh in 1926 by compiling a batting average of .336. Brother Lloyd did not experience the same type of success as his older brother when given a chance to catch on with San Francisco. Lloyd only appeared in a handful of games in 1925 and 1926 before the Seals released him rather than pay a small bonus. Paul talked Barney Dreyfuss into giving Lloyd a tryout by promising: "That kid can hit, run, and field as well as I can."[34]

Dreyfuss heeded the advice of his new star player and signed Lloyd as a free agent after the workout. The younger Waner was farmed out to Columbia of the South Atlantic League, where he hit .345 in 1926 and showed Pittsburgh's brass that he was ready for the big time in 1927.[35] Before that pennant-winning campaign even began, baseball writer George Chadwick was predicting future batting titles for the Waner brothers. His rosy assessment was shared by several former major leaguers. Former Detroit pitcher Bill James raved that Paul Waner was the only young major leaguer who was a pure hitter and also commended him for his astounding catches and an arm that was able to whip a baseball around faster than a mule driver could ply a bull whip. He declared that Pittsburgh's purchase of Paul Waner in 1925 was baseball's biggest bargain since the Yankees acquired Babe Ruth in 1920.[36] Former Chicago White Sox pitcher Bill Wilkinson swore that Paul had a pair of wrists so hard that you could bend steel pipes across them. Wilkinson maintained that if the Waners were not the Siamese twin successors to Ty Cobb, then there likely would be no successor in the next decade. Former Detroit infielder Oscar Vitt agreed with James' assessment for the most part but claimed that Lloyd was well on the road to becoming an even better player than his brother.[37]

After the 1927 World Series, the Waner brothers were able to convert their newfound diamond fame into a lucrative vaudeville engagement during the off-season. After having a successful run on stages in Cleveland, St. Louis, Detroit and New York, Paul and Lloyd brought their show to Pittsburgh for its opening at the Penn Theater on November 7, 1927. Contract discussions were also expected to be part of the itinerary as Barney Dreyfuss planned on attending the show.[38] During a press club dinner in their honor two days later, the Waner brothers announced that they indeed had signed contracts for the 1928 season.[39]

Most baseball experts expected the Pittsburgh Pirates to repeat as National League champions in 1928. Paul and Lloyd Waner gave the team a solid combo from the left side of the plate, while right-handed hitting Pie Traynor and Glenn Wright were equally formidable. Changes were made to the roster prior to the 1928 campaign as two heroes from Pittsburgh's 1925 world championship team were dealt away. Star outfielder Hazen "Kiki" Cuyler, embroiled in a bitter dispute with Pirates management during the 1927 season, was deemed expendable due to the Waner brothers' lightning development and traded to the Cubs on November 28 for infielder Sparky Adams and outfielder Pete Scott.

Pitcher Vic Aldridge followed Cuyler out the door a few months later when he was shipped to the Giants for pitcher Burleigh Grimes on February 11, 1928. Grimes became the rock of Pittsburgh's pitching staff in 1928 as he went 25–14 with a 2.99 ERA, but the Pirates struggled to a disappointing fourth-place finish with an 85–67 record. Pittsburgh wound up nine games behind the pennant-winning St. Louis Cardinals, who were led by former Pirates skipper Bill McKechnie. Pittsburgh's star trio, however could not be blamed for the team's poor season. Pie Traynor batted .337 and led the Pirates with 124 RBIs. Paul Waner slipped one spot in the league batting race as his .370 mark was topped by pace setter Rogers Hornsby's average of .387. Despite the fact that many people inside of baseball believed Lloyd Waner could not duplicate his rookie success due to a newly discovered weakness at the plate, he responded by having another solid year in 1928 and batted .335.

Following two successful seasons, the Waner brothers decided to make their salary demands in tandem for the 1929 season. In February, fans in the Smoky City learned that Paul and Lloyd were not happy with the offer they had received from Dreyfuss, which prompted a report that the New

York Giants were interested in acquiring the star outfielders. It was said that the Gotham magnates were willing to pay $225,000 for the Waner brothers' services. Pirates management quickly denied that any monetary bid had been forwarded for Paul and Lloyd's services.[40]

"The story that the Giants had made us an offer for Paul and Lloyd Waner is ridiculous," said one member of the team's front office. "It is merely a 'pipe dream,' without foundation and we want to deny, as strongly as we can that there has been any talk along this line with any other club. The Pirates won't dispose of the Waners, no matter what turn future events may take. They will sign the contract and play with us next season or they won't play ball at all. The Giants, or any other club for that matter, haven't a chance in the world of prying them away from the Buccaneers."[41]

A prolonged holdout began to look inevitable. Paul Waner, who acted as the official spokesman during these negotiations, stated that at Dreyfuss' request he and Lloyd had passed up making about $28,000 doing vaudeville once again after the 1928 season. He acknowledged that they had been offered a raise, but said that the contracts had been returned unsigned because they felt the amount was too low.[42] "I know of several good fishing places around here and it is my intention to stay here until they place the figure on my contract that I consider I am entitled to," said Paul Waner.[43]

After receiving the unsigned contracts, Dreyfuss asked his player to give a reason for his demand. Paul responded with a letter in which he cited his sterling record during the past three years as the reason behind this request. Dreyfuss then accused Waner of being egotistical, a charge that angered the star outfielder. "It does not look that way to me," Waner declared. "The figures speak for themselves. Why I can name one player whose three-year record did not equal mine and yet he drew more than twice as much money."[44]

Both of the Waners remained on the sidelines without a contract when their teammates returned to Paso Robles, California, for spring training. On March 18, however, Lloyd Waner joined the team in San Francisco and signed his 1929 contract.[45] Terms of the deal remained private, but it was believed Lloyd had demanded $12,000, but settled for $10,000, which was still a significant increase from his 1928 stipend of $7,500.

Paul Waner, however, was still holding out for a sum reported to be $18,000. "Paul won't sign a contract with the Pirates until the club sends for him and agrees to meet his terms," stated Lloyd Waner. "The management of the Pittsburgh club knows exactly how much money Paul wants and where he can be reached if they want to talk business with him. He made it plain to me when I left Oklahoma Tuesday morning that he was determined to stand pat for he believes he is worth every cent he is asking. The fact that I acted independently does not mean that Paul will weaken. There never was any agreement between us, except that we would sign when our terms were met individually or otherwise. I am perfectly satisfied with the terms of my contract which were made known to me when the management asked me to come to San Francisco to join the club. As far as I am concerned, the controversy which began when I first returned a contract last winter is forgotten. I am glad to be with the Pirates again and will give them the best that is in me, as I always have. I am in good shape and should be able to play within a week at the outside."[46]

While owner Barney Dreyfuss was extremely happy to have Lloyd Waner under contract, he remained perplexed and angered by Paul Waner's contract stance. Rumors had Dreyfuss willing to spend a large sum of money securing another high class outfielder rather than continue to battle with Waner over salary.[47] "Of course we could use Paul," said the Pittsburgh owner, "but unless he makes first overtures, we shall have to get along without him. I do not expect to have a conference with him here or anywhere else along the route for he seems determined to remain silent regarding the terms he considers reasonable."[48]

Despite his public stance, Dreyfuss was actually working to get negotiations started once again. He sent a letter to Waner asking him to come to Texas while the Pirates were there playing a series of exhibition games so contract talks could be conducted. Waner initially declined, but soon changed his mind and made the short trip down to Texas.[49] On April 5, 1929, Pittsburgh management announced that Waner had ended his holdout and signed a contract for the upcoming season. As had been the case in other Pirates holdouts, Waner and Dreyfuss refused to divulge the terms of the contract, but it was believed to have fallen somewhere in between Waner's demand for $18,000 a year and Dreyfuss' initial offer of $11,000.[50]

Paul "Big Poison" Waner never seemed to hit his true batting stride during the 1929 season. After an early-season slump, Paul was actually benched for a few games, although it was not done under manager Bush's orders.[51] This left only the two alternatives of Waner asking to sit out a few games or Dreyfuss requesting that his star player ride the pine. Bush eventually tired of Barney's constant meddling and tendered his resignation on August 28, 1929.[52] Bush was replaced as team manager by longtime coach Jewel Ens. In spite of his rough start, Paul Waner finished the season with a .336 average, 15 home runs and 100 RBIs.

Lloyd "Little Poison" Waner topped his older brother in the batting race with a mark of .353. Pie Traynor did even better than his younger teammates, as he led the team with a .356 average and surpassed all of his Pirate comrades with 108 RBIs. Pittsburgh moved up a few spots in the standings from the previous year as they finished in second place with an 88–65 record. This mark left the team ten-and-a-half games behind the pennant-winning Chicago Cubs. A few weeks after the 1929 campaign ended, team vice-president Sam Dreyfuss announced that Paul and Lloyd Waner had signed contracts for the 1930 season and would not be traveling down the holdout road once again.[53]

Shortly after the Waner brothers signed their contracts, the whole country was plunged into economic uncertainty by the stock market crash in late October. While two of Pittsburgh's brightest stars were committed to playing baseball in 1930, shortstop Dick Bartell and veteran pitcher Burleigh Grimes became contract holdouts for the 1930 season. Bartell's case in particular was rather puzzling since he had been the starting shortstop for only one full season after inheriting the spot when Glenn Wright was traded to Brooklyn following the 1928 campaign.

Bartell, who split time between playing second base and shortstop, batted .302 for the Pirates in 1929. When Bartell received his first contract from Barney Dreyfuss in December, the young infielder immediately returned the document without a signature. Further efforts on the part of Pirates management to bring Bartell aboard failed. Dick's teammates were shocked when they found out that he had refused the salary terms tendered and had become a holdout.[54]

"Dick's salary demands are absurd," declared Sam Dreyfuss, "He wants a price for playing in 1930 far beyond what the club offered and far beyond what he could possibly get were he playing on any other club. Negotiations have been going on for several months in the chance that a settlement might be reached. Dick flatly refused ours terms and said if we didn't care to meet his figure, he would not don a uniform. I communicated with him, asking him to come to Paso Robles to talk the matter over. It was then that he gave the club the ultimatum of either meeting his terms or ending negotiations. We have given him what we consider a very good offer. If he does not accept, he will not play with the club this year. He refused to come here to discuss the subject."[55]

It was reported that Bartell was holding out for $10,000, a sum usually demanded by veteran players rather than a 22-year-old youngster who only had two years of major league experience. On March 11, Bartell arrived at Pittsburgh's training camp site in Paso Robles after making the trip from his home in Alameda, California. While there, Bartell and Sam Dreyfuss engaged in spirited negotiations during a conference which saw neither side willing to budge from their position. Pittsburgh management announced that Bartell would be returning to his home the following day. The itch to hit a baseball diamond consumed Dick as he watched his teammates practice that afternoon. Bartell's love for the game was making it difficult to leave camp.[56] The following morning, Bartell telephoned his father, who advised him to sign at the best terms he could get. Bartell requested another meeting with Dreyfuss and it only took a few minutes for him to agree to a 1930 contract that paid him $7,000.[57]

Bartell's signing left veteran pitcher Burleigh Grimes as the only remaining holdout on Pittsburgh's roster. Many fans in Pittsburgh believed Grimes' divorce suit with his wife was delaying contract proceedings from being finalized. This turned out to be a false assumption as an underlying feeling of bitterness between Grimes and Barney Dreyfuss was exacerbated during a conference on April 7. At that point, it was determined by Dreyfuss and manager Jewel Ens that a trade would be in everyone's best interests. On April 9, Grimes was shipped to the Boston Braves for mediocre southpaw pitcher Percy Jones. In the final analysis, Dreyfuss was unwilling to pay Grimes' request of $22,000 for one year or $20,000 a season in a two-year contract.[58]

These two holdouts were only the start of the team's woes in 1930. Pie Traynor was hampered by a sore eye during the spring training session and had to wear stained glasses to protect it from the glaring sun.[59] When his infected eye did not get better, team physician Dr. W.L. Marks pondered the possibility that diseased teeth were the culprit.[60] Eventually, the eye infection was diagnosed as a case of iritis and the ballplayer was ordered to remain in Pittsburgh while his teammates opened the season in Cincinnati.[61] Traynor, who did not appear in a game until May 6, still managed to hit .366 for the season and drive home 119 runs.

Traynor's eye trouble was minor when compared with Lloyd Waner's problems. On January 20, 1930, Waner had his appendix removed by Dr. H.R. Decker during an operation at Pittsburgh's Presbyterian Hospital. The early prognosis among his physicians was that Lloyd would be ready to participate in spring training sessions at Paso Robles. Instead, the star center fielder struggled to muster enough strength to get into shape for the 1930 campaign. During the training trip and spring exhibition games, he was unable to indulge in strenuous workouts and complained of feeling ill in the stomach. As the weeks went by and he failed to gain any weight, Waner became alarmed. After only being able to make one appearance as a pinch hitter during the first few weeks of the season, Lloyd went to Johns Hopkins Hospital in Baltimore in order to receive a second opinion.[62] Amid rumors that he was considering permanently retiring from baseball, Pittsburgh's star player finally started his first game of the season in center field on July 1.[63] Once the youngster kicked it into high gear, there was no stopping him as "Little Poison" finished the season with batting average of .362. Brother Paul had another spectacular season for the Pirates as he led the squad at the plate with a mark of .368.

Strong individual performances from the Waners and Pie Traynor were not enough to offset many shortcomings as the Pirates went 80–74 in 1930 and finished fifth in the National League race. On a positive note, first baseman Gus Suhr had a fine rookie campaign, batting .286, smacking 17 home runs and recording 117 RBIs. The Pirates had obtained Suhr following the 1929 season after he batted .381 for San Francisco. A much less encouraging development occurred at season's end when the tensions between shortstop Dick Bartell and Pirates management finally reached a boiling point. As the squad prepared to leave Cincinnati for a series in St. Louis in late September, Pittsburgh management announced that Bartell had been suspended for the remainder of the season. Owner Barney Dreyfuss also declared that waivers had been requested on Bartell and 20 other players in the Pirates organization.[64]

The idea behind asking waivers on so many Pirates was to gauge trade interest in these players from other teams. Bartell's inclusion on this list seemed to indicate he would not be playing for Pittsburgh in 1931. Dick's attitude during the past summer had peeved Barney Dreyfuss. It seemed that Bartell was more concerned about personal statistics than team success, as he tended to be happy when collecting hits even if Pittsburgh lost.[65] Differences between the two became irreconcilable when Bartell and Dreyfuss became involved in a heated dispute about the player's transportation money to go home at season's end. On November 6, 1930, Bartell was traded to the Phillies for shortstop Tommy Thevenow and pitcher Claude Willoughby.[66]

Barney Dreyfuss' disagreements with his baseball charges paled in comparison with the great tragedy he experienced on February 22, 1931. His son Samuel Dreyfuss, the 34-year-old team vice-president who was being groomed to take control of the franchise, died after he contracted pneumonia while battling a bout of influenza.[67] Barney Dreyfuss, a man whose small stature belied his enormous contributions to major league baseball, was devastated by his son's death. His involvement in baseball was now in question and the future direction of the franchise was in doubt for the first time since he came to Pittsburgh.

2

Bill Benswanger and Arky Vaughan Arrive on the Scene

The untimely death of his only son left Barney Dreyfuss in a dazed and shocked state. His fellow National League magnates and league president John Heydler tried to comfort the grief-stricken father. Men who had been competitors of Dreyfuss for league pennants now felt only compassion for their compatriot.[1] League officials also wondered whether Barney Dreyfuss had the emotional, mental and physical strength to continue to lead the Pittsburgh Pirates franchise.

The answers to some of these questions soon emerged. Dreyfuss placed a call to his son-in-law, William Edward "Bill" Benswanger, who was married to his daughter Eleanor Florence and was a partner in an insurance business that had been started by his father. Even though Benswanger had been a Pirates fan since boyhood, classical music was his main pleasure outside of work. Benswanger and his wife were accomplished pianists, and he was on the Pittsburgh Symphony Orchestra's board and wrote its program notes for many years. This passion, and the insurance business that had become very successful due to 18 years of hard work, became secondary concerns as his inconsolable father-in-law made an emotional request.[2]

"Will you come out here and help me?" asked Barney Dreyfuss.

"If you want me, I'll come," replied Benswanger.

"If I want you!" shouted back Dreyfuss, his nerves strung by his grief. "What in the dickens do you think I called for, if I didn't want you and need you?"

"All right. When do you want me?" said Benswanger.

"Not longer away than two weeks," concluded Dreyfuss.[3]

Bill Benswanger joined the Pittsburgh Pirates front office on February 23, 1931, one day after he turned 39, on a date which also happened to be Barney Dreyfuss' sixty-fifth birthday.[4] Benswanger took control of the duties that had been the responsibility of Samuel Dreyfuss, which included the task of getting Pittsburgh's players signed up for the upcoming season. Fortunately, the winter preceding the 1931 campaign was a relatively quiet one regarding holdouts. Great news surrounding Pie Traynor was trumpeted across the country in early January when the team's star third baseman married Eva L. Helmer of Cincinnati.[5]

Discussion among fans in Pittsburgh shifted from Traynor's wedding to expectations for the upcoming season. Outfielder Forrest "Woody" Jensen's acquisition from Wichita of the Western League after the 1930 season caused many fans to expect the departure of another Pittsburgh player. Rumors over the winter indicated that Paul Waner was coveted by many of Pittsburgh's National League competitors. Team secretary Sam Watters quickly denied that the older brother of the "Poison Pair" was on the market. When reporters specifically asked about Paul Waner's contract status, they were reminded of Barney Dreyfuss's longstanding policy.[6] "If I tell who is signed," Dreyfuss had once said, "it is easy to deduce who is not signed. Then stories go out about this or that man being a holdout, and the publicity causes us a lot of trouble. So we don't announce the signing of players, unless there is some special reason for doing so."[7]

As Pirates players started to make their journeys to Paso Robles for spring training, Paul Waner's name was in the news for other reasons. Word reached the Smoky City on February 25 that Waner was receiving treatment in a St. Louis hospital for an infection in his leg. Paul had been bitten by an unidentified sea creature while swimming in Florida during a vacation several weeks earlier. After undergoing an operation in the middle of February, it was initially feared that the infection would incapacitate Waner for some time.[8]

Fortunately, Paul Waner was soon released from the hospital and he arrived at training camp determined to get in shape for the rigorous season ahead. During the training sessions, Paul protected the injured area of his leg with a catcher's shin guard. When the Pirates packed their gear and broke camp at Paso Robles to begin the team's first stage of the exhibition tour in San Francisco, Waner told reporters that he had been spearing rock crabs in Florida's ocean waters when the accident occurred. "It was a whale that bit me," Waner told his attentive audience with a suspicious wink, "but I handed the whale my card and told him he had made a mistake—for my name wasn't Johah."[9]

While residing in the belly of a whale was not a very attractive scenario, taking up residence in the National League's second division was equally undesirable to baseball men. Unfortunately, that is exactly what the Pittsburgh Pirates did in 1931 as they finished 26 games behind the pennant-winning St. Louis Cardinals with a record of 75–79. An inability to play .500 or better baseball in every month but July and September doomed the Pirates season from the outset. Pie Traynor and Paul Waner saw their batting averages decline significantly as Pittsburgh's two star players batted .298 and .322 respectively. Despite his lowest batting mark in seven years, Traynor still drove in 103 runs. Lloyd Waner enjoyed a solid, bounce-back season after missing much of the previous campaign, batting .314 and leading the National League with 681 at-bats and 214 hits.

Manager Jewel Ens received limited contributions from other members of his fifth-place team. First baseman Gus Suhr had a terrible sophomore season, batting only .211 while appearing in 87 games. New shortstop Tommy Thevenow did not do much better with the stick than Suhr as he batted .213. Rookie outfielder Woody Jensen played to mixed reviews during his major league baptism as he appeared in 73 games after being recalled from the minors in July and batted .243. Ens had only two starting pitchers that he could rely upon as southpaw Larry French went 15–13 with a 3.26 ERA while right-hander Heinie Meine gained staff ace status on the strength of a 19–13 mark supported by an ERA of 2.98.

There seemed to be some hope on the horizon for Pittsburgh's baseball fans who lamented the fact that Thevenow was a huge drop-off at the shortstop spot when compared to Glenn Wright and Dick Bartell. It turned out that the dispute between Bartell and Barney Dreyfuss in 1930 was not the only reason for Dick's trade to Philadelphia. Dreyfuss felt that Bartell was expendable because he had recently secured the services of a youngster from Fullerton High School in California. Floyd "Arky" Vaughan had been accidentally discovered by Pirates scout Art Griggs when he made a trip from his Los Angeles home to scout catcher Willard Hershberger of the Fullerton team. While Griggs was there looking over Hershberger, he became enthralled with Vaughan's play, both at bat and in the field. Griggs quickly signed Vaughan and was so excited over his coup that he forgot all about Hershberger.[10]

Griggs was able to snatch Vaughan out from under the noses of the New York Yankees due to a stroke of good luck. Fellow scout Vinegar Bill Essick of the Yankees was also supposed to be in attendance that day to watch the kid who was nicknamed Arky because he had been born in Clifty,

Arkansas. At the last minute, Essick decided to make a trip to Long Beach to look at another player who only played baseball on Sunday. When Essick arrived in Fullerton the following Sunday to watch Vaughan play, he learned with much regret that the youngster was now property of the Pittsburgh Pirates. Not wanting to have the trip be a total failure, Essick signed catcher Hershberger to a Yankee contract.[11]

Vaughan had a stellar season during his first year playing professional baseball in 1931. The 19-year-old shortstop appeared in 132 games for Wichita, batting .338 while smacking 21 home runs and 16 triples. New York Yankees management continued to keep a close eye on Vaughan while he played for Wichita. Bill Essick's failure to bring Arky to the Big Apple did not deter Yankees business manager Ed Barrow from attempting to pry the talented youngster away from Barney Dreyfuss. At one point, Barrow offered Dreyfuss $40,000 to secure Vaughan's services. When the press caught wind of this proposed deal, Pittsburgh sportswriter Charles "Chilly" Doyle bluntly asked Dreyfuss if he planned on accepting this large amount of cash from the Yankees.[12] "If he's worth $40,000 to Barrow, he must be worth as much to us," responded Dreyfuss very shrewdly. "No, I'll keep Vaughan."[13]

When Wichita became an affiliate of the Chicago Cubs after the 1931 season, Vaughan was shifted to the Tulsa Oilers, a Pittsburgh farm team. Pirates management planned on taking a look at Vaughan by bringing him along for the 1932 training session in Paso Robles. Arky, along with other members of Pittsburgh's squad, would be playing for a new manager: former catcher George Gibson, a member of Pittsburgh's 1909 championship team and Pirate skipper in the 1920s, who had succeeded Jewel Ens. Shortly after Gibson was named as Pittsburgh's new manager, he assured fans in the Smoky City that outfielders Adam Comorosky and Paul Waner would not be traded or sold despite rumors to the contrary.[14]

Baseball experts lauded Barney Dreyfuss for the choice of Gibson. The 1931 season had been a difficult one for Pittsburgh's longtime magnate and questions about his retirement kept popping up. Dreyfuss, however, had signaled his views on retirement when he commented on the decision of a 70-year-old business associate to retire. "He's shortening his span of life," remarked Dreyfuss. "As for me, I am going to die in the harness. I believe a man who has been active for many years and then quits and does nothing is depriving himself of his interest in life."[15]

Barney Dreyfuss' comments turned out to be prophetic. When the time came to attend the December minor league meetings in West Baden, Indiana, Dreyfuss had to remain in Pittsburgh due to a terrible cold.[16] One month later, Dreyfuss was in Mt. Sinai Hospital in New York undergoing a glandular operation. Following the operation, the Pittsburgh owner initially seemed to be on the road to a full recovery. Dreyfuss' status changed, however, when he contracted pneumonia. On February 5, 1932, Dreyfuss passed away, surrounded by his wife Mrs. Florence Wolf Dreyfuss, daughter Mrs. Eleanor Florence Benswanger, her husband William, and daughter-in-law Mrs. Sam Dreyfuss.[17]

Tributes throughout the world of baseball poured in when news of Dreyfuss' death became public. Pittsburgh manager George Gibson spoke for many in offering a stirring tribute for the man who had hired him months earlier.[18] "Throughout my acquaintance with President Dreyfuss, which began in 1905," said Gibson, "I have found him to be an ideal employer and, after serving practically my entire diamond career with his club, I long ago learned to look upon him as a father. We have had differences of opinion, but the most friendly feeling has always existed between us and his passing is indeed a severe blow to me. I know I am going to miss him, but his absence will cause me to work harder than ever to provide what was his foremost wish in life — a winning ball club. It is my resolve to carry on along the lines he mapped out, just the same as if he still was with us."[19]

Baseball writer Edward F. Ballinger of the *Pittsburgh Post-Gazette* succinctly summed up Barney Dreyfuss' contribution to baseball in Pittsburgh one day after the longtime team owner was buried. "When Bar-

Following Barney Dreyfuss' death on February 5, 1932, his widow Florence inherited the Pittsburgh Pirates and Forbes Field. William Benswanger was named Pittsburgh's team president shortly after Mrs. Dreyfuss became director of the board (National Baseball Hall of Fame Library, Cooperstown, New York).

ney Dreyfuss was laid to rest yesterday afternoon in West View Cemetery," wrote Ballinger, "the last chapter was written in the career of a man who brought to Pittsburgh one of the greatest baseball teams of all time and one of the most perfect playing plants ever constructed."[20]

A new chapter in the history of the Pittsburgh Pirates now opened. Many local fans feared that their beloved team would be put up for sale, but to their relief Florence Dreyfuss prevailed upon her son-in-law to assume the organization's presidency, while longtime team executive Sam Watters was named vice-president. For the first time in 32 years, the Pittsburgh Pirates would be participating in a National League pennant chase without Barney Dreyfuss running the ship.

The 1932 season almost had a magical conclusion in Pittsburgh as George Gibson's charges finished the season in second place with an 86–68 record, four games behind the pennant-winning Cubs. Pittsburgh's usual band of sensational performers led the way, with Paul Waner batting .341 and leading the National League with 62 doubles. Pie Traynor rebounded nicely at the plate after a tough year in 1931 to post an average of .329. Lloyd Waner was his usual consistent self, compiling an average of .333. Gibson received better pitching from the 1932 staff than had his predecessor. Larry French continued to solidify his credentials as one of the league's best southpaws, posting an 18–16 record along with a 3.02 ERA. French was complemented by a rookie named Bill Swift who exhibited great poise and composure during his first major league campaign. The 24-year-old Swift went 14–10 and fashioned a 3.61 ERA for the Pirates after his acquisition from Kansas City of the American Association for pitcher Bob Osborn and catcher Eddie Phillips on January 29, 1932.

Swift, however, was overshadowed by fellow rookie Arky Vaughan, who had been given little chance of making the club during spring training. Vaughan was expected to play for Tulsa in 1932, but he got his big chance when regular shortstop Tommy Thevenow's ankle began to trouble him. Given the opportunity to show what he could do, Vaughan was one of Pittsburgh's outstanding players during the team's exhibition tour and earned a spot on George Gibson's squad. After starting the season on the bench because the club believed it needed Thevenow's steadying influence in the infield, Vaughan finally was elevated to a starting position in early May.[21]

Vaughan went through numerous growing pains as a rookie shortstop. Once the young shortstop became acclimated to his big league surroundings, however, his fielding mistakes became less frequent. Arky did not let his problems in the field affect his hitting during the 1932 campaign as he finished the year with a .318 average. Vaughan did experience a late summer batting slump when the pitchers he had terrorized in May and June gained the upper hand. Fortunately, manager George Gibson ignored numerous pleas to replace him with Tommy Thevenow, maintaining that Vaughan would become a better player by getting his struggles out of his system and enduring intense razzing.[22]

The solid nucleus of Pittsburgh's club now seemed destined to expand from a trio to a quartet due to Arky Vaughan's sensational rookie campaign. Fans in the Smoky City also had other reasons to feel optimistic about the team's future. Team president Bill Benswanger wasted little time inking both of the Waner brothers to contracts for the 1933 season. In addition, veterans Freddie Lindstrom and Waite Hoyt were added to the Pittsburgh roster that winter and the loss of a crucial member of the franchise was averted. Speculation had run high that Pie Traynor was a candidate to succeed Dan Howley as manager of the Cincinnati Reds, but in the end former Pirates manager Donie Bush was chosen to succeed Howley. Pirates fans breathed a sigh of relief.

Lindstrom and Hoyt's impact was minimal in 1933 as the Pirates secured second place for the second season in a row. The team finished with an 87–67 record, five games behind the pennant-winning New York Giants. Lindstrom's work was not terrible as he appeared in 138 games and batted .310 for the Pirates. On the other hand, Hoyt's performance seemed to indicate that his best years were behind him, as he pitched mainly out of the bullpen and posted a 5-7 record with a 2.92 ERA. Larry French continued to be manager Gibson's top pitcher as he went 18–13 and posted a 2.72 ERA. Right-handed hurler Bill Swift had another solid season, putting up a 14–10 mark for the second consecutive campaign and lowering his ERA to 3.13. On the battling side, Arky Vaughan's ascent continued as he appeared in 152 games and batted .314. Paul Waner and Pie Traynor each played in every Pittsburgh game and batted .309 and .304 respectively. Lloyd Waner experienced the worst season of his career as he saw his batting mark drop fifty-seven points from the previous year to .276.

After failing to grab the pennant for the second straight year, Bill Benswanger continued to tinker with his roster. On November 17, 1933, Benswanger shipped outfielder Adam Comorosky and second baseman Tony Piet to the Cincinnati Reds for veteran pitcher Red Lucas. The Nashville Narcissus, as Lucas was dubbed, had done great work for some really bad Cincinnati teams during the past few seasons—in 1932, for example, he went 13–17 even though his ERA was a respectable 2.94. Benswanger had a feeling that karma was on his side when he finalized the deal at the minor league meetings in Galveston, Texas. "The deal was made at the Buccaneer Hotel," said Benswanger, "which was a good omen for us."[23]

Good omens and positive signs were in short supply once the 1934 baseball season kicked into high gear. Two of their top players were hampered by early-season injuries as Pittsburgh got off to a sluggish start during the month of April. Pie Traynor was nursing a sore shoulder that had debilitated him throughout spring training.[24] After starting at third base for Pittsburgh in the first four games of the season, Traynor could do nothing more than pinch hit over the next month due to his injury. Making matters worse for manager George Gibson, star right fielder Paul Waner was put on the shelf for a few games after he wrenched a leg muscle in the eighth inning of a game against Cincinnati on April 22.[25]

Things did not get much better for Gibson as the season progressed. The team was playing mediocre baseball and the city's baseball populace was getting restless. On the morning of June 19, the fourth-place Pirates stood at 27–24, seven and one-half games behind the league leading New York Giants. When Gibby showed up at team headquarters that day, he engaged in a discussion with Benswanger about how to shake the team from its slump. Gibson had tried several shakeups to his batting order without getting the desired results. Benswanger and team vice-president Sam Watters had become more concerned with each passing day that Pittsburgh remained entrenched at the bottom of the National League's first division.[26]

When the friendly conference finally ended, both sides agreed that it would be best to relieve Gibson of his duties as Pittsburgh's pilot and for Pie Traynor to take control of the squad.

It later was revealed that the change was not initiated by Pittsburgh's team president. Benswanger was at his desk attending to daily club business when Gibson entered his office looking agitated. "Well," Gibby demanded, "why don't you say something?"[27] Benswanger replied that he would like to know what he was to say about what. "Why don't you tell me you're going to get somebody else to manage the club?" Gibson continued.[28]

Up to that point, Benswanger had given no thought to making a managerial change. Gibson's short remarks changed all of that, as the executive now realized he needed to bring in a new manager to replace one who had lost faith in his ability to lead the Pirates. There was no bitterness or anger during the ensuing ten-minute conversation that resulted in Traynor being named Pittsburgh's manager. Gibson appeared to be relieved when the final decision was made.[29] In Traynor's debut as Pittsburgh's manager against

New York, the Pirates fell to Bill Terry's Giants at Forbes Field by a score of 5–3. The consensus among many Pittsburgh fans who were questioned by a local newspaper writer that afternoon was that Traynor would get the Pirates back in the pennant race. They gave the veteran third baseman their whole-hearted support and believed he would turn things around.[30] "Pie Traynor, through his long, honorable service here and his knowledge of baseball and men," said Joseph N. Mackrell, local register of wills and clerk of the orphans' court, "earned the right to his new role as Pirate manager. Above all, he appeals to the general public, by his fine manhood and clean living habits. He will help increase interest here more than anyone can imagine, through his popularity with the youngsters."[31]

Pie Traynor was not able to get the Pirates back in the pennant race as 1934 turned into a lost season for the famous franchise. Traynor's boys went 47–52 under his watch as Pittsburgh finished the campaign in fifth place with a record of 74–76, nineteen and one-half games behind the pennant winning St. Louis Cardinals. Things did not go smoothly for Traynor during his initiation into the managerial end of baseball as in August he and Bill Benswanger both were required to tersely deny a rumor that dissension was wreaking havoc on the Pirate squad. The strain was so great on Traynor that he lost ten pounds after assuming Pittsburgh's managerial reins.[32]

Things were so bad for Pittsburgh's new manager that he and coach Honus Wagner were forced to evacuate the Alamac Hotel while the team was on a September road trip in New York.[33] Wagner had returned as a coach in 1933 after Benswanger and George Gibson had agreed to add him to the staff when the great player came to team headquarters looking for a job in baseball.[34] Traynor and Wagner were among the first guests to escape the clouds of thick smoke that enveloped the hotel. The two men stood on Broadway and watched firemen extinguish a blaze from a building a half a block from the Alamac. Most of Traynor's players missed the excitement because they had either gone to the horse races or the movies when rain cancelled a game against Brooklyn that afternoon.[35]

While the 1934 Pirates seemed to be jinxed, many players made strong showings individually. Gus Suhr had his best season since the rookie campaign of 1930 as he batted .283, swatted 13 home runs and drove home 103 runs. Arky Vaughan continued to develop into a bona fide star as he hit at a .333 clip, drilled 12 home runs and recorded 94 RBIs. A sore shoulder did not prevent Traynor from pushing his average to .309 in 119 games. Lloyd Waner had another tough season at the plate, batting only .283. Staff ace Larry French also struggled for the Pirates as he could do no better than a

12–18 record supported by a 3.58 ERA. Veteran hurler Waite Hoyt had a phenomenal year pitching as both a starter and reliever for Traynor in 1934, going 15–6 with an ERA of 2.93.

Veteran outfielder Paul Waner was Traynor's go-to guy in 1934 as "Big Poison" won the second batting title of his career with a mark of .362. Waner also led the circuit in runs (122) and hits (217), while belting 14 home runs and driving home 90 runs. In October, the Base Ball Writers Association of America selected St. Louis Cardinals pitcher Dizzy Dean as the National League's Most Valuable Player. Dean topped the ballot with 78 votes and Waner placed second with 50 votes.[36]

In October, Bill Benswanger announced that Pie Traynor would be back to lead the Pirates in 1935. When Traynor had been named player-manager, he had received a small boost in salary. Even though terms of his new contract were not revealed, it was believed that he had been given another raise.[37] Traynor and Benswanger wasted little time getting to work making improvements to the Pirates squad for 1935. On November 22, 1934, Pittsburgh pulled off a blockbuster deal that sent pitcher Larry French and outfielder Freddie Lindstrom to the Cubs for outfielder Babe Herman, plus pitchers Guy Bush and Jim Weaver.[38]

Herman's acquisition seemed a bit odd since the outfield was loaded with Woody Jensen, Lloyd Waner and Paul Waner, while Gus Suhr was entrenched at first base. Indeed Herman did not last very long in Pittsburgh and he was subsequently sold to Cincinnati on June 21, 1935. However, Weaver (14–8, 3.42 ERA) and Bush (11–11, 4.32 ERA) helped give Traynor's pitching staff a boost by pitching steady ball and helping with the development of some younger hurlers. Bush, known as "The Mississippi Mudcat," also showed off his nastier side to fans and teammates during a 12–11 loss against his former team at Wrigley Field on April 29.[39]

A wild donnybrook was staged between these two combatants during the contest's fifth inning. The trouble started when infielder Cookie Lavagetto blasted a double which brought Pie Traynor home and gave Pittsburgh a 6–2 lead. As Lavagetto slid hard into second base, he got tangled up in Billy Jurges' spikes. He immediately leaped to his feet and started throwing punches. Within seconds, players from both squads poured out onto the diamond. Bush, one of the first Pittsburgh players to leave the bench, made a beeline for Cubs pitcher Roy Joiner. After a short verbal encounter, Bush rushed Joiner and sent him to the ground with a few well-placed rights. Bush's attack left Joiner with a bloody nose and a six-inch scratch on the left side of his jaw. As umpires led Bush from the field, manager Charley Grimm attempted to confront his former player. The arbiters prevented any further battles from breaking out and Lavagetto, Jurges, Bush and Joiner were banished for the remainder of the afternoon.[40]

Even though the Pittsburgh Pirates seemed to exhibit more pep and dash during the 1935 campaign and compiled a better record, they still could not climb any higher than fourth place. Pittsburgh finished the slate with a record of 86–67, which left them thirteen and one-half games behind Grimm's pennant-winning Chicago Cubs. Nevertheless, there seemed to be hope for the future as a group of young Corsairs had breakout seasons in 1935. New second baseman Floyd Young finally got a chance to show his ability after languishing on the bench for portions of two seasons. Nicknamed "Pep" by Honus Wagner because of his exceptional spirit, the 27-year-old native of Jamestown, North Carolina, became a starter when Cookie Lavagetto was sidelined with an injury in May. Young went on an immediate tear at the plate, batting .325 in his first 17 games as Lavagetto's replacement. Young, who eventually cooled off to .265 for the campaign, knew he had to make an immediate impression on manager Pie Traynor.[41] "The way it looked to me I would have to do some hitting to stay with the Pirates," stated Young, whose fielding ability had never been questioned. "So I go in there and just keep swinging at the ball."[42]

While Young was a pleasant surprise, it was the play of pitcher Cy Blanton and shortstop Arky Vaughan that was the main baseball story in Pittsburgh during the summer of 1935. Blanton had a phenomenal rookie season on the hill as he went 18–13 and led the National League with a 2.58 ERA. Fellow hurler Bill Swift went 15–8 and placed second behind Blanton with an ERA of 2.70. Vaughan added his name to the list of such Pirates greats as Honus Wagner and Paul Waner by winning the league batting championship with a franchise record mark of .385. Vaughan was hitting .401 as late as September 10 before cooling off and finishing fifteen points below the .400 mark.

Philadelphia Phillies coach John "Hans" Lobert had predicted a great season for both Blanton and Vaughan in late May when his team was in Pittsburgh for a series at Forbes Field. "[Blanton] has a better drop than anyone since Christy Mathewson," Lobert maintained. "They call it a curve now, but when Matty was tossing them it was known better as a drop. Blanton has a ball that takes a sudden swoop from around the batter's shoulders down to his knees. It is sharp breaking. Beyond this the young fellow has speed. I saw him when his curve got a little out of control and he showed me then he has the stuff. He started firing his smoke ball and he has plenty

In only his fourth season as a major leaguer, shortstop Arky Vaughan established a Pittsburgh Pirates franchise record in 1935 when he batted .385 and led the National League in hitting. Vaughan was batting .401 on September 10 before cooling off and finishing 15 points below the magic .400 mark (National Baseball Hall of Fame Library, Cooperstown, New York).

at that, too. I don't agree with the fellows who say Blanton will be good only until the batters get accustomed to him. I think they are going to have a hard time getting used to that hook he owns and to his speed. Give him control at all times and he may beat out both the Deans this year."[43]

Lobert then turned his attention to Pirates star shortstop Arky Vaughan. While Hans was a huge fan of Vaughan's ability as a hitter, he was still skeptical about the Arkansas native's future at short and wondered if a position change may be in his future.[44] "Vaughan," said Lobert, "is going to be hard to beat out for the National League batting honors. He is a wonderful hitter and opposing players like to watch him take his cuts. His trouble is that he is not getting that jump on the ball. He allows too many balls to play him."[45]

Arky Vaughan's supporting cast at the plate included some of the usual suspects. Pie Traynor's playing career was nearing an end and he only batted .279 while appearing in 57 games. However, Paul Waner (.321), Lloyd Waner (.309), Woody Jensen (.324) and Gus Suhr (.272) all had solid seasons with the stick. Rookie pitcher Mace Brown made his debut for the Pirates in 1935 as he appeared in 18 games and posted a 4–1 record. Brown had been purchased from Kansas City of the American Association on November 21, 1934.

William Benswanger and Pie Traynor were encouraged by all of the positive signs and believed the nucleus was present to contend for a National League pennant in 1936. One area of concern was the catching department, where Earl Grace and Tom Padden had shared duties in 1935. Traynor addressed the problem on November 21, 1935, by shipping Grace and young pitcher Claude Passeau to the Philadelphia Phillies for catcher Al Todd. Traynor made the deal figuring that Todd was just reaching his prime and would hold up as a first-string catcher for at least another half-dozen years.[46] With Todd hitting at a blistering clip for the Pirates during spring training in 1936, Traynor ordained the stocky catcher as the "quarterback" of Pittsburgh's pitching staff.[47]

"Last year we finished fourth," mused Traynor. "It wasn't the pitching — it wasn't the hitting. It was trouble behind the plate. We believe we have a solution in Todd. He'll do the 'quarterbacking.' We're counting on him to protect those two and three run leads we blew last year. Look at our pitching staff. It's great, and with a boy like Todd handling it every day, half our troubles are over. It looks as if Cy Blanton and Bill Swift, the league's two leading pitchers in effectiveness last year, will have great seasons. They won 33 games last year and should even do better."[48]

As had been the case on many occasions during the 1930s, things took a turn for the worse for the Pirates just when it seemed that better days were on the horizon. While Todd's acquisition seemed to address one issue, a new set of troubles arose on January 21 when it was reported that Lloyd Waner was seriously ill in an Oklahoma hospital with pneumonia. Waner had a few rough nights in the hospital in which he was unable to recognize visitors but at last he passed the crisis stage of his illness. The veteran outfielder was unable to join his teammates for spring training until an exhibition game in Tyler, Texas, on April 2.[49] By the time Waner finally started a game for Pittsburgh on April 29, the Pirates stood in seventh place with a 4–6 record. This type of performance certainly did not surprise New York Giants manager Bill Terry, who believed that Lloyd's absence severely damaged Pittsburgh's pennant aspirations. "The Pirates will miss Lloyd Waner more than they think they will," said Terry. "Few can compare with Lloyd as a ball hawk!"[50]

Once Lloyd Waner regained his strength, he started batting and fielding just as he had done since debuting with the Pirates in 1927. Lloyd appeared in 106 games and batted .321 for the Pirates. Brother Paul had another stellar season for Pittsburgh and claimed his third National League batting title by hitting a blistering .373. At the beginning of the year, Pittsburgh baseball fans had been worried that Paul loomed as a holdout. After winning the left-handed golf championship at the Miami Biltmore Course in Coral Gables, Florida, at the end of January, Waner had stated that he still had not returned his contract to Pirates management. Paul cautioned everyone that he was not a holdout and stated the contract situation would be fixed in due time.[51] Apprehension had prevailed for over another month until Waner penned his signature to a document in early March and joined his teammates for training in San Antonio, Texas.[52]

First baseman Gus Suhr joined Waner on the list of Pirates who had exceptional years in 1936. Suhr batted a career-best .312, smacked 11 home runs and drove in 118 runs. Bill Brubaker took over for Pie Traynor at third base and hit .289 with 102 RBIs. Veteran pitcher Red Lucas had his best season in years with a 15–4 record and an ERA of 3.18. Sophomore twirler Mace Brown showed equal capability as both a starter and reliever with a 10–11 record buttressed by a 3.87 ERA. While this group of Pirates was able to consider the 1936 campaign a successful one, there were others who underachieved. Staff ace Cy Blanton struggled to a 13–15 record and his ERA ballooned to 3.51. Bill Swift also took his lumps on the mound; he went 16–16 with an ERA of 4.01. Reigning batting champion Arky Vaughan saw his average drop fifty points from the previous year. For many players, a batting mark of .335 would be considered a successful season, but this was not the case for Vaughan.

During the early stages of the 1936 season, Vaughan was mired in a baffling batting slump that prevented him from hitting the .300 plateau until July 23. Things were going so badly for Vaughan in June that he decided to take drastic measures: despite being a man who always had condemned superstition, Vaughan stated that he was going to start carrying a little black cat charm in his pocket. Making the whole matter even more mystifying in manager Pie Traynor's eyes was the fact that Vaughan was hitting the ball hard, only to see those powerful drives head directly to opposing fielders. Vaughan concurred with Traynor's assessment and believed the breaks eventually would go his way.[53]

"I've figured it out from all sides," said Vaughan, "and there's only one answer — luck. I'm using the same stance and the same model bat as last year, a modified Chuck Klein model that hefts about 37 ounces and is 35 inches long. And I'm trying to place my drives just the same as last season. But those balls just don't find the blind spots. Somebody always hangs onto them and I don't get the hits. I'm not a bit superstitious, but when you get desperate, you'll try almost anything — even if you don't believe in what you're trying — even if you do it as sort of a joke. There's always that little glimmer of hope that maybe you're wrong about those charms and maybe you're luck will change. I guess that's the reason."[54]

Luck certainly was not on manager Pie Traynor's side as his Pirates squad finished the 1936 season in fourth place with an 84–70 record, eight games behind Bill Terry's pennant-winning New York Giants. Making matters worse for Traynor were rumors which surfaced in August that his name was on a list of skippers most likely to be fired before the 1937 season. Joining Traynor as possibilities to hit the unemployment line were Philadelphia Phillies manager Jimmy Wilson, Casey Stengel of Brooklyn and Rogers Hornsby of the St. Louis Browns.[55] The consensus among many baseball fans in Pittsburgh was that Traynor was too nice and easygoing to get the most out of his players. Many baseball experts also believed that a hardline stance would yield better results. The big question that remained to be answered was whether Pittsburgh president William Benswanger's thinking was along these same lines.

3

New Blood Offers Hope to Pirates Fans for 1938 Season

Baseball fans who reasoned that Pie Traynor's Mr. Nice Guy approach would lead to his dismissal as Pittsburgh's manager prior to the 1937 campaign saw their theory struck down by team President William Benswanger one month after the conclusion of the 1936 season. Traynor signed a new contract on October 30, 1936, and immediately went to work to improve Pittsburgh's squad.[1] There was no shortage of trade rumors surrounding the Pirates in October and November. While Traynor was in New York watching the 1936 World Series between the Yankees and Giants, he was asked to comment on a far-fetched rumor that had Arky Vaughan headed to the Giants in exchange for pitcher Slick Castleman, outfielder Hank Leiber and a large amount of cash.[2] Traynor sarcastically responded that, if he cared to, he could give away his entire team for practically nothing and then ran out of his hotel to take in a movie.[3]

Vaughan's name came up once again in trade talks when St. Louis Cardinals president Branch Rickey announced that pitching ace Dizzy Dean was available. When Traynor and Benswanger expressed interest, Rickey told them that the price for Dean was Vaughan, outfielder Woody Jensen, catcher Tom Padden, infielder Cookie Lavagetto, prospects Bernie Cobb, Kenneth Heintzelman and Preston Richards, plus $175,000 in cash. Benswanger characterized Rickey's demands as beyond reason. He admitted the Pirates were prepared to bid high for Dean's services but said that he was unwilling to ruin his club to get a deal done.[4] Benswanger added that he would not trade Vaughan even up for Dean. Traynor was skeptical that a deal could be worked out since Cardinals management was unwilling to assuage the Pirates' fears regarding Dean. "We'll take Dizzy all right but not at their price unless they guarantee we'll have no headaches," said Traynor. "They can't guarantee that so it looks like the deal is off."[5]

Pittsburgh's counteroffer of pitcher Cy Blanton and veteran outfielder Paul Waner for Dean's services was rejected by Branch Rickey.[6] So instead, on December 4, 1936, the Pirates shipped Lavagetto and pitcher Ralph Birkofer to the Dodgers for veteran southpaw hurler Ed Brandt. Despite persistent rumors that Traynor was attempting to pry pitcher Hal Schumacher from the New York Giants and trying to convince the Boston Bees to part with slugging outfielder Wally Berger, no other deals were swung by Pittsburgh prior to the 1937 season.[7]

Other events aside from baseball occupied the minds of people in Pittsburgh as a new year dawned. Families throughout the region, who were still suffering the effects of the Great Depression, listened with attentive ears when President Franklin Delano Roosevelt gave his annual address in January. The president's message included implicit criticism of the U.S. Supreme Court for ruling that much of the New Deal's emergency and recovery legislation was unconstitutional.[8] In Spain, a half million inhabitants of Madrid were forced to flee their homes due to aerial raids by Rebel bombers. Volunteers from Germany, Italy, Russia and France offered assistance on both sides as the Spanish Civil War became more brutal and vicious with each passing day.[9] On a positive note, thousands of Pittsburgh football fans jammed the city's Pennsylvania Station to greet Jock Sutherland's Panthers home after they had defeated the Washington Huskies 21–0 in the Rose Bowl on January 1.[10]

Baseball slowly crept back into the forefront of the minds of hopeful Pittsburgh fans. The first party of Pirates players was expected to reach the spring training site at San Bernardino, California, on March 8.[11] By late February, only three players were unsigned: Paul Waner, Gus Suhr and Bill Brubaker.[12] William Benswanger figured he would sign Californians Suhr and Brubaker with ease once Pittsburgh's entourage reached the coast. Waner's situation was a little more complicated as a contract he had brokered with Benswanger over the telephone had fallen apart. The outfielder maintained that the contract he had received in the mail did not include all of the terms agreed upon during that phone conversation.[13] "We talked things over a week ago at which time Paul and the club agreed to everything and he accepted the terms," said Benswanger. "At that time we notified the papers what had transpired. Yesterday we received a wire from Paul. It read 'Sorry, I must have misunderstood our conversation.'"[14]

The disagreement soon turned into a standoff. Paul Waner claimed that Pittsburgh management had promised to give him a $1,000 bonus if he won the batting championship in 1936, but had later reduced the amount to $500. "I'm a sit-down striker," Waner told Pittsburgh sportswriter Ralph Davis. "I'll fish and play golf before I'll sign for what they are trying to pay me. They cut $500 off the contract they agreed over the telephone to send me. Then they called me up and said they had had witnesses listening in on our conversation, and that I'd have to sign at their terms. I don't have to sign for that and I am not going to. I wired them I wouldn't and to tell their witnesses so."[15] Paul threatened to spend the summer crab fishing and playing golf.[16]

The Pirates were taking an equally hard line. Pie Traynor stated that the team could easily get along without Waner in 1937 if need be.[17] An irritated Benswanger was especially outspoken about Waner's holdout. "There is one thing we set out to do when the club came under the direction of Sam Watters and myself," proclaimed Benswanger, "and that was to conduct our relationships with players on the highest possible plane. I remember saying to Sam one day: 'All we have to do is run this team on the same basis that Barney Dreyfuss did, and we're going to do it, no matter whether we finish first or last.' We have tried to hold that line, and we're doing so in Paul Waner's case."[18]

Posturing between both sides continued until April 9, when Waner and Pie Traynor met in a Dallas hotel. The negotiations only lasted 20 minutes before both men emerged from the conference with smiles on their faces— Paul Waner finally had reached a contract agreement with the Pittsburgh Pirates for the 1937 season. As was customary, the details were not announced but both sides claimed they were satisfied with the outcome and tickled to death that Waner finally would be suiting up in a Pirate uniform.[19] Waner was believed to be earning between $18,000 and $20,000 in 1937, which would make him the highest-paid player in team history.[20]

Paul was kidded by his teammates after he played five innings in an exhibition contest against the Chicago White Sox in Fort Worth on Saturday, April 10 and failed to get a hit. After the game, Waner stated he felt great and experienced no soreness after seeing his first baseball action of the season. Traynor joined in on the good-natured ribbing of the veteran star outfielder by taking a shot at Paul's workout regimen during his holdout. "Paul Waner came back to the club saying he had worked out all winter," said Traynor, "but by the showing he made against the White Sox at Fort Worth he looked as if he might have been working out on a ping-pong table; but, laying aside all jokes, with Paul again on the job our outfield appears to be all we could desire — in fact the team looks all right to me aside from the pitchers, who have not so far commenced to click the way I would like to see them clicking."[21]

Concerns surrounding Traynor's pitching staff were alleviated somewhat when the team made two additions prior to the season opener. On April 14, the Pirates purchased 24-year-old pitching prospect Jim Tobin from the New York Yankees. Tobin, who originally had been discovered for the Yankees by veteran scout Joe Devine (who also had been responsible for discovering Paul Waner when he worked for the Pirates in the 1920s), was a five-foot, 11-inch tall speedball hurler who had pitched for Oakland of the Pacific Coast League in 1936.[22] Two days after Tobin's purchase, Traynor swung a deal that sent outfielder Earl Browne to the Phillies in exchange for 26-year-old right-handed pitcher Joe Bowman. After making two deals in three days, Traynor cautioned writers that he was not done altering his team for the upcoming season. "We're not through yet," he declared. "We think we have strengthened our pitching with Bowman and Tobin, who are young fellows with most of their baseball ahead of them, and we have more lines out which we hope to pull in shortly. What has happened this spring has proved that our staff is suffering from too much age. From now on it's produce or get out."[23]

Traynor's team produced like true champions during the first month and a half of the 1937 season. The Pirates won their first four contests and their record stood at 15–4 on May 14. When the month of May ended, Pittsburgh stood in first place with a 23–12 record, while the New York Giants were close on their heels, one and one-half games behind. This turned out to be the high point of Pittsburgh's season — as had happened in so many other baseball campaigns during the past decade, spurts of solid play were ruined by long stretches of ineptitude and ineffectiveness. A combined record of 39–46 in June, July and August doomed the Pirates to another season as also-rans and forced Pittsburgh fans to repeat the familiar mantra of "wait until next year."

The Pirates surged home with a solid month of September and finished the year in third place with an 86–68 record, ten games behind the pennant-winning Giants. Pitching once again was an issue for the Pirates. Cy Blanton was tops on the squad with a record of 14–12 and an ERA of 3.30, while newcomer Ed Brandt posted an 11–10 record supported by an ERA of 3.11. Veteran hurler Waite Hoyt saw his time in Pittsburgh come to an end when he was sold to Brooklyn on June 12. The batting, however, was a bright spot. Pittsburgh's big trio of hitters excelled at the plate as Paul Waner (.354), Lloyd Waner (.330) and Arky Vaughan (.322) possessed excellent batting marks. Catcher Al Todd also put up great numbers: he hit .307, smacked eight home runs, and drove in 86 runs. First baseman Gus Suhr, now a revered veteran of Traynor's squad, chipped in with a batting average of .278 and 97 RBIs.

The most notable event of Suhr's 1937 season, however, was a sad one. Suhr was the reigning iron man of the National League when the 1937 baseball campaign began, having taken part in 784 straight contests since last missing a game on September 11, 1931. Suhr played in Pittsburgh's first 38 games of the 1937 season before his streak came to an end against the New York Giants on June 5 when word reached him from San Francisco that his mother had passed away.[24] Pittsburgh's team captain and undisputed field leader thought of flying to his former home in San Francisco for the funeral. After careful deliberation, Suhr decided not to make the trip, but remained away from the ballpark for the next three days to show respect until his mother was buried. The longest consecutive playing record streak in National League history thus was snapped at 822 consecutive games.[25]

Paul Waner took over for Suhr at first base during his absence and veteran outfielder Fred Schulte was placed in right field. Schulte's time in the starting lineup was brief as he too was forced out of action on June 5 when he was hit in the head by New York's Cliff Melton and knocked unconscious in the eighth inning.[26] Traynor was forced to give youngster Johnny Dickshot a chance to show what he had until Suhr came back. This was one of several instances of Traynor using the summer and fall of 1937 to test out potential contributors for the 1938 baseball season.

Infielder Lee "Jeep" Handley and pitcher Russ Bauers were two of the rookies who received an opportunity to show off their ability. Traynor, who was a big fan of both youngsters, used Handley and Bauers extensively: Handley appeared in 127 games as Pittsburgh's second baseman in 1937 and batted .250, while Bauers went 13–6 in 35 games and topped all Pirates hurlers with a 2.88 ERA. The new Pirates had taken contrasting routes to Pittsburgh.

Handley was a product of Bradley University who had been born on July 13, 1913, in Clarion, Iowa. His family subsequently moved to St. Louis, where he and two younger brothers attended Solden High School. The death of Handley's father in 1931 created financial hardship for his widow Lulu and their three sons. As a result, when Lee and brother Gene entered Bradley, they toiled in a rooming house in order to receive free board, worked in a restaurant for their meals and did odd jobs all over the campus in order to pay for their tuition. While her two sons were in college, Lulu Handley and her youngest son moved to Peoria, Illinois, to be closer to them. When Lee and Gene both embarked on careers in professional baseball in 1935, she returned to St. Louis.[27]

Lee Handley was signed by the Cincinnati Reds and did excellent work for the Toronto Maple Leafs of the International League during his first two seasons. On November 29, 1936, after a season that saw Handley hit .297, commissioner Kenesaw Mountain Landis declared him a free agent who was free to sign with any major league team. Three days later, the Pittsburgh Pirates paid Handley $20,000 to secure his rights. Handley took advantage of his good fortune by generously spending $13,000 to purchase a home for his widowed mother in Peoria.[28]

Born on May 10, 1914, in Townsend, Wisconsin, Russ Bauers lost his father when he was six years old. By then, the family had moved to Lakewood, Wisconsin, where Russ played baseball for Oconto High School and for the Lakewood town team. He started out as a first baseman and became a pitcher by accident. "I was playing first base with the Lakewood town team, when our pitcher was knocked out of the box one day," explained Bauers. "The boys knew I could throw a hard ball, so they asked me to go into the box. I stopped the opposing team from any more scoring, and from that time on, I was the pitcher for our club."[29]

Lee Handley debuted for Pittsburgh in 1937 and batted .250 in 127 games as the team's starting second baseman. The Pirates had paid $20,000 to secure Handley's services on November 29, 1936, after commissioner Kenesaw Mountain Landis declared the youngster from Peoria, Illinois, a free agent. Lee used $13,000 of that sum to purchase a home for his widowed mother (National Baseball Hall of Fame Library, Cooperstown, New York).

Bauers' "hard ball" proved to be equally efficient when he took the hill for Oconto High School. When Russ was 15 years old, he struck out 19 batters in a contest against the West High School team from Green Bay. One factor that contributed to Bauers' power and strength was that he spent the summer months working in a logging camp where his stepfather was a superintendent, which added chiseled muscle to Russ' 204-pound, six-foot-three-inch frame. In 1935, Bauers hooked up with a semi-pro team called the Chicago Mills. Philadelphia Phillies manager Jimmy Wilson, who had been tipped off to Bauers' exploits on the mound, invited the youngster to join his club while they were on a road trip. After taking a look at Bauers for a few weeks, Wilson signed the pitcher to a contract and sent him to his team's Hazleton affiliate in the New York–Pennsylvania League.[30]

The management of the Chicago Mills team protested to Commissioner Kenesaw Mountain Landis that Philadelphia's action had deprived them of a promising prospect. Landis conducted an investigation and then summoned Bauers into his office at the end of the 1935 campaign to inform him that he was a free agent. Pirates manager Pie Traynor, who had seen Bauers in action practicing during his brief journey with the Phillies, wasted little time signing the right-handed twirler. When Pittsburgh secured Bauers, Wilson protested in vain that Traynor had stolen the youngster from him. Russ split the 1936 campaign pitching for Scranton of the New York–Pennsylvania League and Knoxville of the Southern Association before being recalled by the Pirates at season's end.

Given little chance of making the squad in 1937 and expecting to be farmed out to Montreal, Bauers showed enough in spring training to convince Traynor that he belonged in the big leagues.[31] Bauers gave credit for much of his success during that rookie campaign to coach Johnny Gooch, who was back with the organization after being signed by Traynor the previous winter to be his pitching coach. "He's taught me a lot about pitching," said Bauers of Gooch. "For example, he has given me a new delivery — overhand, instead of side-arm. All the fellows have been swell to me. Particularly Pie Traynor and Honus Wagner."[32]

Wagner, Pittsburgh's veteran coach, took Bauers under his wing during the youngster's first major league season. Wagner offered fatherly guidance to Bauers just as he had done to players such as Arky Vaughan when they received their initiation into big league baseball. "Now, there's a comer," commented Wagner on his protégé. "He's got a great curve ball. Fine young fellow, too. But awful bashful. Why, I'm about the only one on the club to whom he'll talk much. Just says 'Yes' and 'No' to most people."[33]

3. New Blood Offers Hope to Pirates Fans for 1938 Season   47

The solid rookie campaigns of Jeep Handley and Russ Bauers gave Traynor confidence that his youth movement was heading in the right direction. He knew that Pittsburgh's fortunes in 1938 would depend on achieving a balance between young players and veterans. The big question was which veteran players would stay and which ones would move aside. Even though Paul and Lloyd Waner had frolicked together in the Pirates outfield for 11 years and were still very productive players, they both were past their prime. If Traynor planned on following through with a rebuilding process, it stood to reason that older star players like the Waners could be included in a trade package.

One of the first hot stove baseball rumors regarding the Pirates suggested that Traynor's job was in jeopardy. A story which started in New York during the World Series claimed that Giants catcher Gus Mancuso was going to be traded to Pittsburgh so that he could replace Traynor as manager. However, Pirates president William Benswanger was quick to deny the rumor.[34] The gossip about Traynor was fueled by the fact that he had not signed a contract for the upcoming baseball campaign, but people who paid attention to such things knew that this was just a formality. It had been customary for many years to announce the appointment of the Pirates manager at the Pittsburgh Sports Writers' dinner in November.[35]

Any doubt about the skipper's status was removed when Traynor represented the team at the annual draft meeting in early October.[36] Traynor added what he believed was another young gem to his roster when 29-year-old pitcher Bob Klinger was acquired in the Rule 5 major league draft on October 5.[37] Klinger was a minor league veteran who had started his professional baseball career with Shawnee of the Western Association in 1929. After toiling for six different squads in baseball's bushes over eight seasons, Klinger finally attracted notice in 1937 when he was one of the Pacific Coast League's top hurlers, going 19–13 with a 3.77 ERA for Sacramento. Traynor was banking on Klinger giving Pittsburgh's pitching staff a boost in 1938 just as Russ Bauers and Jim Tobin had done one year earlier.

William Benswanger decided to break tradition and protocol by not waiting for the baseball writers' dinner in November to announce Traynor's retention as team manager. On October 14, Benswanger announced that Traynor had signed a contract to lead Pittsburgh during the 1938 campaign. He explained that the contract was in line with Pittsburgh ownership's policy of only signing its skipper for one season. The only response from the mild-mannered pilot after news of his signing was made public was to declare that he would keep on plugging away until a pennant winner was brought to Pittsburgh. One day before Benswanger made this announcement, Traynor pulled off a major coup when he acquired star outfield prospect Johnny Rizzo from the St. Louis Cardinals. Rizzo, hailed as another Joe Medwick, had batted .358 in 1937 for Columbus' American Association team as one of the stars of the Red Birds' pennant-winning campaign.[38]

In order to secure Rizzo, Traynor shipped veteran catcher Tom Padden, prospect Bernie Cobb and cash to the Cardinals. On December 15, the Cardinals received outfielder Bud Hafey from Pittsburgh to complete the transaction. The additions of Klinger and Rizzo to Pittsburgh's roster did not mean that Pie Traynor was done reshaping his squad. Traynor's next order of business was to add a veteran pitcher who could assume the role of staff ace. There were rumblings that Pittsburgh was prepared to trade Arky Vaughan and Paul Waner to Brooklyn for pitcher Van Lingle Mungo. Vaughan also was mentioned in a swap with Cincinnati that would bring pitcher Paul Derringer and shortstop Billy Myers to the Steel City. A third rumor had Chicago manager Charley Grimm exchanging infielder Billy Jurges and a pitcher for Vaughan.[39]

When Pittsburgh writer Chilly Doyle asked Traynor if he would be willing to swap Paul Waner straight up for Derringer, Pittsburgh's manager said no because Cincinnati's hurler was suffering from a hernia. He also threw cold water on the proposed transaction involving Vaughan and Jurges. Traynor was also asked the perennial question about whether the Pirates were interested in Dizzy Dean. He responded that he considered Dean a poor risk. "We learned a lesson last winter, and it was never to put too much stress on a single player — especially a pitcher, who can't possibly work more than once every four days," Traynor explained. "If we had bought Dean last winter, we would be panicky now that his future is so uncertain. There are too many poor pitchers with strong arms to go running around looking for the ones whose whips are ailing."[40]

While potential deals for Derringer, Dean and Jurges had been nixed, a transaction involving Van Lingle Mungo of the Brooklyn Dodgers seemed more plausible. On December 4, during the winter league meetings in Chicago, Benswanger, Traynor, coach Jewel Ens and vice-president Sam Watters spent hours in a locked room at the Congress Hotel with Brooklyn manager Burleigh Grimes and team vice-president James Mulvey. Although these negotiations did not render any immediate results, it was believed the foundation had been laid for future discussions. The initial gossip had Mungo coming to Pittsburgh for Paul Waner, pitcher Bill Swift and utility infielder Pep Young. Besides dealing with Pittsburgh, Brooklyn also was fielding offers from the New York Giants and Chicago Cubs.[41]

New York's package to acquire Mungo included catcher Gus Mancuso, outfielder Hank Leiber, infielder Lou Chiozza and pitcher Hal Schumacher. Grimes and Mulvey of the Dodgers requested outfielder Frank Demaree, first baseman Rip Collins, pitcher Clay Bryant, prospect Newell Kimball and cash from the Cubs for Mungo. Cubs manager Charley Grimm turned this bid down and emphatically stated that Demaree was not on the market. This statement meant that another trade rumor by which Pittsburgh would send Arky Vaughan to Chicago with outfielder Woody Jensen and pitcher Red Lucas for Demaree and Bill Jurges was also highly unlikely. However, Benswanger acknowledged that things were progressing in respect to Van Lingle Mungo.[42] "We did talk to Grimes and Mulvey," Benswanger said. "And the name of Paul Waner was brought up. We believe we are further along right now on this deal for Mungo than at any other time."[43]

Mungo was a hot property despite the fact that his numbers had declined considerably during the previous campaign. After winning 81 games for Brooklyn from 1932 through 1936, he could do no better than a record of 9–11 in 1937, although he still posted a solid ERA of 2.91. After spending days fielding offers from other National League clubs at the minor league meetings in Milwaukee and Chicago, Grimes responded to a reporter who asked what was the most attractive proposal by saying that he had not received the best one yet.[44] Meanwhile the Pirates altered their offer for Mungo. Pitcher Cy Blanton and outfielder Wally Berger, who would be acquired from the Giants in a three-team deal with pitcher Bill Swift going to New York, were offered in a final effort to broker a deal.

Yet eight days of talking and haggling by numerous National League team representatives had produced no deal for Mungo. One frustrated baseball mogul who wished to remain anonymous gave his opinion as to why Brooklyn could not afford to trade Mungo. "Brooklyn won't and can't afford to trade Mungo," he declared. "The Dodgers are in debt to the Brooklyn Trust Co. to the extent of $700,000 and the bank is getting ready to close in. The Dodgers have three factions bidding for the franchise. One group is headed by former Mayor Jimmy Walker of New York and I think the deal is going through. Naturally, the ball club will draw a bigger price if Mungo is still with the team. The Dodgers can't afford to turn over the team without its big star. This new syndicate never before has bid for the Dodgers and there's plenty of money behind it. The new group will come whooping into the picture, either by dealing Mungo off as the climax to a long drawn out campaign or return him, with forgiveness, to the bosom of Flatbush."[45]

Even though the Pirates had been unable to make a satisfactory deal to bring Van Lingle Mungo to Pittsburgh, this did not mean team management was not making inroads toward improving the franchise. In an effort to keep pace with teams like the St. Louis Cardinals and New York Yankees, Traynor and Benswanger continued to expand the farm system of the Pirates. In November, Pittsburgh reached option agreements with Knoxville of the Southern Association, Savannah of the Sally League and Hutchinson of the Western Association for the 1938 season.[46] On December 3, Benswanger announced that former major leaguer Joe Schultz, Sr. would be placed in charge of overseeing the Pirates' minor league interests.[47]

The activities of Pirates management did not totally consume the news cycle as winter approached in the Smoky City.

Paul Waner commented on the expected changes to the baseball's construction in the National League by which a reduction in resiliency through tighter stitching was expected to take some of the rabbit out of baseballs. This change seemed to represent more of an aid rather than a hindrance for Pittsburgh as both major league loops were assured of using a uniform sphere for the first time in years.[48] While Waner believed that the new ball would pull down batting averages, he said it would not eliminate the fluke hits that helped accomplished hitters fatten their averages. "Fluke hits," Waner declared, "are just as much a part of the game as home runs. No matter what they do to the ball they won't eliminate them. As a matter of fact, I get as much of a kick out of bouncing flukes over the infield as I do knocking the ball out of the lot."[49]

In mid–December, Pittsburgh baseball fans who had been suffering through a brutal winter storm received a huge dose of encouragement when the Pirates training schedule for the 1938 season was announced. Bill Benswanger revealed that Pittsburgh would play 30 practice games in preparation for the upcoming campaign. The first party of Pirates players, including pitchers and catchers, would arrive at the spring training site in San Bernardino, California, in early March. The remainder of Pie Traynor's squad would follow by train a week later. The first exhibition game was scheduled for March 19 against the Chicago White Sox at Pittsburgh's training site.[50]

Following the game against the White Sox in San Bernardino, the Buccaneers would move on to Los Angeles for a two-game series against Charley Grimm's Chicago Cubs. Beginning March 22, the Pirates were slated to head north to San Francisco and then across the bay to Oakland for eight games with the Seals and Oaks. After completion of that slate of games, they headed down to the state capital for two contests against Sacramento. A return trip to Los Angeles for another game with the Cubs was followed by a final getaway day at San Bernardino before the Pirates started their trip eastward. Games in Fresno, Taft, Bakersfield and Barstow ended the team's stay in California before they stopped to play games in Winslow, Arizona, and Clovis, New Mexico. Pittsburgh hooked up with the White Sox once again after that for contests in Sweetwater, Abilene, Fort Worth and Dallas in Texas; Fort Smith, Arkansas; Shawnee, Oklahoma; Wichita, Kansas and Kansas City, Missouri. That schedule would bring Pittsburgh up to April 14, which was a few days before the National League season opened.[51]

While the hearts of Pittsburgh baseball fans were being warmed by news of the 1938 spring training itinerary, they were also contemplating the harsh words of a former Pirates player. Former pitcher Waite Hoyt gave a very candid assessment of why the Pirates never won a National League pennant during his time in Pittsburgh, which lasted from 1933 to 1937. "When the Pirates open a season," said Hoyt, "they immediately start counting the days until they can return home to resume hunting, fishing or whatever their off-season diversion happens to be. From top to bottom, the members of the club are disinterested [sic] ball players and have a defeatist attitude toward the game. Arky Vaughan could be the greatest shortstop in baseball if he were a hustler, but the only thing that worries Arky, once the season starts, is how soon he can return to California and resume his hunting. The whole club has a hay seeder's awe of New York. Every time the Pirates' train pulls into The Grand Central Station or Pennsylvania Station, Cy Blanton drawls disgustedly: 'Well, here we are in the brickyard again!' The boys are afraid to venture out of their hotel between ball games and one of the players actually got off a subway train from Times Square at 72nd Street, the first stop, because, he said, it went so fast he was afraid it would go off the track. On the train, while traveling between towns, other ball clubs are given to impromptu musicals, practical jokes or card games. The Pirate players just sit there and sulk."[52]

Hoyt added that he did not understand how players who were paid good money could exhibit this type of attitude. He concluded his scathing commentary by stating that Pittsburgh had no hope of getting anywhere in the National League until there was a major housecleaning. Hoyt's comments were big news in New York. "Quite the frankest appraisal of a ball club I've ever heard from the lips of a former member of it was Waite Hoyt's low-down talk on the Pittsburgh Pirates on his radio program," asserted sportswriter Dan Parker. "Leaving nothing to the imagination, Waite took the Pirate machine apart and let his listeners see what made it refuse to work."[53]

Even though Hoyt's comments were harsh, there had been a prevailing sentiment inside baseball that the team's annual failure in the pennant race reflected an unwillingness to do the hard, dirty work required to bring home the flag. Even Pirates fans had echoed these criticisms at times. At the same time, however, loyalty compelled the Pittsburgh faithful to circle the wagons as they always did when some outside force took a shot at their beloved team. In their minds, Hoyt's disregard for players who may not have been as refined as him since they came from the country's heartland was unconscionable. They had no way of knowing just how much the upcoming season would test their loyalty.

4

Bad Luck During Spring Training in San Bernardino

Waite Hoyt's derisive remarks about his former Pirates teammates injected some drama into the Pittsburgh baseball scene at a time of year when stories about the franchise usually fell into the category of mundane and routine.

Even in the dead of winter, however, William Benswanger and Pie Traynor were discussing ways to improve the team and preparing to talk trade with other teams when a second round of league meetings occurred in February. It was no secret that Traynor still was hoping to acquire pitcher Van Lingle Mungo from Brooklyn. While visiting the Smoky City in December, Pittsburgh's skipper commented on why no significant deals had been pulled off weeks earlier when various offers were spurned by the Dodgers. "The scarcity of good infielders in the National League is one reason why there were so few deals enacted at the meetings early this month," Traynor explained. "Everybody wanted infielders, and few clubs in the league have more than their four regulars and a utility man. We're in that boat, too. But in a couple of years, our youngsters out for seasoning will be ready."[1]

Traynor was confident that at least one of the three rookie pitchers Pittsburgh acquired from Class AA teams during the past few months possibly could help the Pirates immediately. These fledglings were Bob Klinger from Sacramento in the Pacific Coast League, Marvin Duke from Montreal's International League squad and Truett Sewell from Buffalo of the same league. Scouting reports received by Traynor from various sources indicated that Klinger was the most likely to be ready.[2] But when asked whether Pittsburgh would make any trades before the 1938 campaign began, Traynor seemed skeptical. "The only way to insure any big trades at this time," he declared, "is to discharge the whole eight managers and appoint new ones in their place."[3]

Traynor also revealed that the league's new baseball would change how his team ran the bases during the 1938 season. Traynor expected his team to become a constant base running threat, as had been the case early in his playing days. He believed that Jeep Handley had great potential in that respect and noted that Handley was already regarded as one of the best in the league at going from first to third or from second to home on singles. A resurgence in the running department seemed plausible since the Pirates had players like Handley, Arky Vaughan and Gus Suhr who always ran intelligently and well.[4] Following his comments, Traynor returned to his home in Brookville, Indiana, where he planned on enjoying the holidays and relaxing for a few weeks before he and his wife left for the West Coast at the beginning of February.[5]

A huge section of America's population found it difficult to enjoy the holidays as 1937 came to an end. An unemployment report released on January 1, 1938, indicated that between 7.9 million and 10.9 million people were out of work on November 20 when a voluntary census had been taken. Census director John D. Biggers advised President Roosevelt that the accuracy of this number was questionable. He stated a house-to-house canvas showed a much larger number of unemployed people than the voluntary postcard census had revealed.[6] Another story with a humorous side to it involving one of baseball's most revered players did help people forget their troubles briefly. After much speculation that Yankees idol Lou Gehrig would be chosen to star in *Tarzan of the Apes,* Principal Productions president Sol Lesser announced that the player's knotty knees had eliminated him as a candidate. It seemed that no leopard could provide enough hide to conceal his gnarled joints. As a way to appease baseball's fan favorite, Gehrig was given a role in a western called *Rawhide* in which he cleared all the villains out of Pleasant Valley and won the girl.[7]

Before long, however, the Waite Hoyt story was back in the news when sportswriter Chester L. Smith of *The Pittsburgh Press* revived the controversy. Smith revealed that Hoyt also had commented that the average Pirates player regarded a training trip as nothing more than an opportunity to move from one city to another in order to check out the gayer night haunts at each stop. He claimed that each opening day brought a huge sigh from many players in the dugout because they realized that six months of hard work faced them before they could go back to fishing, hunting and other forms of loafing in October. It was these claims that led Smith to lambast Hoyt for being a hypocrite.[8]

"Mr. Hoyt intimated that at soaking up a skin full of grog," stated Smith, "the Forbes Field hands were in a class all by themselves. At least, this was the impression he gave, and if he didn't mean it that way, here's begging his pardon. I want to make it plain at this juncture that Mr. Hoyt is a personal friend who is what is popularly known as a swell guy and who used to be a whale of a pitcher. Also, that this is no brief for the Pirates, some of whom are exactly as described by Mr. Hoyt and a lot of whom sold out Skipper Traynor and some of the rest of us who thought they were a better club than they proved to be. But by and large, the Pirates are not so much hell raisers as they are traveling salesmen for the hook worm and boll weevil. They don't, in other words, stagger through hotel lobbies full of suds as often as they stagger through nine innings full of ennui. Again, I doubt if it was the sporting thing to do—for Mr. Hoyt to speak so unkindly of his one-time teammates, for as I recalled the details, he was one of the model kiddies in Mr. Traynor's kindergarten. Even when he was the toast of the invincible Yankees, he was never pointed out as a 10 o'clock guy, and those were the days when he was younger and could stand being on the loose far better than in his later years. No, there are some others of the Bucs who might have spoken the same words and been less open to the accusation that folks who live in tin cans should not go around giving away can-openers."[9]

Baseball fans throughout Pittsburgh had to hope that Smith's comments would be the last they would hear about dissension in the ranks. Instead, the team's longest tenured player went out of his way to criticize Pirates management after team president Bill Benswanger indicated they still were in the running to acquire Van Lingle Mungo from Brooklyn. Benswanger claimed he was willing to trade strength for strength and star for star if it could help improve the team, but that he would not sanction a deal that left a glaring hole. He also predicted that a change of scenery probably would do Mungo a world of good, with a 20-win season even being a possibility if a deal with a first-division squad occurred.[10] Outfielder Paul Waner, dissatisfied with his proposed contract for 1938, responded to Benswanger's remarks by claiming that he was willing to be traded to any club that Pittsburgh chose. "What Mr. Benswanger must mean is cheaper faces from the figures on my contract," Waner stormed. "Maybe he just wants a bunch of two-for-a-nickel players."[11]

Paul Waner's sarcastic comment was rooted in two things that were upsetting him. For the second year in a row, Waner was unhappy with the contract Pittsburgh management had offered him. He also appeared to have felt hurt that Benswanger and Traynor were attempting to deal him to another team. There was no doubt in the minds of those who followed the Pittsburgh Pirates fortunes that Waner was on the trading block. His name had been mentioned in various rumors during the past year and Traynor on one occasion tried to move him to New York for slugging outfielder Mel Ott. Bill Terry had agreed that a change of scenery would have done both players a world of good but declined the offer. Terry cited their age difference and the fact that Waner hit to all fields, while Ott's pull-hitting style was tailor-made for the Polo Grounds' short right-field porch.[12]

Waner's statements did not go over so well with Pirates fans, who felt that his comments were a little out of line.[13] Benswanger did not seem to be as upset as Pittsburgh's faithful baseball followers by Waner's declaration that he would be willing to leave if the team president wanted new faces. "I don't think it is fair to Paul Waner or myself to talk about his statements until he writes to me," said Benswanger. "He should tell us his troubles. We are his employers. If he's dissatisfied with his 1938 contract he hasn't gone to the formality of notifying us. There is too much chance of misunderstanding. I'd rather wait until I hear from him personally." After offering that olive branch, he concluded: "Paul Waner's salary for 1938 is among the highest paid to any players in baseball. At least, it's the biggest contract I've ever offered a player since I became president of the Pirates. Paul is far from an underpaid performer."[14]

While Pittsburgh management did not seem to be annoyed by Paul Waner's attitude, subsequent events were troubling. Benswanger and Traynor were already used to Paul's gripes about his contract, but they had to be surprised when other players started weighing in with similar complaints. Brother Lloyd Waner, possibly feeling underappreciated by Pirates management, also stated that he would welcome a trade to a different team. A few days after the Waner brothers had made their feelings known, fellow outfielder Woody Jensen blasted Benswanger and criticized his handling of the franchise. During an interview with a writer in his hometown of Wichita, Kansas, Jensen sympathized with the Waners and laughed at the suggestion Pittsburgh was in the market to acquire Van Lingle Mungo. "Bill Benswanger wouldn't give $10,000 for two Babe Ruths in their prime," Jensen scoffed. "They say we don't have hustle and pay too much attention to golf. Waite Hoyt, who made that crack about golf, should know that Pirate rules prohibited us playing golf even on days when the team was idle last year."[15]

Jensen claimed that there was nothing wrong with the players on Pittsburgh's roster, but he found plenty of blame in the front office. "President Benswanger was in the insurance business until he succeeded his late father-in-law, Barney Dreyfuss," continued Jensen, "and for five years he tried to run a $4,000,000 athletic plant without knowledge of the game or understanding of player psychology. He ought to let someone who knows the business run it for him. All we get from the business side is criticism and plenty of it. We could win 20 games in a row and then drop one and the front office would want to know what in the hell."[16]

Jensen then expressed his anger about the team's oppressive rules, complaining "that a player isn't allowed to accept a dinner invitation when the

During the off-season prior to the 1938 campaign, outfielder Forrest "Woody" Jensen lambasted team president William Benswanger during an interview with the *Wichita Eagle.* Jensen asserted that Benswanger should let someone who knew something about baseball oversee Pittsburgh's baseball operations (National Baseball Hall of Fame Library, Cooperstown, New York).

team's on the road. And if a player gets a pass for a friend the full price will be deducted from his pay. You'd think that we were running an orphans' home. As for golf, the management seems to think it's better for us to sit around a hotel lobby than to get a little exercise on the links on an off day. Everything is done to irritate the players and then the head office sounds off about hustle and spirit. I say nuts."[17]

In an odd coincidence, Jensen's criticisms of Benswanger's penny-pinching policies appeared on the same day as an article in the *Pittsburgh Press* that painted a much different picture. The article pointed out that Pittsburgh management had forked over $25,000 in cash to acquire Johnny Rizzo and another $12,000 when catcher Ray Berres was purchased from Louisville late in the 1937 season. Pittsburgh management continued their heavy spending during the off-season, when $11,000 went to Buffalo for

Truett Sewell, $11,000 was sent to Montreal for Marvin Duke and Bob Klinger was purchased from Sacramento for $7,500.[18]

Benswanger had been calm in his response to Paul Waner's comments, but he took Jensen's remarks as a personal attack and was furious. "The charges are so ridiculous, I hate to comment and thus dignify them," stated Benswanger one day after Jensen's statements appeared in newspapers, "but I can't leave them go unanswered. This is the same grouch Jensen has carried since he joined the Pirates seven years ago. If he showed half as much spirit in the summer as he does in the winter, he'd be a much better ball player. Why he's popping off now, I can't understand. He hasn't been sent his 1938 contract yet but it will probably go out this week. Of course, Jensen will go to spring training with us. His remarks Saturday won't change his status with us as a player. I take his remarks as a personal issue and he does himself more harm than anyone else could do. It's right easy to have courage when you're 1200 miles from where your remarks are directed. I'm not interested in what Jensen thinks of me or what he thinks of the ball club. I am interested in what the fans think. The fans were highly disappointed in several members of the team last year and the fans know who the bad boys are. As for passes, there is a National League rule limiting each player to two passes each day and we aren't supposed to go over the limit, but we have often done so. Jensen used to bring in six and seven friends at the pass gate in St. Louis and Sam Watters always waived them through. Jim Weaver did the same thing when his friends came to the game in Cincinnati, and we never turned him down. I'm not the smartest fellow in baseball and I don't profess to be, but Jensen shouldn't have said the things he did. He has no basis for the statement. Let's see, he hit .278 last year and drove in about 45 runs. Well, sitting in the president's chair, I believe I hit better than .278."[19]

Most of the baseball fans in Pittsburgh, surprised that Jensen would talk in such a manner, sided with Benswanger. Baseball rooters throughout the city believed Jensen had signed his own ticket out of town and would be traded or released.[20] Pittsburgh scribe Chester L. Smith also took Benswanger's side, writing that Jensen had displayed a lack of spirit and had missed out on stardom as a player because he insisted on taking it easy rather than hustling. He stated that Jensen's lack of hustle was a frequent topic of conversation in the press box.[21] Manager Pie Traynor's response to the controversy was typically succinct. "A mediocre ball player has got to say something pretty sensational to break into print," remarked Traynor. "I could understand if a star player 'popped off,' but it would have to be pretty hot coming from a .276 hitter, wouldn't it?"[22]

4. Bad Luck During Spring Training

Realizing that he had gone too far, Jensen attempted to backtrack by claiming that he had been misquoted in the *Wichita Eagle*. He sent a letter to Benswanger and included the original article, with the portions of it circled in pencil where misquoting occurred.[23] Jensen claimed that he became so angry after reading accounts of former teammate Waite Hoyt's comments about Pittsburgh's players that it caused him to let off some steam to the Wichita writer.[24] In response to Jensen's allegations, *Wichita Eagle* sports editor Pete Lightner stood by the article and stated that the story's first draft contained even more vitriol before he advised Jensen that the final product should be toned down. "We had no interest whatsoever in misquoting anyone and only personal friendship of mine for Jensen held the statement down to milder terms," Lightner added. "He told me personally he held Traynor responsible for bad feeling on the club and would welcome being traded, especially to the Cubs."[25]

The negative stories involving Woody Jensen, Paul Waner and Waite Hoyt overshadowed many positive things that occurred in January. The best news was that signed contracts from many key players had trickled in to team headquarters. The contract of Paul Waner was not among them because he had returned his first contract unsigned to the front office, but the veteran outfielder denied he was a holdout. "I wasn't satisfied with the terms," Waner said. "But feel sure that we can get together. I don't anticipate any trouble."[26]

Waner added that he believed the Pirates could win the National League pennant in 1938 if they were able to make a trade for a slugger. He said that Pittsburgh had had its greatest success in 1937 because of having men like Arky Vaughan and Bill Brubaker who were able to break open games with long-distance blows.[27] Manager Pie Traynor, however, was confident that the acquisition of Johnny Rizzo had already given the team the power boost that it needed. When Rizzo had returned his signed contract, he had included a note that was in stark contrast to the feelings of certain veteran players.[28] "I want you to know that I am certainly well pleased and well satisfied," Rizzo wrote. "You can rest assured that I will be bearing down at all times for our club, both on and off the field. I am very anxious to get started, and sincerely hope for a successful future with the Pittsburgh club."[29]

As spring training approached, player contracts continued to arrive. One of them was from Woody Jensen, who had taken little time signing his contract for the 1938 season after receiving it at his Wichita home in the middle of February. Benswanger had held true to his word regarding the figures that had been agreed upon at the close of the previous season, despite the ballplayer's critical comments. As a result, Jensen gladly accepted the offer, which called for him to make $9,000 in 1938. Along with his signed contract, he included a contrite letter in which he attempted to smooth things over with Pittsburgh's team president though he continued to state that his harsh comments had been taken out of context. Jensen closed the letter by saying he wanted to have a heart-to-heart talk with Benswanger when he reached San Bernardino.[30]

Jensen's signing was followed by that of Paul Waner on February 18. Waner made a special trip to Pittsburgh so he could negotiate a deal with Benswanger in person and prevent the sort of disagreement that had occurred one year earlier when the negotiations had been conducted by telephone. After a two-hour conference with Benswanger and vice president Sam Watters, Waner reached an agreement that was expected to pay him $18,000 for the 1938 season. When the meeting ended, Benswanger asked Paul if the statements attributed to him regarding the Pirates wanting cheaper faces rather than new ones were authentic. After Paul regretfully confirmed their accuracy and offered an apology, claiming that he really did not mean it that way, Benswanger offered an olive branch. "Well," said Benswanger, "I don't want you fellows talking that way about me or the club. I'd rather sit down face to face and have you tell me those things. If you have any trouble with the Pirates, let me know."[31]

Waner's signing left only five Pirates players who had not agreed to terms for the upcoming season: Californians Gus Suhr, Arky Vaughan and Bill Brubaker, plus Lloyd Waner and Bill Swift, both of whom had spent the winter on Florida's links with Paul. None of those players seemed likely to be holdouts and after Paul signed, the Pirates front office stated that they fully expected every Pittsburgh player to be under contract when spring training began.[32]

That prediction came one step closer to becoming a reality when it was announced in late February that Lloyd Waner had agreed to contract terms.[33] Shortly before signing his contract, the veteran outfielder weighed in on all of the off-season controversy. He claimed that the Pittsburgh Pirates had plenty of spirit and that every man on the team was doing his part helping to win ballgames. "It's true the boys don't make a lot of noise and go through a lot of strange antics on the field," Waner said, "but they're out there trying their best to win all the time." However, he echoed his brother's concern that "We need somebody who can knock the ball out of the lot. Paul and I both are punch hitters. So are several others on the team. There're not enough home run smackers."[34]

4. Bad Luck During Spring Training

Two more veteran players followed Lloyd Waner's lead by signing their 1938 contracts after delays which had occurred for two very different reasons. First baseman Gus Suhr wired Benswanger his acceptance of terms from his home in Millbrae, California. In his telegram, Suhr also denied previously published reports that he was at any time unhappy with the terms initially offered by team management.[35] On February 25, veteran twirler Bill Swift accepted his contract terms. It turned out that the original contract had been lost by the air mail service. While Pirates officials had been fretting over Swift's delay, the team's longest-tenured pitcher was trying to enjoy his Florida vacation while worrying over whether he was being tendered a contract. This whole misunderstanding was cleared up when Swift signed his name to a second contract that contained the same salary figure as the lost document.[36]

The Pittsburgh Pirates baseball squad was now prepared to enter the 1938 National League baseball race at full strength. Further alterations to the roster seemed unlikely as previously proposed deals slowly withered on the vine. During early February's National League meetings in New York, William Benswanger had held numerous conferences with representatives from the Chicago Cubs, Cincinnati Reds and Brooklyn Dodgers. It was believed that these discussions centered around Billy Jurges and Frank Demaree of the Cubs, Van Lingle Mungo from Brooklyn and Cincinnati's Paul Derringer. Even though Benswanger had felt that enough progress had been made during earlier negotiations that something could be worked out, Pittsburgh's team president left the Big Apple empty-handed. Talks with Brooklyn general manager Larry MacPhail about Mungo once again yielded no agreement, leaving Benswanger feeling like a jilted bride at the altar.[37]

The club president never revealed who was offered during these talks, but it was believed that Arky Vaughan, Paul Waner and a veteran pitcher was the package that had been proposed in a deal with Chicago.[38]

When *Pittsburgh Press* sportswriter Lester Biederman asked Benswanger if it were true that a potential deal with Chicago involved Arky Vaughan and Johnny Rizzo of the Pirates and Frank Demaree and Bill Jurges of the Cubs, he received a knowing wink. "The Cubs made us two offers," Benswanger said. "They wanted to let us have their star outfielder for one of our star infielders. I'm not going to give you any names, as I go along, but there's nothing that I can do if you guess. We reopened the deal begun last December in Milwaukee, but I refused to weaken the Pirates. I called Pie Traynor at 4 o'clock in the morning and asked him about the new setup. I always ask Pie's okay on any deals. Pie was hesitant, so we dropped it."[39]

Benswanger was also coy about his discussions with New York manager Bill Terry. It was rumored that Terry had offered a catcher for one of Pittsburgh's prize pitchers. When Biederman mentioned New York's Gus Mancuso and Pirates pitcher Cy Blanton, Benswanger did not utter a word as he went about the task of methodically refilling his pipe. However, he did reveal that Terry was interested in prying pitching prospect Ken Heintzelman away from the Pirates.[40] With the names of Rizzo, Vaughan and Blanton being mentioned in trade discussions involving other National League teams, it was not surprising that Benswanger and Traynor remained firm and did not finalize any deals. Traynor believed that Rizzo had great potential and he was not about to trade his best hitter (Vaughan) unless the bounty received was earth-shattering. Pittsburgh's skipper also believed that Blanton was a crucial member of Pittsburgh's pitching staff even though he had regressed a bit since his phenomenal season in 1935.

In spite of their failure to make any trades, Benswanger and Traynor made one roster addition prior to spring training. On February 22, Benswanger announced the signing of veteran infielder Tommy Thevenow, who was expected to perform in the capacity of utility infielder and fill in whenever Arky Vaughan, Jeep Handley, Pep Young or Bill Brubaker needed a break. Thevenow had been living the life of a retired player at his home in Madison, Indiana, when Benswanger contacted him about playing for Pittsburgh in 1938. Thevenow had previously played for Pittsburgh from 1931 to 1935 and had one of the best seasons of his career in 1933 when he batted .312 while appearing in 73 games for the Corsairs.[41]

Now that Pittsburgh's roster was set for the upcoming training session, the team's faithful fans began to grow excited over the prospects of another baseball campaign in Pittsburgh. The team was scheduled to assemble for spring training in San Bernardino, California, in early March to begin a costly and time-consuming exhibition schedule. The team was going to travel a total of 8,372 miles from Pittsburgh to San Bernardino and back again. This mileage total included trips into Arizona, New Mexico, Texas, Arkansas, Oklahoma, Kansas and Missouri for exhibition contests during the homeward excursion.[42] The cost for the entire tour was expected to run around $30,000 for the franchise. Benswanger hoped he could recoup about half of that amount back through exhibition game receipts.[43]

A small group of people connected to the franchise were already in California waiting for Pittsburgh's first unit of players to arrive in San Bernardino. Manager Pie Traynor, team owner Mrs. Florence Dreyfuss, her daughter Mrs. William Benswanger, grandson Billy Benswanger and Pirate trainer Dr. Charles A. Jorgensen made up Pittsburgh's West Coast advance party.[44] The first group of Pittsburgh Pirates players placed under the charge of team president Bill Benswanger left for training camp from the Pennsylvania Station in Pittsburgh on March 2. Included in this group were pitchers Russ Bauers and Mace Brown along with coach Johnny Gooch and scout Bill Hinchman. When the train reached Chicago, pitcher Red Lucas and catcher Ray Berres would be waiting to greet their teammates while a shift was made to the Chicago and Northwestern Railroad. When the Pirates entourage changed trains in Omaha and transferred to the Union Pacific line, pitchers Joe Bowman, Bob Klinger and Kenny Heintzelman, along with coach Jewel Ens, were expected to join their teammates. Pitchers Cy Blanton, Ed Brandt, Marvin Duke, Truett Sewell, Bill Swift, Jim Tobin and Bill Clemensen all made travel plans of their own to make the trip to San Bernardino from their homes.

From Omaha, the Pittsburgh Pirates Express was expected to push forward directly to California with the hope being that the first squad would arrive on March 5.[45] The initial stage of the team's journey was uneventful except for an occasional card game and players trying to sneak in some sleep. Renowned prankster Bill Hinchman refused to allow these naps as he continually kicked coach Johnny Gooch in the soles of his shoes and gave other weary travelers the hot foot treatment. Margaret Doyle, the 79-year-old mother of baseball correspondent Charles "Chilly" Doyle, was the life of the party throughout this long journey. Every bit of politeness and courtesy was afforded Mrs. Doyle during her first journey west with the Pirates squad. She was as energetic as any rookie player and called everybody, including ball players and even porters, by their first names.[46]

Resident lumberjack and potential staff pitching ace Russ Bauers was the traveling party's heaviest eater. Bauers' prowess in the dining car was unparalleled and helped break the monotony of a long trip. He started right in packing away the food during breakfast. After a huge lunch and a giant-sized dinner, Bauers took a break for two hours before he partook in a little evening snack.[47] While Russ used mealtimes as his main diversion during this four-day trip, three other men were able to participate in a baseball-related function when the squad reached Omaha. Bill Benswanger, Red Lucas and Mace Brown all got off the train and were taken into the station waiting room where a radio interview had been arranged. When Benswanger was asked if Pittsburgh would win the pennant in 1938, he responded that the Pirates always finished in the first division and that any such club should be considered a contender.[48]

Then bad fortune intervened. Heavy flooding in California had washed out railroad bridges, damaged highways and blighted the state's beautiful landscape.[49] The excessive rain and subsequent flooding also altered Pittsburgh's travel plans, since one of the destroyed railroad bridges was on the main line of the Union Pacific Railroad.[50]

When the Pirates entourage reached Ogden, Utah, they were re-routed over the Great Salt Lake through a more northern route that eventually would take them to Oakland, California. From there, the Pirates express would be hooked into a streamline special going directly to Los Angeles.[51]

Pittsburgh's players never made it to Los Angeles, as the locomotive stopped at Glendale, California around 2:30 in the morning on March 6.[52] Busses were immediately ordered to transport the party of 18 men to the team's training site in San Bernardino.[53] By 6 o'clock in the morning, every member of the Pirates' first squad was checked into the hotel after having had their arrival delayed by one full day. Manager Pie Traynor hoped to hold a workout that afternoon, but the first practice had to be postponed because all the equipment trunks were delayed in Los Angeles. Traynor then ordered his boys to take in the steam baths at Arrowhead Hot Springs so they could invigorate their bodies after days of inactivity. This plan also had to be called off when it was discovered that flooding had ruined the baths, which would continue to be inoperable for about 10 days.[54]

As a result, the only exercise Traynor's players engaged in during their first day in San Bernardino was a brisk walk around town. A few players also checked out the Perris Hill Ball Park to see if bad weather had ruined the field. Good luck finally seemed to be on the Pirates' side, as flood waters never reached the park and everything was in fine condition.[55] This positive feeling only prevailed for one day, as Traynor and his troops were forced to dodge rain drops during the squad's second practice session on March 8. After a night of heavy showers, the players showed up at the park the following morning, dressed, and then sat idly as it rained some more. When the sun came out, Pie was able to put his players through their paces for about a half hour before another downfall of rain abruptly ended the drill.

The early days of spring training also produced several ominous occurrences. With extra free time on his hands due to the poor weather, catcher Al Todd decided to visit a friend at the San Bernardino courthouse. While Al stood in the corridor, three criminals who were serving anywhere from five years to life staged a jail break as they were being transferred from San Quentin to the San Bernardino jail. Guards, with their guns raised and ready to shoot the escapees, averted a dangerous situation by quickly recapturing the three men. When Todd returned to camp and spoke of his perilous encounter, his teammates gave the catcher some good natured ribbing. "Al," one of the Pirates cracked, "you could have made the greatest catch of your life."[56]

In addition, two Pirates pitchers suffered injuries on March 8. Southpaw Marvin Duke damaged his finger when he awkwardly stopped an infield grounder. Russ Bauers suffered his injury while sitting at a table eating a meal. Bauers, while striking a match to light a cigarette, accidentally ignited the whole pack and painfully burned his hand.[57] While Russ nursed the unusual injury, Traynor continued to be hampered from getting his team ready by the weather. Unless a sudden change in conditions occurred, Pie feared that his pitchers would be in lousy shape when the rest of his squad arrived on March 12.[58]

The arrival of Pittsburgh's infielders and outfielders was also delayed by a day by the flooding.[59] A couple of players, however, had made their own travel arrangements. Pirates second baseman Lee Handley had arrived at camp days before his teammates with his new wife, whom he secretly married on December 28.[60] Rookie outfielder Johnny Rizzo lived in Houston, Texas, so he too arrived separately.[61]

Shortstop Arky Vaughan wasted no time settling his contract issues after he arrived in camp from his ranch in Northern California. One day after celebrating his twenty-sixth birthday, Vaughan signed a contract on March 10 in team president William Benswanger's room. He received a raise that made him one of the highest-paid players on the club.[62] Third baseman Bill Brubaker had also recently come to terms, so Vaughan's signing meant that the entire team was under contract.[63]

Pie Traynor now could turn his attention to making evaluations of players and constructing his roster. Traynor surprised Pittsburgh fans when he announced that veteran outfielder Woody Jensen would alternate with Gus Suhr at first base. This meant that rookie Johnny Rizzo had been ordained as the team's starting left fielder before even playing an exhibition game. Traynor also stated that Pep Young and Tommy Thevenow were slated to handle the keystone sack, that Arky Vaughan was the undisputed starting shortstop, and that Bill Brubaker and Jeep Handley would battle it out at third base.[64] Once practice sessions kicked into high gear, Traynor's decision regarding Rizzo seemed warranted, as his approach at the plate resembled a veteran player and he seemed to handle himself in a very professional manner.[65] After Rizzo was informed that the left field job was his to lose, the rookie outfielder assured Traynor he had no intention of letting the opportunity slip through his hands. "If I don't keep the job," Rizzo told his manager, "it'll be my fault. Now that I've got a chance to stay in the majors, I'm not going to pass it up."[66]

Traynor's excitement over Rizzo's potential was nothing compared to the effusive praise that coach Johnny Gooch bestowed on two members of his pitching staff. Gooch was absolutely ecstatic about the ability of Bill Klinger and Russ Bauers. The Pittsburgh coach believed Klinger would show rapid development, just as Bauers had under Gooch's tutelage in 1937. "I think Klinger has what it takes," said Gooch. "I was with Bob in Columbus in 1934. I was employed as a coach, but a time came when I had to fill in for the regular catchers. I think I caught Bob for something like ten games, and I know he won most of them. This was not on my account, but merely because he had so much stuff that nobody could hit him."[67]

"Do you know," continued Pittsburgh's sorrel-topped coach, "that Klinger's curve ball is as good as the hook owned by Mace Brown? Well, it is. And he should be a much better pitcher, now that he has had several more years of experience in the fastest class of the minors."[68]

Gooch was also convinced that Bauers would have an even better season than his rookie campaign, in which he fashioned the lowest earned run average on Pittsburgh's staff. Johnny also reasoned that Bauers would be less prone to illness and arm issues since he had had his tonsils removed over the winter. Besides being his roommate for the 1938 season, Gooch was Russ' biggest booster. "The kid," said Gooch, "has a 'lively' ball. It sort of floats and jumps just before it reaches the batter. He's learned to 'hide' the ball before he lets it go and that's a big asset. He's part Indian, you know, and instinctively smart. He's learning all the time. Of all the pitchers I've ever seen, he's one of the most promising. He listens well, has improved about 100 per cent since last spring and he's going to be a star."[69]

The time for reports about practice sessions and other baseball hyperbole making up the lion's share of correspondent's articles finally came to an end when Pittsburgh kicked off the exhibition schedule. After being defeated in their first encounter by the Los Angeles Angels of the Pacific Coast League, 10–6, Pittsburgh bounced back on March 19 and defeated the Chicago White Sox, 4–2 in front of 2,000 fans in San Bernardino. Mace Brown was the hurling star on the day, as his efficient three-inning performance served notice that he intended to earn a slot in Traynor's starting rotation. Arky Vaughan was Pittsburgh's batting star, smacking a triple and three singles.[70] Even though the Chicago Cubs destroyed Pittsburgh one day later by a score of 14–7, Johnny Rizzo showed why everybody connected

4. Bad Luck During Spring Training

to the Pirates believed he was improving each day. In the seventh inning, southpaw hurler Larry French decided to cross up the rookie by throwing a screwball. Although this was Johnny's first look at that pitch, he promptly sent the sphere soaring over the left-field fence some 375 feet from home plate.[71]

Pittsburgh's first few exhibition games could best be termed a mixed bag as the Corsairs split their first four contests. One thing that seemed unmistakably evident was that Arky Vaughan was gearing up for a big season in 1938. During a 13–4 victory over the Cubs in Los Angeles, Vaughan crushed two monster home runs into the center-field stands and drove home five runs.[72] Arky continued his blistering hitting when the Pirates reached San Francisco as he batted .437 during a five-game series against the Seals.[73] A sparse turnout of around 1,000 fans showed up for the first game to watch former Seals Gus Suhr, Lloyd Waner and Paul Waner in action. Former Pittsburgh shortstop Glenn Wright also was permitted on the Pirates bench.[74] On March 26, two Pittsburgh players were honored at different California venues. In the morning, pitcher Jim Tobin pitched for the Pirates in his hometown of Oakland while "Gus Suhr Day" was held in San Francisco during the afternoon contest against the Seals.[75]

During the game in San Francisco, Johnny Rizzo drilled a ninth-inning home run that traveled high above the left-field wall some 365 feet from home plate and cleared the barrier by about 25 feet.[76] Johnny also had great success in the series against the Seals, batting .318 during the five-game encounter and belting out three extra-base hits. After Rizzo hit his homer, Seals manager Lefty O'Doul claimed that Joe DiMaggio had never hit a ball that hard in the same park while playing for San Francisco. Veteran Paul Waner could not contain his enthusiasm over Rizzo after he watched the rookie during batting practice prior to a game in San Francisco. "He's going to be a great hitter," Waner said. "Watch him use his wrists. Wrist hitters always are good. Watch how he follows through with one hand on those hits. When he hits a ball, it 'zings.' Rizzo is a good fellow, has a fine arm and can go to either his left or right after a ball."[77]

Two other Pirates players, Arky Vaughan and rookie pitcher Bob Klinger, had their chance to receive accolades when the Pirates played games in Fullerton and Sacramento. As the exhibition season moved into its second phase, games against major league and Pacific Coast League teams were replaced on the schedule with contests against town teams. In California towns like Taft, Bakersfield and Barstow, baseball fans who loved the game were excited over getting a chance to catch a glimpse of greats like Pie

Traynor, Honus Wagner, the Waner brothers, Arky Vaughan and many others. The problem from the perspective of Pittsburgh's players was that field conditions were primitive at times. The grounds were usually barren of grass, while ridges on the infield made playing grounders an adventure.[78]

A few boxes and a bench typically served as a press box for scribes covering the exhibition contests. During many of these games, Pittsburgh played before standing-room-only crowds, since the seating capacity could not accommodate more than a few hundred people. Since admission prices were not high, expenses usually exceeded gate receipts.[79] While the fans from these small towns were very enthusiastic over seeing major league players performing in their town, Pie Traynor's troops had a hard time avoiding boredom. Players who were tired of the monotonous nature of a long training season sometimes tried to find new ways to amuse themselves. Unfortunately for Traynor, one of the players who sought out such diversions was a star pitcher.

5

Bucs Bust Out of the Gate Due to Arky Vaughan's Heroics

The Pittsburgh Pirates' spring training tour soon became a grind. Celebratory banquets and breakfasts honoring Pie Traynor's squad became a thing of the past as the team started making its way east and visits from celebrities like Dick Powell, Joe E. Brown, Pat O'Brien and Bob Hope also became infrequent.[1]

It was now the season for predictions about the upcoming campaign and many experts touted the Pirates as contenders. New York Giants team secretary Eddie Brannick believed everyone should beware of the Pirates. He felt Jim Tobin's addition to the squad made Pittsburgh's pitching staff even more formidable.[2] Cubs manager Charley Grimm and veteran catcher Gabby Hartnett claimed Pittsburgh was the team to beat in the National League. "In the three games we've played with the Pirates this spring," Grimm declared, "they've shown me stronger than last year. The biggest improvements? Why Rizzo in left field should be a great ball player. We tried to get him from Columbus, too, but the Pirates beat us. He certainly has been murdering that ball during the spring, but how he shapes up in the regular championship season is another matter. See what he did yesterday? Homer, single, on base five times. Ray Berres will help the catching department, too. Smart and clever, that fellow. Russ Bauers should have another good year. If Pie Traynor can find another pitcher to help him we'll be in the doghouse."[3]

There was no telling how much Rizzo's play could further impress Grimm once he eliminated a handicap that had plagued him during the exhibition tour's early games. A half dozen bats Rizzo had ordered from the factory had been shipped to Cleveland's Hal Trosky by mistake. As a result, the Pittsburgh rookie was doing heavy damage against opposing pitchers while using Trosky's model war clubs.[4]

Grimm and Brannick's comments about Bauers and Tobin were echoed by manager Pie Traynor's assessment that pitching held the key to the team's success. Traynor reasoned that previous flag winners always had two aces at the top of the rotation who could make life miserable for their National League opponents. "The club that can produce two star hurlers to team up," said the Buccaneers pilot, "usually wins the pennant. I figure Bauers and Tobin can turn the trick for us, providing they pitch the ball of which they're capable. If they can win about 35 or 40 games between them, we're going to be in the race from the opening day. Look at the pennant winners in recent years. The Yanks last season had Lefty Gomez and Red Ruffing as the star team. The Giants showed Carl Hubbell and Cliff Melton. Several years ago the Cardinals brought up Dizzy and Daffy Dean. Our candidates are Bauers and Tobin. If we go along with Bauers and Tobin working smoothly, and one of the others—Blanton, Bowman, Brandt, Lucas, Swift, Duke, Klinger or Sewell—takes up the No. 3 spot, it won't be a hard job to find the fourth starter from our staff."[5]

Traynor believed he had enough candidates to fill the back end of his rotation. He knew, however, that star hurlers Jim Tobin or Russ Bauers were going to have to stay healthy and perform to their potential or there would be trouble. Blanton had ably assumed the responsibility of an ace before, but the rest of Traynor's pitching staff was a mixture of aging veterans and rookies who could not be trusted with such a task. Little did he know that his worst fears were about to become a reality because of the childish behavior of some of his players.

By the time Pittsburgh's exhibition schedule brought them to Barstow, California, on April 4 for a game against the Barstow All-Stars, the Pirate players had wearied of playing games against subpar competition. Even though the Pirates ran their spring winning streak to 11 straight games with a 7–2 victory over the All-Stars, these contests versus town teams had lost all their charm. Primitive conditions irked players who yearned for the championship campaign to begin. Before the game in Barstow, the Pirates were transported from the train station directly to their hotel so they could dress for the game. From there they were driven in a school bus to the baseball field, which also acted as the town's airport and which consisted entirely of sand. As the game progressed, windy conditions created a sandstorm that drove sand into the eyes and hair of players and spectators.[6]

The brisk wind made chasing fly balls an adventure for players on both teams. Pirates pitchers Cy Blanton, Jim Tobin and Truett "Rip" Sewell's only concern that afternoon was to throw strikes and try to end each inning as quickly as possible. There were no more than 200 spectators standing or sitting in their automobiles watching the game from the outfield. Jackrabbits mingled with baseball players throughout the afternoon. When the contest ended, Pirate trainer Doc Jorgensen had to use plenty of eyewash to cleanse the afflicted orbs of Pittsburgh's players. One of the oddest aspects of the afternoon was that the large majority of the male spectators who attended the game sported mustaches, goatees and sideburns. It seemed that "Calico Days," scheduled for the carnival in Barstow on May 14 and 15, included a contest where the men with the longest sideburns and bushiest goatees would be awarded trophies. Making matters worse from the players' perspective after this travesty was that cold weather and snow awaited them at an upcoming barnstorming stop in Winslow, Arizona.[7]

The players had six or seven hours to kill before their train left for its next destination. In anticipation of the visit of the ball club, many of Barstow's local business owners had spruced up their establishments to make them more alluring. Barstow's best billiard parlor and saloon was the choice of one group of Pirates players while another contingent took in a motion picture show at the local theater. Most of Pittsburgh's players had sipped a glass or two of beer to wet their parched throats before they ended the evening's entertainment and left for the station to board the midnight train. Most of Traynor's players were already aboard the train and nestled under their covers when the final six or seven men arrived at the train station around 11:30 p.m. Pie, who was among those who had turned in early, was so sound asleep that he never heard the ensuing tomfoolery that took place in one of the cars carrying Pittsburgh's players.[8]

The usual entertainment during train trips included pranks on traveling secretary Lawrence Collier involving sneezing powder and some musical melodies by Cy Blanton and Arky Vaughan with a harmonica.[9] On this night, some of the Pirates who had been drinking decided to break the monotony by attempting to pin Russ Bauers on the floor. The friendly scuffle had devastating consequences.[10] Bauers injured his right knee during the playful tussle and by morning his knee was irritated, very swollen and red.[11]

The initial report Traynor received was that Bauers had slipped on the train overnight and injured his knee. Further inquiries on his part brought to light the truth about the impromptu wrestling match. Traynor called on Doc Jorgensen to examine Bauers' swollen knee and then made plans for the pitcher to consult with Dr. Robert F. Hyland in St. Louis.[12] When the Pirates reached Clovin, New Mexico, for their next game, the manager called for a meeting at which he plastered fines on Bauers and five other players

who had participated in the senseless brawl. Traynor did not mince any words as he read his squad the riot act.[13] "I'm through fooling with you fellows," exclaimed Traynor in a terse tone. "From now on we want hustlers and the laggards will have to go. We've got our best pitcher laid up with a wrenched knee and he may be out of action for a month, maybe two months. I'm going to fine the fellows that were tussling in that Pullman and the money comes out of the first paycheck. Bauers stands suspended and will draw no pay from the Pirates until he proves he's able to pitch. In addition Bauers must pay his own hospital expenses all the time he's out."[14]

The loss of Pittsburgh's star hurler left Traynor in a foul mood and he gave his players every indication that the Mr.

Pittsburgh pitcher Russ Bauers incurred the wrath of manager Pie Traynor after injuring his knee while wrestling with two teammates on the team train after an exhibition game in Barstow, California, on April 4, 1938. Bauers suffered a torn ligament in his knee during this senseless tussle and was fined by Traynor for his reckless behavior (National Baseball Hall of Fame Library, Cooperstown, New York).

Nice Guy label usually attached to him was ancient history. However, he did eliminate the fines on three players when further investigating revealed that those players were not even in that Pullman car when the wrestling match took place. Pie refused to reveal the other two players' identities involved in the incident.[15] Bauers and team president William Benswanger left immediately for Amarillo, Texas, where they would board a plane for St. Louis. Once they arrived there, Bauers would be placed in the care of Dr. Hyland at St. John's Hospital and Benswanger would rejoin the team in Dallas.[16] Benswanger also seemed to be in total agreement with his manager in respect to those players who did not take their work seriously. "I'm back of Pie 100 per cent," Benswanger announced. "We're going to have everybody in line or they go off this team. I don't care if we finish in last place, we're going to get along without the non-producers and bank on the youngsters who will hustle for us and take this game seriously. We are sure this move will bring us beneficial results."[17]

Benswanger also cautioned the press that the whole affair involving Bauers and his two teammates was nothing more than a friendly wrestling match and did not transpire during a wild party. He intimated that Traynor used strong language to hammer home his point that players needed to curb their desire to have fun using such rough methods. Pirates management received some good news after Dr. Hyland examined Bauers in St. Louis. Hyland stated that a preliminary examination showed his injury was not as serious as was initially believed. X-rays revealed that Russ had suffered a sprain and a torn ligament. Hyland believed the injury would sideline Pittsburgh's star pitcher for a week to ten days before he could resume getting in condition for the upcoming campaign. Bauers was to remain in St. Louis during that time to undergo treatment on his lame knee. The prognosis was welcome news even though Bauers would not be ready to start on opening day as had been planned.[18]

Traynor remained concerned as the team moved forward on its exhibition tour in preparation for the season opener that was less than two weeks away. First up was the Phillips 66 Oilers in Clovis on April 6, but the game was called in the fifth inning with Pittsburgh trailing, 2–1, when a dust storm made visibility non-existent. The weather was so cold that Al Todd and Arky Vaughan wore gloves while they batted.[19] More bad luck plagued Pittsburgh when they reached Sweetwater, Texas, for a game against the Chicago White Sox on April 7. A desert snowstorm that packed a huge Texas punch led to the contest being postponed.[20] Players from both squads decided to hold an impromptu hunting expedition after a local sporting goods store supplied the shotguns and ammunition. Chicago defeated Pittsburgh 27–20, with jackrabbits being counted instead of runs.[21]

Idle time for Pittsburgh's players did not mean that manager Pie Traynor's mind was not constantly working on mapping out a path for his squad. The Pirates skipper wasted little time laying down some new rules for his players after the Bauers injury: he prohibited liquor and poker games and decreed that players had to be in their hotel rooms by midnight on road trips.[22] He still seemed a bit agitated over the whole incident as he informed his players that these rules would be strictly enforced. "Acting like a lot of wild schoolboys is no way to get ready for a major league season," Pie said. "If you fellows don't think enough of your jobs to run no chances of hurting yourselves, you are the ones who are going to suffer."[23]

As Pittsburgh prepared to play the final slate of games on their exhibition schedule, fans in the Smoky City were still wondering if a two-week-old rumor meant that Traynor was unhappy with his options for the third base position. The Pirates had been rumored to be interested in veteran third baseman Arthur "Pinky" Whitney from Philadelphia. Phillies manager Jimmy Wilson and Traynor supposedly had held discussions regarding a deal involving Whitney. The transaction never gained any traction since Wilson was insisting on receiving one of Pittsburgh's young hurlers.[24] While Pie seemed to be worried about using either Bill Brubaker or Jeep Handley at third base, the brilliant play of Arky Vaughan and Johnny Rizzo during the exhibition season continued to put a huge smile on his face. Vaughan blasted a home run and barely missed smacking a second against the White Sox in Fort Worth, Texas, on April 9. Rizzo banged out four hits and raised his average to .450 for spring training. Brubaker even shook loose from a slump as he smacked a single, two doubles and a triple.[25]

Following Pittsburgh's 13–8 victory over the White Sox in Fort Worth and another 9–2 triumph in Dallas one day later, Sox manager Jimmy Dykes offered his assessment of the Pirates. Dykes cautioned baseball writers that a three-game sampling was not enough time to pass judgment, but when pressed he stated that Pittsburgh had everything necessary to be a solid squad. Dykes then proclaimed that the Pirates were his choice to win the National League pennant. He believed Traynor's squad superior to Charley Grimm's Cubs team, which had played 13 exhibition contests against his White Sox. Veteran White Sox catcher Luke Sewell was even more adamant than Dykes in ordaining Pittsburgh as the National League's prohibitive favorite. "I've never seen such a strong hitting club," said Sewell. "The Pirates have been murdering that ball and distributing the hits all through the lineup. Rizzo looks like a natural in left field and if Pie Traynor can dig up a good pitcher to pair with Bauers, the Pirates should step out and stay there."[26]

Traynor's troops continued to impress Dykes and Sewell even though the Pirates were defeated by the White Sox, 7–4, at Fort Smith, Arkansas, on April 11. Pitcher Bill Swift was Pittsburgh's star for the day as he tossed five shutout innings and allowed only three hits.[27] After the game at Fort Smith, both teams moved on to Shawnee, Oklahoma, for another bout on April 12. A hearty group of rabid baseball fans turned out to pay tribute to hometown favorite Cy Blanton and fellow Oklahomans Paul and Lloyd Waner. Blanton's wife, daughter, mother and father were in attendance, while Paul and Lloyd's parents and two married sisters made the 16-mile trip from Harrah to watch the game.[28]

A crowd of 2,500 turned out to watch Blanton pitch the first inning as Pittsburgh destroyed Chicago by a score of 10–2.[29] Prior to Blanton's homecoming, manager Pie Traynor announced that he would be the Pirates starting pitcher on opening day against St. Louis. Jim Tobin was chosen to hurl the series' second contest on April 20, while either Bill Swift or Mace Brown would pitch the finale against the Cardinals.[30] While Traynor's pitchers were busy working to get in shape so that they could fill the void left by Russ Bauers' absence, Arky Vaughan continued his torrid hitting pace during the game in Shawnee. Vaughan launched two home runs over an advertising sign at the Shawnee Park and was awarded with a pair of five-dollar hats by the company marketing their goods on that billboard. Arky immediately sent one of the hats to his father.[31]

When the Pirates entourage moved into Kansas to play a game in Wichita, numerous luminaries were part of the crowd of 6,000 people. Kansas Governor Walter A. Huxman and Governor Frank Murphy of Michigan were in attendance. Former Pirates great Fred Clarke also made the trip from Winfield, along with oil mogul Lew Wentz of Ponca City, Oklahoma.[32] Battles against major league foes were no longer on the docket as Pittsburgh prepared to play its last three exhibition contests. Following the game in Wichita, Traynor's boys would finish with further contests in the state of Kansas against Hutchinson in Manhattan and then Salina and Hutchinson once again in their respective hometowns.[33]

The Pirates' ten exhibition skirmishes against the Chicago Cubs (three games) and Chicago White Sox (seven games) could be classified as a rousing success from a hitting standpoint. Arky Vaughan batted .516 against the two clubs, while smacking five home runs, two triples and a double. Second baseman Pep Young followed Vaughan with a .447 average, while first baseman Gus Suhr drilled four doubles, two triples and hit .366 during those ten games.³⁴

The Pirates had scheduled two spring games against the Hutchinson team because it was a crucial minor league affiliate for which Pittsburgh held the right of first refusal for any player on the roster. Third baseman Frankie Gustine, an 18-year-old Traynor had discovered in Chicago, was an intriguing member of the Hutchinson nine who seemed to have a bright baseball future ahead of him. When Gustine was 14, he used to come around and shag fly balls whenever the Pirates played at Wrigley Field.³⁵

The game in Salina was cancelled due to rain, so Pittsburgh finished off its exhibition schedule with two contests against Hutchinson.³⁶ Traynor handed over the managerial reins to coach Jewel Ens for the final game in Hutchinson so he could travel to St. Louis one day early to participate in a nationwide radio broadcast along with the National League's seven other managers.³⁷ After their final exhibition game in Hutchinson, the Pirates squad rushed to Pullmans that would deliver them to St. Louis on Monday morning, April 18. Traynor planned on putting his players through a long, spirited practice session that afternoon in preparation for the opener on Tuesday.³⁸ Despite all of the pitfalls and bad luck that had befallen Traynor and his charges during spring training, his team had won a majority of its exhibition games and had lost only two players to injuries. One of these was Russ Bauers and the other was pitcher Joe Bowman.³⁹

Bowman seemed to have developed a kink in his pitching arm during the Corsairs early exhibition series in San Francisco. Joe remained there for a couple of days and received treatment from a specialist who worked on his arm. When Bowman rejoined the Pirates, Traynor was very cautious with his veteran hurler, allowing him only to chase fungoes and toss lightly on the sidelines. Traynor reasoned that the rest would do Bowman a world of good and permit him to be ready by opening day.⁴⁰ News on the Bauers front was also encouraging, as Dr. Robert Hyland had cleared the big right-hander to rejoin his teammates on the eve of Pittsburgh's opener. Heat lamp treatment on Russ' knee had worked wonders, enabling him to jump, run and take long walks without experiencing any pain. Bauers also kept his pitching arm strong by participating in some workouts with the St. Louis Cardinals.⁴¹

Hyland believed that Russ had made so much progress that Traynor could use the pitcher without any restrictions in the opener against the Cardinals on April 19. When Bauers arrived in St. Louis, he greeted his teammates at the Kings Way Hotel and announced he was ready for action and fit once again.[42] With the opening of another regular season only one day away, the time for official predictions by baseball writers had arrived. New York sportswriter Joe Williams predicted that Pittsburgh would finish the 1938 National League campaign in second place behind the New York Giants. Williams felt the Pirates were strong in every area except for defense. He also reasoned that Traynor handled his pitchers poorly during the 1937 season by not relying more on Mace Brown, Jim Tobin and Russ Bauers. The clincher for Williams was New York's supremacy in head-to-head contests with Pittsburgh during the past five seasons.[43]

While Joe Williams' opinions made for interesting reading, baseball fans in Pittsburgh cared a lot more about the views of the man at the helm of the Pirates. Prior to the opening contest, *Pittsburgh Press* columnist Chester L. Smith called Traynor on the telephone and asked for his assessment of the 1938 campaign. When the phone operator finally told Smith she had Traynor on the other end of the wire, Pie immediately joked that it was a devil of an hour to be getting an honest man out of bed. Traynor asked Smith if he could wait for a minute while he put on some slippers and lighted a cigarette. After the usual pleasantries had been exchanged, they got down to business.[44]

"What is it you want to know?" Traynor inquired.

"Where do you think the Pirates will finish this year?" Smith inquired.

"In Cincinnati on the second of October," quipped Traynor using some of that sardonic wit he had become known for.

"Pardon me, maybe you want the real answer, and you'll get it," continued Traynor in a more serious tone. "We've got the stuff this time. If we don't land higher than all of you fellows say, I'm going to be disappointed."

Smith reminded Traynor that such a conclusion could only mean one thing — a pennant. Was Traynor willing to go out on a limb and predict Pittsburgh would be crowned as champions of the National League in 1938?

"Sure — I figure the Pirates or the Giants and I'm not going to take a back seat for Bill Terry until he shoves me into it," continued Traynor. "I don't think Dizzy Dean will pitch the Cubs ahead of us. In fact, they look like a third-place team to me. And I gave the Cardinals fourth place, the Bees fifth, the Dodgers sixth, the Reds seventh and the Phillies last. This is the best team I've ever had in my four seasons as manager."[45]

Traynor's reference to Dizzy Dean being a member of the Chicago Cubs was the result of a blockbuster deal that had been brokered a few days before the season opened. On April 16, 1938, Dean was shipped to Chicago in exchange for pitchers Curt Davis and Clyde Shoun, outfielder Tuck Stainback and $185,000 in cash. Some believed that the deal made the Cubs a pennant favorite, but Traynor disagreed. He reasoned that Dizzy still had not recovered from his arm problems since St. Louis had given up on him at a time when they desperately needed pitchers of his caliber.[46] Traynor's prediction during his interview with Smith that Pittsburgh would battle New York for the National League pennant was bold given his comments earlier in the spring. During a previous chat with Chicago baseball scribe Ed Burns about the Pirates' reputation as underachievers, Traynor questioned why his team had been projected as a pennant winner in several prior seasons. He also wondered why his pitching staff always was touted too highly by baseball experts across America.[47]

"When I was a player in the ranks," commented Traynor, "I was a much better judge of prospective players than I now am. As a player, I could tell the first day whether a prospect was going to make good and usually could gauge the exact extent to which the young man would help us. In some of those years when the optimists were awarding us the pennant, I was amazed at their perspectives—at the reasons they gave why we were going to win the pennant. Since I have been a manager, my judgment in making appraisals has been lessened to an enormous extent. A manager must always be looking for the best. Managers hope for miracles, just like the fans frequently do. I have to be an optimist and must join with our friends who wish us well, insofar as the future is concerned. However, my power to analyze the failures after they have happened has not been distorted."[48]

When the Pirates' 1938 roster was announced, it included five rookies. The twelve-man pitching staff consisted of Russ Bauers, Cy Blanton, Joe Bowman, Ed Brandt, Mace Brown, Marvin Duke, Ken Heintzelman, Bob Klinger, Red Lucas, Rip Sewell, Bill Swift and Jim Tobin. The catchers responsible for developing this young staff were Ray Berres and Al Todd. Pittsburgh's infield aggregation included Bill Brubaker, Lee Handley, Gus Suhr, Tommy Thevenow, Arky Vaughan and Pep Young. Traynor's outfield unit was heavy with experience as veterans Paul Waner and Lloyd Waner would be flanked by rookie Johnny Rizzo, while Woody Jensen and Johnny Dickshot would be available to give those starters breathers when necessary.

Disturbing off-season rhetoric, past contract haggling and stupid behavior by some Pittsburgh players during the spring exhibition tour was all forgotten by devoted baseball fans in the Smoky City who were overjoyed that the baseball season was finally beginning. Pie Traynor and his players, along with 13 other teams in the National and American leagues, hoped that their squad would be the one to dethrone the two teams from New York.

The Pirates players looked slightly different when they took the field at Sportsman's Park for the opener against St. Louis on April 19. Pie Traynor and team officials had decided to change the team's uniform style for the 1938 campaign: square lettering on the jerseys used in 1937 had been replaced by script calligraphy. On Pittsburgh's white home jerseys, the word "Pirates" appeared in navy blue script lettering and edged with cardinal, while the color scheme was reversed on the team's grey road jerseys. Single piping on the neck of both jerseys matched the script lettering color, while a double band of navy and cardinal appeared on the sleeves of both the home and traveling uniforms. Belt loops on each respective jersey also matched the lettering color. The hat worn by players at all venues remained the same as the previous year. The cap was the usual "Pirate Special," solidly blue except for the letter "P" on the front in cardinal.[49]

While the Pirates looked resplendent in their brand-new uniforms, playing solid baseball right out of the gate was manager Pie Traynor's top priority. Traynor took his first step toward achieving that goal by going with a balanced lineup against southpaw opening day starter Bob Weiland of the Cardinals. The following was Traynor's lineup: 1. Lloyd Waner (CF), 2. Paul Waner (RF), 3. Johnny Rizzo (LF), 4. Arky Vaughan (SS), 5. Gus Suhr (1B), 6. Al Todd (C), 7. Bill Brubaker (3B), 8. Pep Young (2B) and 9. Cy Blanton (P). Prior to the game, United States Senator Bennett Clark assumed the position of catcher behind home plate while Governor Henry Horner of Illinois stood in the batter's box as the first ball was pitched by St. Louis mayor Bernard F. Dickmann.[50]

Things started smoothly for Traynor's boys as they jumped out to a quick 2–0 lead against St. Louis after three innings. Pirates hurler Cy Blanton pitched magnificently until he tired in the fifth and a Pep Young error helped St. Louis take the lead by pushing three runs across the plate. The Cardinals maintained that 3–2 advantage until the ninth inning when Pittsburgh's star player pulled off some spectacular opening day heroics.

Paul Waner started off the frame by banging out a single to center for his third hit on the day. Waner quickly was erased from the basepaths when Johnny Rizzo grounded into a force play. Shortstop Arky Vaughan stepped up to the plate and worked the count to three balls and one strike against Weiland. Correctly anticipating a fastball on the next pitch, Vaughan whipped his bat around and sent the ball soaring into the right-center-field bleachers. The 400-foot home run scored Rizzo as well and gave Pittsburgh a 4–3 lead. Rookie reliever Bob Klinger made that score hold up by tossing his second shutout inning of ball in the ninth inning to preserve Pittsburgh's victory.[51]

There were many aspects of the exciting opening game victory that put a smile on manager Pie Traynor's face. He was ecstatic over the way Klinger and Mace Brown pitched shutout ball in their respective relief stints. Paul Waner showed that he still was one of the top hitters in the National League, while there also could be no doubt there was still some power in Vaughan's big bat. Johnny Rizzo's major league debut was also a smashing success as he was magnificent both at the plate and in the field.[52] Rizzo, along with former Columbus teammate Enos Slaughter of the Cardinals, both made fine impressions during their first taste of big league baseball.[53] Slaughter went 3-for-5 at the plate while Rizzo went 2-for-3, scored one run and drove home one. Rizzo also missed hitting home runs by inches on two occasions when he blasted balls into the left-field stands that were foul by the narrowest of margins.[54]

Rizzo's first game as a major leaguer was so impressive that representatives of Pittsburgh's Italian Professional Association wasted no time in honoring the Pirates rookie. After Dr. D.S. DeStio of the Italian Professional Association wired Rizzo asking him if he would be their honored guest at a dinner party on Sunday, April 24, the young outfielder immediately accepted this invitation.[55] Rizzo gave his admirers more reason to be proud of him on Wednesday, April 20, when he went 2-for-4 at the plate, scored two runs and poled a long triple in Pittsburgh's 9–4 victory over St. Louis. Lloyd Waner, Arky Vaughan and Al Todd recorded three hits apiece and accounted for four runs scored and four RBIs. The Pirates feasted on St. Louis pitching as they banged out 20 hits. Pittsburgh starter Jim Tobin needed all of that run support, as he allowed 14 hits while also pitching a complete game.

Right fielder Paul Waner was the only Pirate player who did not record multiple hits as Cardinals manager Frankie Frisch trotted five hurlers out to the mound. Even though Waner only went 1-for-6 during the contest, he continued a trend of making brilliant, heady plays in the outfield. While Waner and Bill Benswanger had been at odds on a few occasions over the years during contract negotiations, the team president had earned the respect and admiration of the veteran outfielder and his teammates. Prior to the season, Waner had wagered a chapeau with Benswanger that pitcher

5. Bucs Bust Out of the Gate Due to Vaughan's Heroics

Bob Klinger would post the best earned run average of any rookie hurler during the 1938 season. Following the game against St. Louis on April 20, Benswanger approached Paul in the hotel lobby that evening and praised him for his play during the season's first two games. "Paul," the Pirate president said. "You looked pretty good the first day, three hits. And out there today, you only got one hit in six times. But listen, the opening day you cut off Slaughter going to third base, stopped a rally and saved us some runs by that play. The second day, when you came up with a great shoe-string catch on Pepper Martin's short fly, you stopped another rally that looked dangerous. I just want you to know that those fielding plays you make are as good as hits in my books."[56]

Benswanger's squad made the season opening road series a complete success with a 6–5 victory over St. Louis on Thursday, April 21, that enabled them to sweep the three-game set. Mace Brown picked up the victory in relief even though he allowed two runs and four hits during two and two-third innings of work. Johnny Rizzo and Arky Vaughan continued their assault on Cardinals pitching; each player went 2-for-5 at the plate, recorded one double and one RBI apiece while also scoring half of Pittsburgh's runs. Through the first three games of the season, Rizzo had hit safely in each contest, while Vaughan had collected six hits against Frankie Frisch's squad.[57] While everyone connected to Pittsburgh's baseball franchise was ecstatic over the squad's effort in this series, Frisch was in a foul mood when he addressed his players in the clubhouse after their third straight defeat. "How can big, strong, able-bodied guys stand up there with runners on bases and look at a fast one, right over the middle, for a third strike?" thundered Frisch.[58]

When the triumphant Pirates reached the Pennsylvania Station at 8:25 a.m. on April 22, the players were welcomed by a committee from Pittsburgh's Chamber of Commerce. The KDKA radio station set up a microphone so that Pie Traynor and his players could be introduced to the throng of rooters. After the introductions, the players were escorted to automobiles and paraded through the downtown streets. Shortly after noon, rookie outfielder Johnny Rizzo was given a proper introduction to baseball fans in the city during an interview with Chester L. Smith at the new Press-KDKA studio.[59]

Everything seemed to be going smoothly for Pie Traynor and his players as the Pirates prepared to face Cincinnati in the home opener at Forbes Field on Friday, April 22. In spite of the fact that local weatherman W.S. Brotzman called for cold weather and rain showers, the sun was shining brightly on more than 20,000 Pittsburgh patrons as they filed through the turnstiles. Brotzman was partially correct about the weather, as those who sat in shaded portions of the stands could attest to biting cold throughout the afternoon. Pittsburgh's opening day ceremonies were subdued as had long been the tradition at Forbes Field.[60] Manager Pie Traynor was presented with the traditional giant apple pie at home plate by members of the Dormont Boosters' Club prior to the contest.[61] Then, with Danny Nirella and his band playing, both teams marched to the center-field flag pole for the flag-hoisting ceremony. A new season at Forbes Field was officially ordained when mayor Cornelius D. Scully threw out the ceremonial first pitch.[62]

Even though the infield was dry and fast, the previous night's rain made for treacherous footing in the outfield that forced players from both teams to be cautious.[63] Manager Traynor received a scare in the first inning when starting pitcher Red Lucas was involved in a play at first base. After retiring Cincinnati's first two batters, Dusty Cooke smacked a ground ball to first baseman Gus Suhr. When Lucas came over to the bag and took Suhr's toss, Cooke became entangled with the veteran Pirates hurler and fell on top of him. Lucas walked around a bit to shake off the pain, rubbed his back and then requested an opportunity to toss a few warm-up pitches. The collision did not seem to affect Lucas, as he appeared to have his usual stuff the remainder of the afternoon.[64]

Lucas battled the Reds through seven and two-thirds innings and picked up his first win of the campaign as Pittsburgh prevailed by a score of 7–4. Second baseman Pep Young was money in the clutch as he went 2-for-4 and knocked in four Pirates runs. Gus Suhr, Bill Brubaker and Al Todd also banged out two hits apiece, with both of the Pirates catcher's safeties being triples. Russ Bauers saw his first action in 1938 when he relieved Lucas in the eighth inning and choked off a potential Cincinnati rally.[65] Russ then set down the Reds in the ninth inning to preserve the victory. Rookie outfielder Johnny Rizzo failed to record a hit for the first time in a big league game, going 0-for-4 at the plate.

Rizzo's hitless day during the home opener did not dampen the excitement about the young power hitter. When he came to bat in the first inning, Forbes Field's fans gave him a rousing round of applause and Danny Nirella's band played "O Sole Mio." The Italian-American outfielder from Texas got a huge kick out of this reception.[66] Several thousand lines about Rizzo already had been written by baseball pundits across America during the season's first week. After Pittsburgh's win over Cincinnati in the home opener, Pie Traynor added a few comments of his own regarding Rizzo's indis-

5. Bucs Bust Out of the Gate Due to Vaughan's Heroics

putable fighting spirit. "He's going to be a good ball player because he doesn't scare easily," Traynor said. "The White Sox pitchers tried knocking him down a couple times but when Johnny climbed back on his feet and combed their hair with line drives they quit. I'll string along with anyone who can do that."[67]

Rizzo wasted no time getting back on track at the plate by tormenting the Reds during a 6–2 Pittsburgh victory on Saturday, April 23. Johnny blasted two triples and one single during four trips to the plate while knocking in three of the Pirates runs.[68] A crowd of 8,550 fans also watched Rizzo field his position in left field exceptionally. Cy Blanton pitched shutout baseball through the eighth inning until the Reds touched him up for two tallies.[69] Prize fielding plays by Bill Brubaker, Pep Young and Paul Waner greatly aided Blanton's cause during the contest. Waner's fielding gem was the game's most crucial play—he came running toward first base in the eighth inning and made a diving catch of Nino Bongiovanni's drive that ended the frame. Ray Berres started his first game behind the plate because regular catcher Al Todd was sidelined with a mild charley-horse injury that had occurred on Friday during a collision with Reds first baseman Frank McCormick.[70]

Pitcher Jim Tobin supplied the main storyline during Pittsburgh's final game of the series against the Reds on Sunday, April 24 as the Pirates attempted to win their sixth game in a row.

Tobin outdueled Cincinnati's Peaches Davis as Pittsburgh pulled off a second consecutive series sweep with a 2–1 victory. Tobin tossed a complete game, gave up one run and scattered five hits. Jim also went 2-for-2 at the plate, smashing a triple and a single and scoring a run. Tobin's triple off Davis to the deepest part of Forbes Field traveled 410 feet. Cincinnati center fielder Harry Craft was able to get his glove on the baseball but failed to hold onto the sphere; nobody in the press box disputed official scorer Ed Balinger's decision when he held up three fingers to indicate that Tobin's blast was a triple.[71]

Pittsburgh's three-game sweep over Cincinnati ran their winning streak over manager Bill McKechnie's team to 20 straight games. Pittsburgh now had won 21 consecutive contests against the Reds at Forbes Field since the Rhineland crew last had pulled out a victory at the Oakland ballpark on August 11, 1936.[72] A big banquet at the Balbo Restaurant at 444 Wood Street was held on Sunday night to honor one of the players most responsible for Pittsburgh's strong start out of the gate.[73] Johnny Rizzo was honored by the Pittsburgh Italian Professional Association, whose members were impressed with the player's friendliness, sincerity and baseball ability. During the event, his friends and admirers decided that they would honor the player with a "Johnny Rizzo Day" at Forbes Field on Saturday, June 4 when the Buccaneers played Brooklyn. Association president Dr. D.S. DeStio acted as toastmaster for the event while Bill Benswanger offered some kind words about Rizzo as one of the guest speakers. "Your success is ours and ours is yours," Benswanger told Rizzo. "Keep up the good work."[74]

Success continued to be the Pirates' battle cry as they made it seven wins in a row with a comeback victory over the Chicago Cubs on Monday, April 25. Staff ace Russ Bauers was unimpressive during his first start of the year as he allowed six earned runs during seven innings of work. In the eighth inning, with his team trailing, 6–4, Traynor relieved the tiring Bauers with Mace Brown. Since Jim Tobin had pinch-hit for Ray Berres in the previous frame, he placed Brown in the eighth slot of the batting order and allowed new catcher Al Todd to hit ninth so he would lead off the eighth inning. This tactic is commonplace today but it was not used as much during that era. It reaped immediate results when Todd responded by slashing a single to center to start the eighth inning. Since southpaw hurler Bob Logan was pitching for Chicago, Traynor selected Johnny Dickshot to bat for Lloyd Waner even though Waner had gone 2-for-4 on the day.[75]

Dickshot hustled up to the plate and drew a walk that put the tying run on first base. Paul Waner got a pitch to his liking that he attempted to pull to left-center, but shortstop Tony Lazzeri fielded it and forced Dickshot at second base. Johnny Rizzo worked Logan for a free pass that loaded the bases. Arky Vaughan stepped up to the plate and promptly dumped a single to left, scoring both Todd and Waner with the runs that tied the game. Gus Suhr lashed out his third hit on the day, a single to center field that brought Rizzo home and gave Pittsburgh the lead. Bill Brubaker greeted new pitcher Bill Lee after he replaced Logan by ripping a double to left-center that scored Arky Vaughan. As Pep Young stepped to the plate, Traynor had Todd stand in front of the dugout swinging his menacing war bludgeon even though Mace Brown was due to hit next.[76]

Traynor's ruse almost fooled Lee as he started pitching to Young. Chicago's hurler finally caught on to what Traynor was doing and called for an intentional walk that would set up a force at any base. This strategy paid off when Brown grounded into a double play. Brown then retired the Bruins without any player hitting a baseball out of the infield. Brown was credited with his second victory of the year in a relief role as Pittsburgh defeated Chicago, 8–6. Traynor's players celebrated heartily in the dressing

5. *Bucs Bust Out of the Gate Due to Vaughan's Heroics*   85

room after this exciting contest as they discussed their skipper's brilliant maneuvers and the great victory that had resulted.[77]

Prior to the second game of the series against the Cubs on April 26 at Forbes Field, Traynor announced that pitcher Joe Bowman was ready to go once again. The hurler had been nursing a sore arm for some time, but Pie was impressed enough with what he had recently seen of Bowman during practice to officially reinstate him to the active roster.[78] Traynor, however, had little reason to be enamored with the performance of starting pitcher Ed Brandt in that afternoon's contest against Chicago— the southpaw twirler was pulled after he allowed two runs, three hits and three walks in one-and-a-third innings of work. Bill Swift came on and did an admirable job in relief until the Cubs got to him for two runs in the tenth inning as Pittsburgh was handed its first defeat, 5–3. Swift's performance was so impressive that Traynor was giving strong consideration to adding him to the starting rotation. Rookie Johnny Rizzo had his first tough day of the season as he fanned twice with two runners on base each time. He also grounded into a double play, although a run did score on that occasion.[79]

It looked like the Pirates were headed for their second consecutive defeat on Wednesday, April 27 after the Cubs chased Pittsburgh starter Cy Blanton out of the box after five innings. Mace Brown and Bob Klinger did solid work in relief to avert further disaster. Chicago pitcher Larry French was cruising along with a 4–0 lead until the Pirates finally made a statement in the bottom of the seventh inning. Bill Brubaker walked to start the parade and then moved over to third on Pep Young's blistering single to deep left field. Brubaker scored Pittsburgh's first run of the afternoon when he tagged up from third on pinch-hitter Johnny Dickshot's fly ball to center field. Woody Jensen followed with a single and Johnny Rizzo walked to load the bases for Arky Vaughan.[80]

Vaughan was in the midst of a perfect day at the plate thus far against French, having singled two times and drawn a walk. The southpaw twirler had a count of three balls and two strikes on Vaughan when he decided to cut loose with a fastball. The left-handed-hitting Pirates shortstop sent French's pitch into the second tier of Forbes Field's right field stands. It was Vaughan's second home run of the season and, as had been the case on opening day in St. Louis, it gave his team a dramatic victory.[81] Klinger pitched the ninth inning to preserve a 6–5 victory. In the clubhouse after the game, Vaughan minimized his great effort saying that it was all in a day's work. "French just gave me a good pitch and I hit it right," stated Vaughan.[82]

The euphoria of Pittsburgh's come-from-behind victory quickly wore off the following day when St. Louis came to town and handed the Pirates their second loss of the season. The Cardinals easily handled Buccaneer starter Jim Tobin and cruised to a 5–3 victory. Tobin did not make it out of the seventh inning, allowing five runs and 12 hits. Rookie hurler Truett "Rip" Sewell made his major league debut and showed great stuff as he fanned five Cardinals during two and two-third innings of work.[83] Sewell did make a little history of sorts when he threw a wild pitch on his first pitch that allowed Johnny Mize to scamper home with his team's final run. Longtime baseball men could not recall another pitcher who had made his National League debut in such a fashion.[84]

Arky Vaughan continued his power hitting feats in defeat by blasting his third home run of the year. Vaughan easily could have hit two more homers if the wind had not been blowing from right field across to left. His blistering drives in the second and sixth innings carried to the right-field wall before Enos Slaughter hauled them in. After being put out of action for one game due to a left leg injury, Lloyd Waner pinch-hit for Pep Young in the ninth inning and was called out on strikes. Lloyd's vehement protest with plate umpire Beans Reardon over the call prompted many of his teammates to claim that they had never seen him squawk so loudly over a disputed play.[85] Manager Pie Traynor planned on using Woody Jensen against right-handed pitchers and Johnny Dickshot when Pittsburgh faced southpaws until Waner recovered from the injury.[86]

The second contest of this two-game set on April 29 was postponed due to wet grounds and cold weather. The Cardinals immediately left for St. Louis while the Pirates packed their gear and traveled to Cincinnati to open a three-game stand against Bill McKechnie's Reds.[87] Traynor sent Russ Bauers to the hill on April 30 in an effort to secure Pittsburgh's twenty-first consecutive victory over Cincinnati. Bauers deserved a better fate for his six innings of work — the Reds' Peaches Davis stymied Pittsburgh's batters and claimed a 2–0 victory. Paul Waner recorded two of his team's five safeties. Third baseman Bill Brubaker had a brutal day at the hot corner, committing four errors. One of Brubaker's gaffes was the muff of a throw that would have completed a triple play. After recording the first two outs in unassisted fashion, Bill dropped a throw during a rundown on the third man.[88]

Oddly enough, Brubaker's ineptitude at third base had no effect on Cincinnati putting their two runs on the board. Both of the Reds' markers were earned, with one of them coming on a booming home run off the bat of Ival Goodman in the seventh inning.[89] Despite the fact that Pittsburgh had struggled somewhat during their past four games, the Pirates still found themselves in second place with an 8–3 record when April ended. Pittsburgh trailed first-place New York by two games as Bill Terry's troops were off to a blistering 10–1 start. The battle for National League supremacy seemed to be shaping up as another showdown between these two longtime rivals.

6

Paul Waner's Slump and Talk of Rebuilding for Next Year

After spending years as the National League's doormat, the Cincinnati Reds seemed to be a reinvigorated squad under new manager Bill McKechnie's guidance during the first few weeks of the 1938 campaign. McKechnie had a fine track record, having won a championship as Pittsburgh's pilot in 1925, led the St. Louis Cardinals to a World Series appearance in 1928 and vastly improved the fortunes of the Boston Braves/Bees during his eight-year tenure as their pilot. Cincinnati's players showed the Pirates that their previous dominance was a thing of the past as Pittsburgh dropped their second game in a row against the Reds on Sunday, May 1. Reds pitcher Al Hollingsworth was brilliant as McKechnie's boys defeated the Pirates, 4–1. Bill Brubaker was the only Pirate who could do anything at the plate, smacking two doubles and driving home Pittsburgh's only run. Worse, Traynor lost the services of starting catcher Al Todd when a foul tip off the bat of Harry Craft tore skin and part of the nail off his forefinger.[1]

Pittsburgh's third consecutive loss prompted sportswriter Sid Feder to announce that the Pirates were doing their annual stumbling act after their customary fast getaway. Feder noted that it usually was Pittsburgh's custom to keep up their hot opening pace a little longer than this. In 1937, for instance, they had waited until the middle of May before the sleeping sickness took over. Feder reasoned that Pie Traynor had not given his squad that little extra jolt of inspiration in the spring to see them through at least one month of the season. Final proof for the sportswriter had come when Pittsburgh dropped two straight games to a team they had manhandled in 1937.[2] While there is no reason to believe that Traynor was swayed by comments in the press, he was concerned enough over his team's recent losses that a lineup change was made for the game against Cincinnati on May 2. Lee Handley replaced Bill Brubaker at third base and was placed in the leadoff spot. Expected to follow Handley in the order were Woody Jensen, Paul Waner, Johnny Rizzo, Arky Vaughan, Gus Suhr, Pep Young, Ray Berres and pitcher Cy Blanton.[3]

Traynor's changes did revitalize Pittsburgh's hitting attack, as they banged out 10 hits and pushed six runs across the plate, Unfortunately, this newfound offense was not enough as Cincinnati knocked around three Pirates hurlers and claimed an 8–6 victory. Cy Blanton did not make it out of the fifth inning and gave up five runs and seven hits. Mace Brown and Bob Klinger were not much better in relief, as each pitcher failed to suppress the Reds' onslaught. Gus Suhr led the Pirates' rejuvenated offense and pushed his average to .304 by going 2-for-3, scoring one run, rapping a double and driving home two teammates. After going hitless in the first two games of the Cincinnati series, Johnny Rizzo went 3-for-4 and scored two of Pittsburgh's runs.

While Traynor was hopeful that Rizzo was finally pulling himself out of the minor batting slump that had followed his blazing start, his concern over veteran outfielder Paul Waner's hitting woes was growing. Through Pittsburgh's first 13 games, Paul's average stood at a lackluster .235. Even though Traynor believed that Waner's problems were only temporary, the possibility that this could be the year his great career went into decline obviously worried Pittsburgh's manager. Rizzo was also an enigma because the rookie resembled a world beater some days and a minor leaguer on others.[4] This was to be expected from a man who was playing his first season of major league baseball. Overall, Rizzo seemed to be doing a good job of handling the huge expectations which had been placed upon him.

Rizzo had been under intense scrutiny since reporting to spring training because he was the first true power hitting prospect ever to wear a Pittsburgh uniform. John Costa Rizzo had been born on July 30, 1912, in Houston, Texas. As a teenager playing baseball in his home state, his prowess was so overwhelming that by 1930 he was one of the area's best semi-pro players.[5]

He began his professional career in 1931 by toiling for teams in Corpus Christi, La Feria and Galveston. In 1932, Rizzo split time between Muskogee, Hutchinson and Bartlesville, batting a combined .341 for the three teams. After being shadowed by agents of Cincinnati's front office for weeks, Johnny was purchased from Bartlesville by the Reds.[6]

Rizzo was confident that he would be playing the outfield for Cincinnati in 1933. Instead, he was traded to the St. Louis Cardinals as part of a package that included 11 players and cash so that Cincinnati could secure veteran first baseman Jim Bottomley. Rizzo turned out to be the real find out of the list of unknown minor leaguers St. Louis received in the Bottomley deal by appearing in 133 games for Elmira of the New York–Pennsylvania League in 1933 and batting .307. The young Texan improved on that mark in 1934; he led the league in hitting with a .379 average and then was moved to the Cardinals' Texas League affiliate in Houston for the final weeks of the season. Rizzo was now a legitimate major league prospect, but as he was to discover it was difficult to progress in the vast farm chain of the Cardinals.

Before the 1935 season, St. Louis management arranged for Rizzo to play for their minor league affiliate in Rochester. Johnny balked at this move and went against the wishes of Branch Rickey and Cardinals owner Sam Breadon by refusing to report to Rochester.[7] The young outfielder cited money concerns as his reason for wanting to remain in Houston. Rochester was willing to pay Rizzo $275 per month to play for them, but this was only a $25 monthly increase over what he was making playing for Houston. So Johnny reasoned it would be more practical to play for less in his hometown in order to save a few dollars. He got his way and continued his hard hitting for the Buffaloes in 1935, batting .312 in 150 games and recording 100 RBIs. He followed that up with another solid season in 1936 in which he played in 144 games, hit .307 and drove home 84 runs. This earned Rizzo a promotion to Columbus in 1937, where he teamed up with Enos Slaughter to form a deadly combination in the outfield. Rizzo batted .358 while Slaughter won the American Association batting crown with a mark of .382. The pair combined to drive home 245 runs, with Rizzo accounting for 123 of them.[8]

Rizzo's proven ability as a run producer led Pirates management to make the deal that brought him to Pittsburgh after the 1937 campaign. Even though it would have been natural to compare Rizzo to Slaughter since they had accomplished so much playing together in Columbus, Pittsburgh's rookie outfielder was a prototype of Al Simmons at the plate. He used a spread stance much like Simmons. Even though he did not brandish his bat in such a robust fashion as Simmons before each trip to the plate, Rizzo poised his hickory in a way that was just as menacing to opposing pitchers.[9] While Johnny's batting style was comparable to Simmons, Pie Traynor believed the young player had the potential to be Pittsburgh's best left fielder since an all-time great. "Johnny Rizzo is not only a good hitter and a smart hustler—he is a fine fielder," stated Traynor. "I think he will be Pittsburgh's best left fielder since Fred Clarke."[10]

While Rizzo was not ready to be placed in the same category as a superb player like Clarke, he took great pride in trying to uphold the standards established by fellow players of Italian heritage like Tony Lazzeri, Ernesto Lombardi and Tony Cuccinello. Indeed Rizzo seemed to be brimming with self-confidence. When he found his first contract offer from the Pirates unacceptable, he responded in a letter asking Bill Benswanger if he had heard of Joe DiMaggio of the American League. The former Columbus outfielder added that he planned on being the Johnny Rizzo of the National League. Impressed with the rookie's boldness, Benswanger upped the salary amount in a second contract that Rizzo quickly accepted and signed.[11]

Rizzo's average stood at .313 as Pittsburgh returned home to face the Brooklyn Dodgers on Tuesday, May 3. Even though the Pirates had just been swept by the Reds, panic was not setting in among the players, who remained loose. Infielder Lee Handley paid a visit to Municipal Judge William E. Handley during the team's trip to Cincinnati. Even though the two were not related in any way, Judge Handley was in the habit of joking with his friends that his oldest boy was an infielder for the Pirates. One of those friends arranged for Lee to visit the judge. When Handley arrived at the courthouse, he found the proper courtroom and strolled up to the bench to greet the judge.[12]

"Good morning, pop," said Handley.

"How are you doing this morning, son," the judge replied. Both men carried on a father-and-son conversation for a couple of minutes as a puzzled group of people watched the cordial exchange. Finally they both had a good laugh about the gag and Lee then handed Judge Handley a baseball that was signed by every member of the Pittsburgh Pirates squad.[13]

Handley was one the few bright spots for manager Pie Traynor in the Pirates' first contest against Brooklyn on May 3 at Forbes Field as the Dodgers whipped Pittsburgh, 7–2. Handley went 2-for-4 at the plate, while fellow infielder Arky Vaughan banged out three hits for the Pirates. Starting pitcher Jim Tobin pitched a brilliant game until things fell apart in the seventh frame. With one out and the score tied 1–1, Brooklyn positioned runners on first and third on singles by Leo Durocher and Woody English. Durocher came around to score when Roy Spencer grounded out to Vaughan at short. Brooklyn's inning was given further life when Tot Pressnell's grounder rolled through Vaughan's legs. A single by Buddy Hassett and a double by Johnny Hudson sent Tobin to the showers as Truett Sewell was summoned to the mound.[14] Sewell was unable to get the job done as

Ernie Koy drew a walk and Dolph Camilli rapped a single to right. When Paul Waner muffed Camilli's drive, Koy came around to score Brooklyn's sixth run of the inning, giving them an insurmountable lead. Ed Brandt finished the game in brilliant fashion; during the game's last two innings, he induced four batters to be retired on infield grounders and struck out two Dodgers.[15]

Mired in a five-game losing streak and teetering on the brink of being deemed as irrelevant in the National League race after only one month, the Pirates needed a hero to step forward. Prior to Pittsburgh's game against Brooklyn on May 4, Lloyd Waner turned to brother Paul on the bench and stated the time had come for him to do something about their combined batting slump.[16] "I think I'll do the hitting today for the Waner family," Lloyd said to his older brother.[17]

Lloyd's prediction was not an idle boast as he led the Pirates to a 9–5 victory over Brooklyn that ended their five-game skid. Waner went 4-for-4 at the plate, blasting a home run, two triples, a single, driving home five runners and scoring a trio of tallies.[18] After both of Lloyd's triples, brother Paul drove him home with long fly balls. Waner's seventh-inning home run into the right-field stands marked only the second time he had reached that section of Forbes Field during his 12-year career in Pittsburgh. As Lloyd touched home plate after his prodigious blast, the Dodgers bench began to give him some good-natured ribbing. Waner just grinned and pointed to the muscle on his arm. Waner's two triples certainly were not cheap hits either, as the first cleared Gil Brack's head in center while the second blast was rifled down the right-field line with ferocious velocity.[19]

Pitcher Joe Bowman also gave a heroic effort in his first appearance of the year. After starter Russ Bauers struggled, Bowman allowed only one hit during five innings of shutout relief work. Solid pitching was the key ingredient once again the following day when Pittsburgh made it two victories in a row as Red Lucas cruised to a 4–2 win over the Dodgers. Lucas hurled a complete game and held Brooklyn to five hits on the afternoon. Johnny Rizzo went 2-for-4 at the plate for the second consecutive day, while Pep Young also banged out two hits and drove home three runs.

Young let his hitting do the talking against Brooklyn one day after his solid fielding dazzled fans at Forbes Field. In the second contest, Young had made two spectacular plays that thwarted Dodger rallies. In the fourth inning, with Roy Spencer and Buddy Hassett on base, Pep turned a slick double play after he grabbed a Johnny Hudson grounder that had bounded off Arky Vaughan's chest. With two out in the seventh, Dolph Camilli slashed a drive that caromed off first baseman Gus Suhr's glove. Young grabbed the ball and fired to Bowman covering first for the out.[20]

Paul Waner assumed Young's role as a defensive wizard in the third game against Brooklyn by making a crucial catch in the second inning that robbed Cookie Lavagetto of a potential extra-base hit. Waner resembled a mountain climber as he scaled Forbes Field's right-field wall and stretched his glove above his head to snare Lavagetto's drive. A solid defensive contribution from Waner was crucial since he was mired in one of the worst batting slumps of his exceptional career. In spite of the fact that Paul had only collected one hit in his last 18 times at bat, he did not seem to be worried about the tailspin. "I'm hitting the ball better now and my timing is improving," reasoned Paul, "so I'll be getting started most anytime now. Say, today when the Giants come to town, wouldn't be a bad time to get going, would it?"[21]

Bill Terry and his New York Giants made their first trip to Pittsburgh for the start of a two-game series on May 6. In 1937, New York had dominated Pie Traynor's Pirates by going 16–6 during head-to-head competition. Prior to the first battle between these two longtime antagonists, Terry told Pittsburgh baseball scribes that he believed this was the best club he had ever managed and that the Giants should win their third consecutive pennant in 1938 without much trouble. When one of the writers mentioned Pittsburgh as a team that could possibly circumvent those plans, Terry responded by letting out a hearty laugh.[22] New York's manager had good reason to chuckle since his squad currently held down first place in the National League with a 13–3 record. Playing ball at a blistering .813 clip gave the Giants a three-game edge over Traynor's crew, who held down third place with a 10–6 mark.

On the same day, Bill Benswanger announced that nearby McKeesport of the Class D Pennsylvania State Association had been added as the seventh franchise in Pittsburgh's minor league chain.[23] Benswanger added that the Pirates would appear in McKeesport for the first time in almost 40 years when they played a charity game at Tuber Field on Monday, June 27. This contest against an all-star team from the McKeesport City League would be sponsored by the McKeesport Academy of Medicine and all the proceeds were going to be donated to the McKeesport Hospital.[24] While the Pirates were solidifying their relationship with a neighboring municipality, Pie Traynor was taking part in another community outreach project by serving as the guest speaker at Shadyside Academy's morning assembly.[25]

That afternoon, however, New York continued its dominance over the

Pirates with a convincing 11–7 victory. Mace Brown was soundly thumped during his first start of the season as Pittsburgh's premier reliever was chased in the first inning after he allowed four runs on three hits. New York pitcher Cliff Melton improved his record to 5–0 on the season, even though the Pirates touched him up for 14 hits. Lloyd Waner continued his torrid hitting for Pittsburgh by going 2-for-4 at the plate, while Lee Handley and Arky Vaughan also rapped out two hits apiece. Johnny Rizzo smacked a double, two singles and drove home three runs. Rizzo's three hits gave him 11 safe blows in his last 21 trips to the plate and raised his average to .354.[26]

While Rizzo was starting to break out of his minor slump, fellow outfielder Paul Waner went hitless at the plate once again. In the midst of the worst batting slump of his career, Waner saw his average plummet to .197. When manager Pie Traynor suggested to Paul that he give way to a pinch hitter during Pittsburgh's four-run ninth-inning rally, the struggling veteran endorsed the decision to let Bill Brubaker bat for him.[27] Despite a round of boos from fans when Waner was lifted, Brubaker responded by lashing a single that drove home two runners.[28] This was only the second time during Waner's illustrious career that he had been removed for a pinch hitter. (Brother Lloyd had batted for him on one other occasion.) After the game concluded, Paul asked numerous people for any piece of advice that would cure this slump. Even though he was taking extra batting practice before games, Waner's struggles with the bat continued to plague him.[29]

Paul Waner finally connected for a hit in the second contest of this series against New York on Saturday, May 7, when he collected a triple in five trips to the plate. Brother Lloyd once again was the Pirates' top player, going 3-for-5 and recording two RBIs, while Johnny Rizzo continued to sizzle with two hits and two runs batted in. The Pirates seemed to be headed for a victory until Mel Ott delivered a clutch eighth-inning triple that secured New York's 6–5 victory. Giants starting pitcher Hal Schumacher had to leave the game in the sixth inning after he was struck in the chest by a line drive off the bat of Gus Suhr.[30] Even though the force of the drive knocked Schumacher off the mound, he recovered momentarily and threw out Suhr while kneeling on the ground. Dr. J. Huber Wagner left his box behind the first base dugout and attended to the injured pitcher, who was taken to St. Francis Hospital where X-rays confirmed that he had contusions of the chest and bruised ribs.[31]

While Schumacher had his injured ribs taped up so that he could accompany his teammates to Chicago, the fragile Pirates awaited the arrival of the Boston Bees for a three-game series at Forbes Field. The two losses

6. Paul Waner's Slump and Talk of Rebuilding for Next Year   95

against their archrival had left Pittsburgh in third place with a 10–8 record. Prior to the contest on Sunday, May 8 against Boston, Pie Traynor contemplated making some changes to his lineup. Traynor strongly considered sending the slumping Paul Waner and Gus Suhr to the bench. Pie had a change of heart when Boston manager Casey Stengel opted to use a right-handed hurler in the series' first game. Had Stengel gone with a southpaw, Traynor probably would have countered by playing Johnny Dickshot in right field and Bill Brubaker at first base.[32] Pie's decision to continue using two players who desperately needed a day away from the diamond did not pay off, as Waner and Suhr went a combined 0-for-8.

In fairness to both players, hitting was in short supply that afternoon because Boston's Lou Fette and Pittsburgh's Russ Bauers were brilliant. Bauers allowed Boston to score only one run in the second inning while a Jeep Handley double and Lloyd Waner's single tied the game for Pittsburgh in the seventh inning. Once again, Lloyd upheld the honor of the Waner family name by recording two hits. Handley was brilliant as Pittsburgh's lead-off batter as he reached base in his last four times at-bat and rapped out two singles and a double. Jeep was also phenomenal in the field, making plays around the hot corner that reminded fans of Traynor during his heyday. He came up with defensive gems in the second, third, fourth and ninth innings. In the eleventh frame, he struck once again when he gobbled up Johnny Cooney's slow roller with his bare hand and recorded the out by throwing a perfect strike to Suhr at first base.[33]

The score remained tied at one run apiece as the game entered the twelfth inning. Reliever Mace Brown made quick work of Boston in the top of the frame by tossing his fourth shutout inning since coming in after Woody Jensen pinch hit for Russ Bauers in the eighth. Catcher Al Todd, who had come into the game when starter Ray Berres was lifted for pinch-hitter Red Lucas, led off the home half of the twelfth inning by swinging at Lou Fette's first offering and sending the baseball soaring over the left-field wall. Fette walked off the mound while the crowd of 7,500 people at Forbes Field cheered heartily as Todd rounded the bases to give Pittsburgh a 2–1 victory.[34]

Smoky City rooters who believed that this dramatic win would be the tonic for a struggling Pirates squad were disappointed when lackluster baseball returned to Forbes Field on May 9. This time it was the Bees who pulled off some extra-inning heroics by scoring two runs against reliever Ed Brandt in the tenth inning to earn a 7–5 victory. Pirates hurlers were roughed up all afternoon as Boston connected for 16 hits against Cy Blanton, Truett

Sewell, Jim Tobin and Brandt. Rookie Bob Klinger was the only twirler who was able to stymie the Boston bats, as he tossed two frames of shutout relief. For the second time in the past week, Pie Traynor lifted the struggling Paul Waner for a pinch-hitter when Johnny Dickshot batted for him and forced Lloyd Waner in the tenth inning. Paul had now gone hitless in 13 straight trips to the plate while recording only one hit in his last 24 at-bats.[35] This stretch of futility at the plate dropped the former batting champion's average down to .175.

Pirates fans were spared more disappointment when the series finale against Boston on Tuesday, May 10, was postponed due to cold weather and wet grounds.[36] Unseasonably cold weather in Pittsburgh also forced the postponement of the first game of a series against Philadelphia on May 11.[37] While the Pirates were idle, local sportswriters started dissecting the team's current slump. They noted that Jeep Handley had been one of the few bright spots. His play at third base conjured up memories of Traynor's days covering the hot corner for scores of old-timers. In addition, since replacing Bill Brubaker at third on May 2, Handley was 15-for-34 at the plate for a blistering average of .441.[38]

Mired in one of the worst batting slumps of his illustrious career, star outfielder Paul Waner saw his batting average plummet to .175 after a loss against the Boston Bees on May 9, 1938. Things got so bad for Waner that his nine-year-old son, Paul, Jr., even asked his father during a telephone conversation when he planned on getting started hitting once again (National Baseball Hall of Fame Library, Cooperstown, New York).

On the flip side, Paul Waner's current struggles were something that fans who had rooted for Paul throughout his long career had never seen before. Waner even received a special gift in the mail from 13-year-old Jimmie Kehr of Pittsburgh. Since

Waner was Kehr's favorite player, he sent the slumping Pirate his own good luck charm, a penny imbedded in a lucky token. Young Jimmie wished Paul good luck and recommended that he keep the token in his pocket so he could experience better days while playing baseball. Waner also received a phone call from his nine-year-old son in Sarasota, Florida, in which the subject of the batting slump came up immediately.[39]

"Hello," uttered Paul Waner, Jr., over the phone to his father. "Hello, Dad, how are you?"

"I'm okay, son," responded his father, "how are you?"

"Say dad," the child responded. "When are you going to start hitting?"[40]

While Waner claimed that he was not letting the slump get him down, it was evident to anyone who had watched him play for the past 12 years that it was having an adverse effect. Waner felt genuine guilt over the fact that he was consistently failing Pie Traynor and his teammates. During an interview with Pittsburgh baseball writer Lester Biederman, Paul was very candid. "You know, a few years ago," said Waner, "I used to walk up to the plate with men on bases, look at the pitcher and start pitying him. I'd say 'I'm sorry, pal, but I've got to do it. We need some runs.' Then I'd get the base-hits. Now the pitchers are pitying me. I've been using a different bat almost every time I go to the plate. I go out to the park early and hit for about an hour. All I got out of that was a pair of blistered hands."[41]

One explanation put forward by some baseball experts was that Waner was pressing at the plate because he had never experienced such a slump before. Paul definitely was not as relaxed at the plate as he used to be in the past.[42] "There are five or six games I could have won for the Pirates with my bat," continued Waner, "and take those games out of the lost column and put them on the won side, and see where we'd be today. But I'll make up for them, you watch and see. Sometimes I feel like chucking the whole thing and retire. But I don't want anybody to think I'm yellow. I've heard a few boos lately and I probably deserved them. But I've always cherished the memory of the cheers I've received here and before this season's over, you can make a bet right now I'll hear 'em again."[43]

No cheers or boos were heard at Forbes Field on Friday, May 12, as the final contest of the two-game set against Philadelphia was also postponed due to cold weather. The Pirates left for Chicago that night to begin a long road trip that was to include their first eastern swing of the 1938 campaign.[44] During the team's short break away from the diamond, a story regarding a possible rebuilding process on Manager Pie Traynor's part began to gain some traction. It seemed that Traynor was giving serious consideration to forgetting about the current campaign and doing a complete team overhaul with an eye on the future. It was reported that Pirates president William Benswanger was of the same mindset and would stand behind Traynor no matter what course of action was taken.[45] When New York had been in town one week ago, Pie was rebuffed by Bill Terry when he attempted to swing a deal with the Giants manager. "That's the way it is in baseball," Traynor remarked. "When you're down the other teams don't want to help you. They'd rather apply the boot. But that's the idea in this game — don't help the other fellow and it's dog eat dog. I'd probably do the same thing."[46]

On May 13, the Pirates at last returned to the diamond at Wrigley Field after four days of inactivity. Pittsburgh earned a 4–1 victory in ten innings that worked wonders at lifting their spirits. Reliever Mace Brown upped his record to 5–1 on the season by tossing three innings of shutout ball after relieving Red Lucas in the eighth inning. Traynor finally made the crucial changes to his lineup that he had been mulling for days: Bill Brubaker was installed at first base over Gus Suhr and Johnny Dickshot replaced Paul Waner in right field. The two veterans accepted their fate philosophically. "What's the use of worrying over it?" Waner remarked with a smile on his face. "Perhaps we will be able to look back a few weeks hence and laugh at what seems a serious matter."[47]

Waner's replacement in right field got the ball rolling for Pittsburgh in the tenth inning when he singled to center against Chicago starter Larry French. Mace Brown moved Dickshot over to second with a beautiful sacrifice and he came around to score when Jeep Handley belted a base hit to left field. Handley advanced to second base after Phil Cavarretta hauled in Lloyd Waner's long drive to the right-field wall. After Johnny Rizzo was walked intentionally, Arky Vaughan drove Handley home with a single. Charlie Root replaced French on the mound and promptly surrendered a single off the bat of Al Todd that drove Vaughan home with Pittsburgh's final run.[48] Hopes of carrying over this momentum for Saturday's game were squashed when a steady rain throughout the morning resulted in the series' second game being cancelled.[49]

Extra-inning heroics were the norm once again when action resumed on Sunday, May 15, and Pittsburgh defeated Chicago, 4–3, in eleven innings. Dickshot and Brubaker were key factors in the victory, while Waner and Suhr remained chained to the bench for a second consecutive game. Dickshot's single in the eleventh inning drove Vaughan home from second base with the game's winning run. Brubaker hit a clutch home run in the fifth inning off Chicago hurler Bill Lee with one teammate on base. Another key contributor was Johnny Rizzo, who tied the contest in the sixth inning with his first major league home run. Chicago almost won the game in regulation during their half of the ninth — Pittsburgh's hopes were kept alive when a brilliant throw from Lloyd Waner in center field nailed pinch runner Clay Bryant at the plate after he tried to score from second on Stan Hack's single.[50] Bill Swift picked up his first victory of the season by hurling shutout ball over the game's final four innings.

When the Pirates left for Boston to begin the second leg of their road trip, manager Pie Traynor made two moves to reduce his roster to the required 23-player limit before the May 23 deadline. Southpaw hurlers Ken Heintzelman and Marvin Duke were both sent to Montreal of the American Association. In Heintzelman's case, the Pirates retained a 24-hour recall option, but with Duke the Pirates would have had to pay $25,000 to retain the 29-year-old and they elected not to do so.[51] Duke was very irked by the decision and demanded to know how his ability could be properly assessed if Traynor never gave him a chance to pitch.[52] "This is the queerest thing that has ever happened to me in my baseball career," Duke said. "I never got a chance, that is the kind of chance I deserved. Then, for no apparent reason, I am sent away. I got very little opportunity during the training trip and never had a chance in the big league. There's something screwy about this thing — and I'm going to try find out what it is before I consent to spend another year in the minors when it has not been proved that I am a failure in the majors."[53]

Duke held true to his threat by meeting with Commissioner Kenesaw Mountain Landis to talk about what he deemed to be unfair treatment on the part of Pittsburgh management. Landis offered his sage advice and recommended that Marvin hurry to Montreal immediately. Duke took this wise counsel to heart and prepared to leave for Canada after he tied up a few loose ends with the Pirates front office.[54]

Meanwhile the Pirates were at Braves Field in Boston, where they were unable to solve Milt Shoffner in the game on Tuesday, May 17. While they were recording only three harmless singles, Russ Bauers was handcuffing the Bees on a single hit. Unfortunately for Russ, that lone safety translated into the game's only run. First baseman Elbie Fletcher led off the bottom of the first frame by drawing a walk. Third baseman Debs Garms followed Fletcher with a single to Lloyd Waner in center field. Fletcher challenged Lloyd's arm by trying to make it from first to third on Garms' hit. Waner's accurate throw would have nailed Elbie by more than ten feet at third if the baseball had not caromed off the Boston first baseman's back and allowed him to score.[55]

After the disheartening loss, Traynor decided to restore Paul Waner and Gus Suhr to the lineup for the second game of the series on Wednesday, May 18. While Traynor originally announced that Waner would bat third with Suhr hitting sixth, the manager had changed his mind by the time he handed in his lineup card.[56] Pie's new batting order still had Jeep Handley and Lloyd Waner at the top, followed by Arky Vaughan, Johnny Rizzo, Gus Suhr, Al Todd, Paul Waner, Pep Young and pitcher Bob Klinger. The rookie hurler acquired from Sacramento after the 1937 season was making his first major league start.[57]

On the night before game two of the series, Handley and Vaughan visited a friend of theirs from the Boston Police Department. Both players were photographed with an identification number and fingerprinted like any criminal who was brought to the station. The Pirates infielders made sure their policeman friend did not keep the mug shots or the prints.[58] Manager Pie Traynor should have asked the two players to bring some of Boston's finest to their game the following afternoon so that a missing person's report could be filed on Pittsburgh's hitters. Despite the lineup changes, the Pirates could only muster five hits during a 2–1 loss to Boston in fourteen innings. Klinger was absolutely brilliant for Pittsburgh, allowing only one run and five hits during twelve-and-a-third innings of work. Mace Brown took the loss for Pittsburgh in relief, while Boston's Jim Turner tossed a complete game.

Turner made only one mistake all afternoon, allowing Lee Handley to smack his second pitch of the game for a lead-off homer in the first inning. Boston claimed victory in the fourteenth frame when they scored an unearned run against Brown. With the bases loaded and one out, Boston catcher Ray Mueller drove a long fly to right field that was caught by Paul Waner. Gene Moore's slide home caused catcher Al Todd to drop Waner's perfect peg to the plate and gave the Bees their second straight victory over the Pirates in as many days.[59] Manager Pie Traynor was not around to see the final innings of another disappointing loss due to his seventh-inning ejection by umpire Lee Ballanfant for protesting a decision.[60]

The Bees completed a three-game sweep on Thursday, May 19 when they scored against rookie hurler Truett Sewell in the eleventh inning to claim a 4–3 victory. Lloyd Waner led the way for Pittsburgh, going 3-for-6 with a double, one run scored and one RBI. One positive development gleaned from this game was that Paul Waner and Gus Suhr each had their best game at the plate in weeks. Suhr doubled in the first and singled in the eighth, while Waner singled during his last two trips to the plate before being intentionally walked in the tenth inning.[61] Paul took Bees pitcher Ira Hutchinson's decision to walk him as a positive sign. "I must be getting out of my slump," Waner cracked, "when they start walking me to get to the next hitter. That's the best compliment I've had paid me all season by any pitcher."[62]

Suhr and Waner's possible resurgence at the plate could not have come at a better time since recent trade gossip linked the two veterans to potential deals with Chicago and New York. Pie Traynor was discussing a trade that would either bring Frank Demaree of the Cubs or Hank Leiber of the Giants to Pittsburgh. However, negotiations between Traynor, Charley Grimm and Bill Terry never got beyond the preliminary stage.[63] On May 20 the Pirates dropped their fourth game in a row in Brooklyn. The Dodgers sent starter Red Lucas to the showers early and rapped out 12 hits in manhandling Pittsburgh, 7–5. This latest defeat dropped the Pirates into a fourth-place tie with Cincinnati.[64]

While the losing skid was becoming alarming, Traynor was pleased by Paul Waner and Gus Suhr's batting resurgence. Waner had a great day at the plate in the first game in Brooklyn, going 3-for-4 and driving home two runs. Suhr also seemed to be breaking loose from his funk; the Pirates first baseman had knocked in three runs in the past two games with a double and two singles while also reaching base six times. Prior to Pittsburgh's second game against the Dodgers, Waner expressed confidence that the worst batting slump of his 13-year career was finally over. Now that he had raised his average up to .207 for the season, Paul was in a buoyant mood. "I don't want to predict I'm going to win the batting championship or anything like that," he said, "but I think I've got my confidence back. I'm hitting the ball better than at any time since the opening game when I got a single, double and triple. Watch me go from now on."[65]

Waner's jubilation was shared by his teammates after the Pirates finally put a game in the win column on Saturday, May 21, by defeating Brooklyn, 5–4. Arky Vaughan was Pittsburgh's hitting star, going 2-for-4, slamming a double and scoring two runs. Jim Tobin was the afternoon's pitching hero, pitching three-and-one-third innings of shutout ball in relief of Russ Bauers. Pie Traynor was ejected for the second time in three days when umpire Larry Goetz banished him from the diamond. Prior to the 1938 campaign, Traynor had only been thrown out of a game by an umpire on one occasion since having become Pittsburgh's pilot in 1934.[66]

As Pittsburgh prepared to open a series against the Giants at the Polo Grounds on May 22, rumors about a three-cornered deal involving the Pirates, Dodgers and Phillies began making the rounds.[67] No deals materialized during a conference at the Atlantic Hotel between Pittsburgh's Bill Benswanger, Philadelphia's Gerry Nugent and Brooklyn's Larry MacPhail. When the meeting ended, none of the three executives were willing to divulge what had transpired during their discussions.[68]

In the Pirates' first game against New York, Bill Terry's players did all of the talking with their bats as Traynor's troops were crushed, 18–2. Lloyd Waner was the lone Pirate who acquitted himself well; the veteran center fielder went 3-for-4, scored one run and drilled a double. The day's only positive news for Pittsburgh involved two things with no connection to playing bad baseball. Prior to the contest, Pirate coach Honus Wagner was honored by the Huron Club of Greenwich Village and presented with a wrist watch at home plate.[69] Veteran pitcher Bill Swift also received welcome news when he was notified that his wife had given birth to a healthy seven and one-half pound son at a hospital in Lakeland, Florida.[70]

Pittsburgh finally found a way to beat New York in the final contest of this two-game set on Monday, May 23. Mace Brown pushed his record to 6–2 for the year in relief of a faltering Cy Blanton and Russ Bauers closed out the victory as Pittsburgh defeated the Giants, 4–3. Brown and Bauers combined to pitch five and two-third innings of shutout baseball after Blanton had given up most of a 4–0 first-inning lead. While a win over New York should have been big news back in Pittsburgh, the result took a back seat to a decision that Bill Benswanger and Pie Traynor had reached during a long conference on Sunday night. The two men responsible for crafting a squad that could compete for a National League pennant each year had come to the conclusion that the present team was sadly deficient in many areas. They determined that a rebuilding process was necessary.[71]

The nucleus of this new-look Pirate squad was expected to include Russ Bauers, Jim Tobin, Joe Bowman, Bob Klinger, Jeep Handley, Arky Vaughan, Johnny Rizzo and Al Todd. Traynor's biggest areas of need seemed to be at first base, second base and right field, where it was believed that younger players would be brought in to replace Gus Suhr, Pep Young and Paul Waner.[72] Two days after Benswanger conferred with Traynor about the future of Pittsburgh's squad, he explained their intentions:

6. Paul Waner's Slump and Talk of Rebuilding for Next Year 103

I had a long conference with Manager Traynor in New York last Sunday night and after we had talked the whole thing over from every conceivable angle we came to the decision that we ought to start immediately to build a new team — and build it around younger men. It is to our advantage that we have a good many young players on the team at the present time. Now a few of them are showing the kind of improvement that leads us to believe they are fully up to major league standards — winning major league standards if you please.

In launching this program we do not want the public to get the idea that we will be able to show it a new team next week, or the week after. Because we have mapped out a plan for rebuilding is no guarantee of immediate success. The fortunes of other clubs in both our own and the American League are proof that rebuilding is 50 per cent enterprise and 50 per cent good fortune in picking up the key players needed. We promise to provide the enterprise; we hope the luck lights on our shoulders.

During a game against the Brooklyn Dodgers on May 4, 1938, outfielder Lloyd Waner was the catalyst behind Pittsburgh's 9–5 victory by going 4-for-4 and driving home five runs. Already known by such nicknames as "Little Poison" and "Sprout," Waner was given the moniker of "Pro" by teammates in 1938 because of his professional approach (National Baseball Hall of Fame Library, Cooperstown, New York).

Merely to go out and bring in all the ball players we could find would be no guarantee of a pennant or even a first-division contender. You can't find Rizzos, Handleys or Paul Waners on every bush, and the general average is one good player out of every 10 that are produced in the minor leagues.[73]

Despite the fact that veteran outfielder Lloyd Waner's name was not mentioned as one of the foundations of the rebuilding process, there was no denying that he had been Pittsburgh's steadiest performer in 1938. Known at times by nicknames like "Little Poison," "Sprout," and "Pee Wee," Lloyd was given the moniker of "Pro" in 1938 by a teammate because by comparison he made all of the other Pirates look like amateurs. Waner's solid play to date had earned him a spot among the National League's top five hitters with a nifty .364 average. Lloyd, who had recently collected hit number 2,000 of his career, said that he planned on striving toward collecting 2,000 more safeties. Lloyd also had been responsible for upholding the Waners' family honor because of brother Paul's subpar campaign. "My brother Paul taught me how to hit," Lloyd said, "but now it looks like I'll have to teach him some of the things he's forgotten."[74]

The rookie flanking Lloyd Waner in left field was also having a solid season despite a paltry .171 batting average on the current road trip. Johnny Rizzo was a few notches below the .300 mark with 34 hits in 114 trips to the plate. He led the major leagues with five triples and was tied with Arky Vaughan for the team lead in RBIs with 20.[75] Players like Waner and Rizzo who hoped to fatten their averages by playing a few games in the hitter-friendly Baker Bowl were forced to wait an extra day when rain cancelled the first game of the series on May 24. This postponement actually was good news for Pie Traynor, since ace reliever Mace Brown was unavailable due to an injury he had suffered against New York. Pittsburgh's top pitcher was struck on the right side by a line drive off the bat of Mickey Haslin on May 23. After the incident, Brown was helped to the locker room.[76]

This was only the latest in a string of encounters that the unfortunate pitcher recently had had with baseballs struck by the bats of opponents. Right before being knocked out of the game, Harry Danning's drive had nicked him in the shins. In Chicago one week earlier, Gabby Hartnett had drilled a ball that belted Brownie in the right knee.[77] The diagnosis from Pirate trainer Dr. Charles Jorgensen was that Brown had a severe rib injury that would sideline him for one week.[78]

Pittsburgh's players got back on the field once again on Wednesday, May 25 against Philadelphia and wasted a strong effort by pitcher Jim Tobin. Even though Tobin tossed a complete game and only gave up two runs and five hits, the Pirates were defeated, 2–1, as Phillies hurler Bucky Walters harnessed the Corsairs hitting attack. Gus Suhr was the only Pirate who experienced much success against Walters, going 2-for-4, smacking a double and a triple and driving home Pittsburgh's only run.

Pittsburgh's final game of the eastern swing on May 26 was cancelled due to rain. The Pirates immediately left Philadelphia and arrived in Pittsburgh that evening to start a long home stand at Forbes Field, beginning with the Chicago Cubs.[79] The Pirates had compiled an abysmal 2–6 record

6. Paul Waner's Slump and Talk of Rebuilding for Next Year 105

during their first battles against the National League's eastern clubs, while the 10-game road trip netted them a 4–6 record overall. A dearth of hitting doomed Pittsburgh, as the Waner Brothers were the only two Pirates who hit above .300 during the trip: Lloyd checked in at .318 and Paul hit .312 while seeing less action than his younger brother. The numbers for the remainder of the starting squad were pitiful, as Arky Vaughan (.264), Gus Suhr (.259), Jeep Handley (.195), Johnny Rizzo (.152) and Al Todd (.135) struggled mightily at the plate. Pep Young was the biggest disappointment among the regulars, batting .088 during the road trip, grounding into seven double plays, failing to drive home a single run, and striking out on numerous occasions. For the season, Handley, Lloyd Waner and Johnny Dickshot were the only Pirates hitting above .300.[80]

Things got even worse for the Pirates in the first game of the home stand on Friday, May 27. Bill Lee tossed a shutout and Gabby Hartnett went 3-for-4, blasted a home run and recorded three RBIs as Chicago won easily, 5–0. Arky Vaughan was the only Pirate who solved Lee, going 2-for-4 at the plate. Rookie outfielder Johnny Rizzo was given the day off when he reported to the park late after having to take his wife to the doctor. Manager Pie Traynor took one look at the concerned look on Rizzo's face and decided that a day of rest would be the best option for the youngster. When Paul Waner stepped to the plate for his first at-bat, most of the 3,000 fans in attendance showed their appreciation for the veteran by giving him a round of applause.[81]

The Pittsburgh Pirates dressing room always was a cheerful place when the team was winning. During tough times, the atmosphere became frayed and players wondered if the slump would ever end while they gloomily sat at their lockers. One team leader offered words of encouragement after the latest setback. "We'll get out of this," he told his teammates. "When we do, we're going to pay back some debts."[82] Pie Traynor tried to inject some levity into the tense dressing room. "You fellows had better snap out of it soon," he told his charges, "before the pitchers quit speaking to you."[83]

The Pirates struggled through another tough day at the plate in the series' second contest on May 28, but for a long time it looked as though strong pitching would lift them to victory. Starter Russ Bauers was phenomenal through six and one-third innings, allowing only two singles and nursing a 1–0 lead. Everything turned sour in a matter of minutes, however, as the result of a series of pitching and fielding lapses. Chicago had scored nine runs by the time the side was retired, while disgruntled fans walked out on their beloved team during the atrocious seventh stanza.[84] The Cubs gained their ninth victory in the past ten games by defeating Pittsburgh, 9–3. Pittsburgh broke a 21-inning scoring famine with a run in the fourth inning following an error by Cubs third baseman Stan Hack.[85]

Official standings in the National League at the close of play on Saturday, May 28 showed that Pittsburgh had tumbled into the second division. The Pirates stood in fifth place with a 15–17 record, eight-and-one-half games behind the league-leading New York Giants, who were cruising along at a 24–9 clip. The recent strong showing of the Cubs had propelled them into second place with a 23–13 record. The great start by the Pirates was now forgotten and with each passing day the chances of a pennant looked more remote. The sleeping sickness that Sid Feder referred to at the beginning of the month had now manifested itself. A rebuilding process seemed to be the only logical solution for the Pirates.

7

Pirates Regroup as Benswanger and Traynor Nix Deal with New York Giants

Poor hitting by most of the Pirates was a big reason why Pie Traynor's squad was mired in the National League's second division after one-and-a-half months of the 1938 season. Lloyd Waner (.341) and Arky Vaughan (.306) were the only starters above the .300 mark; they were followed by Jeep Handley (.284), Johnny Rizzo (.279), Gus Suhr (.276), Al Todd (.244), Pep Young (.235) and Paul Waner (.187). Just when Paul Waner seemed to be out of his slump, another 0-for-12 skid again dropped his average below .200. In spite of the tough season, Waner was not ready to quit on himself. "This looks very serious, but I really believe that before many weeks have passed a lot of us will look back on my slip and smile," said Waner. "I feel great, I have picked up five pounds on the bench, which ought to benefit me, in that I have been a bit light. All in all, I feel that I will soon be back where I was. A batting slump is a terrible thing, but on the other hand, when the batter holds the whip hand, he often wonders how in the deuce the pitcher gets him out."[1]

It seemed unlikely that Waner would be given the opportunity to bust out of his slump if Pie Traynor and Bill Benswanger followed through on their intention to scrap the current season and rebuild for the future. While losing had become common during the season's early weeks, Pittsburgh's players angrily denied a report that the squad was loaded with malcontents.[2] While it seemed unlikely that the Pirates were dogging it on purpose, this did not mean that Benswanger was not prepared to eliminate players whose play was not meeting expectations. "We must keep enough of the veterans in the lineup to hold a balance," stated Benswanger, "but manager Traynor and I both agree that we must show preference to young players in some of the key positions, inasmuch as the veterans in some of these spots appear to have gone over the top in the matter of their skill."[3]

In the final contest of the three-game series against Chicago on Sunday, May 29, starting hurlers Red Lucas and Larry French locked horns in a brilliant pitchers' duel. Pirates shortstop Arky Vaughan was the afternoon's hero as Pittsburgh won a tight contest, 2–1. Vaughan plated both runs as he blasted a home run in the second inning that gave Pittsburgh a 1–0 lead and then smacked a double in the sixth stanza that drove home Jeep Handley with the game's winning run.[4]

Handley scampered home with the winning run once again one day later in the first game of the Memorial Day doubleheader at Forbes Field as the Pirates defeated St. Louis, 5–4. Handley scored the game's deciding marker in the seventeenth inning when he raced home from second after Cardinals second baseman Stu Martin's wild throw. This game was the longest of the major league season to date, lasting four hours and 19 minutes.[5] Pirates fans witnessed an interesting confrontation in the fourth inning as Pittsburgh pushed four runs across the plate. As Arky Vaughan and Gus Suhr executed a perfect double steal, umpire George Barr's foot stopped the catcher's wild throw from careening into left field. Pirates coach Jewel Ens immediately rushed Barr and reminded the beleaguered arbiter that he had also interfered with Pep Young during a game in New York several weeks earlier.[6]

Pittsburgh did not fare so well during the nightcap of the twin bill as St. Louis prevailed, 9–6. Fans who decided to remain at Forbes Field for both games finally were able to start for home when the final out was recorded at 9:15 p.m.[7] The holiday split saw some Pirates excel, while others struggled. During the first game, Pep Young singled four straight times and was passed intentionally in the sixteenth inning. Johnny Rizzo's futility with the bat continued as he took the collar during both contests and now had gone hitless in his last 24 plate appearances. In the second game, he grounded into a double play during a crucial at-bat when the Pirates had the bases loaded with one out. Lee Handley was excellent in the nightcap, going 3-for-5, while Paul Waner conjured up memories of his brilliant past by slashing out two hits.[8]

Pie Traynor's troops continued to show more life as they opened the month of June with a 4–1 victory over Bill Terry's New York Giants at Forbes Field. Russ Bauers made masterful use of his assortment of pitches while tossing a complete game and allowing only five hits to earn his first win of the 1938 season. Russ was at his best in the sixth frame, immediately after the Corsairs had scored three runs off Giants starter Cliff Milton. Jo-Jo Moore led off the inning with a single and was followed by the pesky Dick Bartell, who ran the count to three balls and no strikes. Bauers threw two quick strikes before Bartell fouled off seven straight pitches. But Bauers refused to give in and the three-minute battle finally ended when Bartell grounded into a force out.[9] Bauers also contributed to his own cause at the plate by banging out two hits and scoring one of Pittsburgh's runs.

Gus Suhr was the only other Pirate to record multiple hits, going 2-for-4 and scoring a run. Prior to the game, Suhr had been honored by the East Liberty Lions Club on behalf of the other 37 Lions Clubs in Pittsburgh and its surrounding municipalities. Gus, who was a Lions member in his hometown of Millbrae, California, had received a similar honor from the San Francisco Chapter during Pittsburgh's spring training excursion. The East Liberty Lions hosted all the visiting club members during a special luncheon at the Ritz Hotel.[10] While Suhr was being honored by admirers and seemed to be back on track at the plate following a minor slump, outfielder Johnny Dickshot was given a rare start in the first game against New York when starting left fielder Johnny Rizzo was unable to play because of a sprained right wrist. Rizzo had suffered the injury on May 30 while chasing a fly ball off the bat of St. Louis' Johnny Mize. Jeep Handley remained in the lineup even though he was hobbled by a slightly swollen left ankle. "It's swollen and a little sore," remarked Handley, "and I don't even know how I got it."[11]

The second game of the series between Pittsburgh and New York on June 2 was postponed when heavy rain interrupted the contest while Bill Terry's men batted in the second inning.[12] Since there was no baseball game for local sports scribes to dissect stories that ran in Pittsburgh's newspapers on June 3 centered around Pie Traynor approaching Terry about possible trades before the series' first contest. Traynor was interested in acquiring either Hank Leiber or Wally Berger from the Giants, while Terry coveted Pirates second baseman Pep Young.[13] After some intense discussions, Terry proposed a deal for Young that included Berger and Giants second baseman Lou Chiozza. Traynor told Terry he wanted to take a little time to consider the transaction from every angle. Bill Benswanger trusted his manager with making a decision that was in the team's best interests.[14] "The decision rests entirely with Pie," said Benswanger when he was asked to offer his opinion about a potential deal. "If he is for it, I am for it."[15]

Terry desperately needed a second baseman of Young's caliber to replace Burgess Whitehead, who was out for the year after having had his appendix removed. Some baseball writers suggested to Terry that he ought to consider purchasing someone currently playing in the minors who already had major league experience. Bill scoffed at this notion by pointing out that Branch Rickey referred to such men as "anesthetic players." Terry explained that they were called anesthetic players because when a team got a few of them on its roster, the manager in question usually woke up in September and found his squad in seventh place.[16] So the Giants manager reasoned that his problem could only be solved by making a deal that brought in a second baseman from another National League squad. "Whitehead is out for the year, perhaps for good," commented Terry. "I tried to get Tony Cuccinello from Boston but Bob Quinn said 'No business.' So I've been working on a couple of other deals. There isn't a young infielder anywhere in Class A or Double A ball ready to move up. I've checked them all."[17]

While Traynor mulled over Terry's proposal, the Pirates and Giants concluded their shortened series at Forbes Field on Friday, June 3. The day held special significance for Pirate right fielder Paul Waner as his three hits included number 2,500 of his illustrious career. At the start of the 1938 campaign, Waner's lifetime average of .348 was the best of any active National League veteran.[18] When Paul connected for his milestone hit, he became the thirtieth player in major league history to gain entry into the "2,500 Hit Club." While Waner had slumped at the plate throughout the 1938 campaign, if he could catch fire and bang out 200 hits for the season, he would establish a National League record and tie Ty Cobb's major league mark by accomplishing that feat in nine different seasons.[19]

The game was a wild one as Pittsburgh built up a huge lead and hung on behind rookie pitcher Bob Klinger to defeat New York, 6–5. Besides Waner's scintillating day at the plate, Jeep Handley went 2-for-5, scored one run and drove home two, while Arky Vaughan also recorded two hits on the afternoon. In addition to celebrating a second consecutive victory over New York, Pittsburgh's players were also in high spirits due to a joyous occasion in third baseman Bill Brubaker's life. Brubaker passed out cigars to his teammates after his wife gave birth to an eight-and-one-half-pound baby boy in Los Angeles one day earlier. In honor of roommate Lloyd Waner, Bill named his new son Lloyd Robert Brubaker.[20]

There were other signs that Pittsburgh's players were bonding with each other and the local fans. During the Memorial Day doubleheader, 12-year-old Robert Arke of Pittsburgh had been permitted to sit in the Pirates dugout as a guest of Arky Vaughan. Arke had become a Vaughan rooter many years earlier while the youngster was a hospital patient recovering from leg injuries. When Vaughan heard about Arke's devotion to the Pirates, he invited the lad to join him on the bench and gave him an autographed baseball after the second game concluded.[21] Possibly realizing that his team was beginning to develop some chemistry after a rough stretch in May, Bill Benswanger had a change of heart and decided against the proposed deal with New York. Before the Giants left for their next series in Cincinnati, Benswanger and Pirates vice president Sam Watters recommended to Traynor that the transaction be nixed.[22]

The final deal would have shipped outfielder Wally Berger, infielder Lou Chiozza and $35,000 in cash from New York to Pittsburgh for second baseman Pep Young and outfielder Johnny Dickshot. Traynor reasoned that once this transaction was finalized, he could then use the $35,000 to purchase an infielder to replace Young. When Giants manager Bill Terry learned the news, he expressed his surprise to a New York newspaperman that Benswanger had intervened. "It was the first time I knew that Pie Traynor didn't have a free hand in making deals for the Pirates," lamented Terry.[23]

After being rebuffed by the Pirates, Terry was able to broker a deal for a second baseman with the Reds when his squad arrived in Cincinnati. Terry secured second baseman Alex Kampouris in exchange for outfielder Wally Berger. When Traynor was approached for his reaction, Pittsburgh's manager claimed that he was not willing to weaken his club to acquire Berger. Traynor and Benswanger both were irritated by Terry's claims that Pittsburgh's team president had overruled his manager regarding this deal. Pittsburgh's front office hierarchy stated that Traynor never had been restrained at any time since he became manager from making any trades that improved the Pirates. During an interview with the press, Pie assured everyone he made the final decision not to trade Young under the terms that had been offered by Terry.[24]

"In the first place," said Traynor, "a switch of Young to the Giants would enhance their flag chances greatly, and we are not trying to win another flag for any other club. Secondly, it would not be wise to try strengthen one department of your club while weakening another department in a marked degree. We would like to have Berger for our outfield, but the departure of Young, without a promise of some new infield strength would have a tendency to unsteady our first line of defense. And in the third place, the Pittsburgh club has never been in the business of selling players for money considerations. It hasn't been done in Pittsburgh through the years and money returns for players here will continue to play an incidental part in deals."[25]

When the Pirates returned to action on Saturday, June 4, Pep Young showed the baseball world why he was a hot property. Days after Terry had claimed that Young was the best all-around second sacker in the National League, Pep smacked two singles, a double and a triple as Pittsburgh defeated Brooklyn in 11 innings, 4–3. He also sent Ernie Koy close to the Barney Dreyfuss memorial in deep center field on a blistering drive on the only occasion that he was retired by Dodgers pitchers. His ninth-inning triple drove home Gus Suhr from second with the game's tying run. In the eleventh frame Young crushed a lusty double that moved pinch-runner Bill Brubaker over to third base. After Brooklyn pitcher Tot Pressnell retired Bill Swift, Jeep Handley pounded the first pitch he saw into right-center field for the game-winning hit.[26]

A poor Saturday crowd of only 4,168 fans saw Pittsburgh's heroic effort against Brooklyn. Lousy weather contributed to the poor turnout as rain fell intermittently during the game.[27] The 6,800 Pirate rooters who were in attendance at Forbes Field for Sunday's contest against Brooklyn have to have believed that Pittsburgh was about to claim its fourth consecutive victory when the Pirates took a 5–2 lead into the sixth inning. Pirate starter Russ Bauers had been cruising along up to that point, but suddenly everything fell apart for Pie Traynor's crew as Brooklyn sent 11 batters to the plate and pushed across six runs. Bauers, Joe Bowman and Ed Brandt were knocked around freely by the Dodgers before Truett Sewell stopped the bleeding in the ninth inning. Brooklyn claimed a 10–5 victory.[28]

Brooklyn defeated Pittsburgh again during the series finale on Monday, June 6. Pittsburgh starter Red Lucas was knocked out of the box after allowing six runs and five hits during only one-third of an inning of work. The Dodgers cruised to an easy 9–4 victory. Pep Young led the way for Pittsburgh by going 3-for-4 at the plate, while former Buccaneers Kiki Cuyler and Cookie Lavagetto banged out three hits apiece for Brooklyn. Young was absolutely brilliant during the three-game series against the Dodgers, lashing out seven hits during 12 trips to the plate and reaching base on nine occasions. In addition to his three safeties in the final game, Young's blistering drive in the ninth frame sent Buddy Hassett to Forbes Field's scoreboard to make the catch. Young, Paul Waner and Al Todd accounted for seven of the 10 hits Pittsburgh recorded in the series' final contest.[29]

The Pirates were forced to wait an extra day to try get back in the win column when their first game against the Boston Bees on Tuesday, June 7

New York Giants manager Bill Terry desperately tried to obtain second baseman Pep Young from the Pittsburgh Pirates in early June to fill a void on his team. Terry's efforts failed when Pie Traynor and William Benswanger decided that moving Young would leave the Pirates vulnerable. On June 4, 1938, Young showed everyone why he was a coveted property by smacking a triple, a double and two singles during a 4–3 victory over the Brooklyn Dodgers (National Baseball Hall of Fame Library, Cooperstown, New York).

was postponed by rain. One day later, the Pirates played one of their best games of the season. Bob Klinger was exceptional on the mound for Pittsburgh, tossing a complete game and defeating Boston, 4–1. The Pirates attacked Boston starter Lou Fette immediately as Jeep Handley led off the bottom of the first with a single. Paul Waner followed with a run-scoring triple and came home with Pittsburgh's second run on a double by Arky Vaughan. The Pirates added their other two runs in the third inning when Lloyd Waner and Vaughan each singled and both scored on Gus Suhr's triple.[30]

Rookie hurler Bob Klinger improved his record to 4–1 on the young season and lowered his ERA to a minuscule 2.06. Klinger seemed to be one of the season's true finds and Traynor believed the youngster was ready to assume more responsibility as one of his key starting pitchers. "You know," Klinger remarked as he peeled off his sweatshirt on the bench following the victory over Boston, "a pitcher in the minors has to go through, well—almost hell. Most of the games are at night and when you're out there pitching at night, you're trying to throw 'em past the batter and he ups and hits it where it hurts the most. The nights are usually cool and that's tough on the arm. But the major leagues? Now there is the spot. Sure the hitters are better, but you have major league support and you can mix your pitches. I've always thought in my own heart I could pitch in the big leagues, but this is really the first chance I've had. Each spring I'd go with the Cards but it was almost a foregone conclusion that I'd be back as soon as their minor farms started training. Now I've got the break of my life. Don't think for a minute I'm going to pass it up."[31]

The Pirates made it two wins in a row against Boston on Thursday, June 9 with a 5–3 victory that was paced by the solid hitting of Gus Suhr and Paul Waner. Suhr banged out a double during Pittsburgh's three-run first inning and scored what proved to be the winning run in the sixth after leading off the frame with a single. Suhr was now Pittsburgh's leading hitter with an average of .320 after 42 games. In his past 13 games, Gus was hitting a robust .434 with three doubles, three triples, one home run and ten RBIs. Paul Waner was also on a tear, pounding a double and two singles against Boston's Jim Turner and raising his average to .241. While Suhr and Waner finally were hitting their stride after protracted slumps, Lloyd Waner and Arky Vaughan had been the model of consistency all season. Lloyd was batting .315, while Vaughan was smacking the ball at a clip of .302 and led the Pirates with 26 RBIs.[32]

Solid hitting was not the only ingredient that brought about Pittsburgh's second victory against Boston. Strong relief pitching from Mace Brown had kept the Bees from blowing the game wide open in the third inning. Brown performed his standard rescue act when he relieved starter Jim Tobin after Boston loaded the bases. Mace allowed only one of the inherited runners to score and then topped off his great day by driving home Pittsburgh's final two markers in the sixth inning with a single off shortstop Rabbit Warstler's glove.[33] Brown improved his record to 7–2 for the year as he gave up one run on two hits during seven innings of work. Fireman Brownie's win put him among the National League leaders in victories. Loyal rooters at Forbes Field referred to Mace's route from the bullpen in right field to the pitcher's box as "Brown's Lane" since the pitcher always seemed to walk the same straight line from the pen to the mound.[34]

The Pirates were now two games above .500, but Traynor's squad regressed in a game against Philadelphia on Friday, June 10. A strong pitching effort by Russ Bauers was wasted when four Pirates errors allowed the Phillies to claim a 3–2 victory. This shoddy display by Traynor's men gave them 53 miscues in 43 games and made them the National League's most error-prone team.[35] A frustrated Traynor was hard pressed to explain why the Pirates looked like world beaters some days but resembled cellar dwellers other times. Aside from Jeep Handley and Pep Young, Pittsburgh's squad did not possess relentless performers in the Pepper Martin mold whose never-say-die attitude could be counted on to boost a team's morale. Traynor referred to some of his players' style as a "dinner-bucket attitude" that could not be altered since they were so set in their ways.[36]

While Traynor was busy lamenting some of his team's shortcomings, he was able to take solace in the fact that Gus Suhr and Paul Waner were blazing a path of destruction at the plate. Suhr had rapped a single against Philadelphia to extend his hitting streak to 12 games while Waner collected two hits and extended his streak to 10 games. Younger brother Lloyd "Pro" Waner's work had been so consistent that Pittsburgh theatrical agent Steve Forrest started a drive to have "Little Poison" chosen to start in the All-Star Game in July.[37] Prior to the second game against Philadelphia on Saturday, June 11, Traynor announced that Johnny Rizzo would be back in left field after having been sidelined with a sprained right wrist. He also reported that Cy Blanton, who had not appeared in a game since May 23, was confined to his home with an attack of influenza.[38]

Pitcher Bill Swift helped bring home a Pirates victory in the series' second contest by tossing a complete game and outdueling Phillies hurler Bucky Walters, 4–3. Swift scattered 11 hits after Traynor returned him to the starting line following a short stint in the bullpen. Bill also smacked a crucial hit in the second inning. Walters was a bit wild in the frame, walking Pittsburgh's first two batters. A double play eliminated two Pirates runners before Pep Young drew another free pass. Walters ran the count against Swift to one ball and two strikes before he tried to bring the inning to an end by throwing a strike on the inside corner. Swift put all of his weight behind a prodigious swing and smacked a long drive that cleared Forbes Field's left field fence to the right of the scoreboard for a three-run home run.[39]

Two veteran Pirates kept their hitting streaks going as Paul Waner scorched a first-inning double while Gus Suhr used an infield single to push his streak to 13 games. Waner was hitting a blistering .450 during his 11-game streak and had pushed his season's batting average close to the .250 mark.[40] Both players kept the parade moving when Pittsburgh handily defeated Philadelphia on Sunday, June 12 by a score of 11–5; Suhr went 1-for-3 and Waner drilled three line drive singles in five trips to the plate. Fireman Mace Brown was brilliant once again, winning his eighth game in relief of starter Bob Klinger.[41] Brown hurled six-and-two-thirds innings of relief, giving up two runs on seven hits. Mace also collected two hits, scored one run and recorded an RBI.

Poor weather conditions almost prevented this game from being played. Head groundskeeper Jack Fogarty had to burn gasoline on the infield and dump bags of sawdust on the basepaths before the contest could get underway. Even so, Forbes Field's infield was soggy and featured scattered puddles, while the outfield grass was saturated with water. The 7,800 fans who had waited patiently for the rain to stop were rewarded for their patience when rookie Johnny Rizzo struck a crucial blow during Pittsburgh's six-run fifth inning. Pittsburgh's rooters practically tore the roof off the park when Rizzo connected with an Al Smith fastball and blasted a grand slam home run. Johnny's shot was driven like a tee shot from home plate and was just starting to rise as it soared out of sight over the left-field fence.[42]

Pie Traynor hoped the Pirates could use their recent success at Forbes Field to climb the National League standings during their second eastern swing in 1938. Standings at the close of play on June 12 showed Pittsburgh in fourth place with a 24–21 record. The Pirates trailed the first-place Giants by five-and-a-half games and were within three-and-a-half games of the second-place Cubs. Traynor's squad was scheduled to open the road trip with a key three-game series against New York that could go a long way in shaping Pittsburgh's season. Besides these huge games against Bill Terry's squad, Traynor was also attempting to improve his team before the trade deadline on June 15. While the Phillies were in Pittsburgh, Traynor had made an offer to Philadelphia skipper Jimmy Wilson that included either Johnny Dickshot or Woody Jensen, plus a pitcher and cash in exchange for slugging outfielder Chuck Klein. Pie was prepared to begin a 48-hour vigil beside the telephone in his room at the Alamac Hotel so a potential deal could be finalized.[43]

Traynor finally left his hotel room on the afternoon of June 14 to lead his Pirates against New York at the Polo Grounds. Pittsburgh's manager could only hope that trade discussions over the next two days would produce better results as the Giants prevailed, 5–3. Russ Bauers took the defeat for Pittsburgh, with two unearned runs turning out to be the difference in the tightly contested game. Paul Waner and Gus Suhr both kept their hitting streaks alive. Pittsburgh's veteran first baseman went 2-for-4, slammed a double, a triple, scored one run and drove home a teammate, while Arky Vaughan and Johnny Rizzo also recorded two hits apiece. It took Waner until the eighth inning to extend his hitting streak to 13 games.[44]

Two fourth-inning incidents left the Pirates fuming. When New York's Jimmy Ripple took a three-quarter swing at a pitch that plate umpire George Magerkurth called a ball, Pirates catcher Al Todd went ballistic. Pie Traynor rushed out to join Todd in arguing the call. Eventually Todd went too far and Magerkurth told him that a fight would ensue if he used that name again. Ripple returned to the batter's box and promptly hit a ground ball to shortstop Arky Vaughan. Gus Suhr made a spectacular play at first base to snare Vaughan's wild return throw, but umpire Tiny Parker ruled that Suhr's foot had left the bag and called Ripple safe. Suhr threw his glove down to the ground in disgust after Parker's ruling.[45]

The Pirates rebounded quite nicely for the second battle between these two antagonists on Wednesday, June 15. Pittsburgh claimed a 2–0 victory as Jim Tobin tossed a complete game, allowing five hits, four walks and striking out two. Lloyd Waner, Gus Suhr and Al Todd were Pittsburgh's catalysts at the plate, each going 2-for-4. Suhr also scored a run while Todd drove home one teammate.

When the afternoon contest with New York ended, Traynor hustled back to the Alamac Hotel hoping to pull off a deal before the midnight trade deadline. While Traynor waited patiently by the phone hoping to hear from the St. Louis Cardinals, Bill Benswanger hustled over to Ebbets Field to talk with Philadelphia manager Jimmy Wilson and team president Gerald Nugent before they played a night game against Brooklyn. When the clock struck midnight, however, no changes had been made to Pittsburgh's roster composition.[46]

Pittsburgh's management team had pondered a few swaps before they decided that the transactions in question would weaken their squad too much. The Pirates had offered the Phillies outfielder Woody Jensen, pitcher Ed Brandt and $10,000 in cash for slugging outfielder Chuck Klein. When Wilson and Nugent countered with a proposal that included pitcher Russ Bauers, the Pirates said no thanks and walked away from talks. Traynor was called to the telephone at a late hour on June 15 to discuss a trade with Branch Rickey of the Cardinals involving pitcher Bill Swift of the Pirates and St. Louis' Frenchy Bordagaray. Pie ended the dickering between these two men before it really had a chance to get started with a terse, witty response. "Oh, so you want one of my starting pitchers for a fellow who plays in the Mudcat band?" queried Traynor in a sarcastic tone. "Sorry."[47]

This failure to add any new faces meant that the 1938 Pirates would stand or fall with the current roster. Now that concern over being moved to another National League squad no longer existed for Traynor's players, they could relax and concentrate on just playing baseball. The Buccaneers certainly looked at ease as they dismantled the defending National League champions at the Polo Grounds on Thursday, June 16 by a score of 10–2. Pitcher Bob Klinger went the route for Pittsburgh, giving up two runs on five hits, striking out eight and pushing his record to 5–1. Jeep Handley was Pittsburgh's hitting star; he went 3-for-5 at the plate, scored two runs, knocked in four teammates and clubbed a three-run homer off Jumbo Brown in the ninth inning. Lloyd Waner also connected for a four-bagger in the fourth frame, while Johnny Rizzo was 2-for-4 and Al Todd went 3-for-4, scored two runs, blasted a triple and recorded three RBIs.

Pittsburgh's latest victory against New York meant that the team had taken five out of nine games against its archrival, including four of the past five meetings. Baseball writer Sid Feder, who had claimed over a month ago that Pittsburgh was falling into their annual state of slumber earlier than usual, now believed that the Pirates and Cincinnati Reds were capable of making a strong push to supplant New York and Chicago atop the National League. Feder gave much of the credit for Pittsburgh's sudden rejuvenation to pitchers Bob Klinger, Jim Tobin and Mace Brown, who had accounted for 17 of Pittsburgh's 26 victories. He also claimed the hitting of Lloyd Waner and Arky Vaughan was another big reason why the Pirates had surged recently.[48]

Pitcher Mace Brown added to his victory total on Friday, June 17, when the Pirates moved on to Philadelphia and defeated the Phillies, 4–3. Pittsburgh claimed victory in the tenth inning when Jeep Handley scampered home with the winning run on a wild pitch by Phillies hurler Al Hollingsworth. Hollingsworth had also uncorked a seventh-inning wild pitch that presented Pittsburgh with its first run. Brown pushed his record to 9–2 on the season when he replaced starter Bill Swift in the eighth inning and choked off a potential Philadelphia rally by fanning Phil Weintraub with the bases loaded.[49] Veterans Paul Waner and Gus Suhr starred at the plate as each player recorded two hits apiece and scored one run each.

Philadelphia gained some revenge against Pie Traynor's troops the following day by blitzing starter Russ Bauers and holding on for a 5–3 victory. Bauers' record dropped to 1–6 on the year as he pitched six-and-one-third innings and gave up five runs on ten hits while also walking five batters. Jeep Handley did all of Pittsburgh's scoring, crossing home plate three times, going 2-for-4 at the plate and smacking his fourth home run of the season against Hugh Mulcahy in the fifth inning. Lloyd Waner chipped in by going 2-for-5, while Gus Suhr raised his batting average to .335 with a 2-for-3 performance at the plate.

The Pirates concluded their series against Philadelphia at the Baker Bowl with a doubleheader on Sunday, June 19. The ballpark lived up to its reputation as a hitter's paradise from the Pittsburgh players' perspective as the Pirates bombarded five Phillies pitchers to the tune of 30 runs and 34 hits during the twin bill. Pittsburgh won the opening contest, 14–4, and then claimed the nightcap, 16–3. Left fielder Johnny Rizzo recorded six hits in nine trips to the plate during the doubleheader, blasting one home run in the first game and two more four-baggers during the second contest. Rizzo's superb power hitting display allowed him to drive home nine runs on the day. Veteran outfielder Paul Waner was also smoking hot at the plate, collecting seven clean safeties in 12 times at bat, including two home runs and eight RBIs.[50]

In the first game of the doubleheader, Philadelphia starter Pete Sivess was chased from the mound in the first inning before he recorded an out. The Pirates continued to pound Wild Bill Hallahan and Sylvester Johnson as neither Phillies pitcher could subdue the onslaught. Jim Tobin picked up his fifth victory of the season while holding Philadelphia to nine hits. Tobin only experienced trouble in the fourth inning when home runs by Morris Arnovich and Spud Davis accounted for two runs. Any doubt regarding the outcome of the nightcap was erased in the first inning when the Pirates scored five runs off starting pitcher Wayne LaMaster.[51] Cy Blan-

First baseman and team captain Gus Suhr went on a tear at the plate after having been benched for a few games in May due to a protracted batting slump. Suhr proceeded to hit safely in 16 consecutive games from May 28 through June 15. Suhr's hot streak helped push his average up to a team-leading .328 as of June 19 (National Baseball Hall of Fame Library, Cooperstown, New York).

ton gladly accepted all the support he received from his mates as the Pirates right-hander made his first mound appearance in nearly one month. Blanton was brilliant following his exile due to a stubborn bout of influenza, tossing a complete game, recording his second victory of the season and giving up two earned runs on ten hits.

Pie Traynor's troops enjoyed a well-deserved day off following their impressive doubleheader sweep over Philadelphia prior to the start of a short series against Brooklyn. Pittsburgh's recent hitting surge had done wonders in boosting the batting averages of many members of the squad. Gus Suhr led the way for Pittsburgh with a .328 average, while center fielder Lloyd Waner was the only other player that topped the .300 mark, checking in with a mark of .307. Paul Waner had lifted his batting average to .265, while Arky Vaughan (.292), Jeep Handley (.284), Johnny Rizzo (.278), Pep Young (.272) and Al Todd (.265) all had been wielding a wicked war club in recent days. While the team's batting had improved significantly, the work of the pinch hitters had been pitiful during the season's first two months. Through June 21, Pirates pinch hitters had only registered four hits in 45 official at-bats for a pathetic average of .089.[52]

Pittsburgh played its first night game of the season on Tuesday, June 21. Prior to the game at Ebbets Field, Dodgers management staged the first event of a series of races aimed at determining the National League's fastest runner. The Dodgers planned on staging races during various night games throughout the summer with $500 in prize money being offered as an incentive. Brooklyn's Ernie Koy, Gibby Brack and Goody Rosen participated in the first heat against Pittsburgh's Arky Vaughan, Jeep Handley and Johnny Dickshot. Koy was crowned the race's winner after he covered the 80-yard distance in 8.05 seconds. Vaughan finished second, followed by Handley and Brack.[53]

Once the actual game got started, the Pirates quickly fell behind the Dodgers when Kiki Cuyler blasted Bob Klinger's initial offering for a home run in the bottom of the first inning. That was one of the few things the Ebbets Field crowd of 25,527 had to cheer about, as Pittsburgh tied the game at two in the third inning before Russ Bauers replaced Klinger on the mound.[54] Bauers kept Brooklyn at bay for the remainder of the evening as Pittsburgh's bats thrashed four Dodgers hurlers for 14 hits and claimed a 9–3 victory. Russ pitched seven innings of stellar one-run relief, scattering four hits and striking out seven Dodgers, to improve his record to 2–6. Al Todd and Pep Young were Pittsburgh's hitting leaders with three hits apiece. Todd also hit a solo four-bagger off Vito Tamulis in the fifth inning, while

Young connected for a two-run homer against Max Butcher in the seventh stanza.

After another idle day away from the ballpark, Pittsburgh and Brooklyn locked horns once again on Thursday, June 23. Pie Traynor's troops were never in the game as Dodgers hurler Tot Pressnell cruised to an easy 8–1 victory. Johnny Rizzo was the only Pirates player who offered any resistance against Pressnell as Pittsburgh's rookie outfielder went 2-for-3 at the plate. Bill Swift was knocked around freely and was pulled in the fifth inning after allowing five runs and six hits. Mace Brown was not much better during his three and one-third inning relief pitching stint. Brooklyn catcher Babe Phelps was a headache to the Pirates all day, going 3-for-4, driving home six runs and blasting a home run off Brown in the eighth inning.

Pittsburgh returned to action on Saturday, June 25 against Boston on the final stop of this eastern trip. The Pirates looked like they were headed to an easy victory when they drove Bees starter Johnny Lanning from the mound with five runs in the first inning. Unfortunately, Corsairs starter Jim Tobin had surrendered much of that lead by the time Mace Brown was summoned in the fifth inning. Brown allowed two additional runs, but he improved his record to 10–2 for the season when Pittsburgh hung on to defeat Boston, 8–7. Brown's seventh-inning double drove home Pittsburgh's final two runs and Russ Bauers preserved the victory by thwarting a Boston rally in the seventh and then tossing two scoreless innings. Pittsburgh's eastern trip ended prematurely when their final game against Boston on Sunday, June 26 was postponed due to rain.[55]

Standings at the end of play on June 26 showed that Pittsburgh's recent surge had put the team back in the thick of the National League pennant race. The Pirates stood in fourth place with a 31–24 record, three games behind league-leading New York, who checked in with a mark of 37–24. Pittsburgh, who was only one game behind second-place Cincinnati, had played 55 games so far while the top three teams had participated in anywhere from five to seven more contests. The Pirates' eastern trip had been a rousing success; by going 7–3 during their sojourn through New York, Boston and Philadelphia they had made up crucial ground in the standings. Johnny Rizzo was blazing hot with the bat, having batted .425 during the eastern swing. Rizzo's great power surge had catapulted him to the team lead in RBIs with 38, while his average now stood at .287. Paul Waner also reached a personal milestone during the trip by belting the 100th home run of his major league career.[56]

While the Pirates were in Boston finishing up their road trip, manager

Pie Traynor revealed that he had nominated three of his players—Mace Brown, Lloyd Waner and Arky Vaughan—to represent the National League at the All-Star Game in Cincinnati on July 6. The final decision, however, was in the hands of league president Ford Frick and Bill Terry. Vaughan was the only player from this trio of Pirates who had previously appeared in this clash between the best players from the American and National leagues.[57]

Before Pittsburgh returned to action against Cincinnati at Forbes Field, the team played a tune-up exhibition contest against the McKeesport City League All-Stars at the World War Memorial Field in McKeesport. Traynor chose Rip Sewell to pitch the 5 p.m. game, which was staged as a benefit for the McKeesport Hospital.[58] The upcoming three-game series against the Reds to close out June was being viewed as a critical engagement since Bill McKechnie's team currently occupied second place in the National League. This clash also was being observed with much anticipation by local baseball fans since Pittsburgh and Cincinnati were two of the league's hottest teams. The Pirates had won 16 of their last 23 contests and had not lost two games in succession during the streak. While McKechnie was still a long shot to win the National League flag in his first season as Cincinnati's skipper, the former Pirates manager believed his team could be a factor in the race. "The race is tightly bunched," said McKechnie, "and I think there's a great chance for us. We're playing our games day by day and looking no further ahead than our next contest. So far on our eastern trip we won nine games and lost four, but we've taken ten out of our last 15. We slumped a little after beating the Giants, but as long as we can take those New Yorkers, we'll be in the race."[59]

McKechnie's squad looked like true pennant contenders when they opened the three-game series at Forbes Field on Tuesday, June 28 with a 5–2 win over the Pirates. Reds southpaw Johnny Vander Meer, fresh off his consecutive no-hit performances earlier in the month against Boston and Brooklyn, doused Pittsburgh's flaming bats by tossing a complete game and scattering six Pirate hits. Russ Bauers' struggles continued as his record dropped to 2–7, even though he sported a respectable ERA of 3.62. One of Bauers' problems was shoddy fielding by the man Pie Traynor expected to be the pitching staff's ace. While Bauers certainly had not lost his stuff during the past year, he also did not possess the poise or polish that big leaguers usually acquired through constant teaching and coaching.[60]

Bauers displayed his fielding deficiencies once again in the defeat against Cincinnati. Such fielding gaffes had been a contributing factor in four of his seven losses—Bauers looked confused when an opponent bunted against him and he still had not mastered the art of positioning himself properly when balls were hit to the outfield with men on base. He seldom backed up home or third base to prevent runners from taking an extra base on overthrown baseballs from the outfield. The fact that Bauers had begged for help on numerous occasions showed that he was confused rather than just lazy. After the latest incident, Traynor had worked with Russ prior to the second game against Cincinnati. Bauers reported to Forbes Field at noon and was given one hour of instruction fielding bunts, throwing to the proper bases and backing up at third and home following hits to the outfield.[61]

Devoted Pirates rooters were delighted when their favorite baseball team rallied from a four-run deficit and claimed an exhilarating 5–4 victory from Cincinnati on Wednesday, June 29. Starting hurler Jim Tobin was knocked from the box after only three-and-one-third innings of work while the Reds pushed across four runs on nine hits. Pittsburgh refused to fold and tied the game with four runs in the fifth inning. The Waners sent patrons home happy by pulling off the kind of hitting stunt that had been witnessed at Forbes Field on many occasions during the past decade. Lloyd Waner doubled to left in the seventh inning and then scored the game's winning run when brother Paul followed suit with a two-bagger to the opposite field. Manager Pie Traynor had shuffled his lineup a bit in an effort to shake Arky Vaughan from a minor batting slump: Vaughan was bumped from the cleanup spot to sixth, while Gus Suhr was elevated to the fourth hole with Johnny Rizzo following in the fifth spot. Vaughan responded with two solid raps that netted him a single and a double.[62]

While Vaughan and the Waner brothers were Pittsburgh's batting heroes for the day, their exploits would not have mattered had Bill Swift not given a masterful pitching performance after relieving Tobin. Swift hurled five-and-two-thirds innings of shutout baseball, allowing only one hit, and striking out three Reds batters while improving his record to 4–3. Swift dedicated the victory to his four-week-old son, whom he still had not seen. Swift's wife, who gave birth to the boy while Pittsburgh was traveling in the east, was due to arrive in Pittsburgh with Bill, Jr., in another week. When Swift was in the locker room showering after Pittsburgh's victory, he caught sight of writer Lester Biederman of *The Pittsburgh Press*. As the water beat on his head and shoulders, Swift wiped the soap from his eyes and gave Biederman a simple six-word quotation for his newspaper article. "That game was for Bill, Jr.," Swift proudly announced.[63]

Pie Traynor's troops were again victorious in the key rubber match of the Cincinnati series and claimed the undisputed title of hottest team in the National League by brushing aside the Reds, 3–1, on Thursday, June 30. Cy Blanton was brilliant for the second consecutive outing, going the distance and hurling a three-hitter. The Pirates held a slim 1–0 lead in the eighth inning when they touched up Cincinnati's Bucky Walters for two runs on a Gus Suhr double, an Arky Vaughan triple and a single by Al Todd.[64] Shawnee Cy kept the Reds off balance all afternoon by mixing fastballs and curves with his famous "downer" pitch. Blanton allowed only one Cincinnati hit through eight innings before the Reds finally pushed a run across the plate during the final frame.[65]

Arky Vaughan's resurgence at the plate continued as Pittsburgh's shortstop went 3-for-4 and recorded two RBIs. Since Traynor had dropped Vaughan into the sixth slot of his batting order, the shortstop had pounded three singles, one double and one triple in two games against Cincinnati.[66] Pittsburgh's manager seemed to be pushing all of the right buttons in recent weeks as Pittsburgh followed up a disastrous month of May with a record of 16–7 in June. Key performers such as Vaughan, Paul Waner, Gus Suhr and Johnny Rizzo were finally hitting their stride at the plate and contributing along with men like Lloyd Waner who had been the model of consistency throughout the 1938 campaign. Pie's pitching corps was slowly rounding into shape after tepid results from some starting hurlers that would have doomed Pittsburgh to the second division if not for Fireman Mace Brown's quality work. The confident Corsairs had slowly risen in the standings and now had their sights set on first-place New York. Pittsburgh finally was on a roll as they staked their claim to the National League flag that had eluded them for so many years.

8

Johnny Rizzo Shines as Pirates Climb into First Place

Pittsburgh's victory over Cincinnati on the twenty-ninth anniversary of Forbes Field's opening on June 30 allowed Pie Traynor's squad to jump ahead of the Reds into second place behind New York.[1] The Buccaneers now trailed Bill Terry's team by four games as the season moved into the summer's hottest months. Beautiful, sunny weather certainly was not evident on July 1 as Pittsburgh prepared to play St. Louis in the first contest of a four-game series. Rain prevented the two teams from doing battle at Forbes Field, giving the Pirates yet another idle afternoon. Since Traynor's boys were on a hot streak, such interruptions couldn't come at a worse time.[2]

The Pirates won their third straight game when Pittsburgh and St. Louis resumed action on Saturday, June 2. Rookie hurler Bob Klinger was magnificent on the mound, tossing a complete game and improving his record to 6–1 while Pittsburgh defeated the Cardinals, 5–1. Lloyd Waner, Gus Suhr and Johnny Rizzo led Pittsburgh's hitting attack with two safe blows apiece, while second baseman Pep Young struck the key blast that broke the game wide open. Trailing 1–0 in the second inning after St. Louis scored an unearned run against Klinger in the first, Pittsburgh roughed up pitcher Bill McGee and took control of the contest. After Suhr drew a walk, Rizzo drilled a single that moved him over to third base. McGee walked Arky Vaughan to fill the bases. The St. Louis pitcher seemed to settle things down when he struck out Al Todd on three pitches, but then Young drilled a double to deep left field that cleared the bases and gave Pittsburgh a 3–1 lead.[3]

Young's clutch hit at the plate occurred before he single-handedly retired St. Louis in the third frame by figuring in on all three putouts. Pep's final assist was the afternoon's gem. With Enos Slaughter occupying first base, Ducky Medwick rifled a ball to Young's left that seemed destined to land in the outfield for a single. Pep raced across the diamond, picked up the hot smash in his glove and made a perfect throw that retired Medwick at first base.[4] The small crowd of 3,893 in attendance at Forbes Field witnessed a bizarre protest by Cardinals manager Frankie Frisch in the seventh inning when he claimed that Pittsburgh had more players in uniform than the rules allowed. Frisch reasoned that the presence of prospects Lenny Levy, Johnny Mize and Andy Lipscomb in Pittsburgh's dugout with uniforms on pushed the Pirates roster to 26 players. The fact that none of these men were under contract and that such amenities had been extended to prospects for years by every National League team did not seem to faze Frisch.[5]

While Frisch was busy being childish, Pie Traynor was ecstatic that Bob Klinger had performed brilliantly in his first appearance since he had injured his back and had a finger mashed against Brooklyn on June 21. Klinger's ailing back had prevented him from properly following through with his pitches. Another Pirates rookie continued on a rampage with a bat as Johnny Rizzo pushed his hitting streak to 12 consecutive games, during which he had cranked out 20 hits in 47 trips to the plate for a .425 average.[6]

With pennant enthusiasm now reaching a feverish pitch, a crowd of 20,866 rooters, the largest turnout to date at Forbes Field in 1938, witnessed the doubleheader between St. Louis and Pittsburgh on Sunday, July 3. Pirates fans were entertained to a thrilling pair of games as Pittsburgh pushed its winning streak to five games by sweeping the afternoon twin bill. The Corsairs claimed the first contest in 12 innings, 6–5, as reliever extraordinaire Mace Brown picked up his eleventh victory of the season. After the Cardinals had tied the game in the ninth frame when they touched up starter Jim Tobin for two runs, Pittsburgh claimed victory in the twelfth on Pep Young's bases-loaded single that drove Gus Suhr home with the winning run.[7] Suhr was Pittsburgh's hitting star during the first contest as he went 3-for-6 and scored three runs. Lloyd Waner, Johnny Rizzo, Arky Vaughan and Pep Young rapped out two hits apiece and combined to drive home four of Pittsburgh's runs.

Hits were scarcer during the nightcap as Pittsburgh and St. Louis combined for 11 safeties. The Pirates bunched their six blows off Cardinals hurler Roy Henshaw effectively as Pie Traynor's troops won, 6–2, in a contest that was shortened to eight innings due to travel issues. Russ Bauers cruised to his third victory of the season as he tossed a complete game and gave up one earned run on five hits. Henshaw survived a four-run fourth inning before he was sent to the showers by Frisch after Johnny Rizzo hit a 429-foot triple in the fifth and scored on Arky Vaughan's home run.[8] After the two victories, three crucial performers were recognized for their brilliant work during the 1938 season. All three of Pie Traynor's nominees, Mace Brown, Lloyd Waner and Arky Vaughan, were selected to represent the National League at the All-Star Game on July 6.[9]

Before the remainder of Traynor's squad could embark on a three-day All-Star Game vacation, there was still a holiday doubleheader on July 4 in Cincinnati to be played. In the opener, Cy Blanton tossed a complete game and bested the Reds, 2–1, while Bill Swift also went the route in the nightcap and claimed a 3–2 victory. The doubleheader sweep extended Pittsburgh's winning streak to seven games. The red-hot team had earned 23 victories in its past 31 games. While the Pirates felt energized by their recent success, they had not been able to close the gap with New York because Terry's team was feasting on the weak eastern teams.[10] As the National League prepared for the All-Star break, New York stood atop the league with a 45–25 record, while Pittsburgh was three and one-half games behind with a mark of 38–25.

Manager Traynor remained in Cincinnati with the team's three All-Stars. Coach Jewel Ens escorted the remainder of the Corsairs squad back to Pittsburgh, where he would put the boys through a few rigorous practices at Forbes Field before they resumed play in St. Louis on Friday, July 8.[11] While the Pirates were not on the field practicing in preparation for the second half of the National League campaign, Pirates farm system director Joe Schultz, Sr. was conducting a baseball school for 400 applicants at the ballpark. Helping Schultz run the one-week baseball clinic were scout Bill Hinchman, coach Honus Wagner, Leo Mackey and former Pirates Wilbur Cooper and Tom McCreery.[12] The Pittsburgh Pirates baseball school attracted sandlot players between the ages of 17 and 23 from all over the country. Sessions were held from 9 a.m. to 12 p.m. and 1 p.m. through 5 p.m. Second base candidate Bud Bridwell from Ventura, California, traveled the greatest distance to attend.[13]

While Schultz and his crew were hoping to unearth a few nuggets of baseball gold for the future, Pittsburgh's current gems represented the Steel City in the sixth annual All-Star Game at Crosley Field in Cincinnati. Unlike the current-day event, managers from both squads treated the contest like

8. Johnny Rizzo Shines as Pirates Climb into First Place

any other game and only used substitutions when strategy dictated it was prudent. Thus Arky Vaughan and Lloyd Waner remained on the bench because manager Bill Terry preferred to use shortstop Leo Durocher and center fielder Mel Ott for the full nine innings. Terry did summon Pittsburgh's other representative from the bullpen in the seventh inning with the National League leading, 2–0. Fireman Mace Brown responded with one of the steady performances he had delivered on so many occasions in 1938 as the National League prevailed by a 4–1 score.

The National Leaguers, victory-starved in their recent encounters against the American League in both the mid-summer and October classics, were counting on Brown when he took the mound to begin the seventh inning. Awaiting Brown after he tossed his customary practice pitches to catcher Ernie Lombardi was slugger Jimmy Foxx of the Boston Red Sox. Shortstop Durocher, expecting Foxx to pull the ball, moved closer to third baseman Stan Hack. Jimmy foiled this strategy by smacking a single between Durocher and second base. Had Leo been standing in his standard spot, he would have gobbled up the grounder without any problem instead of having it carom off his glove for a base hit. Mace remained calm and cool under pressure as Joe DiMaggio stepped to the plate and recorded the inning's first out when Foxx was forced on a ground ball to second baseman Billy Herman. Brown quickly made it two outs for the American Leaguers when Bill Dickey was retired on a popup to Hack.[14]

DiMaggio then swiped second base and Brown followed by walking Cronin and allowing the tying run to reach first base. Things got tougher for Pittsburgh's star relief pitcher when Lou Gehrig of the Yankees reached first on a slow roller that eluded Durocher, who had been fading the slugger toward third base. With the bases loaded and two out, manager Joe McCarthy selected Detroit's Rudy York to pinch hit for pitcher Johnny Allen.[15]

Brown used a mixture of curves and fastballs in an effort to retire the Tigers slugger. The suspense in Crosley Field reached nerve-racking heights when the count went to three balls and two strikes. Lombardi and Brown both seemed to recognize that Mace's curve was not as sharp as usual. The catcher, realizing that Brown also possessed a blazing fastball, called for the "swifter" on this crucial 3–2 pitch. Mace stepped back and heaved a low pitch from his powerhouse right arm that was headed somewhere below York's knees. Not wanting to risk taking a called third strike at such a critical juncture of the game, York cut down on his swing and attempted to put the ball in play. Rudy's wooden weapon failed to make contact as Brown's pitch nestled into Lombardi's glove with a loud thud. The fans who had packed Crosley Field broke out with the wildest and loudest cheer of the game for Brown.[16]

Despite surrendering one run in the ninth inning, Brown stole the show away from other players like Johnny Vander Meer, Bob Feller, Ival Goodman and Frank McCormick who had been expected to play leading roles in the 1938 All-Star Game. After Mace dressed and signed autographs for fans following the game, he searched for a telephone in order to call his wife and discuss his great achievement. When Mace finally gained a phone connection to Pittsburgh, his wife informed him that she had listened to the game on the radio at their home. She admitted being apprehensive at times, especially during the precarious seventh inning when she was very scared when the American League loaded the bases. Mace assured his wife that such theatrics were part of the game for a relief pitcher who was responsible for extinguishing rallies. "Now dear," said Brown over the telephone, "I don't want you to be that way. Please don't get excited when I seem to be in trouble. Why, I just don't feel at home out there unless I look around and see a few runners on the sacks."[17]

Brown's magnificent performance in Cincinnati thrust him into the national spotlight. Born on May 21, 1909, in North English, Iowa, about 100 miles from Bob Feller's home, Brown actually had been a track and field star at his high school before he started to show an interest in baseball. He attended the University of Iowa, where former Chicago Cub Otto Vogel managed the college baseball team and helped mold Mace into a promising pitcher. A scout from the St. Louis Cardinals started following Brown around whenever he pitched and eventually signed the youngster to a contract in 1929. Mace decided to forego his senior season at Iowa to pitch for St. Joseph of the Western League. After experiencing tough times during five years playing baseball at different levels, Brown finally had a breakthrough season with Tulsa's Texas League team in 1934 when he won 19 games and fanned 168 batters.[18]

After Brown finished up the 1934 campaign pitching for Double A Kansas City, Pittsburgh purchased him from the Blues on November 21. Mace certainly was not an overnight pitching sensation once he reached the National League, going 4–1 in 1935 and 10–11 in 1936. Used as a spot starter and reliever during his first two seasons, Brown then pitched almost exclusively as a reliever for Pie Traynor in 1937 and posted a 7–2 record with an ERA of 4.18. Even though it had taken Brown many years to reach star status on a baseball diamond, he never lost confidence in his ability. Mace always

8. Johnny Rizzo Shines as Pirates Climb into First Place

believed that his curve and fastball would allow him to excel at the major league level once he got the chance. Even though he suddenly was being toasted throughout America after his stint in the All-Star Game, Brown took his newfound celebrity status in stride. Before Brown left the ballpark to rejoin his Pirate teammates for the second half of the 1938 season, he made one last comment to reporters regarding the American Leaguers' powerful hitting exhibition during batting practice before the game. "Well, I'm darn glad I was not out on the field when Foxx, Gehrig, Johnson and DiMaggio were losing balls over the fences," said Brown. "From what I hear, they must have been smacking them plenty. As far as I am concerned, they were hitting them too hard inside the park in the last inning."[19]

Sporting News editor J.G. Taylor Spink wrote that the American League's batting practice display reminded him of when the New York Yankees put on a home run show at Forbes Field prior to Game One of the 1927 World Series.[20] If Brown had witnessed the American League's hitting prowess during batting practice, it's unlikely the star pitcher would have been fazed one bit, since he always exhibited cool, calm behavior during a crisis. As the conquering hero made his triumphant return to rejoin teammates in St. Louis, Bill Benswanger arrived in Pittsburgh after participating in the National League's mid-season meeting in Cincinnati and found that he was part of a false story regarding the All-Star Game. Two local radio stations claimed that Benswanger had asked Commissioner Kenesaw Landis to refuse them permission to broadcast the All-Star Game on July 6. Benswanger wasted no time firing back against this accusation, which deeply surprised him when it reached his attention.[21] "The assertion that I, or any other person connected in any way with the Pittsburgh club," Benswanger said, "had anything to do with the banning of the All-Star game broadcast from any Pittsburgh radio station, or with suggesting or requesting that order, is entirely and absolutely false. Nothing ever was farther from my thoughts. Far from having had any part in keeping any radio station from broadcasting the game to the fans of this territory. I did not even know that the proposed broadcast had been stopped until I was informed of the action on my arrival at home in Pittsburgh late this afternoon."[22]

Thoughts about the All-Star Game were banished from the thought of most Pittsburgh fans as the Pirates prepared to begin the second half of the 1938 campaign against St. Louis on July 8. The Pirates' recent surge in the standings had persuaded Broadway betting commissioner Jack Doyle to rework his baseball odds at the mid-season point. While Doyle still believed a third consecutive subway series between the Yankees and Giants was inevitable, Pittsburgh was now quoted at 5:2 to win the National League pennant while the odds for Bill Terry's favorites stood at even money.[23]

Pie Traynor selected Bob Klinger to take the hill against St. Louis, which allowed a group of Klinger's friends from Allenton, Missouri, to sit behind the Pirates dugout at Sportsman's Park and cheer loudly throughout the contest. Indeed it seemed as if the game were being played at Forbes Field since Pittsburgh was applauded and the Cardinals were booed throughout the afternoon.[24] Klinger certainly did not disappoint the rooting section from Allenton, as he pushed his record to 7–1 with a complete-game victory over the Cardinals, 6–2. Johnny Rizzo punished the organization that never gave him a chance at the major league level by smacking two singles, a double and drawing a walk.[25] Lloyd Waner, Paul Waner, Arky Vaughan and Pep Young also aided the Pirate attack by rapping out two hits apiece, while accounting for four runs scored and three RBIs.

The Pirates made it nine wins in a row when they won a thriller over St. Louis on Saturday, July 9 by an 8–7 score. Pittsburgh's latest victory cut New York's lead to two-and-a-half games as the Giants were shut out by Boston. Mace Brown secured his twelfth win of the season when he relieved Jim Tobin after Pittsburgh's starter faltered in the third inning.[26] There were only a couple of thousand fans in attendance at Sportsman's Park due to temperatures that hovered around 100 degrees on that hot July afternoon.[27] Johnny Rizzo's bat continued to blaze as Pittsburgh's rookie outfielder hit home runs number six and seven during successive at-bats in the second and third innings.[28] Rizzo's blast in the second stanza was a line drive that traveled about 400 feet into the left-field stands, while his third-inning wallop followed almost the exact same trajectory.[29]

Even though heavy hitting such as Rizzo's had allowed Pittsburgh to build a 7–5 lead, the Cardinals tied the game in the seventh frame when they pushed across two runs against Brown. The Pirates went ahead for good in the eighth when Pep Young singled to start the inning, was sacrificed to second by Brown, moved to third on Jeep Handley's single and scored on Lloyd Waner's high chopper to second baseman Jimmy Brown.[30]

Pie Traynor's troops concluded their series at Sportsman's Park with a doubleheader sweep over St. Louis. Pittsburgh claimed the first contest, 5–2, as Cy Blanton improved his record to 5–1 for the season, while Russ Bauers was credited with a victory in the nightcap as the Pirates won a 4–3 thriller. Bauers needed assistance from veteran hurler Joe Bowman who pitched two innings of shutout relief to nail down the victory after rookie Rip Sewell made the game interesting when he allowed single runs in con-

8. Johnny Rizzo Shines as Pirates Climb into First Place 133

secutive innings. The highlights of game one included Blanton's eight-hit hurling, the Corsairs turning double plays in three consecutive innings and Johnny Rizzo's two singles and a double. Pittsburgh's four-run seventh inning was the key to the second victory as Arky Vaughan's walk, Pep Young's double, an intentional pass to pinch hitter Al Todd, a pinch-hit double by Jim Tobin and Jeep Handley's fly ball out secured the Pirates' victory.[31]

Besides Rizzo's continued excellence during his rookie campaign, Paul Waner, Blanton and Bauers acquitted themselves quite nicely during the Sunday afternoon twin bill. After hitting into two force-outs against St. Louis' Max Macon in the opener, Paul connected for a pair of singles.[32]

In July, writer Charles "Chilly" Doyle of the *Pittsburgh Sun-Telegraph* proclaimed that Pie Traynor's 1938 squad was the strongest the city of Pittsburgh had seen for many years. Doyle also considered the Pirates' infield quartet to be the best in the National League. In this photograph, from left to right, are third baseman Jeep Handley, shortstop Arky Vaughan, second baseman Pep Young and first baseman Gus Suhr (National Baseball Hall of Fame Library, Cooperstown, New York).

Waner then went 2-for-4 in the nightcap and raised his batting average to .260 on the season. Bauers seemed to be bringing the heat more frequently than usual in the second contest, as St. Louis' batters were swinging late at his high, hard pitches during the early innings.[33]

Baseball scribe Charles "Chilly" Doyle, who was a *Sporting News* correspondent and covered the Pirates for the *Pittsburgh Sun-Telegraph*, believed Pie Traynor's squad was shaping up as one of the strongest in Pittsburgh in many years. Doyle reasoned that Pep Young and Arky Vaughan were the best middle infield combination in baseball, propelling Pittsburgh to the National League lead in double plays. He also believed the Pirates were every bit as solid at the corners, with Jeep Handley and Gus Suhr rounding out an infield unit that supplied airtight defense. With Johnny Rizzo and Mace Brown added into the mix, Doyle reasoned that the elusive National League pennant was not a far-fetched notion. "The infielders clicking like four champions," wrote Doyle, "the kid pitchers, together with Mace Brown, coming through like the midnight mail, and Johnny Rizzo playing a Joe Medwick engagement in left field and at the plate, the Pirates of Pie Traynor look like the best Pittsburgh club to come over the baseball horizon since Donie Bush's 1927 Buccos won the last pennant for Pa Pitt."[34]

The team's sudden rise to pennant contention put Pie Traynor in an odd position. Before his squad hit their recent hot streak and started climbing in the National League standings, Traynor had been adamant that a rebuilding process was the only proper course for the franchise. Such a course of action was no longer practical because Pie was reluctant to tamper with the chemistry of a team that was playing so well. Pittsburgh moved to within one-and-a-half games of first-place New York and claimed their twelfth straight victory by defeating Chicago, 5–3, on Monday, July 11.[35]

Things got nasty in the contest's seventh inning. A contingent of angry Pirates surrounded umpire George Barr after he called Johnny Rizzo out on a close play at the plate with what would have been the tie-breaking run. Barr took all of the jabbering in stride and let the Pirates have their say in protesting what they believed was a blown call. After their grievances had been aired, Barr ordered play to resume and ejected coach Jewel Ens for having charged toward him. When the Cubs came up to bat in their half of the seventh, Pirates catcher Al Todd again showed his displeasure with Barr's decision by kicking dirt on home plate. The umpire dusted off the dish, only to have Al kick more dirt over the cleaned area. After this exchange went on for a few rounds Barr, who was obviously tired of bending over, informed Todd that he was ejected from the festivities.[36]

Instead of retreating, Todd started giving Barr a piece of his mind. The umpire began backing away, but the catcher persisted in lambasting the arbiter who always seemed to be front and center in disputes involving the Pirates. When it seemed that Todd was prepared to start arguing with his fists, fellow umpire George Magerkurth stepped in between both men. As Todd walked off the field, he stripped off each piece of his catcher's gear and threw it into the air. He then strolled to the Pirates dugout and released his last few ounces of pent-up rage by throwing a few bats onto the infield before some of his teammates intervened and calmed him down.[37]

Pie Traynor's brigade trailed, 3–2, heading into the ninth inning but they never gave up the fight. Cubs hurler Larry French recorded the inning's first out when he fanned Gus Suhr. Johnny Rizzo got things started when he blasted his second double of the afternoon. French, remembering that Arky Vaughan had connected for a game-winning homer against him earlier in the season, walked Pittsburgh's shortstop for the second time that afternoon. Catcher Ray Berres then beat out an infield grounder to Stan Hack to load the bases. Rizzo scored the game's tying run when Pep Young's ground ball forced Berres at second. Young promptly pilfered second to put two Pirates in scoring position. Pitcher Jim Tobin followed with a single to left-center that drove home Vaughan and Young. Jeep Handley then connected for a double, but Tobin was thrown out at the plate attempting to score a run that proved irrelevant. Mace Brown relieved Tobin after Chicago's leadoff batter reached first in the ninth and preserved the victory without any further damage.[38]

Fighting spirit was something that Pirates teams from previous years sorely lacked, as many of Traynor's players had been accused of being too docile in the past. The 1938 version certainly seemed to possess more spirit. Pittsburgh claimed its thirteenth consecutive victory and closed out one of the most successful road trips in team history with a resounding 14–6 victory over Chicago on Tuesday, July 12. Ed Brandt claimed his first victory of the season in relief after Bob Klinger was knocked out of the box during the third inning. Brandt hurled five-and-two-thirds innings and gave up one earned run on six hits, while also walking six Cubs. Al Todd was Pittsburgh's catalyst at the plate, stroking a single, a double, a home run and knocking in five runs.[39]

The Pirates connected for 17 hits against five Chicago pitchers as Paul Waner continued his pursuit toward the .300 batting mark by going 4-for-6 at the plate. Johnny Rizzo and Pep Young also chipped in with two hits apiece and combined to drive home four runs. Pittsburgh now had three batters who were part of the heralded .300 club: Gus Suhr (.327), Johnny Rizzo (.307) and Lloyd Waner (.303). The Pirates were a perfect 8–0 on this road trip and had now won 20 of their last 23 games and 29 of the past 37. Pittsburgh's latest victory over Chicago, coupled with New York's defeat at Brooklyn's hands finally propelled the Pirates into first place by three percentage points. New York, who had played five more games than Pittsburgh and was up three games in the win column, had also suffered two more losses than the Pirates.[40]

Pittsburgh triumphantly returned home to Forbes Field for a long home stand against the National League's eastern teams. When the team's train pulled into Pennsylvania Station, the players were greeted by 200 enthusiastic baseball fans.[41] Before the Pirates played four critical games with the New York Giants, they had to play a three-game set with Brooklyn. Prior to Pittsburgh's first encounter versus the Dodgers, Pirates officials placed 7,500 more reserved seats on sale for the upcoming Sunday doubleheader with New York due to high ticket demand.[42] The little more than 6,600 people who showed up at Forbes Field to watch the first game against Brooklyn had to wonder if Pie Traynor's troops were looking ahead to the upcoming New York series. Pittsburgh went down hard as Brooklyn connected for six runs against Mace Brown after he relieved starter Russ Bauers in the eighth inning and claimed a 10–5 victory.

While the Pirates were unable to win their fourteenth straight contest, Arky Vaughan showed off his hustle and heady play on two occasions in an effort to manufacture runs. Vaughan's first piece of sharp baseball strategy occurred when he tagged up from first on a short fly to left field and easily made it into second base because he knew that Brooklyn's Buddy Hassett did not have an accurate arm. Vaughan's second display of sharp baseball came at the expense of Dodgers first baseman Dolph Camilli. Arky had moved to third on an infield out as Johnny Rizzo crossed home plate with a run. Realizing that Camilli seemed to be napping at first with the baseball in his glove, Vaughan continued running at full speed around third and crossed home plate without a throw. Camilli was stunned since the Pirates had not attempted such daring maneuvers earlier in the season.[43]

Vaughan also collected four hits against Brooklyn. Arky's recent revival at the plate pushed his season's average to within two points of the magical .300 mark. Gus Suhr, Johnny Rizzo and Lloyd Waner were still members of that charmed class, while Pep Young was closing in with a mark of .288. Jeep Handley (.269), Paul Waner (.266) and Al Todd (.264) rounded out Pittsburgh's hitting attack, which had played a huge role in the team's recent

8. Johnny Rizzo Shines as Pirates Climb into First Place

winning streak. The Pirates' mantra prior to their game against Brooklyn on Thursday, July 14 was: "At least 13 more in a row!" As his squad prepared to begin another long stretch of putting games in the win column, Pie Traynor gave a simple reason for his team's recent success. "We were getting some excellent pitching," explained Traynor, "both from starters and relief men and our hitters were clicking. That's all."[44]

On the same day that Pittsburgh's winning streak came to an end, coach Jewel Ens and catcher Al Todd were informed by National League president Ford Frick that they had been fined $50 for abusive conduct toward umpire George Barr in the game against Chicago on July 11.[45] When play resumed at Forbes Field on July 14, it looked like Pittsburgh was headed for a second straight loss as Brooklyn carried a 2–0 lead into the ninth inning. After pitcher Freddie Fitzsimmons recorded the first out, the Waner brothers connected for back-to-back singles against Brooklyn's veteran hurler. Both runners moved up one base when Gus Suhr was retired for the inning's second out on a long line drive to right-center field. Johnny Rizzo stepped to the plate with Pittsburgh's final hope for the afternoon hanging in the balance.

As Rizzo waved his bat menacingly, Fitzsimmons started his peculiar delivery, which involved turning his head and body toward second base and then firing toward home plate. His first pitch was a bit wide of the dish and it eluded catcher Merv Shea, bouncing all the way to the screen. Lloyd Waner scampered across home plate and was followed by brother Paul as Pittsburgh tied the ballgame. When Fitzsimmons finally received the ball back from Shea, he kicked it in disgust before Rizzo was retired on a popup to Dolph Camilli at first base. After Jim Tobin made quick work of the Dodgers in two consecutive innings, Pittsburgh's first two batters in the bottom of the eleventh frame brought the game to a sudden end. Jeep Handley crushed a leadoff triple that rattled off the left-field wall and then scored when Lloyd Waner cracked a single down the right field line. Rookie outfielder Johnny Rizzo's exuberance was evident when he gave his impression of Pittsburgh's exciting comeback. "Well, if we can win those kind of games, nothing is going to stop us from now on!" proclaimed Rizzo.[46]

Pittsburgh's come-from-behind victory allowed the team to retain the National League lead over New York by one-half game.[47] Traynor's troops were unable to use the momentum from this game to start another winning streak, however, as Brooklyn claimed the rubber game by thrashing the Pirates, 9–4, on Friday, July 15. Luke Hamlin of the Dodgers kept the Pirates in check all afternoon as he tossed a complete game and scattered eight hits. Paul Waner had a solid day at the plate for Pittsburgh, going 2-for-5 and blasting his third home run of the season in the eighth inning. Even though the Dodgers were in sixth place, they led Pittsburgh in the season series with seven victories against six losses.[48]

Nearly 5,000 boys and girls showed up at Forbes Field for the final contest against Brooklyn for the weekly Kids Day, which was scheduled during every Friday summer home game. Most of the youngsters on hand that day were there to catch a glimpse of legendary slugger Babe Ruth, now a Brooklyn coach. The youngsters jeered the Dodgers and stomped their feet in approval for Pittsburgh's players. Many of the children waited outside Forbes Field after the game hoping to meet the great Ruth. The kids congregated in front of the press gate and mobbed various Pirates players while they continued their vigil. The Babe and his wife, after being informed that a large crowd was waiting at the press gate, exited a special gate on the park's opposite side so that they could get back to their hotel safely. But the kids got word of his departure and ran after him.[49]

As the Pirates attempted to break loose from a minor slump before they prepared to play the most important series of the 1938 campaign against New York, veteran outfielder Paul Waner placed his stamp of approval on the current Buccaneer aggregation. Waner, a player who was usually reticent and rarely gave in to the temptation of making predictions, spoke openly of the belief in the Pittsburgh locker room that they were the team to beat in 1938. During an interview with baseball scribe Charles "Chilly" Doyle, Waner stated: "We have had a nice winning streak and nobody seemed to feel the strain to any great extent. I look for us to have some bad days when we will get trimmed plenty, but I don't see any other club in the league that has as much chance to win the pennant."[50]

On the eve of the big series against their longtime rivals, this statement by Waner was a bold proclamation. In the old days when John McGraw and Fred Clarke had butted heads, it was open season on the Giants whenever they came to town for games at Exposition Park. During those grand days of yesteryear, boys and girls used to congregate at Fifth Avenue and Market Street to playfully toss rocks at the Giants as they were driven across the river to Exposition Park in horse-drawn carriages. The energetic youngsters even developed a scoring system to make the whole affair more competitive. A child was awarded two points if a New York regular was struck, while five points were given to the youngster whose toss connected against McGraw. While current Pirates rooters had become slightly more refined, disgruntled fans at Forbes Field were still prone to throwing pop bottles at umpires after an unfavorable call.[51]

8. Johnny Rizzo Shines as Pirates Climb into First Place 139

Pittsburgh drew first blood in this heavyweight matchup against Bill Terry's squad as Bob Klinger continued his domination over New York before 15,197 raucous fans at Forbes Field on Saturday, July 16. Klinger improved his record to 8–1 on the season by limiting the Giants to eight hits as he cruised to an easy 7–3 victory. Bob was all but untouchable until the ninth inning when New York pushed two meaningless runs across the plate.[52] The top of Pie Traynor's batting order terrorized Giants hurlers Cliff Melton, Bill Lohrman and Jumbo Brown by accounting for eight of Pittsburgh's 13 hits. Jeep Handley, who had two singles and a double on the afternoon, might have recorded a fourth safety if he had run out his slow tapper down the third-base line in the eighth inning. He slowed up when the ball curved foul, but then it scooted back into fair territory and he was thrown out easily by Mel Ott.[53]

Another hitting star was Lloyd Waner, who smacked an inside-the-park homer, rapped out two singles, scored three runs and knocked home three runners. Brother Paul hit safely twice during the game and might have recorded five hits on the day if not for several great plays by Giants fielders. In the first inning, right fielder Jimmy Ripple robbed Paul of an extra-base hit. During the fifth frame, Bob Seeds made a great backhanded catch after having traveled a great distance to the left-field foul line. It was Hank Leiber's turn in the eighth stanza when he galloped back in deep center field and speared Waner's wicked drive.[54] While Handley and the Waners were largely responsible for crushing the Giants' chances during the first game of this pivotal series, newspaper correspondents from New York spent most of their time talking to All-Star Game hero Mace Brown. When asked to explain his recent success, Mace broke it down in simple terms by claiming he was always ready, willing and able to help when called upon. "I'm lucky that's all," said Brown about his phenomenal record. "I've been getting the breaks. I'm satisfied to be the relief guy, the 'fireman' who saves games, but my ambition still is to be a starter. That's the life. Pitch every fourth day. Lots of rest. Me for that. And I'll win, if I get the chance again."[55]

Rabid rooters who planned on attending the doubleheader between Pittsburgh and New York on Sunday, July 17, were urged by Pirates management to arrive at Forbes Field early since a capacity crowd was expected. Team officials planned on opening the gates at 11 o'clock in the morning to alleviate mass congestion prior to the 2 P.M. start time for the first game. This plan would allow those with reserved tickets to arrive early at the ballpark and reach their seats with minimal hassle. The various general admission windows also opened early so that fans who purchased these tickets could get to their seat locations well before the afternoon's double battle began. Pittsburgh management also had extra police and ushers on duty to ensure that everything ran as smoothly as possible, while the full cooperation of patrons was being requested.[56]

The heat at Forbes Field was so blistering that 17 pop vendors had to be given medical attention before the first game even began.[57] Once the contest started, the 43,241 fans who had paid to gain admission to Pittsburgh's baseball palace quickly forgot about the sweltering heat as the Pirates and Giants engaged in a tight, nail-biting affair. This crowd fell 569 short of breaking the park's attendance record of 43,810, set during Game Six of the World Series between Pittsburgh and Washington on October 13, 1925. When fans started showing up at 9 a.m. to purchase general admission seats, the Pirates actually opened their ticket windows a half hour early to begin processing orders. An estimated 10,000 people were turned away when the game sold out and 2,000 fans stood in roped-off areas on the field as special ground rules were established by which any ball hit into the massive throng of people was a double.[58]

New York claimed the afternoon's first game, 2–1, as Jim Tobin and Carl Hubbell locked up in a classic pitching duel. A poor managerial decision by Pie Traynor in the ninth inning prevented Pittsburgh from tying the game when a golden opportunity presented itself. Hubbell retired the Pirates first two batters before Al Todd connected for a single. Traynor allowed the slow-footed Todd to remain in the game as Pep Young stepped to the plate. Young lined Hubbell's three-two pitch to left field for a single that moved Todd over to second. If Pittsburgh had a runner with more speed on the bases, it was likely that runners would be occupying first and third with two out. Traynor belatedly decided to send Woody Jensen in as a pinch runner for Todd.[59]

Facing Jim Tobin with two on and two out, Hubbell uncorked a wild pitch that set the runners in motion. The ball caromed off the low wall at Forbes Field behind home plate and bounced 30 feet back toward the dish into catcher Gus Mancuso's hands. His snap throw to Hubbell covering the plate caught Jensen for the final out of the game.[60] If Traynor had chosen to place Jensen in as a pinch runner immediately after Todd singled, Woody probably would have been at third and scored the game's tying run on Hubbell's wild pitch. The Pirates still would have been playing and hoping to pull out a victory, rather than sitting in the locker room waiting to play another game. The twin bill's second contest was declared a 7–7 tie after nine innings after a 4–1 Pittsburgh lead was wiped out by Mel Ott's seventh-inning grand-slam home run off Russ Bauers.[61] Pirates slugger Johnny Rizzo was ejected from the contest by umpire Larry Goetz when he left the bench and argued a third strike call on pinch-hitter Jim Tobin.[62]

Prior to the final game of this series against New York, Rizzo was informed by league president Ford Frick that he had been fined $25 for coming out of the dugout and verbally berating Goetz when he had no business doing so.[63] This punishment put Rizzo in a foul mood that spelled disaster for New York in the final game on Monday, July 18. The rookie took out his anger against Giants hurler Harry Gumbert in the sixth inning. Johnny busted open a scoreless game when he connected on a Gumbert curve ball and blasted a three-run homer that sailed over the left-field wall and seemed to cut the scoreboard in half. Rizzo's latest four-bagger pushed his team-leading RBI total to 54.[64] Cy Blanton improved his record to 6–1 for the season as Pittsburgh claimed a 7–4 victory that gave them two wins in this crucial series against New York.

National League standings as Pittsburgh prepared to play Philadelphia at Forbes Field on Tuesday, July 19 showed the Pirates clinging to a lead of a half game over New York: Pittsburgh checked in with a 47–28 record while the Giants stood at 49–31. By winning two out of three games against their most bitter rival, the Pirates now had won 12 of their past 15 series.[65] Pie Traynor even sounded surprised when asked about his team's recent success. "The gang suddenly got the idea that it could win the pennant," Pie explained. "That bright thought struck it about the time we were halfway through our winning streak of 13 games, and it has stuck ever since. I've noticed the difference more when we were behind and trying to pick up a few runs when there were only one or two innings to play. Some of the players who used to hope we could catch up are sure of it now, and that makes a big difference in the way they go after a pitcher at the plate."[66]

Johnny Rizzo was one Pittsburgh player who had given the team a large dose of enthusiasm with his lusty drives and timely hits. The rookie outfielder, who had pushed his batting average up to .308 during the New York series, personified the team's new attitude that Traynor talked about. Rather than use his own words to praise Rizzo, Traynor referenced the comments of Dodgers pitcher Freddie Fitzsimmons after the game on July 14 when he threw a wild pitch past Rizzo and allowed two Pirates to cross home plate and tie the game in the ninth inning. "I tightened up on the ball," Fitzsimmons admitted, "and Rizzo was the reason. I never looked at a batter who was any more determined to knock the stitching off the ball. I felt sure he would knock it out of the lot if I gave him anything good to hit, and I tried to put so much on the pitch that it got away."[67]

Rizzo's determination to become one of the National League's top players and lead Pittsburgh to a pennant continued in the first contest of a four-game set against Philadelphia on July 19 that saw him go 4-for-4 at the plate and score four runs. Southpaw Ed Brandt was absolutely brilliant on the mound after two months of uneven pitching, tossing a five-hit shutout and defeating the Phillies, 8–0.[68] Shortstop Arky Vaughan also had a perfect day at the plate, going 3-for-3, blasting two triples and driving home three runs. Philadelphia extracted revenge in the first game of a doubleheader one day later by driving Bob Klinger from the mound in the fifth inning and cruising to an easy 11–0 victory. Relievers Mace Brown and Rip Sewell failed to record an out as the Phillies pushed ten runs across home plate during the fifth stanza. The resourceful scoreboard boy at Forbes Field did not have a slate with the number ten imprinted on it, so he credited the Phillies with one run in the fourth and nine tallies the following inning.[69]

During a doubleheader against Philadelphia at the Baker Bowl on June 19, 1938, rookie outfielder Johnny Rizzo hit three home runs and recorded nine RBIs. Rizzo's torrid pace at the plate continued in July as the Pittsburgh Pirates moved into first place. On July 18, Rizzo busted open a scoreless game against the New York Giants at Forbes Field when he blasted a three-run homer in the sixth inning as Pittsburgh won the game, 7–4 (National Baseball Hall of Fame Library, Cooperstown, New York).

Pittsburgh responded like a team that considered itself a pennant contender as they gained a twin bill split in the nightcap. Russ Bauers pitched like a staff ace in tossing a five-hitter and defeated the Phillies, 4–1. The day's

8. Johnny Rizzo Shines as Pirates Climb into First Place

big blow occurred in the sixth inning when Gus Suhr connected for an upper-deck home run against Philadelphia's Pete Sivess.[70] Arky Vaughan's 3-for-3 day at the plate gave him four hits for the afternoon, while Jeep Handley went 2-for-5, scored one run and drove home a teammate. Vaughan's solid day at the plate pushed him into the team batting lead with an average of .318, while Suhr (.316) and Johnny Rizzo (.314) followed closely behind the National League's top shortstop.[71]

Pittsburgh made it two victories in a row against the last-place Phillies on Thursday, July 21 by pulling off a late comeback to claim a 5–4 victory. Trailing the Phillies 4–2 heading into the ninth, Pittsburgh didn't look poised for a rally when southpaw Al Smith retired Vaughan for the first out. A glimmer of hope emerged when Phillies shortstop George Scharein allowed Al Todd's ground ball to roll through his legs for an error. Pep Young followed with a single to left before Woody Jensen was sent in to run for Todd and Bill Brubaker pinch-hit for Mace Brown. Brubaker walked to load the bases and manager Jimmy Wilson brought in Claude Passeau to relieve Smith. Jeep Handley looked at Passeau's first pitch for ball one and then connected with the second offering and drilled a sizzler to right field. Outfielder Gil Brack attempted to make an impossible shoestring catch but missed as the ball bounded to the wall and caromed away toward center field. Jensen, Young and Brubaker all scored as Handley was credited with a triple.[72]

Following Handley's late-game heroics, Pie Traynor left his station at the first base box and walked more deliberately than usual so he could be the first man in Pittsburgh's clubhouse. As his players arrived moments later laughing and cheering, Traynor greeted them as he stood at the door by singing, "You're driving me crazy." Once Pittsburgh's manager was finished belting out his ballad, he found a mirror in order to count the new grey hairs that had been added during this latest stressful game. If Traynor's hair turned snowy white, close games certainly were a valid reason since the victory over Philadelphia was now the twenty-third game Pittsburgh had won in 1938 by one run.[73] While these harrowing experiences on the diamond probably aged Traynor a bit, his current situation was better than that of former teammate Charley Grimm. On July 21, Chicago owner Phil K. Wrigley announced that Grimm was being replaced as Cubs manager by veteran catcher Gabby Hartnett. Always the gracious team player, Grimm wished Hartnett luck and expressed hope that Chicago would win the National League pennant.[74]

Wrigley decided to make the change because the Cubs were languishing in third place, five-and-a-half games out of first place before play started that day.[75] Although it looked as though the Cubs' season was spinning out of control to some observers, Traynor still believed the team would be a formidable foe during the campaign's final months. While Pie was confident that Pittsburgh was the team to beat in the National League, he believed the hardest punches in the fight would come from Hartnett's squad rather than Bill Terry's Giants. "Their pitching is fair enough, they have good hitting, and it's a tough defensive outfit, even though the outfield could be improved," explained Traynor. "And don't forget, those Cubs are one bunch we can beat."[76]

One day after 7,259 women attended Ladies Day at Forbes Field for the final game of the Phillies series, over 6,000 children filled Forbes Field's right field stands for a Friday matinee against Boston. Dubbed Wanerville because these youngsters passionately cheered the veteran outfielder's every move during the weekly Kids Day, this section of the ballpark was particularly vocal as Pittsburgh defeated Boston, 4–3. When Waner hit a fourth-inning home run into the upper deck off Jim Turner of the Bees, the applause lasted for five minutes as the youngsters repeatedly chanted: "Yeah Paul! Yeah Paul!"[77] Arky Vaughan was Pittsburgh's other hitting star, driving home two runs with a double in the fourth and a single in the eighth inning.[78] Cy Blanton recorded his seventh victory of the season, including six straight, against one defeat. Blanton kept Boston at bay until the ninth when Vince DiMaggio connected for a homer with Max West on base.[79]

Boston reversed the tables against Pittsburgh on Saturday, July 23 as Danny MacFayden defeated Russ Bauers, 4–2. After having looked prepared to assume the mantle of being Pittsburgh's staff ace in his previous outing against Philadelphia three days earlier, Bauers gave up three runs and seven hits during four-and-one-third innings of work. Bees first baseman Elbie Fletcher was the day's star, as he went 3-for-4 at the plate and launched a solo home run off Bauers in the third inning. Gus Suhr was the only Pirate who recorded multiple hits as he accounted for two of Pittsburgh's ten safeties.

On July 24, 25,557 jammed Forbes Field for a Sunday doubleheader against the Bees. Pittsburgh gained an afternoon sweep by claiming the first contest in 15 innings, 5–4, and then winning the nightcap, which lasted only six frames due to the 6 o'clock Pennsylvania Sunday Law, 4–2. In the initial contest, Boston did all of its scoring off Bob Klinger during the first four innings before Jim Tobin was brought into the game by manager Pie Traynor. Pittsburgh knocked out Boston starter Lou Fette with a three-run

8. Johnny Rizzo Shines as Pirates Climb into First Place

attack in the fifth inning and then tied the score in the ninth frame with a single tally.[80]

Pittsburgh won the game in the fifteenth inning when Johnny Rizzo came through in the clutch once again by belting a double to right-center field that drove home Gus Suhr.[81] Ed Brandt won the afternoon's second contest, surrendering two runs on five hits during six innings of work. Paul Waner was Pittsburgh's hitting star, going 2-for-3, cracking a double, scoring one run and driving home a teammate. Woody Jensen received a rare start in center field and matched Paul's work for the day exactly except for the little detail of scoring one more run. This doubleheader sweep gave the Buccaneers 22 victories in their last 27 games and allowed them to capture their fourteenth series out of their past 17.[82]

The Pirates' latest victories over Boston also pushed their lead over second-place New York to four games.[83] Pittsburgh's 9–5 record during this home stand at Forbes Field had helped them pad their lead a bit and Pie Traynor's boys were looking more and more like the prohibitive favorite to win the National League flag with each passing day. An upcoming road trip in the east that included three games against New York certainly could go a long way in cementing Pittsburgh's position as the team attempted to claim its first pennant in 11 years.

9

Pittsburgh Feels the Pressure and Starts to Wilt in the Summer Heat

Before the Pirates embarked on their eastern excursion, Pie Traynor's squad had to fulfill an exhibition obligation in Warren, Pennsylvania, on July 25 against the Warren Moose team.[1] Most of the players were praying for rain for this contest and the other two remaining exhibition battles left on their schedule. Traynor's men preferred a chance to rest and recharge their batteries to going through the motions against town teams.[2] The game itself was actually secondary in importance, since the festivities' main event was Pittsburgh coach Honus Wagner being honored by the Warren Moose Club. Players such as Tommy Thevenow, Bill Brubaker, Rip Sewell, Johnny Dickshot, Woody Jensen and prospect Andy Lipscomb saw action as Traynor rested most of his starters.[3] Wagner was presented with a traveling bag from his admirers as 2,000 fans watched Warren defeat Traynor's water-downed unit, 6–3.[4]

A train carrying the Warren contingent was expected to hook up with a special coming from Pittsburgh transporting Al Todd and Traynor's regular pitchers at a station in Harrisburg before embarking for Philadelphia.[5] There was growing concern in Pittsburgh that some of the players were becoming fatigued due to a heavy workload during the first three-and-a-half months of the season. Some baseball followers in the Smoky City believed the Pirates' smaller players were beginning to feel the physical strain of a pennant race that offered few open dates and included bargain doubleheaders played in sweltering heat. These worries certainly were valid since second baseman Pep Young had played practically every inning of the 1938 campaign and veteran Lloyd Waner had been used almost exclusively by Traynor in center field.[6]

Pittsburgh looked poised to secure a victory during the first game of this road trip in Philadelphia on Tuesday, July 26, before shoddy ninth-inning play doomed the Pirates. Traynor's squad held a 5–4 lead with Fireman Mace Brown on the mound for Pittsburgh. Things started going badly for the Pirates when Philadelphia's Bill Atwood hustled into second base after his ground ball bounced through shortstop Arky Vaughan's legs. The Phillies put runners on first and third when Atwood was called safe on a close play after Brown fielded Emmett Mueller's bunt and threw a perfect strike to Jeep Handley. Pinch-hitter Cap Clark tied the game when he singled to right and drove in Atwood. The Phillies loaded the bases when Buck Jordan singled to left.[7]

Pittsburgh recorded the second out of the inning when Mueller was forced at home plate on pinch-hitter Chuck Klein's grounder to Handley. Mace worked carefully against Gil Brack and ran the count to three balls and two strikes. He then tossed the decisive pitch wide for ball four and forced home pinch runner Hugh Mulcahy with the final tally that gave Philadelphia a 6–5 victory. Veteran Pirates fans who had witnessed jittery behavior from past teams that eventually wilted during various pennant races hoped this first game against the Phillies was not a bad omen.[8] Rookie outfielder Johnny Rizzo certainly did not resemble a player who was destined to fold under pressure. The youngster continued his personal assault against Philadelphia by going 2-for-3, blasting his ninth home run of the season and recording three RBIs. Rizzo now had homered in two different Philadelphia ballparks, since the Phillies were finishing their 1938 schedule in Shibe Park after making a decision to abandon the Baker Bowl.

Pie Traynor's boys responded quite nicely after this disappointing loss by claiming a 4–2 victory over Philadelphia on July 27. Russ Bauers was brilliant on the mound for Pittsburgh: he tossed a complete game, scattered four hits and pushed his record to 6–8. Arky Vaughan was Traynor's offensive catalyst, converting two walks into a pair of runs that aided Pittsburgh's victory. In the second inning Arky drew a base on balls, then stole second base and scored on Pep Young's single. Vaughan added a crucial insurance run in the ninth frame when he walked, raced to second on Al Todd's ground ball to shortstop George Scharein, stole third base and then raced home with another tally when second baseman Emmett Mueller grabbed Young's slow roller and tried to catch him at the plate.[9]

While the victory helped ease some of the tension felt by baseball fans back in Pittsburgh and raised the team's lead over second-place New York to five games, some bad news regarding one of Pie Traynor's most dependable starters tempered any celebration. Rookie hurler Bob Klinger visited a Philadelphia specialist who examined his arm and diagnosed a sprained muscle in his pitching elbow. Klinger paid a second visit to the doctor one day later and was advised not to touch a baseball again until the following Monday and then gradually work his arm back into shape. Klinger had been complaining of slight soreness in his right elbow since having been called upon to toss a few innings of a night exhibition contest in San Francisco during the team's spring training tour. Nevertheless, Klinger had persevered and fashioned a fine record of eight victories against two defeats. The pain had become excruciating during his previous two outings, when he was knocked out of the box by Philadelphia and Boston. "My arm bothered me several times this season but I usually managed to pitch the soreness out," said Klinger when he addressed the press about his injury. "In one game against the Giants it pained like a toothache and all I did in the last few innings was try to get the ball over the plate and hope the fielders would protect me. They did. The last two games I started I didn't last very long and I decided to look up this doctor in Philadelphia and find my way out of trouble. I'll be ready in a week."[10]

One day later, Pittsburgh made it two victories in a row against its cross-state rival by defeating the Phillies, 9–2. Philadelphia hurler Al Hollingsworth was clinging to a 2–1 lead over Jim Tobin when the Pirates exploded for seven runs in the seventh inning. Paul Waner and Gus Suhr walked to get the inning rolling before Hollingsworth, Al Smith and Syl Johnson were savagely battered by a barrage of Pirates hits.[11]

Pittsburgh did not come out of the game unscathed as second baseman Pep Young suffered a slightly sprained thumb on his right hand while chasing Chuck Klein's double in short right field. Those fans who were worried that Young might become the latest Pirate to be sidelined by injury were relieved when Pep announced that his thumb would have to be cut off before he left Pittsburgh's lineup. On a lighter note, Paul and Lloyd Waner received a letter from a female fan in St. Louis who had admired the skill of the Oklahomans for years. She had recently given birth to twin boys and had named them Paul Glee and Lloyd Robert. Paul Waner also had been recently informed by a racing stable owner that he had named one of his horses "Big Poison." Through the years, Paul and Lloyd were honored by having baseball teams, cats, dogs, chickens, pigs and hogs named after them.[12]

The final game at Shibe Park had been witnessed by many of the players from the Chicago Cubs, though most of them left during Pittsburgh's seven-run seventh inning. Chicago pitcher Dizzy Dean could not resist the urge to make a provocative comment. "Those Pirates ain't so tough," said Dean. "We'll slow them down with an assortment of Dizzy stuff. They're fast ball hitters. Yeah, with my luck we'll be on top in a month."[13]

As Pittsburgh prepared to play its next game in Brooklyn, the ballclub was involved in bizarre litigation back in Pittsburgh. Judge F.B. Schoonmaker had been asked by Pirates ownership to prevent radio station KQV from peeking into Forbes Field from a vantage point it had leased on the outside and broadcasting Pittsburgh's games.[14] Earlier in the season, club investigators had discovered that the station was working out of a two-story house on a street adjacent to Forbes Field and a large canvas had been erected to obscure the view of the KQV announcer. But the canvas proved to be an inconvenience for many patrons at the ballpark and was taken down before the twin bill with New York on July 17, enabling KQV to resume its broadcasts.[15]

This latest development prompted Benswanger to file an injunction in federal court to prevent KQV from continuing its bootleg activities. Besides broadcasting Pirates games without the club's permission, the station was also breaking a rule Pittsburgh's management had established for KDKA and WWSW, the two stations that could legally broadcast games from Forbes Field, that forbid them from broadcasting Sunday and holiday contests.[16] KQV's attorney, Judge Elder W. Marshall, declared that if Pittsburgh management wanted to prevent outsiders from interfering in their affairs, they should take the proper steps to prevent them from looking into Forbes Field. "If we can observe what transpires inside and wish to broadcast what we see, that is the hard luck of the Pirates," proclaimed Marshall.[17]

Hard luck almost pulled defeat from the jaws of victory at Ebbets Field on Friday, July 29 as Pittsburgh barely hung on to claim a 7–6 victory over the Dodgers. The Pirates banged out 13 hits as Pep Young went 3-for-3 while Jeep Handley, Gus Suhr, Johnny Rizzo and Arky Vaughan chipped in with two hits apiece. The outcome became precarious when Fireman Mace Brown was called from the bullpen in the fourth inning after starter Ed Brandt was overcome by the 90-degree heat. Mace only faced three batters, as Buddy Hassett and Dolph Camilli ripped back-to-back singles before Cookie Lavagetto connected for a 365-foot home run into the left-center field stands that tied the game, 5–5. Joe Bowman then came into the game and held Brooklyn in check before being forced from the contest with a pain in his side.[18] Bill Swift took over on the mound and tossed two innings of shutout relief to wrap up the victory.

Many baseball experts added Brown's name to a list of players that included Johnny Vander Meer, Lefty Grove and Johnny Allen who seemed to be haunted by the All-Star Game jinx. All four of these pitchers had experienced various hardships since participating in the grand mid-summer event at Crosley Field.[19] Since Brown had become the toast of baseball for his performance at the All-Star Game, Pittsburgh's star reliever had gone 2–2 in his last eight appearances and watched his ERA balloon from 3.43 to 4.56. Brownie seemed to be philosophical about the whole thing, as he always considered himself lucky when a victory occurred while never offering alibis after a loss. "I can't explain it," Brown said. "You know, I had more stuff than I've had all year out there, but I guess the Dodgers wouldn't believe it. No more All-Star Games for me. I guess they're just evening up a little. I got a good start and was due for a setback. But watch me go from now on."[20]

After pitcher Mace Brown gained national attention by starring in the 1938 All-Star Game at Crosley Field in Cincinnati, he struggled in his first eight appearances when league play resumed. Brown saw his ERA balloon from 3.43 to 4.56 as many baseball experts believed he was haunted by the All-Star Game jinx, much like fellow hurlers Johnny Vander Meer, Lefty Grove and Johnny Allen (National Baseball Hall of Fame Library, Cooperstown, New York).

Brown rebounded to hurl two and two-thirds innings of shutout baseball in a 9–2 victory over Brooklyn on Saturday, July 30.[21] Starter Cy Blanton improved his record to a sterling 8–1 for the season and he was victorious for the seventh consecutive time.[22] The Waners were front and center for the Pirates as each brother unloaded two singles and one triple. Jeep Handley was excellent in a supporting role as he blasted a double and two singles, while Al Todd contributed by rapping out two hits. Paul, Lloyd and Johnny Rizzo each drove in a pair of runs. The National League standings after all games had been completed that day showed Pittsburgh in first place with a 57–31 record while New York was second, five games out, at 54–38 and Chicago held down third, eight games behind the Pirates, with a mark of 50–40.

Pittsburgh's modest four-game winning streak came to an end on Sunday, July 31 when Brooklyn claimed a 4–3 victory in the first game of a doubleheader. Red Lucas pitched well in his first appearance since June 6, giving up two runs and six hits during seven innings of work. Bill Swift was tagged with the loss after allowing the Dodgers to score two runs in the eighth inning. Dolph Camilli was Brooklyn's batting star, as his home run with a man on base gave the Dodgers a 2–0 lead in the first frame. In the eighth, his double drove in Brooklyn's third run before he scored what proved to be the winning tally when he was driven home by Cookie Lavagetto. The nightcap of the scheduled twin bill was postponed on account of rain.[23] On a positive note, Johnny Rizzo slammed his tenth home run of the season and now had clubbed round trippers in every National League ballpark except Crosley Field, Braves Field and the Polo Grounds.[24]

In spite of suffering a defeat on the last day of July, the month had been a rousing success for Pie Traynor's troops as they posted a 24–7 record. Before the Corsairs could continue their march toward the National League pennant with a series in Boston, they had to play an exhibition contest on August 1 in Springfield, Massachusetts. Traynor's regulars were scheduled to play in the game while the battery men went directly from New York to Boston. It was a bit puzzling why these games were even scheduled, since Pittsburgh's players complained about such exhibitions and preferred to skip them, while fans in those towns certainly were not witnessing quality baseball. Some of the New York baseball writers kidded the Pirates front office by asking if exhibition games would be scheduled from the time the regular season ended until the World Series started.[25] Springfield's patrons did receive an unexpected treat when Traynor played part of the game at third base while Pittsburgh claimed a 5–0 victory.[26]

The Pirates looked like a tired baseball team when they hit the diamond against Boston on Tuesday, August 2. Jim Tobin pitched magnificent ball but was tagged with a 3–1 loss when a Pep Young error allowed the Bees to score three unearned runs. Tobin's record dropped to 9–5 on the season even though he matched Boston's Johnny Lanning pitch for pitch. Al Todd was the only Pirate who did any damage against Lanning, as he blasted a solo home run in the second inning. Many of Traynor's regulars were in desperate need of a rest, both physically as well as mentally. Young and Jeep Handley were in particular need of time off. Handley was playing with both of his ankles wrapped while Young was still nursing a swollen right hand.

Since July 7, the Pirates had played 28 games in 24 consecutive afternoons.[27] Nevertheless, one unidentified player assured Pittsburgh's fans that the team would be ready to go when important games were on the docket. "We'll be in shape for the exhibition next Monday," cracked a Pirate player after their loss against Boston.[28]

Disgust over useless exhibition games was quickly forgotten when Pittsburgh banged out 28 hits during a doubleheader sweep against the Boston Bees on Wednesday, August 3. The Pirates won the first game, 9–4, as Cy Blanton secured his eighth straight win even though he was forced to retire from the heat after seven innings of work. Pittsburgh claimed the afternoon's second contest, 5–3, and widened the lead in the National League race over second-place New York to five and one-half games.[29] The city of Boston experienced some of the hottest weather it had seen in many years—temperatures in the stands reached 95 degrees, while it was at least 100 degrees on the diamond. In addition to pitchers on both squads suffering from the heat, Jeep Handley had to be replaced in the eighth inning of the nightcap. Handley had been overcome with cramps in the opener but gutted it out until he became sick once again late in the second game.[30]

Al Todd was one of Pittsburgh's hitting stars on the afternoon, belting three line singles and a double in the first game of the doubleheader. Todd's hitting barrage came one day after he had switched to a lighter bat for the first time in 1938 and had blasted a homer.[31] Al was given a breather in the afternoon's second contest and Ray Berres worked behind the plate. Lloyd Waner was also given a rest in the nightcap, while Johnny Rizzo played even though his left hand was swollen after being hit by a pitched ball in the first game.[32] Many of the Pirates players lingered in the showers a little longer than usual after earning the sweep on the hot and sticky afternoon. Joy was the prevailing theme as these men sang, shouted and cheered while cool water hit their bodies.[33]

Joe Bowman, who had pitched four-and-two-third innings of shutout relief in the twin bill's nightcap and picked up his third victory of the season, was the only player still in the clubhouse when Traynor prepared to leave. Traynor walked up to Bowman and offered the type of compliment that Pittsburgh's manager usually was reluctant to bestow on his players. "Nice goin', Joe," said Traynor as he praised the veteran pitcher. "I've called on you three times now in the last 10 days and you've delivered every time. I'm going to start you soon, great work."[34]

Traynor's elation over the doubleheader sweep was short-lived, as the Bees gained a split of the four-game series with a 4–3 victory at Braves

Field on Thursday, August 4. Danny MacFayden turned back the league leaders for his tenth victory of the campaign by allowing only two earned runs, even though the Pirates collected 12 hits. The Bees did most of their damage in the fifth inning when Vince DiMaggio connected for a three-run homer against Bill Swift. Boston claimed victory in the eighth stanza against crack reliever Mace Brown when Johnny Cooney and Debs Garms singled, Elbie Fletcher walked, and Joe Stripp's long fly ball brought home the deciding run.[35] Brown's record dropped to 13–5 on the season; Jeep Handley led the way for Pittsburgh at the plate by going 3-for-5.

Pittsburgh finished the current eastern road trip with a critical series against the New York Giants at the Polo Grounds. A crowd of 18,000 turned out on August 5 as Bob Klinger pitched his first game since suffering an elbow injury two weeks ago against New York's Cliff Melton. Klinger, who had defeated the Giants three consecutive times, was not up to the task as New York prevailed, 5–3.

The heatedly contested game included a disputed call and a beanball incident. New York pitcher Cliff Melton dusted off Johnny Rizzo with a tight pitch during his first trip to the plate. When Johnny rose to his feet, he shouted angrily at the Giants pitcher.[36] Rizzo extracted his revenge in the sixth inning when he blasted a prodigious shot that travelled 425 feet for his eleventh home run of the season.[37] As Rizzo continued his meteoric rise to stardom, the rookie outfielder took every opportunity that presented itself to bash the St. Louis Cardinals organization for hindering his debut as a major league player. "I should have come up to the big time in 1935," Rizzo maintained. "I was ready then, just as I am now. If I had come up then, my salary now would be in five figures. The Cardinal system did not permit me to come up when I should have, but kept me chained in the minor divisions."[38]

Rizzo said he was not surprised to be hitting over .300 against major league competition. He believed that there were a thousand capable men in the minors who would never be given the opportunity to show their ability because of chain store organizations like the Cardinals. "I got on the big time through a trade," Johnny continued. "But I still insist that there are a lot of players in the minors who could get into the majors and replace big names, and do better than them."[39]

Rizzo and his teammates were forced to wait an extra day to face New York because the game on Saturday, August 6 was postponed when a thunderstorm broke out just as the contest was about to get underway. This cancellation meant a Sunday doubleheader would be played instead, with Giants management estimating that 50,000 people might pack the Polo Grounds for the day's festivities. Over 10,000 fans had been on hand for Saturday's contest when the barrage of heavy rain and lightning ruined their fun afternoon at the ballpark. While the rain cheated Pittsburgh out of an opportunity to even the series, Pie Traynor's players were mighty happy to finally get some much needed rest.[40]

Even though no game was played on Saturday afternoon, there were plenty of subjects to digest surrounding the Pittsburgh Pirates. One topic was the pressing need for a capable left-handed pinch-hitter for Pie Traynor's bench. Red Lucas was having one of the worst seasons of his career in that role, batting a mere .067 for the season and having failed on numerous occasions even to hit the ball out of the infield when called upon. Woody Jensen was not doing much better, as his average stood at a skimpy .152 on the year. This poor work from left-handed hitting substitutes prompted many people to look toward former American League star Heinie Manush as an alternative. The 37-year-old veteran outfielder currently was with Toronto of the International League after having hit .333 for Brooklyn in 1937.[41]

A second story that received intense scrutiny from Pittsburgh's players centered around comments attributed to New York catcher Gus Mancuso. "The Pirates can't beat us with the pitching staff they have," Mancuso had reportedly proclaimed. "Only Cy Blanton can throw hard and he can do it only just so long. Tobin. Klinger? Soft stuff; home run pitching."[42] As a result, the Pirates were full of fire and ready to fight when they arrived at the Polo Grounds for their doubleheader on August 7.

Prior to the first contest of the afternoon, Pirates pitcher Joe Bowman approached Mancuso and warned him that he better watch out. "Soft pitching, eh," Bowman told him. "If you bat today, see how soft it is. Wish I were pitching against you fellows today."

"You can't scare me," responded Mancuso.

"Why, Gus, you've nothing to be afraid of," said Bowman. "If we don't have fast ball pitchers, you won't get hurt. You said we're softball pitchers."[43]

Bowman's veteran leadership had been of great benefit to the Pirates during their recent rise to the top of the National League standings. Bowman had the utmost confidence that Pittsburgh would claim the pennant and was constantly encouraging his teammates and lifting their spirits when times got tough. Bowman was passing the things he learned from his time with New York years ago along to his Buccaneer brethren. When the Pirates hit a rough patch in Philadelphia, he went around and told the boys to forget about it. After a player suggested that the Pirates might not be able to stand such a brutal pace, Joe quickly made sure that man's mind was set right. "That game is gone," said Bowman after a loss to the Phillies. "There's nothing we can do about it. Let's forget it and start in tomorrow. We have the best team in the league and we're going to win this pennant. Just get that idea into your head. Okay. If you don't have any confidence, I do. I'll buy your World Series share right now. This team can't miss winning that pennant."[44]

While Joe Bowman was a beacon of positive energy for his teammates, the Pirates received some encouragement from an unexpected source. On the afternoon of the series opener, Pirates batboy Porky Cohen had been a dejected soul when he learned that New York had won. Cohen decided to take matters into his own hands and called up an older friend who had a car to ask him

Pitcher Joe Bowman supplied veteran leadership for the Pittsburgh Pirates in 1938. Bowman assured his teammates when times got tough that he believed they would ultimately win the National League pennant. He also challenged New York Giants catcher Gus Mancuso for making disparaging remarks about Pittsburgh's pitching staff (National Baseball Hall of Fame Library, Cooperstown, New York).

if a trip to New York City was a possibility. Porky's friend agreed to make the trip, but informed the loyal batboy that he would be making a stop in Atlantic City rather than returning to Pittsburgh on the way back. This was fine with Cohen who was sure that the Pirates needed him at the Polo Grounds as a good luck charm in this crucial series. "You drive me over to the Polo Grounds so I can give the Pirates some luck, and I'll get you into the games," Porky told his friend. "Then you can go to Atlantic City and I'll get home some way."[45]

Cohen arrived in the Pirates clubhouse as the players were getting dressed for Saturday's contest that eventually was cancelled. The players' spirits were uplifted greatly when they saw Porky enter the locker room. "Hey fellows," Bill Brubaker shouted. "Here's Porky. Everything's under control."[46]

Porky hit the field with Pittsburgh's players during practice before Sunday's doubleheader at the Polo Grounds dressed in his Pirates home uniform. He grabbed his glove and helped the Giants players kill time during their fielding practice. Even Bill Terry, a man who hardly ever cracked a smile, laughed at Porky scooping up grounders as the fans cheered him on. The Polo Grounds faithful were treated to an exhibition that was witnessed by Forbes Field patrons at every home game. During those contests, Cohen always entertained Pittsburgh's fans by scooping up hot grounders off the bat of coach Jewel Ens during the conclusion of infield practice. Porky invariably stationed himself at the hot corner, a slab of ground he considered to be hallowed since his hero Lee Handley plied his craft there.[47] Like many of the batboys who worked for the 16 major league teams, Porky was also considered a good luck charm besides taking care of the players' sacred equipment.

Good luck and inspiration on Cohen's part, combined with domination by Pie Traynor's brigade of swashbuckling baseball players, enabled Pittsburgh to run roughshod over New York during an afternoon sweep at the Polo Grounds. A crowd of 50,466 people watched their Giants fall six-and-one-half games behind the Pirates as Pittsburgh claimed the first contest, 5–1, and then shellacked star hurler Carl Hubbell, 13–3, in the nightcap.[48] Jim Tobin improved his record to 10–5 on the season in the first contest, with his only mistake occurring in the second inning when Mel Ott connected for a home run. Jim held the Giants to one hit between the second and the sixth frames as Pittsburgh clung to a 2–1 lead. Gus Suhr put the game out of reach in the ninth inning when he drilled a homer with two teammates on base against New York's Dick Coffman.[49]

The Pirates battered Hubbell in the second contest as they connected for 10 hits against the star southpaw. Pep Young went 3-for-4, scored two runs, stroked a double and blasted his third home run of the season. Jeep Handley and Al Todd also connected for circuit blasts against Hubbell, while Lloyd Waner, Gus Suhr, Johnny Rizzo and Ed Brandt recorded two hits apiece and combined to drive home five of Pittsburgh's 13 runs. Brandt was brilliant in relief of starter Cy Blanton, allowing one run during seven innings of work and picking up his fourth victory of the season. Pie

9. Pittsburgh Feels the Pressure

Traynor's pitchers also exacted some revenge for the Rizzo dusting incident two days earlier. In the first contest, Tobin knocked down Ott in retaliation. When Gus Mancuso came to bat in the second contest after having not played in the initial battle, Brandt gunned a pitch that whizzed past the Giants catcher's ear. After the two games concluded, Mancuso made a special trip to the Pirates hotel to seek out manager Traynor and deny that he ever made disparaging remarks about Pittsburgh's pitchers.[50]

Pittsburgh's latest eastern trip was an undeniable success as Traynor's squad had won eight games against five defeats. They had claimed three series during the road trip, split one and had added two-and-one-half games to their league-leading pace over second-place New York. Prior to the doubleheader defeat on August 7, the Giants had been confident that they had Pittsburgh on the ropes and eventually would reclaim the top spot.[51] This now seemed like an unlikely scenario, as the Pirates were playing their best baseball of the season while New York was mired in a slump. While there were many players who had performed admirably during this trip, Traynor believed young third baseman Lee "Jeep" Handley was the man most responsible for putting the flag spark in his Pirates. "Last year, Lee was just another young player trying to break in," said Traynor. "Early this spring, Brubaker again showed signs of folding up at third base and I put Handley in his place. Ever since, we have been winning regularly, so I must give Lee credit for putting in the spark that started us on our way to what I hope will be Pittsburgh's first pennant in 11 years."[52]

Before the Pirates opened up a short home stand, they had to play a 5 p.m. make-up exhibition game on August 8 at Cycler Park in McKeesport that had been postponed by poor weather in June.[53] Pittsburgh's players finished off the exhibition portion of the 1938 season by participating in their third practice game over the past two weeks. Pittsburgh defeated an all-star semi-pro lineup featuring players from McKeesport, 9–2, with all of the proceeds from the contest being donated to the McKeesport Hospital.[54] Following the game, Bill Benswanger announced that his club would not play any more exhibition contests during the remainder of the season, while also pointing out that the three contests to date all had been charity affairs.[55] "Nobody knows better than I do that players get dead tired, especially at this season of the year," stated Benswanger, "and on any remaining open dates in our schedule our players will be permitted to take things easy."[56]

On the same day that Traynor's squad spent the afternoon in McKeesport, Federal Judge F.P. Schoonmaker announced his decision in the case between radio station KQV and the Pittsburgh Pirates. Judge Schoonmaker granted the Pirates and three other plaintiffs—a preliminary injunction restraining KQV from broadcasting accounts of baseball games at Forbes Field.[57] Judge Schoonmaker rejected KQV's claim that the games fell under the purview of news and ruled that the station could not broadcast them without paying for the right to do so. "The Pittsburgh Athletic Company acquired and maintained a baseball park, and have a right to capitalize on the news value of their games by selling exclusive rights to companies as advertising media of their merchandise," said Judge Schoonmaker in his opinion. "This right KQV interferes with while using different broadcasting facilities for giving out the identical news obtained by its paid observers at points outside Forbes Field for the purpose of securing information that it can't otherwise acquire."[58]

The two radio stations that had paid for the rights to broadcast Pirates games at Forbes Field got the opportunity to describe an exciting game against St. Louis on Tuesday, August 9. Russ Bauers outlasted Roy Henshaw of the Cardinals as Pittsburgh secured a 1–0 victory. Bauers tossed a complete game, allowed only two hits, struck out five and also scored the game's only run when he crossed home plate after Lloyd Waner singled in the third inning. St. Louis made the game interesting in the ninth frame before Bauers buckled down with Fireman Mace Brown warming up in the bullpen. Terry Moore drew a walk to start the inning. Bauers seemed unfazed by having the tying run on first as he fanned Stu Martin on three pitches. Enos Slaughter took a strike before he lined out to Paul Waner in right field for the stanza's second out. Ducky Medwick walked to the plate and smashed Russ' first offering foul by inches into the left field bleachers. Bauers tossed a second strike past Medwick before one of the league's most dangerous hitters grounded out to Pep Young to end the game.[59]

When visiting teams like the Cardinals went to the clubhouse after a game at Forbes Field, they were usually greeted by Socko McCarey, who had been curator of the opposing team's locker room for almost 20 years. McCarey had been one of the first people to proclaim that the 1938 season would see the pennant return to Pittsburgh. When a New York sportswriter had insinuated that the Pirates were lazy, Socko became so infuriated that he wrote a scathing letter to the publication's editor and told him he'd see him at the World Series in Pittsburgh. When the Pirates had played their in-season exhibition games, McCarey usually packed his uniform along for the trip. During the game in McKeesport, Socko finally got his chance to play when Traynor told the longtime Pirate employee to bat for him.

9. Pittsburgh Feels the Pressure

McCarey drew a walk and went in as a replacement for Pie at third in the next inning. "Just imagine," Socko said, "McCarey batting for Traynor, Gosh, I wait 20 years for the chance to play and then I go up to hit for the greatest third baseman that ever lived. Well, I always did say, everything comes to him who waits!"[60]

The Cardinals extracted revenge against the league-leading Pirates on Wednesday, August 10. Lon Warneke was brilliant for the visitors, scattering four hits and shutting out Pittsburgh, 5–0. Bob Klinger surrendered three earned runs before he gave way to Mace Brown after six-and-a-third innings of work. This first contest of a scheduled doubleheader ended up being an abbreviated seven-inning affair when inclement weather interrupted proceedings at Forbes Field for the remainder of the day. While Pie Traynor's boys were losing to St. Louis, Bill Terry's troops suffered a similar fate against Boston. The Corsairs finally had their first scheduled day off in over a month and got some much needed rest and relaxation on August 11 before opening a series against Chicago. This was the first day they had not dressed for a game since July 7, the final day of the All-Star break.[61]

The crowd of 16,712 at Forbes Field on August 10 took the rain and subsequent delay in stride even though some of the fans tossed cushions on the diamond and booed the umpires when they decided to call the game. Cy Blanton, who was slated to pitch in the afternoon's second contest, watched the first game from the press box which happened to contain many other sports celebrities. Pittsburgh pro football star and future Supreme Court justice Whizzer White was sitting nearby along with his coach Johnny Blood, while Canonsburg native and Wisconsin line coach Bob Reagan also was a guest.[62] Traynor decided to push Blanton back for the series' second contest against Chicago so Jim Tobin could still face Gabby Hartnett's squad in the opener.

This was the first time Pittsburgh had faced the Cubs since Hartnett replaced Charley Grimm as the team's manager on July 21. Chicago was in third place with a record of 56–45, trailing first-place Pittsburgh by seven-and-a-half games. The Cubs easily chopped one game off Pittsburgh's lead by cruising to a 9–3 victory on Friday, August 12. After Jim Tobin was knocked out of the box in the seventh inning, Fireman Mace Brown struggled once again as Chicago feasted on his offerings for three runs on seven hits. Augie Galan, back in the Cubs lineup after being sidelined for several weeks with a knee injury, smacked a triple and two singles. Hartnett also contributed to the cause with two doubles and a single, while pitcher Bill Lee went the distance and won his fourteenth game of the season. Lee had little difficulty subduing the Pirates with the exception of Lloyd Waner, who collected three of his team's seven hits.[63]

Worse than the loss for the Pirates was that second baseman Pep Young was forced from the contest in the ninth inning with a pulled muscle in his left leg. Veteran Tommy Thevenow replaced the peppery second sacker, whose steadying influence had contributed greatly to Pittsburgh's success thus far in 1938. Traynor expected Young to be ready for the series' second contest on Saturday, August 13. Trainer Charles Jorgensen worked on Young's leg for a half-hour after the game and then took heat lamps to his home that night and gave him additional treatments.[64] Young was back in Traynor's lineup as the Pittsburgh Italian Professional Association honored teammate Johnny Rizzo before the Saturday afternoon contest against Chicago. The popular rookie left fielder was presented with a shotgun and roses during ceremonies at home plate prior to the game. Johnny hoped the special adulation would not act as a jinx since he already was mired in a minor batting slump.[65] "Ball players are a bust on days they're honored," claimed Rizzo.[66]

Instead, Rizzo performed like a Roman god on the day he was honored, blasting a triple, a double and driving in his 70th run of the season.[67] Unfortunately, the Pirates pitching was a bust as Chicago slaughtered Traynor's team for the second straight day. Despite the fact that Pittsburgh rapped out 13 hits, they were crushed by the Cubs, 11–5. Dizzy Dean, who had not pitched a game in more than two weeks, used an assortment of curves and floaters to hold Pittsburgh in check through six innings. By the time Traynor's squad plastered Dean for four runs and five hits in the seventh frame, it was too late. Cy Blanton's winning streak ended at eight games as he was chased from the box in the first inning and took the loss.[68] Chicago's Frank Demaree had a perfect day at the plate, going 4-for-4 and blasting a home run off Joe Bowman in the fifth inning.

Pittsburgh salvaged the final game against Chicago on August 14 before a Sunday crowd of 24,193 people. The contest was a nerve-wracking battle that Pittsburgh claimed, 2–0, thanks to the brilliant work of Russ Bauers and Mace Brown. The contest seemed to be in doubt when Chicago loaded the bases with none out in the ninth inning, but Mace exhibited his usual calm and recorded three outs without a single runner crossing home plate. Johnny Rizzo launched the day's biggest hit when he blasted a 400-foot home run over Forbes Field's left-field fence in the second frame.[69] Johnny's twelfth circuit blast of the season was a wallop which cleared the left field wall about three panels to the right of Forbes Field's scoreboard.[70] When the game ended, Brown gave all the credit for staving off Chicago's rally in the final frame to his infield unit, which turned five double plays on the afternoon.[71] "I had great stuff out there and when Galan got a hit off me I felt like calling it off," said Brown. "But Handley, Vaughan and Young pulled me out of the hole and now everybody says great pitching. You need breaks in this game."[72]

On a day when a stellar victory should have been the main storyline in Pittsburgh's newspapers, bad news wedged its way to the forefront once again in the form of a report that rookie pitcher Bob Klinger's arm was still bothering him. The pain which first had settled in his elbow had now moved up to the shoulder. Even though Klinger initially felt great after visiting a Philadelphia specialist, his discomfort quickly returned. Pirates management decided to send Bob to another doctor to have his teeth X-rayed. If bad teeth possibly were contributing to his arm problems, the troublesome ones would be removed through surgery. The fear that Klinger could be sidelined for several weeks was a huge blow to Traynor's staff, which already had been stretched thin.[73]

The X-rays of Klinger's teeth did not shine any light on his sore shoulder since no diseased molars were detected. Now that dental surgery was ruled out, the decision was made to have Pirates trainer Charles Jorgensen work on Klinger's shoulder for about a week. Jorgensen promised the rookie pitcher would be ready to go after seven to ten days of rubbing and massaging.[74] Pie Traynor's Pirates certainly could have used a man with Klinger's pedigree during the first game of a short series with Cincinnati on Monday, August 15. The Reds pulled out a 6–2 victory when ace reliever Mace Brown committed two crucial errors that led to three unearned runs crossing home plate in the ninth inning. Brown's record dropped to 13–6 on the season as he struggled through one-and-two-thirds innings of work before giving way to Bill Swift. Johnny Rizzo was Pittsburgh's star at the plate, going 4-for-4, knocking in both runs and connecting for his thirteenth home run of the season against Lee Grissom in the second frame.

This loss to Cincinnati sliced the Pirates' lead in the National League race to four games and was their fourth loss in the last five games. Pittsburgh's tepid hitting during this minor slump prompted Pie Traynor to make some changes to his lineup. Bill Brubaker was installed at first base as a replacement for Gus Suhr, while Ray Berres took over behind the plate so that Al Todd could step away from the game for a few days. During the past 20 games, Suhr was batting .213 while Todd checked in at .208. Both men had been guilty of leaving crucial runners stranded on the bases numerous times.

Traynor's new batting order continued to have Jeep Handley and the two Waners at the top, while Johnny Rizzo was elevated to the cleanup spot, Arky Vaughan batted fifth, Brubaker sixth, Pep Young seventh and Berres eighth.[75]

Traynor's new lineup produced immediate results on Tuesday, August 16 as his team smacked 14 hits off Cincinnati's Peaches Davis and Jim Weaver en route to a 10–0 victory. Cy Blanton tossed a complete game and improved his record to 10–2 by scattering eight hits and striking out five Reds batters. When the Pirates scored six runs in the third frame, it was the team's first hitting outburst since the Corsairs had bombarded New York for seven runs in the seventh inning of the second game of the twinbill on August 7. The crucial blows came off the bats of Arky Vaughan and Bill Brubaker. Vaughan blasted a triple with two teammates on board, while Brubaker drilled a two-run homer over the left-field wall. Johnny Rizzo also ran his streak of consecutive hits to six with two singles before being forced to retire from the contest in the fourth inning due to the afternoon's excessive heat.[76]

Lloyd Waner also starred at the plate with two hits and four RBIs and also continued an odd streak of hitting home runs on the sixteenth of the month. When Lloyd legged out an inside-the-park homer in the eighth inning, it marked the third consecutive month that he had connected for a circuit blast on that calendar date. Waner continued his torrid pace at the plate when Pittsburgh left the cozy confines of Forbes Field and started a short road trip against two of the National League's western teams. Lloyd went 3-for-5, smacked two doubles and scored two runs as the Pirates defeated St. Louis, 4–3, on Wednesday, August 17. Trailing by one run going into the ninth frame Pittsburgh tied the score on a Bill Brubaker single, Pep Young's double and pinch-hitter Johnny Dickshot's single. The Pirates claimed victory in the tenth inning when Lloyd Waner led off with a double and scored on Johnny Rizzo's one-out single.[77] Bill Swift improved his record to 6–5 for the year by pitching two innings of shutout relief.

Cardinals southpaw Bob Weiland ended Pittsburgh's modest two-game winning streak on August 18 by thwarting the Pirates attack and claiming a 5–1 victory. Russ Bauers and Jim Tobin were abject failures on the mound for Pie Traynor. Cardinals slugger Johnny Mize made Tobin pay dearly for a blunder in the fifth frame when his three-run, two-out homer landed on top of the right-field pavilion and gave St. Louis a 5–1 lead. For the second time in 1938, Lee Handley connected for a home run to lead off a baseball game. In both of those instances, that was the only run Pittsburgh put on the board.[78] Pirates slugger Johnny Rizzo just missed picking up his fourteenth home run of the season when he blasted a 400-foot drive in the first inning that landed just foul in the left-field stands. Bob Klinger was honored before the contest by fans from his hometown in Allenton, Missouri. The entourage of royal rooters even brought the Allenton High School band with them as Klinger was presented with a watch and a shotgun during ceremonies at home plate.[79]

Pie Traynor's troops had a day off before a four-game series against the Chicago Cubs began at Wrigley Field on Saturday, August 20. The National League standings showed Pittsburgh in first place with a record of 65–40, four-and-a-half games ahead of the Giants and eight games up on the Cubs. The Pirates easily took care of Dizzy Dean and Chicago in the series' first game, rapping out 11 hits to earn a 5–2 victory. Gus Suhr was sent back to first base for Pittsburgh while catcher Al Todd was called upon to replace Ray Berres, who could not go because of a bruised right hand.[80] Suhr and Todd responded brilliantly after their short exile on the bench: each rapped out three hits and also drove home two runs apiece. Veteran hurler Red "Old Rosebud" Lucas improved his record to 4–2 on the season by pitching six solid innings and Bill Swift preserved the victory in relief.

When the Pirates hit the field for a Sunday doubleheader on August 21, the tables were turned as Chicago pulled off a sweep in front of 40,402 fans. It was estimated that half the crowd at Wrigley Field was from out of town since many of the fans who came through the ballpark's turnstiles carried shoe box lunches. Cubs management permitted these rural rooters to use the concession shelves for refrigeration and also supplied mustard, horseradish and relish for their sandwiches.[81] These fans who came from far and wide to watch the Cubs were sent home happy as Chicago won the opener, 6–4, and then claimed the nightcap, 6–1.

Relatives of various Pirates players were among those who viewed the Sunday afternoon festivities. Over 400 fans came from Kenosha, Wisconsin, to honor Ray Berres and present him with a 47-pound bat and a shotgun. Jeep Handley's mother, grandparents and brother also took in the game, while Russ Bauers' mother and stepfather made the trip from Lakewood, Wisconsin to watch Russ pitch.[82] Bauers failed to deliver the goods during the second contest: his record dropped to 8–10 after he gave up four runs on six hits during four innings of work. Handley had a slightly better day than Bauers in the first game, going 2-for-2 at the plate before his afternoon of work ended when umpire Ziggy Sears ejected him in the seventh inning. Various family members and more than 1,200 people that made the trip from Peoria, Illinois, watched Lee exit the game after he supposedly bumped into Sears during an argument.[83]

The reason for Handley's disenchantment was a call at third base in which Chicago's Phil Cavarretta was called safe although the Pirates were adamant that he had been tagged out a foot from the bag.[84] Sears ejected Handley from the contest for jostling him when the Pirates rushed the umpire after this horrible call. In fact, this ruling also appeared to be in error since another player seemed to have bumped into Sears. Handley ranted and raved to the heavens when he realized the umpire had thrown him out of the game. Johnny Rizzo and Pie Traynor initially had also been ejected, but they were permitted to remain on the grounds when Sears changed his mind. Before Lee left the diamond, he used a little quick thinking in an effort to avert a fine and suspension by talking to senior arbiter Bill Klem.[85]

"Bill," said Handley as he graciously addressed Klem, "I think Sears made a mistake. I didn't push him and I was only arguing for what I thought was right. He shouldn't have put me out."

"Are you telling me the truth, young man?" Klem asked in a manner which indicated that mercy was in his soul.[86]

The doubleheader sweep did not damage Pittsburgh's lead drastically as they still were five games ahead of the New York Giants. The Cubs' two victories had allowed them to pull into a third place tie with Cincinnati. Over in the American League, it looked as if the New York Yankees were a lock to claim their third consecutive pennant, having built an eleven-game lead over second-place Cleveland.[87] Despite the fact that the Pirates had struggled somewhat during the past few weeks, they still seemed to be in great shape as the season moved into its final phase. Star shortstop Arky Vaughan offered his assessment as to why Pittsburgh would not fold up in 1938 as they had done in the past.

"It's easy to play ball behind good pitching and we sure are gettin' it," explained Vaughan. "We're never more than a run or two behind in important games and it's easy to go out after a short lead like that. We always got plenty of hits and runs before, but it took a lot to win ball games. Good pitching changed all that. Lee Handley made our infield this year. He didn't play much on third base last year, but this season he's the tops. I'll rate him along with any in the league and it's a simple job to play behind him."[88]

Handley was in Pittsburgh's lineup as Pie Traynor's boys gained a split in the four-game series against Chicago by claiming the final contest on Monday, August 22 by a score of 4–2. Pep Young led Pittsburgh's hitting attack with two doubles and a single, while Johnny Rizzo pulled out of a mild slump with two rattling singles. Jim Tobin hurled a five-hit masterpiece as he improved his record to 11 victories against six defeats. One of Tobin's teammates pointed out that he was a pitcher who excelled in important baseball games against quality opponents.[89] "When Tobin has control he is the best pitcher in the League," claimed the unnamed teammate. "When he's good, he can't be touched. When he's bad, he gets knocked all over the field. But he is a money pitcher. He has always managed to be great against the tough teams."[90]

Pittsburgh's position atop the National League did not seem to be in jeopardy despite having posted a 3–3 record during their short road trip through St. Louis and Chicago. The Pirates still held a five-and-a-half game lead over New York as they returned to Pittsburgh for a long home stand that saw them playing at Forbes Field through Labor Day. The time had come for this team to lay claim to the National League pennant.

10

Traynor's Boys Attempt to Hang on While Chicago Surges

Pie Traynor and his first-place Pittsburgh Pirates were confident as they began a two-week home stand at Forbes Field in which they played every National League team except for Cincinnati. Playing in front of cheering, screaming rooters was expected to help lift the players' spirits as they fed off the crowd's energy and dismantled the opposition. Instead, Traynor's troops were left shocked and bewildered when the exact opposite happened during a doubleheader against the Boston Bees on Tuesday, August 23.

The doubleheader itself was a split, with Boston claiming the day's first contest, 6–0, and Pittsburgh winning the nightcap in fourteen innings by a score of 4–3. Boston's Johnny Lanning held the Pirates to six hits in the initial game while Pittsburgh starter Bob Klinger did not make it out of the first inning, giving up two runs on three hits during his first mound appearance in two weeks. The Pirates pulled the second game out of the fire as Mace Brown upped his record to 14–6 on the season by tossing six solid innings after relieving starter Ed Brandt. Traynor's squad claimed victory in the fourteenth frame when Jeep Handley singled, moved to second after Bill Brubaker grounded out on a hit-and-run play, and scored from second when pitcher Dick Errickson dropped Elbie Fletcher's throw to first after Fletcher had gobbled up Paul Waner's hot smash.[1]

On two different occasions, a Pirates pitcher barely escaped serious injury. In the second contest, Ed Brandt received a bruise to his left leg after a drive off the bat of Lou Fette struck the southpaw and sent him dancing in pain around the infield. Later in the game, Mace Brown could not dodge a blast from Vince DiMaggio's bat that struck him on the right knee and left a painful bruise. Also ailing was shortstop Arky Vaughan, who participated in both contests even though he was handicapped by a lame leg.[2] While the Pirates were lucky that these three players were not forced to the sidelines by their injuries, the entire squad was perplexed and hurt when a small minority of the 12,000 fans in attendance booed the league leaders.[3]

During the second game of this doubleheader, these fans showed their displeasure toward Johnny Rizzo, Al Todd, Pie Traynor and other Buccaneers with vociferous catcalls and boos. The disgruntled rooters began their attack on Todd when he replaced Ray Berres and then shifted their attention to Rizzo who was in the midst of a batting slump (while ignoring the fact that he was leading the team with 13 home runs and 76 RBIs). Traynor became the target of Forbes Field patrons when he sent the right-handed Bill Brubaker in to pinch hit for Lloyd Waner against a southpaw pitcher. Pie was booed again when he pulled a tiring Ed Brandt after he had run the bases in the eighth frame and replaced him with Mace Brown.[4]

The Pirates pulled out the second game just as umpires were preparing to call the contest a tie due to darkness. Nonetheless, the mood in Pittsburgh's clubhouse afterward was subdued as the result of the booing. Instead of shouting, cheering and slapping each other on the back because of a great victory in the second game, Pittsburgh's players were sullen and quiet. Prior to the final game of this short series on August 24, umpire Babe Pinelli, a former big league player, did not mince words about the surprising turn of events. "Say, what kind of town is this?" Pinelli remarked. "In all my 22 years in baseball, I've never heard anything like that booing the fans here gave the Pirates yesterday. I'll grant the fans have a right to boo or cheer. They pay for that privilege. But, I think they abuse that privilege in this town. Why, do you realize the Pirates were 'put on the spot' after they had lost the first game, 6 to 0? They saw the figures on the scoreboard with the Giants beating the Cubs and the Bucs just had to win that second game to save their big lead. Yet, the boys hustle, the manager tries to shift his lineup and batting order for the best results and what happens—the fans second-guess him before he has a chance to put his plan into operation. The fans should give this team a lift. They deserve it. Any team that can leave 22 men on the bases and not become discouraged, but instead, rear back fighting, is a team that is worthy of support."[5]

While the devoted baseball rooters who cheered on their Pirates through thick and thin patiently waited to see how the team would react to this unfortunate jeering, Bob Klinger proclaimed that his arm had felt fine the previous day despite having been knocked from the pitcher's box.

Klinger maintained that his arm had never felt better and that he was now pain free. He added that he had lots of stuff on the ball against Boston.[6] If Klinger's shoulder problems did return during the season's final weeks, Fireman Mace Brown said that he would volunteer his services to replace the rookie pitcher in Pittsburgh's starting rotation. Brown had appeared in 40 games for the Pirates so far in 1938, but had only started one game. While discussing his desire to help the team as a starter, he pointed out that relief pitching brought special challenges. "It's warming up," said Brown. "When one of those pitchers throws a few bad balls, out I go to warm up. Then maybe he settles down and so do I for a few minutes until something else happens. If he gets into enough different trouble, I get almost as tired warming up as I would pitching three or four hard innings. You notice it the next day, especially if you're called into work."[7]

Brown's services were not required during the final contest on August 24 against Boston as Pittsburgh cruised to an easy 6–2 victory. Russ Bauers tossed a complete game and improved his record to 9–10 on the season as he gave up two runs on nine hits. While hurling one of his best games of the year, Bauers fanned eight Bees, including Vince DiMaggio three times. Pittsburgh's fans showed their fickle nature as boos early in the contest had turned to cheers in the sixth inning. The jeering was especially noticeable in the fourth frame when Pittsburgh only scored one run after they loaded the bases. Those jeers turned to cheers when Pep Young put the game on ice with a three-run triple between Vince DiMaggio and Max West. Besides being a consistent dynamo at the plate throughout the 1938 campaign, Young had also combined with Arky Vaughan to turn a league-leading 125 double plays.[8]

Pittsburgh's two-game winning streak became a distant memory when Pie Traynor's troops suffered the humiliation of dropping both games of a doubleheader to lowly Philadelphia on Thursday, August 25. The Pirates lost the first contest, 2–1, as Max Butcher of the Phillies tossed a complete game and scattered seven hits. Philadelphia claimed the second game, which lasted 11 innings, by the same score. Cy Blanton took the loss for Pittsburgh in the first game, while Red Lucas' record dropped to 4–3 even though he was brilliant in the nightcap. Lucas pitched all eleven innings, giving up two runs on seven hits. Philadelphia would have wrapped up the second game in regulation if not for some bad defense. After Johnny Rizzo had walked in the seventh frame, Gus Suhr bunted a pop fly to pitcher Bill Hallahan while attempting to sacrifice Rizzo to second. Hallahan, who unexpectedly dropped the ball, quickly recovered his faculties and threw to first base.[9]

10. Traynor's Boys Attempt to Hang on 169

Phillies first baseman Phil Weintraub made a bone-headed play that prevented his team from pulling off a double play. Instead of tagging Rizzo and then the first base bag, Wientraub stepped on the base first and only recorded one out since he had now eliminated the force play. Rizzo scored Pittsburgh's only run of the game moments later when he crossed home plate after Pep Young tripled.[10] The only bright spot on a day when Pittsburgh scored two runs during 20 innings of play against the last-place Phillies was a new attendance record for Ladies Day at Forbes Field. A total of 11,907 women turned out and filled both the lower and upper decks of the right-field stands. They showed their allegiance and spirit throughout the afternoon by cheering favorite Paul Waner and jeered Chuck Klein of the Phillies. The women got so excited on one occasion that a fight broke among four of them. This short battle reached its conclusion when one of them took off her opponent's shoes and tossed them onto the field.[11]

There was no cheering in the Pirates clubhouse when this double debacle reached its painful conclusion. Pie Traynor's boys were silent as they pondered the potential consequences of the two losses to Philadelphia. Pittsburgh's players, who realized they were struggling collectively at the plate, could only wait and hope that this batting slump would soon end. Manager Traynor had more options at his disposal and on August 26 he decided to make two changes in his lineup. Johnny Rizzo, who was mired in an 0-for-17 batting slump, was replaced in Pittsburgh's starting lineup by Johnny Dickshot. Traynor also sent Bill Brubaker out to third base in place of Jeep Handley. Rizzo and Handley showed they were consummate team players by endorsing Pie's moves.[12] "I hope Bill starts hitting and brings us out of our slump," said Handley after being notified by Traynor that he was being benched.[13]

Handley's ability to strike the ball with authority had been hampered by a sore right shoulder that he had injured in a game against Brooklyn on the recent eastern trip.[14] Brubaker proved to be a worthy replacement, going 2-for-4 at the plate and driving home two runs. Unfortunately, Paul Waner was the only other Pirates player who accomplished anything at the plate by also banging out two hits. Phillies starter Al Smith throttled the other Pirates hitters as Philadelphia made it three wins in a row over their cross-state rival with a 6–4 victory. Phillies manager Jimmy Wilson made good on a bet that evening when he treated Smith, Max Butcher and Bill Hallahan to champagne. Wilson had promised each of these starters that they would receive a bottle of the bubbly if they prevailed against the Pirates. Surprised that the players had earned the champagne, Wilson was more than happy to pay off his bet. Jimmy also planned on giving twirler Al Hollingsworth his bottle on the train Saturday evening if he could defeat Pittsburgh during the series' final game.[15]

Even though the Pirates were experiencing some problems during their current home stand, the second-place New York Giants were also struggling and had only made up one game. Chicago and Cincinnati were closing in on Bill Terry's Giants as each team now was poised to move ahead of the defending National League champions. Despite the fact that New York was only trailing Pittsburgh by four-and-a-half games, Terry believed his team was in no position to mount any challenge. While in St. Louis playing the Cardinals, Bill all but counted his team out of the race, while also claiming that Cincinnati had the best chance to overtake Pittsburgh.[16]

"If the Giants win the pennant now," Terry said, "I'd have to believe in baseball miracles. Our outlook is dismal and I might as well admit it. We have been shot by injuries and illness and now our whole pitching structure is falling all around us. I've tried to do something about it, but I'm afraid it's too late. We'll have to worry through as we are, having Hal Schumacher's arm go bad just as Carl Hubbell went out as a crusher. I'm going to start relying on the rookies to go out and try to win for me. I wish it were late September instead of late August. The butchering may be brutal in the final weeks. If we only had our full strength. A team at this stage of the particular National League race that really had strength and confidence could go to town. If I had the team I thought I was going to have, I'd cop easily. The best way to describe our ailment is that we were caught out in the rain without an umbrella, having no pitching to speak of now."[17]

While Pittsburgh's players felt no sympathy after reading Terry's sob story in local newspapers, they had to be annoyed by his insinuation that Cincinnati could pass them to win the National League pennant. The Pirates took out their anger on the Phillies as they made sure that Al Hollingsworth was not going to receive his bottle of champagne. Pittsburgh ended their three-game losing streak with a 6–1 victory over Philadelphia on Saturday, August 27. Southpaw Ed Brandt stymied the Phillies all afternoon by scattering seven hits, fanning five and walking one. Manager Pie Traynor was forced to juggle his lineup once again because Johnny Rizzo remained home, sick in bed with a cold and sore throat. Jeep Handley went back to third base, Bill Brubaker took over at first and Woody Jensen replaced Rizzo in left field.[18]

Handley did not remain in the contest very long. After Lee beat out a hit to shortstop George Scharein in the first frame, he had the wind knocked

10. Traynor's Boys Attempt to Hang on

out of him sliding into third while advancing on Lloyd Waner's single. Even though he was slightly incapacitated, Handley had the presence of mind to scamper home with a run when the ball was muffed. When Pittsburgh took the field to start the second inning, however, Tommy Thevenow replaced Handley at third base. Lloyd Waner was busy at the plate for Pittsburgh all afternoon, rapping out three hits, while Al Todd and Woody Jensen each contributed a pair of blows.[19] Before Philadelphia left the Smoky City after having claimed three out of four games in this series, manager Jimmy Wilson cautioned everyone who rooted for the Pirates not to worry about their team. Wilson reasoned that it was better to lose against his Phillies, rather than Bill Terry's Giants in a few days. "You fellows will have to quit worrying," said Wilson. "You've got the best team in the league and you're in one of those slumps that hits every team sometime or another. We're playing our finest ball of the year. The Pirates are playing their poorest. The Phils are up there free and easy. Nothing on their minds. No lead to protect. The Pirates happen to be tightened up a little and that's where we have the advantage. But class will tell in the long run and you'll see the Pirates way out in front."[20]

The Pirates continued to look out of sorts when Brooklyn came into town on Sunday, August 28 for a two-game series and whipped Pie Traynor's team, 8–5, in the first contest. A crowd of 16,045 watched the Dodgers push six runs across the plate in the first two innings. Russ Bauers started for Pittsburgh and gave up two markers in the initial frame before Joe Bowman was called in from the bullpen. Bowman held Brooklyn in check for the remainder of that frame but was tagged for four runs in the second inning. An unusual battle of wits between managers Pie Traynor and Burleigh Grimes took place in the fifth inning with Dodgers starter Freddie Fitzsimmons pitching to Gus Suhr. When the count went to two balls and one strike, Grimes yanked Fitzsimmons and replaced him with southpaw Vito Tamulis. Traynor countered Grimes' strategy by sending the right-handed Bill Brubaker up to the plate to finish Suhr's at-bat. Pie won this particular round as Brubaker connected for a two-run home run. After Tamulis retired Pep Young, Tot Pressnell entered the game and held Pittsburgh in check for the remainder of the afternoon.[21]

Baseball fans at Forbes Field were a little more lenient on their team than they had been during the doubleheader against Boston five days earlier. The only time they rode a Pirates player came in the second inning when Woody Jensen misjudged a fly ball off the bat of Cookie Lavagetto that dropped for a three-run double. Most of the loyal rooters at Forbes Field tried to lift the team's spirits by rooting earnestly throughout the day.[22] Compounding the Pirates recent difficulties was the fact that shortstop Arky Vaughan was suffering from a mild charley-horse in his left leg. Arky, who had thus far played every inning of baseball for Pittsburgh in 1938, refused to let a substitute take his place because he could still hit and run the bases. Vaughan was the consummate team player who was revered by teammates and opponents throughout the National League. Arky always liked to keep his fellow Pirates loose by telling jokes, even though he usually ruined the punch line by laughing before he was finished.[23]

Vaughan was in the lineup once again on August 29 as Pittsburgh turned the tables on Brooklyn and scored a decisive 10–1 victory. Arky went 2-for-4 at the plate and stroked a double as part of the Pirates' 15-hit attack. Paul Waner also rapped out two hits, while Al Todd went 3-for-4 and scored two runs as pitcher Cy Blanton tossed a complete game and improved his record to 11–4. Johnny Rizzo returned from his sick bed and contributed two hits.[24] While all of these players were key contributors during Pittsburgh's lopsided victory, second baseman Pep Young was the batting star of the day. Young celebrated his thirty-first birthday in grand style by going 3-for-5 at the plate.[25]

As the month of August wound down and the Pirates prepared to play the first contest of a vital four-game series against Bill Terry's Giants, Pie Traynor's squad held a five-and-a-half-game lead over New York and Chicago.[26] Pittsburgh extended its lead over New York with a decisive 7–1 victory over Terry's Giants on Tuesday, August 30. Dick Coffman, making his first start for the Giants since October 2, 1937, was strafed for six runs on eight hits during six innings of work. Gus Suhr's bat caught fire after being benched recently for light hitting, cracking a triple, a double and a single.[27] Suhr also drove home five of the Pirates' seven runs. Lloyd Waner chipped in by going 3-for-5 and scoring two runs, while Arky Vaughan rapped out two hits and scored twice. Jim Tobin improved his record to 12–7 on the season by tossing a complete game and scattering five hits.

While Pie Traynor was ecstatic that his squad had dismantled the Giants in relatively easy fashion, he was absolutely euphoric when he informed Pittsburgh's baseball scribes that Heinie Manush had been purchased from Toronto of the International League. Pie planned on using the veteran Manush as an insurance outfielder and pinch hitter during the final month of the pennant drive. Heinie would not be eligible to appear on the Pirates bench until September 1 when the 23-player roster limit expired. If the Pirates did make it to the World Series in October, Manush would not

10. Traynor's Boys Attempt to Hang on

be permitted to play since he had not been added to the roster before the deadline of August 31. Pie explained to reporters why he was so pleased by the new acquisition. "We've lost at least five games in the last month," Traynor observed, "which we could have saved with a hit or even a long fly. Woody Jensen isn't hitting the ball for us and Red Lucas is going to concentrate on pitching. Red, the world's champion pinch hitter, has had only three hits this season, but none in a pinch. In fact, Red hasn't even driven the ball out of the infield in a pinch this year."[28]

While Jensen had been an abject failure as a hitter for Pittsburgh in 1938, he was doing yeoman's work behind the scenes in an area that generally went unnoticed by fans. On a day when the Pirates were scheduled to face a southpaw hurler, Jensen took the mound during team batting practice and mimicked the opponent's starting pitcher that day. Woody went to great lengths to impersonate these twirlers accurately so that the Pirate batters were prepared for the pitches they would see that afternoon. When the Pirates faced New York's Carl Hubbell, for example, Jensen made sure the screwball was part of his repertoire — no easy feat, since the screwball is a notoriously difficult pitch to throw. Woody's work was easier when the Pirates opposed Cliff Melton of the Giants, a more conventional pitcher. When Jensen's contribution to the team in this manner was featured in an article that appeared in *The Pittsburgh Press* on August 18, Pittsburgh had either defeated or driven a southpaw from a game early on 21 out of 26 occasions after he had pitched batting practice.[29]

Jensen's services in batting practice were required by manager Pie Traynor on Wednesday, August 31 since Melton was scheduled to oppose Pittsburgh in the second game of a doubleheader. Over 40,000 shrieking, howling, yelling spectators were on hand at Forbes Field to cheer on their Pirates.[30] Pirates fans were disappointed in the outcome of the first game as New York prevailed, 6–5. The Waner brothers conjured up memories of the 1927 National League pennant drive as they harassed New York the whole game by recording three hits apiece, while each scored one run and smacked one double. Paul also drove home two of Pittsburgh's runs. Jeep Handley and Johnny Rizzo pitched in with two hits apiece as Russ Bauers saw his record fall to 9–12, even though he only allowed one unearned run during four-and-two-thirds innings of relief work.

Controversy marred the first contest. The Pirates front office forwarded a written protest to National League president Ford Frick over a decision made by umpire Ziggy Sears in the sixth inning. With runners on second and third, Russ Bauers smacked a ground ball to New York shortstop George

Myatt, who quickly threw to catcher Harry Danning. When Gus Suhr realized he was trapped between third and home, he hustled back to third base. Gus reached the bag just as teammate Pep Young was arriving at third base. Danning ran up the line and tagged both men. Under baseball rules, Young was out since Suhr already had possession of third base. When Suhr then walked off the bag and Danning touched him again, Sears ruled that both runners were out. Suhr argued vehemently that he only had started walking to the dugout because Sears had called him out while he stood on third base.[31]

A 17-minute argument involving players from both teams ensued, as Sears and fellow umpires Bill Klem and Lee Ballanfant held a series of conferences before issuing a final ruling. It was initially their contention that Suhr was out and Young was safe at third. This led Bill Terry and his entire team to descend upon the three umpires to point out the error of their ways. Five minutes later, the arbiters changed their ruling and declared both runners out. This caused Pie Traynor to argue for an additional five minutes, while an irate Gus Suhr had to be restrained by Al Todd. When it all ended, Young finally walked off third base, where he had remained stationed throughout the drawn-out argument.[32]

Many of the paying customers in Forbes Field's stands showed their displeasure with this decision by tossing pop bottles on the baseball diamond. Umpire Sears' explanation regarding this sequence of events only made the whole situation more confusing, as his contradictory comments indicated that he informed Suhr twice that he was out even while he was claiming that he only said this to the Pittsburgh first baseman on one occasion. "The only time I said 'You're out, Suhr,' was when Danning tagged Young on the bag," claimed Sears. "Then Suhr walked off the bag — and Danning tagged him also. Then I said, 'You're out Suhr.' That's the first and only time I called Suhr out on that play. Suhr knew he was trapped — because when he was being run down he shouted to Young to get back on the bag. The Giants came out to claim they had a double play. Then I went over to Umpire Bill Klem and we agreed that it was a double play. But, I only called Suhr out once, and that was when Danning tagged him — and then afterward, tagged Young."[33]

The Pirates rebounded from this adverse decision in the afternoon's second contest to destroy Cliff Melton and the Giants, 12–3. Pie Traynor's charges slammed out 16 hits behind Red Lucas, who tossed a complete game and improved his record to 5–3. Pep Young, Al Todd and Johnny Rizzo banged out three hits apiece for the Corsairs. Rizzo and Paul Waner each

10. Traynor's Boys Attempt to Hang on

recorded five hits during the double bill with Waner driving in four runs and Rizzo five. Johnny also launched his fourteenth homer of the season over Forbes Field's left-field wall in the second contest.[34] The doubleheader drew a record crowd of 43,586 for a regular season game at Forbes Field.[35]

Pie Traynor's Pirates had gone only 16–16 in August, yet had increased their National League lead from five games to six and a half over the second-place New York Giants.[36] Rookie pitcher Bob Klinger made sure Pittsburgh got off on the right foot in the month of September as he shut out Bill Terry's squad during the finale of the four-game series. Klinger improved his record to 9–5 on the year as Pittsburgh claimed a 6–0 victory. The Waners were front and center once again for the Pirates: Lloyd went 4-for-5, scored two runs and drilled a triple, while Paul was 2-for 4 and drove home one run. In leading Pittsburgh to three wins in four games against New York, the two brothers had combined for 19 hits in 37 at bats.[37] Lloyd Waner's performance in this series was remarkable considering that he was playing with a slightly sprained left wrist and had large chunks of skin missing from one of his legs.[38] Lloyd, who had been the model of consistency throughout the year, was batting .313 for the season. Paul, who had been mired in the worst slump of his career during the campaign's early stages, was now hitting .283.

Following his masterful performance, Pirates pitcher Bob Klinger proclaimed that he had completed the game without experiencing pain for the first time all season. This good news was short lived, however, as Klinger's arm was ailing him once again by the following day.[39] New York manager Bill Terry certainly could relate to having a top pitcher with arm problems. Giants ace Carl Hubbell was on the shelf after having bone chips removed from his left arm. Before New York left the Smoky City, Hubbell expressed confidence that Pittsburgh had enough pitching and punch to defeat the Yankees in a potential World Series matchup. "The Yanks," said Hubbell, "will be prohibitive favorites, but the Pirates have some punch of their own, especially when Johnny Rizzo is in there swinging. The Yanks won't hit so many home runs at Forbes Field. It's too large — much larger than Yankee Stadium."[40]

While Hubbell believed that Pittsburgh could defeat the New York Yankees in the 1938 World Series and extract some revenge for what happened in 1927, New York baseball writer Dan Daniel thought Joe McCarthy's boys would prevail in the October Classic. Since Daniel was a scribe who usually covered the Yankees, his decision to travel with the Giants on their latest western swing had allowed him to see teams in person that he usually only

Despite persistent arm problems throughout the 1938 season, rookie hurler Bob Klinger gutted it out and performed admirably down the home stretch. On September 1, Klinger continued his dominance over the New York Giants and pushed his record to 9–5 on the season with a 6–0 shutout at Forbes Field (National Baseball Hall of Fame Library, Cooperstown, New York).

read about in the newspapers. "It's the only club I've seen in this league," wrote Daniel of the Giants. "Until we came to Pittsburgh, I hadn't looked at a team that could get a runner from first base to third on a single. There's speed there, and no one seems to be asleep. In Chicago, St. Louis and Cincinnati, the boys are enjoying a quiet nap, and the rest of the mob can be wrapped up and thrown into the most convenient river."[41]

When Pittsburgh sportswriter Chester L. Smith asked Daniel if the Yankees would march through the Buccaneers in four straight games like they had done in 1927, he responded that a sweep would not happen. "It will go six games," continued Daniel. "Blanton will stand a great chance to win at least one game in the Series and if Bauers has the stuff he had on Wednesday, he can win another."[42]

While Hubbell and Daniel were a bit measured in their comments, New York Giants manager Bill Terry spoke very candidly to Pittsburgh scribes about where the National League pennant was heading during the season's final month. Terry announced that he no longer harbored any fantasies about the Giants claiming their third consecutive pennant. He even admitted that his team would be hard pressed to prevent a slide into the second division during the campaign's final weeks. Terry believed that the Pirates were the best team in the league. He also felt that Pittsburgh would easily win the pennant and give the Yankees a tough battle in the World Series. "If the Pirates do not win, they should quit playing ball," said Terry.[43]

Terry's frank remarks did not sit well with Pie Traynor. He believed that Terry had placed him in a difficult position if Pittsburgh were unable to bring home the National League pennant in 1938. A minor feud between the two pilots had developed just days earlier when Traynor made a sarcastic remark after being asked to comment on New York's signing of right-handed hurler Manuel Salvo from San Diego. Pie did not pull any punches when he responded to Terry's comment about what the Pirates players should do if they did not win the National League pennant. "I recollect in 1934 the Giants had a bigger lead than we now have, at a much later stage of the season, and yet blew the pennant," said Traynor. "Looking over the line-up of the Giants, I find that many veterans of that sad experience still are playing for the New York club. They did not see fit to retire from baseball. How come?"[44]

Traynor had bigger problems than Terry's opinion as the Pirates prepared for a three-game series against St. Louis at Forbes Field. Shortstop Arky Vaughan was forced to the sidelines with a swollen right thumb that had been injured during the final game of the Giants series when Vaughan was spiked while tagging out New York speedster George Myatt on an attempted steal. With Vaughan unable to grip a bat or throw a baseball, Bill Brubaker replaced him at shortstop. The infield seemed out of sync all afternoon in the first contest against St. Louis on Friday, September 2. Pep Young allowed an easy grounder to roll through his legs. Several hits bounced off Jeep Handley's glove, while a couple of grounders to Brubaker that would have been gobbled up by Vaughan eluded his substitute for singles.[45]

St. Louis had built an 11–3 lead in the sixth inning and then hung on to win, 11–10.[46] Pittsburgh connected for 15 hits against two Cardinals pitchers, but the game was lost due to the ineffectiveness of Cy Blanton and Joe Bowman before Bill Swift stabilized things during the last two innings. Lloyd Waner, Gus Suhr and Pep Young were the Pirates batting stars for the day, each recording three hits. Johnny Rizzo also was a beast at the plate: he went 2-for-4, scored three runs, knocked in five runs and drilled his fifteenth home run off Bob Weiland in the first inning. Things got worse for the Pirates on September 3 when Cardinals hurler Max Macon tossed a five-hitter and claimed a 6–0 victory against the National League's pacesetters. Gus Suhr was the only Pirate who dented Macon as he accounted for Pittsburgh's only two hits during the first six innings and finished with three on the day.[47]

The Pirates received inspiration on Sunday, September 4 when Arky Vaughan bandaged his swollen right thumb and trotted out to his post at shortstop to compete against the Cardinals. The 12,187 fans in attendance gave Pittsburgh's star shortstop a rousing round of applause.[48] Pie Traynor's troops seemed to be energized by Vaughan's return as they ended a two-game losing streak and claimed a 5–3 victory. Pittsburgh did all of their damage against Cardinals starter Roy Henshaw during two separate innings. The Pirates scored three runs in the second frame when Gus Suhr walked, Pep Young tripled, Al Todd doubled and Russ Bauers singled. Two more runs crossed home plate in the sixth inning on Johnny Rizzo's single, Young's two-bagger and Ray Berres' single.[49] Rizzo also hit the longest drive of the season at Forbes Field in the third inning when he blasted a Henshaw offering that traveled 440 feet before Cardinals outfielder Terry Moore hauled in the drive near the center-field flagpole.[50]

While the Pirates were in the midst of trying to expand their National League lead during this long home stand at Forbes Field, a bizarre story started making the rounds claiming that the Pittsburgh franchise might be sold before the coming winter. This rumor stated that a prominent resident of Pittsburgh who had made a fortune in the motion picture business was about to make a bid to purchase the Pirates. The story also claimed that Florence Dreyfuss would be receptive to selling the team if she received a suitable offer. While this report seemed speculative, it was common knowledge that Mrs. Dreyfuss had pondered selling the team because she was getting along in years. It seemed logical that Barney Dreyfuss' widow would attempt to liquidate her baseball holdings while the property was at peak value, both financially and as a collection of baseball talent.[51]

These rumors were ignored by Pittsburgh's players as they geared up for a big Labor Day doubleheader, scheduled to begin at 1:45 p.m. against the Chicago Cubs at Forbes Field. Pittsburgh still was six games ahead of the second-place Cincinnati Reds as they prepared to meet Gabby Hartnett's third-place Cubs.[52] Chicago handed the Pirates a critical pair of defeats as they recorded a 3–0 victory in the opener, and claimed the nightcap, 4–3, in front of an overflow crowd of 42,545 fans that had jammed into Forbes Field. The Buccaneers record dropped to 0–4 with Arky Vaughan on the sidelines when the star shortstop's afternoon ended after only two-and-a-half innings of the initial contest. Arky was suffering from a brand-new ailment, as he was knocked out of action by a stiff neck and sore back.[53]

The Pirates were unable to score on Chicago hurler Bill Lee in the afternoon's first game, even though they banged out ten hits. Veteran Ed Brandt was saddled with a disappointing loss when fielding miscues by his teammates allowed Chicago to score three unearned runs in the third inning. Brandt's record dropped to 5–3 even though he tossed a complete game and gave up only five hits. Pittsburgh looked poised to claim victory during the second game after they scored three runs off Cubs starter Clay Bryant in the fifth inning to take a 3–1 lead. Bryant settled down from that point, however, while Chicago added single tallies in the sixth, eighth and ninth innings to claim a 4–3 victory. Jim Tobin took the loss for Pittsburgh after he relieved starter Red Lucas and allowed one run during one-and-one-third innings of work. Even though left fielder Johnny Rizzo was held hitless by Chicago pitchers all afternoon, he did nail some blistering line drives that made their way directly at Cubs fielders. Rizzo also made several circus catches in the outfield that brought cheers from the crowd.[54]

Chicago's sweep over the first-place Pirates, coupled with Cincinnati's two victories over St. Louis, tightened the National League pennant race as Pie Traynor's troops prepared to embark on a long road trip after an 8–10 home stand.[55] Pittsburgh held down the top spot with a record of 75–52, while Cincinnati was four games behind in second place with a mark of 72–57. Chicago was close on the Reds' heels in third, five games out of first place with a record of 71–58, while New York held down the fourth position, six-and-one-half games back at 69–59. The Pirates were afforded the opportunity to rest and recharge their batteries after arriving in Cincinnati on September 6. Traynor took in that day's game at Crosley Field and watched St. Louis defeat the Reds, 8–0.[56] While Traynor's club enjoyed a day away from the baseball diamond, National League president Ford Frick announced that he had ruled against the Pirates' protest of Ziggy Sears' umpiring decision in the game on August 31 against New York.[57]

Pittsburgh spoiled Cincinnati ace Paul Derringer's effort to record his twentieth victory of the season on September 7 by earning a 7–1 victory. Bob Klinger and Paul Waner were Pittsburgh's stars. Klinger improved his record to 10–5 by tossing a complete game and allowing one unearned run on six hits. Traynor's revised lineup, which had the Waners in the first two slots, knocked out 14 hits as Paul had a perfect day at the plate with a double, three singles and a walk in five plate appearances.[58] Johnny Rizzo was 2-for-5 at the plate and blasted his sixteenth homer of the season against Gene Schott in the eighth inning. Tommy Thevenow also played brilliantly in place of the injured Arky Vaughan at shortstop, rapping out two singles and starting three lightning double plays in the field. Thevenow's solid work gained the admiration of Vaughan as he sat in Pittsburgh's dugout with a sore neck. "You know, the more I watch Thevenow, the better my neck feels," cracked Vaughan. "I'll be ready to play right away if that guy keeps on going like that. I don't want to lose my job."[59]

Thevenow's tale of finally getting a chance to play was a feel-good story, as the veteran infielder had figured his playing days were over after the 1937 season. Tommy went back to his farm in Indiana after being released by the Boston Bees in February. Just when it seemed retirement was his only option, Pie Traynor called him on the phone and informed Thevenow a contact was on its way in the mail. When the Pittsburgh press corps got wind of Traynor's plans to bring the veteran infielder back to Pittsburgh, one scribe incredulously asked what good he expected to get out of Thevenow. "Not much — but the day we need Tommy — if it even comes — will be too late if we don't get him now," Traynor replied. "And, if it ever happens that we want someone to go in and play for a few days or a week, I don't know anyone I'd prefer."[60]

That prudent decision finally paid dividends for the Pirates in September as Tommy Thevenow ably replaced Vaughan at shortstop. Nevertheless, on Thursday, September 8, the Reds, faced with the possibility of sliding into fourth place, pulled out a 5–3 victory over Pittsburgh.[61] Cincin-

10. Traynor's Boys Attempt to Hang on 181

nati's Johnny Vander Meer made his first start since August 10 and tossed his first complete game since July 20. Vander Meer held Pittsburgh to five singles and one run through the game's first eight innings before Johnny Rizzo blasted his seventeenth home run of the season in the ninth with Paul Waner on board. While Rizzo knocked in all three Pirates runs, he also committed three errors in left field.[62]

Cincinnati sealed the outcome in the sixth inning by scoring three runs against Cy Blanton. After Wally Berger doubled to start the stanza, Blanton retired Ival Goodman and Frank McCormick before Traynor ordered an intentional pass to Ernie Lombardi. A hit behind third base by Harry Craft allowed Cincinnati to load the bases. Lew Riggs' single drove home Berger and Lombardi, and when Rizzo booted the ball in left field, Craft also came around to score.

During an off day on September 9 before opening a series against St. Louis at Sportsman's Park, Traynor announced that Red Lucas was temporarily leaving the team to go to his home in Nashville, Tennessee. Lucas had been given a leave of absence after learning that his wife was battling pneumonia. Red planned on rejoining the Pirates in New York if his wife's condition improved.[63] The Pirates also lost the services of young man who was not on the roster, but had made a minor contribution to the squad's effort during the 1938 campaign. Lieutenant Andy Lipscomb, a West Point graduate who had been with Pittsburgh all summer as a batting practice hurler, was ordered to report to Fort Hamilton in Brooklyn by commanding officer Colonel Fay W. Brabson. Lipscomb had requested that his leave of absence be extended until the World Series concluded. Manager Pie Traynor also had written to Army officials requesting an extension for Lipscomb, who intended to follow a career as an infantry lieutenant.[64] If oddsmaker Jack Doyle was correct, Lipscomb would miss out on a chance to be part of the 1938 World Series with Pittsburgh. Doyle's latest betting line favored the Pirates and New York Yankees meeting in the upcoming Fall Classic. Doyle had already stopped taking bets on the Yankees, who were now 15 games ahead of the second-place Boston Red Sox. Jack also stated that he did not see how Pittsburgh could blow its lead with such an advantage in the loss column with so few games left to play.[65]

Arky Vaughan's return against the Cardinals was expected to aid Pittsburgh's cause. On September 10, St. Louis grabbed a quick 6–0 lead against Russ Bauers and Bill Swift. Pie Traynor's troops fought back to close the gap to 7–6 and then exploded for eight runs in the eighth inning and claimed a 14–7 victory.[66] Al Todd was the main catalyst of Pittsburgh's 16-hit attack, going 2-for-5 at the plate, while blasting a triple, a home run and driving in five runs. Jeep Handley went 3-for-4, scored four runs and recorded two RBIs, while Johnny Rizzo was 3-for-5 and drove home two runs. Mace Brown improved his record to 15–6 by hurling four innings of hitless relief. On the road trip, Rizzo had connected for six hits, while also blasting his sixteenth and seventeenth home runs of the season. His eight runs driven in during the three contests had pushed his season total to 96.[67]

Since Pittsburgh had won nine out of ten games at Sportsman's Park in 1938, superstitious manager Pie Traynor did not change his routine one bit prior to the game on Sunday, September 11. This meant that Pie once again had to hike the three-mile trip from the Chase Hotel to the Cardinals ballpark on foot.[68] Traynor had to be optimistic about the chances of making it 10 victories out of 11 games, since St. Louis was sending Paul "Daffy" Dean to the mound for the first time in 1938. This decision looked suspiciously like a publicity stunt to lure customers into Sportsman's Park, since Dean had spent the summer pitching for Dallas of the Texas League and had posted an 8–16 record.[69]

The Pirates bolted out of the gate in superb fashion against Dean, jumping to a 3–0 lead after three innings. Lloyd Waner singled to start the first inning and then stole second base when his brother was fanned by Dean. Lloyd then trotted across the plate when Johnny Rizzo blasted his eighteenth home run of the year. Pittsburgh added a third marker in the third inning after two men were retired when Rizzo walked and came around to score after Arky Vaughan and Gus Suhr followed with back-to-back singles.[70] However, Pirate starter Jim Tobin was not up to the task of holding this lead and had allowed St. Louis to tie the game before exiting in the fourth inning. Russ Bauers replaced him and allowed three runs, two which were unearned, during five innings of relief. Pittsburgh made it interesting in the ninth inning when Al Todd blasted a home run into the left-field stands but Dean set down the Pirates to claim a 6–4 victory.[71]

Things did not end quietly from Pittsburgh's perspective as Johnny Rizzo had a verbal confrontation with home plate umpire George Magerkurth. The incident occurred while Paul Waner was at bat with two out in the ninth frame. The count went to three balls and one strike when Waner took a pitch that appeared to be outside. Magerkurth did not agree and called the pitch a strike. Rizzo, who was standing nearby waiting to take his turn at bat if Waner got on base, gave the umpire a tongue-lashing, accusing him of trying to bring the game to an end because the sun was too hot for him. Rizzo hoped for a chance to tie the game with another home run, but instead Waner swung at a 3–2 pitch and sent a liner to left-center field that was caught by Frenchy Bordagaray.[72]

Cardinals fans were thrilled to see Paul Dean win his first major league game since 1936, but to their surprise the contest also was a farewell for a longtime National League performer. St. Louis manager Frankie Frisch had been rumored to be on the hot seat after four full seasons and parts of two others, but the manner in which the announcement was made was shocking. Cardinals' owner Sam Breadon announced that Frisch was being released during the middle of the game. Breadon stated that coach Mike Gonzalez would assume the managerial duties and run the squad for the remainder of the season.[73]

At that point, Frisch was in uniform on the first-base coaching line. Moments later, the inning ended and he made his way through the dugout to the clubhouse to pack up his belongings. Frisch was immediately besieged by reporters who wanted to know his feelings now that he was not going to be involved in major league baseball for the first time in two decades. "I haven't a thing to say," Frisch told the numerous scribes gathered around him. "I'll probably be around St. Louis for a day or so, then leave for my home in New Rochelle, New York. Mr. Breadon and I are still on the friendliest terms. I hope we will remain that way. We just had a salary difference, that is all there is to it."[74]

Meanwhile, Pie Traynor and his troops returned to Pittsburgh for a few hours before departing on their final eastern swing, which was slated to begin in the Polo Grounds on September 13. How well the Pirates did during this 13-game journey was expected to go a long way to determining whether Pittsburgh would claim the 1938 National League pennant.[75] Pittsburgh was now clinging to a three-and-a-half-game lead over the second-place Chicago Cubs, who had won seven out of their past eight games and now looked like the greatest threat to Pittsburgh's pennant aspirations. The Pirates held down first place with a 77–54 record, while Chicago was second at 75–59, Cincinnati third with a mark of 74–60 and New York still mathematically in the hunt at 73–61.

When Pie Traynor and his team arrived in the Big Apple, they found the city was shrouded in rain. Giants management canceled the game scheduled for September 13 and announced that a doubleheader would be played the following afternoon. This scenario was troublesome to Traynor, since Pittsburgh would now be playing four twin bills in eight days. When he did an impromptu interview for New York sportswriters, he seemed nervous and fidgety throughout the discussion. Pie joked that being a National League manager had caused this condition.[76]

Traynor stated that his players believed they would win the National League pennant but that they were not taking anything for granted by looking ahead to the World Series. In this interview, Traynor also gave a lot of credit for Pittsburgh's success to rookies Johnny Rizzo and Bob Klinger, saying that they had made the difference between a good ball club and a pennant contender. When asked if the Giants still looked tough to Traynor, the Pirate skipper diplomatically responded that every National League club was an obstacle in securing a pennant.[77]

Bill Terry's Giants proved to be a major obstruction for the Pirates, as they claimed both games of the doubleheader on Wednesday, September 14 at the Polo Grounds. Hal Schumacher was magnificent in the first contest, holding Pittsburgh to seven hits and earning a 3–0 decision over Cy Blanton. In the second game, New York pummeled Pirates hurlers Ed Brandt and Bill Swift to claim a 10–3 victory. Jeep Handley was the only Pirate who nicked Schumacher in the first game as Pittsburgh's peppery third baseman smacked two doubles.

During the second affair, Johnny Rizzo and Paul Waner were the only Corsairs who solved New York's Harry Gumbert, combining for half of Pittsburgh's ten hits.

Manager Pie Traynor was despondent after the lost doubleheader. Traynor tried to eat that night but only touched the pieces of food on his plate sporadically with a fork before giving up. He attempted to turn in early, but instead found himself pacing about his room all night. Traynor was still lamenting the fact that Bob Klinger had been unable to go in the first contest against New York because of developing a sore arm while warming up in the bullpen prior to the game. Pie had to unexpectedly turn the starting assignment over to Cy Blanton. National League president Ford Frick, who seemed to be secretly pulling for Cincinnati to claim the crown, made a comment unbecoming for a man in his position by criticizing Klinger after watching both games at the Polo Grounds.[78] "Pitchers nowadays aren't like the old-timers," Frick said. "With their team in the pennant race, they don't care whether they pitch or not. Dolf Luque used to grab the ball and announce he was going to pitch. Carl Hubbell is the same way. Look at Schumacher out there now. Sore arm, but he's pitching and winning, too."[79]

Meanwhile in Pittsburgh, diehard fans were becoming alarmed. If the Pirates did not hang on, most of the blame probably would be heaped upon

Traynor, who looked like a tired, dejected soul as the losses continued to mount. Team president Bill Benswanger, however, grabbed Pie outside the dressing room after the double loss against New York and gave him a pep talk.[80] "Win or lose," Benswanger told Traynor, "you're going to stay as manager. You've done remarkably well this season and if you don't win the pennant, it won't be your fault. But quit worrying. We're still in first place and the time to fret is when we go into second place."[81]

Pie Traynor felt more comfortable in the dugout on Thursday, September 15 as the Pirates defeated New York, 7–2, in the last contest of this three-game series. A season's high for home runs in the major leagues was set in this game as four Pittsburgh players combined to smack five balls out of the Polo Grounds. Paul Waner hit two, while Johnny Rizzo, Pep Young and Lloyd Waner also went deep for Pittsburgh. "Little Poison" decided to break from his tradition of hitting a home run on the sixteenth day of the month by drilling a four-bagger one day early. New York's Mel Ott also tied a major league record when he was hit three times by Pirate pitcher Jim Tobin.[82] Despite his wildness, Tobin tossed a complete game and improved his record to 13–9.

Pittsburgh's lead over second-place Chicago remained at three games as the team left New York and prepared to play consecutive series against second-division representatives Boston and Philadelphia. Buoyed by the strong showing in the final game against Terry's Giants, the Pirates seemed more relaxed as they prepared to feast on two of the National League's bottom feeders. Even though it was evident Traynor's troops had been pressing recently, a strong showing against these two teams could pretty much guarantee that a pennant flag would fly in Pittsburgh. Former Pirates manager Fred Clarke, who had guided Pittsburgh to four National League pennants between 1901 and 1909, offered his opinion on this subject from his ranch in Winfield, Kansas. "A great many players set themselves to thinking too much of the importance of each game," explained the former Pirates great, "and thus they bear down or press too much. When they do so they are not natural. I trust that Pie Traynor can keep the Pirates free and easy. I am sure that if he can do that, they will come through."[83]

Pie Traynor could only hope that Fred Clarke's assessment was accurate.

11

Pittsburgh's Final Collapse and the Homer in the Gloamin'

The strain of the National League's exciting pennant race was beginning to take its toll on Pie Traynor as his squad prepared to play a doubleheader in Boston on September 16. Twin bills were particularly worrisome for Traynor, since the Pirates had been swept by Chicago twice, while New York and Philadelphia had turned the trick one time each during recent doubleheaders. Pittsburgh's record was a dreadful 2–10 over the past six doubleheaders.[1] While Traynor was exhibiting nervousness, some baseball experts perceived that his players were tightening up and choking under the pressure.

"If ever a club tightened up like a Scotch trap drum under pressure, it's the not-so-bold Bucs," declared sportswriter Dan Parker. "There's more tension on Pie Traynor's team than in Ringling's big top. Traynor, himself, looks like a pie from which all the filling has been extracted. Early this season, he confided in friends that he had to win the pennant this year to save his job. But if saving his job means losing his health, Pie can ask 'What price glory?' Right now, manager Traynor is so thin the Pirates can use him for a pennant pole, if they win. As for his players, it isn't safe to come up behind them and say 'boo,' for they all act as if they expect to be shot in the back any minute. This reaction isn't peculiar to the Pirates. In fact, there is hardly a first-place club that hasn't undergone the same experience when trying to protect a slim lead going down the home stretch. However, the Pirates are so devoid of dash, even in their most devil-may-care moods, that an attack of the pennant jitters is far more noticeable when it hits them. It has been suggested that what frightened the Bucs so much at the Polo

Grounds wasn't the Giants or the slimness of their lead, but the proximity of the Yankee Stadium, where, if all goes well, they have a date with an executioner early in October. There may be something in that, too."[2]

Tight or not, Pittsburgh's players knew that fellow National League competitors were not going to cry for them if a pennant slipped through their fingers. They realized that games were won and lost on the field and not in newspapers. The task of claiming the elusive pennant resumed when Pittsburgh clashed with Boston in a twin bill at Braves Field on Friday, September 16. The Pirates pulled out an exciting 7–6 victory in the afternoon's initial contest. Trailing 6–4 heading into the eighth inning, Pittsburgh scored two runs to tie the game and send it into extra innings, where Johnny Rizzo won it with an eleventh-inning home run into the left-field stands. After Rizzo smacked the circuit blast, his teammates raced off the bench to give their hero a proper celebratory greeting once he reached home plate.[3]

Hurler Bill Swift made sure Johnny's clutch hit would be the final storyline surrounding this game as he finished off Boston in the bottom of the eleventh frame. Swift improved his record to 7–5 by pitching four innings of shutout relief and allowing only one hit. Besides hitting the home run that won the game, Rizzo also reached a few milestones that were quite impressive for a rookie. To begin with, Johnny recorded RBI number 100 on his game-winning blast. Pittsburgh's left fielder also set a new team record for four-baggers in a season: his twentieth round-tripper of the 1938 campaign broke Arky Vaughan's all-time Pirate mark of 19, established in 1935. By finally connecting for a homer at Braves Field, Rizzo had now smacked a circuit blast in each of the National League's nine ballparks, making him the first player to do so that season.[4]

In the second game, Mace Brown was exceptional in his second start of the season, allowing only two runs on ten hits during eight innings of work. Brown looked to be assured of picking up his sixteenth victory of the season when Woody Jensen's two-run single gave Pittsburgh a 4–2 lead in the ninth inning. Manager Pie Traynor just needed Joe Bowman to record three outs to give Pittsburgh their second victory of the afternoon. Unfortunately, Bowman was not up to the task as he was only able to retire one Bees batter. Bill Swift relieved Joe and gave up the game-winning hit that enabled Boston to pull out a dramatic 5–4 victory.[5] After the game ended, Jensen bemoaned that an opportunity to finally produce a heroic moment in 1938 had been thwarted. "I have a chance to be a hero for the first time this year," said Jensen. "My luck is all bad. I just got through calling my wife in Wichita. Wished her a happy birthday. Then she hangs up on me after telling me her birthday was on Wednesday."[6]

Pie Traynor was now being referred to as the thin man from Somerville, Massachusetts, as he seemed to lose more weight each day.[7] Meanwhile, Joe Bowman was involved in a harrowing incident that paled in comparison to losing a baseball game. On the evening following Pittsburgh's doubleheader split with Boston, Bowman was robbed at gunpoint. Joe stepped out of the team hotel after dinner and walked down one block to a drug store. When on his way back to the hotel, an automobile drove up to the curb and a middle-aged man got out. The man pointed a gun in Joe's ribs and demanded his wallet. Bowman obliged and handed over the billfold, which was empty since he was carrying money in his pockets. Joe later told teammates that the gun resembled a cannon, while he also explained his reasoning for not getting the car's license number. "No sir," said Bowman, "I don't want to see those guys again. They're liable to come back when they find out there wasn't anything in that pocketbook."[8]

Losing a pitcher to foul play probably would have been the last straw for Pie Traynor as he was having a hard time finding capable hurlers during this stretch that included many doubleheaders. Traynor did receive some good news when rookie Bob Klinger agreed to give it a try on the mound against Boston during the final contest of this three-game affair on Saturday, September 17. This announcement came as a pleasant surprise since it seemed that Klinger would be lost for the remainder of the season after being unable to lift his right arm following a ten-minute bullpen session before a game against New York on August 14. Klinger surpassed all expectations as he tossed a six-hitter and claimed a complete-game 2–1 victory over the Bees.[9]

A lucky break helped the Pirates pull out the victory. Boston carried a 1–0 lead into the ninth inning, but Pittsburgh gained a new lease on life when outfielders Vince DiMaggio and Johnny Cooney collided while chasing Gus Suhr's fly ball and allowed the Pirates first baseman to be credited with a double. Pep Young laid down a beautiful sacrifice that moved Suhr to third. Jeep Handley drove Suhr home with the tying run by smacking a single to left field. Al Todd kept the inning going by lining a single to left field. Klinger grounded out to shortstop Rabbit Warstler, but his hustle averted a double play and left runners at first and third with one out. Todd also had a hand in preventing the twin-killing by legally taking out second baseman Tony Cuccinello as he pivoted to make the throw to Elbie Fletcher at first. Lloyd Waner put Pittsburgh ahead for good when his single to center field drove Handley home with the go-ahead run.[10]

Klinger shut the door during the bottom half of the ninth. Cuccinello grounded out to Arky Vaughan for the first out. Fletcher kept the hopes of the Bees alive by singling to right field. Klinger ended the game by getting Joe Stripp to fly out to Paul Waner in right and inducing Al Lopez to hit a dinky pop fly to Suhr.[11] After the game, as Al Todd stripped off his catcher's gear, he marveled at how well Klinger pitched after having been plagued by a sore arm for much of the 1938 campaign. "That guy had as much stuff and as much heart as I've seen in a long, long time," beamed Todd. "Nothing flusters that Klinger. Gosh, he must have a heart as big as that baseball diamond. And he can pitch in the clutch."[12]

The celebration in Pittsburgh's clubhouse following this exhilarating victory resembled a scene that had been witnessed in 1925 and 1927 after the Pirates clinched those pennants. Pie Traynor's players were shouting, laughing, slapping one another with bath towels, patting each other on the back and rushing into the showers half-clothed to pump one another's hands.[13] It seemed that much of the tension of the past few weeks had melted away in a matter of seconds as a result of one of their biggest victories of the season. Team president Bill Benswanger entered the clubhouse after the game with a big smile on his face. From his pocket came the same type of little black book that Barney Dreyfuss had been known to carry with him during his time as Pittsburgh's owner. Bill made a secret notation in the book as he jokingly told the players that their heart-stopping exploits were wreaking havoc on his nerves. "I like to see you fellows win," remarked Benswanger, after telling the players that he had only seen the final three innings against Boston, "but please don't make me so nervous. Gosh, you fellows saved the run scoring until I could get down from the front office, but it was all I could do to stand the pace. But what the hell, as long as you win, I'll fight it out with my own heart. It isn't that bad."[14]

Despite this great triumph, the Pirates' lead over second-place Chicago was reduced to two-and-a-half games when the Cubs knocked off New York in both ends of a doubleheader, 4–0 and 4–2. Pittsburgh was now four-and-a-half games in front of the Reds, while New York dropped to six games back.[15] The Pirates shuffled out of Boston and grabbed a train for Philadelphia, where Pie Traynor's boys were scheduled to play consecutive doubleheaders on September 18 and 19. Russ Bauers and Ed Brandt both followed Bob Klinger's lead by pitching brilliantly during the first doubleheader on Sunday, September 18. Bauers edged the Phillies 1–0 in the initial contest as the big right-hander pushed his record to 11–13 on the season by tossing a four-hit shutout. Brandt was cruising along in the second contest until the umpires halted the game in the fifth inning due to darkness with the score tied 1–1.[16]

Bauers and Philadelphia's Al Hollingsworth were locked in a scoreless pitcher's duel through eight innings in the initial contest before Pittsburgh broke through with the game's only marker in the top of the ninth frame. Al Todd led off the inning with a sizzling single. Pie Traynor decided to get a little more speed on the basepaths by sending Johnny Dickshot in as a pinch runner for Todd. Bauers tried to sacrifice Dickshot over to second, but failed in his effort to lay down a bunt and was called out on strikes. Lloyd Waner successfully moved Dickshot to second with a beautiful bunt. This put the whole outcome of the game on Paul Waner's shoulders. The man whom many Pirates fans considered to be one of the top players in franchise history wasted no time taking care of business as he almost took Hollingsworth's cap off with a blistering line drive into center field that scored Dickshot.[17]

Any hope of getting the afternoon's second contest completed before darkness descended upon Shibe Park was ruined when the first game was delayed for an hour and a half so groundskeepers could prepare the rain-soaked field for play.[18] There was more rain on September 19, forcing the postponement of that day's games as well, giving the team's overworked pitching staff some much-needed rest. With Cy Blanton still unable to take a turn on the mound due to a slight case of indigestion, Traynor was very pleased when veteran Red Lucas rejoined the team after a 10-day absence to be at the bedside of his wife in Nashville. He reported that she now was feeling much better.[19]

The rainstorm that had washed out the games in Philadelphia also forced the cancellation of a twin bill between Brooklyn and Chicago. When Cubs management requested to reschedule the doubleheader for Friday, September 23, when both teams had an open date on their schedule, Bill Benswanger filed a protest with the National League. According to league rules, the request could not be approved unless every club in the National League consented. Pittsburgh's three-and-a-half-game lead over Chicago was starting to look insurmountable.[20]

Brooklyn was the next stop for the Pirates and on the night before the first game coach Jewel Ens escorted many of the players to Madison Square Garden to watch a bike race.[21] Meanwhile, back in Pittsburgh, arrangements to expand the seating capacity at Forbes Field were underway. On September 19, the Pirates filed an application with the Pittsburgh Bureau of Building Inspection to erect additional bleachers that would seat 2,500 fans, which would push Forbes Field's capacity to between 41,000 and 42,000.[22] Team vice-president Sam Watters issued a short statement explaining that "the bleachers already have been built and all we have to do is to put them up and win some more games."[23]

On Tuesday, September 20, rain once again made baseball impossible and the scheduled doubleheader between Pittsburgh and Brooklyn was postponed. This latest cancellation meant the Pirates would play back-to-back twin bills against Burleigh Grimes' Dodgers on Wednesday and Thursday afternoon. Consecutive days off were expected to reinvigorate Pie Traynor's pitching staff in spite of the fact that Cy Blanton still was under a physician's care with an upset stomach and sore side. Traynor did not anticipate Cy being able to pitch in any of the four games in Brooklyn.[24]

The rain continued on September 21, forcing the Pirates to endure a third straight day of idleness. The series against Brooklyn now would be condensed to a two-game affair—if Ebbets Field could be dried out adequately for a doubleheader on September 22. Given the fact that it had been raining for three consecutive days and nights, field conditions were expected to be atrocious. It was rumored that Ebbets Field was under a foot or two of water.[25] The culprit responsible for this stretch of poor weather was a destructive hurricane packing 100-mile-an-hour winds that had been battering the New England coast. Later referred to as The Great New England hurricane, this powerful storm's path of destruction had accounted for 296 deaths by September 21 in New England, New York, New Jersey and Quebec.[26]

The storm had washed out every game involving first-division clubs since Sunday afternoon. As baseball writer Sid Feder explained, the rainouts placed the Cubs and Reds at a huge disadvantage as they tried to overtake the Pirates. Feder pointed out that the Pirates already had a lead large enough that, if they played .500 ball during their final 12 games, Chicago would have to go 10–3 to catch them.[27] Each additional cancellation would eliminate another chance to narrow the gap.

Pittsburgh finally was able to get back on a baseball diamond on Thursday, September 22 when Ebbets Field was deemed playable for a doubleheader despite three days of rain.[28] Pie Traynor's day got off to a bad start when Jeep Handley was injured before the first game even started. A flying bat, which slipped out of Jim Tobin's hands during batting practice, sailed into the Pirates dugout and struck Handley on the arm after it just missed hitting Lloyd Waner and Johnny Dickshot.[29] Jeep's left bicep muscle was so bruised and sore that he was unable to take his position at third base.

Traynor installed Bill Brubaker at the hot corner with the hope that Handley would be ready to go against Cincinnati the following day, since the injury seemed to be more painful than serious.[30]

Despite Handley's absence, Pittsburgh swept the afternoon twin bill. Jim Tobin shut out Brooklyn during the first contest and claimed a 6–0 victory. The Pirates ace scattered four hits as he improved his record to 14–9. Pep Young starred for Pittsburgh at the plate, going 3-for-4, scoring two runs and driving home two teammates. Lloyd Waner, Arky Vaughan and Al Todd contributed two hits apiece. Young also left his mark all over the afternoon's second game, going 2-for-5, scoring one run, smacking a double and recording four RBIs as he led Pittsburgh to an 11–6 victory. Arky Vaughan chipped in with four hits, three doubles and three runs batted in. The Waner brothers combined to smack four hits and score five runs. Bob Klinger pushed his record to 12–5 with relief help from Mace Brown.

Pittsburgh's two victories were critical since the Cubs swept their doubleheader with Philadelphia, enabling them to remain three-and-a-half games behind the Pirates. As Pittsburgh prepared to return for their final home series of the 1938 season against Cincinnati, support for Arky Vaughan for Most Valuable Player of the National League was growing. Vaughan's recent stellar work at the plate had pushed him to second in the league batting race with a mark of .333, six points behind Cincinnati's Ernie Lombardi. When Vaughan was informed by a reporter that he was closing in on Lombardi, the shortstop cut him off. "Don't tell me that," Vaughan responded. "All I'm interested in is winning games and winning that pennant. Hits that I make don't mean a thing unless we win the game."[31]

If the Pirates were able to manage enough wins to clinch the pennant, they would be facing Joe McCarthy's New York Yankees in the World Series in a rematch of Pittsburgh's last appearance in the Fall Classic in 1927. A potential World Series encounter between Pittsburgh and New York also offered possible vindication for one member of Pie Traynor's squad. Pitcher Jim Tobin was not a big fan of McCarthy, maintaining that his mother could manage those Yankees to an American League pennant. When a reporter asked Tobin for an explanation, he left no doubt that the matter was personal.[32]

"Because he never gave me the chance," said Tobin. "The Yanks owned me for nearly five years and never gave me a chance. Finally, they took me down to their St. Pete training camp in the spring of '37. Did I get a tryout? Yeah! I pitched a couple of times in batting practice. They didn't even take me on the exhibition trip. McCarthy tried to send me to Newark — back to

11. Pittsburgh's Final Collapse and the Homer in the Gloamin'

Pitcher Jim Tobin was purchased from the New York Yankees on April 14, 1937, after having toiled in the minor leagues for five years. Tobin was anxious to get an opportunity to pitch against New York in the 1938 World Series because he held a personal grudge against Yankees manager Joe McCarthy for not giving him a chance while he was in New York's farm system (National Baseball Hall of Fame Library, Cooperstown, New York).

the minors. Nearly five years — and that was the chance I got. If I'd belonged to any other club, I'd been up in the majors a couple years earlier. No, I didn't go to Newark. I talked the Yanks into sending me back to Oakland; my home town, in the Coast League. So, when I get to Oakland, I tell the Yanks I don't want to play anymore. I'm quittin' the game for good. They threatened to suspend me if I don't play. They couldn't scare me. So, finally they sold me to Pittsburgh."[33]

Before Tobin could be afforded the opportunity to extract his revenge against Joe McCarthy, Pittsburgh still had to complete the final ten games of the regular season. That task began on Friday, September 23 as Bill McKechnie's Cincinnati Reds came to Forbes Field for a three-game series. Prior to the first contest at Forbes Field, manager Bill McKechnie made it clear that his team hadn't given up. "Just suppose," said McKechnie, "That we start on a winning streak against the Pirates. We have seven games left with them — including the three here. Should we suddenly get hot, where would the Pirates be?"[34]

In the opener, the Reds ended Pittsburgh's four-game winning streak with a 5–4 victory in 12 innings. Bucky Walters of Cincinnati tossed a complete game and held Pittsburgh to seven hits, while Wally Berger and Ernie Lombardi each blasted a two-run homer off Cy Blanton in the sixth inning. Fireman Mace Brown saw his record drop to 15–7 when a close play in the twelfth inning secured Cincinnati's victory. With two out and Harry Craft occupying second base for the Reds, Walters lined a single to Paul Waner in right field. Waner grabbed Walters' shot on the first bounce and fired it home on a line toward catcher Al Todd. Paul's toss landed about halfway between the mound and home plate. When it struck the soft grass, the baseball seemed to die and reached Todd a fraction of a second after Craft reached home plate.[35]

Pittsburgh narrowly missed out on chances to win the game in regulation on two occasions. Johnny Rizzo just missed his twenty-first homer of the season in the sixth inning when his blistering liner hit a foot from the top of the left-center field fence and went for a double. In the eighth frame, Johnny chased Craft to deep left-center field before Cincinnati's outfielder hauled in the 460-foot drive.[36] While Pittsburgh was dropping their contest against Cincinnati, Chicago was sweeping a doubleheader against Philadelphia at Shibe Park. Benswanger's strategy of preventing the Cubs from playing a twin bill against Brooklyn on September 23 may have backfired since the rules allowed Chicago to play two postponed games with the last-place Phillies because it was the continuation of a series already in progress. Pie Traynor believed Chicago was entitled to play every scheduled game that remained during the season's final week. "We want to play every day down to the finish, and we hope Chicago gets the same dose," said Traynor.[37]

While many baseball scribes proclaimed that washed-out games were floating the Pittsburgh Pirates to a National League pennant, Benswanger was not happy with the numerous postponements that had left his team idle for most of the present week. Even though he had tried to hinder Chicago's effort to play a few postponed games, the team president echoed Traynor's sentiment when the Pirates experienced their short layoff in the East. "I would rather that our team was playing than loafing," said Benswanger. "If we don't play, we can't win the games we should be winning to make sure of the pennant and likewise give the Yankees a good battle in the World's Series."[38]

No matter which team represented the National League in the upcoming World Series, they would be playing the New York Yankees, who had clinched a third consecutive American League crown. Yankees owner Colonel Jacob Ruppert acknowledged having received a congratulatory telegram from Benswanger after his team secured the pennant. Ruppert also expressed his desire to see Pittsburgh win the National League title and oppose his team in the Fall Classic.[39] The Pirates moved one step closer to doing so with a 4–1 victory over Cincinnati on Saturday, September 24. Their latest victory was their fifth in the last six games, and the sixth in their past eight contests.[40] Russ Bauers improved his record to 12–13 by tossing a complete game six-hitter.

The Pirates scored all the runs they needed in the second inning when they batted around against Johnny Vander Meer. Arky Vaughan started out the frame by working out a walk and then Gus Suhr beat out a hot grounder to Reds shortstop Nolen Richardson. Vander Meer recorded the inning's first out when Suhr was forced at second base on Pep Young's grounder to Richardson even though Billy Myers initially dropped the throw. Jeep Handley stepped to the plate and rattled a sharp single to shallow right field, scoring Vaughan.[41] Al Todd drilled a single to center field that scored Young and moved Handley over to third base. Russ Bauers followed with a fly ball to Wally Berger in short left field. Handley made a mad dash for the plate and scored when Berger's throw hit him in the back. After Lloyd Waner walked and Paul Waner reached on an error by Richardson to load the bases, Vander Meer finally ended the inning by getting Johnny Rizzo to lift a high fly behind second base.[42]

Even though Rizzo failed to keep that stanza going, he did smack one of the longest triples ever seen at Forbes Field in the seventh inning when his towering drive struck the top of Forbes Field's left-center field fence and bounded back onto the field. Rizzo's two outfield mates made the day's fielding gems: Lloyd made a sensational shoestring catch on Lew Riggs' drive in the fourth inning and then doubled Ernie Lombardi off first, while Paul matched his brother's great play by snagging Berger's drive off his shoetops near the right-field line in the eighth frame.[43]

Chicago kept pace with Pittsburgh by defeating the St. Louis Cardinals, 9–3. The Pirates' chances in their final home game of the season on Sunday, September 25 looked good since Red Lucas had been tabbed by manager Pie Traynor to pitch. Lucas owned a thirteen-game winning streak over his former team and had never been beaten by Cincinnati since joining Pittsburgh in 1934. The veteran was making his first start in over a month after being away from the team for ten days to tend to his sick wife.[44] The crowd of 27,147 that gave the Pirates a rousing send-off before their final road trip of the season was treated to a grand home finale as Lucas defeated Cincinnati, 5–3. This large crowd pushed Pittsburgh's aggregate attendance at home to almost 700,000 in 1938, which was not a bad figure considering so many people were out of work.[45]

Pittsburgh cruised to a 5–1 lead through eight innings before Lucas gave way to Bill Swift in the ninth frame. The Pirates' offensive barrage was spearheaded by Arky Vaughan's home run, Al Todd's triple and Jeep Handley's three hits, which included a double.[46] While the Pirates were wrapping up their home slate at Forbes Field, Chicago defeated St. Louis at Wrigley Field, 7–2. Even though the Pirates had gone 8–2 in their past ten games, Chicago had gained a half-game in the standings by posting an 8–1 record over that same time period. Pittsburgh's victory over Cincinnati gave the team a final record of 44–33 at Forbes Field in 1938. While their record at home was quite satisfactory, the Pirates were even better on the road with a mark of 41–25. Their season now rested on series in Chicago and Cincinnati.

As the team boarded its Chicago-bound train at Pennsylvania Station, Pie Traynor was informed that the Pittsburgh Chamber of Commerce planned a huge celebration for his team when they returned to Pittsburgh in another week. The Chamber, having already conceded the National League pennant to the Pirates, announced that a victory breakfast of ham and eggs would be held at 8:00 a.m. on Monday, October 3, to celebrate this achievement. Smoky City baseball fans with good memories harkened

11. Pittsburgh's Final Collapse and the Homer in the Gloamin' 197

Prior to being chosen by manager Pie Traynor to hurl the final home game of the season on September 25, 1938, veteran pitcher Red Lucas had won 13 consecutive games against the Cincinnati Reds. Lucas made it 14 in a row when he defeated his former team, 5–3, as Pittsburgh finished their home slate with a record of 44–33 at Forbes Field (National Baseball Hall of Fame Library, Cooperstown, New York).

back to another year that the Chamber had made a similar announcement when the pennant seemed to be guaranteed, only to see the Pirates blow their lead. Traynor and one of his players were aghast when the information about this breakfast was presented to them. "Omigosh!" moaned Traynor as he fell into his train berth. "That settles our hash," commented another Pirate.[47]

While Traynor was a superstitious sort who did not like to change his daily routine when his team was in the midst of a winning streak, he still adamantly believed that the Pirates would claim the National League pennant despite the Pittsburgh Chamber of Commerce's ill-timed announcement. Pie planned on going with pitching aces Jim Tobin, Bob Klinger and Russ Bauers in the crucial three-game series against Chicago. Pittsburgh's manager did not seem to care who Gabby Hartnett countered with to pitch against his squad. Pie could not see any Cubs hurler having more on the ball than Cincinnati's Paul Derringer had when Pittsburgh's players hit him hard the previous game. Traynor also was confident he would not be seeing top pitchers Bill Lee and Clay Bryant, who were used as starters by Hartnett in the series against St. Louis.[48]

Traynor listened to the game between Chicago and St. Louis on Monday, September 26 as Pittsburgh waited to open their crucial series against the Cubs on Tuesday.[49] Star hurler Bill Lee pulled his team within one-and-a-half games of the first-place Pirates by defeating St. Louis, 6–3. A few days prior to the final meeting between these top two teams, Gabby Hartnett had opened himself up to a lot of scrutiny and second-guessing by claiming that his team would take care of everything, including the pennant, when this series commenced at Wrigley Field.[50] Hartnett selected Dizzy Dean, who had gone 6–1 in limited pitching duty, to go against Pittsburgh's Jim Tobin on September 27.

It was evident during the early stages of this game that Dean had absolutely nothing on the baseball. Yet the veteran pitcher got by on nerve and junk pitches and held the Pirates at bay all afternoon. Dizzy threw only one or two fastballs all game but his slow offerings bewildered the Pirates. Dean's gutsy performance and some timely hitting by his teammates gave the Cubs a 2–1 victory and earned them their eighth consecutive win and an 18–3 record in their past 21 games. Chicago scored single runs off Tobin, who pitched gallantly for Traynor, in the third and sixth innings. Dean was masterful in the clutch as Pittsburgh pushed runners over to third base on three different occasions, but failed to bring any of those runners home.[51]

Pittsburgh finally got something going in the ninth inning when Arky

Vaughan was struck by a Dean pitch to get things started. Dean seemed to be headed toward pitching a complete game when he retired Gus Suhr on a popup to Billy Herman at second and pinch hitter Woody Jensen forced Vaughan at second. Jeep Handley kept Pittsburgh's hopes alive when he slashed a double that moved Jensen over to third. Hartnett decided to make a switch to Bill Lee, who had warmed up on several occasions during the past few innings. As Dean walked from the mound, tears started to stream down his cheeks as the crowd of 42,238 fans at Wrigley Field gave the veteran hurler an inspiring ovation. Dean stopped en route to the dugout long enough for photographers to snap some pictures of the afternoon's hero. Lee took the hill and ran the count to 0-2 on Al Todd before uncorking a wild pitch that allowed Jensen to scamper home with Pittsburgh's first run and moved Handley over to third. Pittsburgh's rally ended there as Lee regained his composure and struck out Todd.[52]

Chicago's huge victory knocked Pittsburgh's National League lead down to a half game. The Cubs had been able to pull out a tight victory even though numerous good luck charms were in attendance to root for the Buccaneers. Batboy Porky Cohen had driven to Chicago on Monday to lend his moral support, while Socko McCarey and former Pittsburgher Lew Wentz, who currently was an Oklahoma oil operator, also were on hand to cheer for the Pirates.[53]

One person who was not in Chicago watching Pittsburgh battle for the National League pennant was Pirates owner Florence Dreyfuss. Even though Mrs. Dreyfuss was not rooting for her beloved Pirates in person, she did attempt to keep track of the latest game by listening on the radio. After Chicago took a 1–0 lead, she turned the radio off and did other things in an effort to divert her attention from the game. When sportswriter Claire M. Burcky of *The Pittsburgh Press* called on the National League's only female baseball magnate at her home at 5:30 p.m., the radio was still turned off. Burcky and Mrs. Dreyfuss listened to the remainder of the game together as Pittsburgh's rally came up short in the ninth inning. Remembering that Pie Traynor had been confident that Pittsburgh would take two out of three in Chicago before the team left Pittsburgh, Mrs. Dreyfuss pondered the possibility that a World Series appearance might not happen. "Oh, it would be terrible if they lose now," she said. "They've led so long, and we've done so much work getting ready for the World Series. It's hard to lead for such a long time, you know. It's better to come up from second or third. It would be a dreadful disappointment now if they were beaten out. But if they are, I guess I'll just have to be disappointed. If we hadn't lost those easy games to Philadelphia — but I guess that's baseball."⁵⁴

Mrs. Dreyfuss readily admitted that she had been very nervous during the past few days. If the Pirates did make it to the World Series, she planned on attending the championship games. Mrs. Dreyfuss never missed a home game at Forbes Field and first had fallen in love with the Pirates when she used to take her little son and daughter on a streetcar over to Allegheny for games when they were played at Exposition Park. In respect to recent rumors regarding the Pittsburgh franchise being put up for sale, Mrs. Dreyfuss claimed she knew nothing about it and was not aware of how the false story got started.⁵⁵

Mrs. Dreyfuss and thousands of diehard baseball fans from the Smoky City prepared to root their Pirates to a National League pennant once again as Pittsburgh opposed Chicago on Wednesday, September 28. Pie Traynor selected Bob Klinger to pitch for Pittsburgh, while Gabby Hartnett chose Clay Bryant, who was making his second start in the past three days. Pittsburgh looked like a tight baseball team that was hanging on to prevent one of the most monumental collapses in baseball history as 34,500 screaming fans at Wrigley Field cheered on their Chicago Cubs. Four Pirates — Paul Waner, Arky Vaughan, Al Todd and Jeep Handley — committed errors. Todd and Handley's mistakes were the most costly as they led to Chicago scoring an unearned run in the second inning. After Carl Reynolds fanned and Hartnett flied out to Paul Waner in right field, Rip Collins singled. It looked as though Klinger had ended the inning when he also struck out Billy Jurges, but the ball popped out of Todd's glove and allowed the batter to reach first base, while Collins advanced to second. Pittsburgh still looked to be in good shape when Bryant hit a grounder to Handley down at the hot corner. Unfortunately, Handley uncorked a wild throw that soared over Suhr's head and allowed Collins to score Chicago's first run.⁵⁶

The score remained 1–0 until Pittsburgh pushed three runs across the plate in the sixth inning and chased Bryant from the mound. Pirates slugger Johnny Rizzo was right in the middle of this uprising as he connected for his twenty-first home run of the season. Klinger did not hold the lead very long as Chicago countered with two runs in the bottom half of the frame. Pittsburgh mounted a rally in the seventh inning, only to have it come to nothing as the result of a controversial umpiring decision. Lloyd Waner connected for a one-out single against Chicago's Vance Page and his brother followed with another single that moved the speedy Lloyd over to third. Rizzo stepped to the plate with a chance to drive home the go-ahead run. Page worked the count to two balls and one strike before committing what

11. Pittsburgh's Final Collapse and the Homer in the Gloamin'

the Pirates considered to be an obvious balk.[57]

Third base coach Jewel Ens immediately noticed the illegal motion and shouted to Rizzo at home plate to let Page's pitch go by. Over in the first-base coaching box, Pie Traynor saw umpire Dolly Stark rush past first baseman Rip Collins with his hand upraised, indicating that he was ready to call the balk. Unfortunately, Rizzo did not heed Ens' advice as he swung at the pitch and grounded into a double play. After the twin killing was completed, Stark returned to his station near first base and acted as though nothing had happened. Even though four umpires were on the field for this vital contest, none of the arbiters were willing to make the balk call. Traynor immediately protested to Stark while Ens pleaded his case with home plate umpire George Barr. At one point, 20 Pirates were on the field trying to get any umpire to see things their way. Even the fans in attendance at Wrigley Field seemed to know that it was a balk because many of them groaned when Page made the illegal move.[58]

If Stark had followed through with his original intention and called Page's pitch a balk, Lloyd Waner would have scored, while Paul Waner would have been stationed at second with Rizzo still batting and one out. As it was, Pittsburgh's inning ended without any runs. In the press box, National League president Ford Frick was asked his opinion of the play and he claimed that he did not see a balk. He could hardly have said otherwise, since second-guessing them would have been unseemly. Ens was not willing to be so kind as he vehemently protested the umpires' negligence in failing to call a balk.[59] "The president of the league sends us quantity in umpires but no quality," he declared angrily. "You can bet Bill Klem would have called it. Why even some of the Cubs knew it and they were afraid Page was going to be called on it."[60]

Pie Traynor's players remained focused even though they believed that the umpires had given them a raw deal. They chased Page from the game in the eighth inning and added two runs before Bill Lee recorded the last out. Pittsburgh's lead was short-lived once again, as Klinger and Bill Swift each allowed one run in the bottom of the eighth inning before Fireman Mace Brown ended Chicago's threat. Pittsburgh was retired quietly in the ninth frame as veteran hurler Charlie Root only gave up one harmless hit. As semi-darkness enveloped Wrigley Field, Brown took the mound hoping to retire Chicago in order during the bottom of the ninth frame. Brown easily retired Phil Cavarretta and Carl Reynolds before Gabby Hartnett stepped to the plate. If Fireman Brown were able to retire Hartnett, the game would probably end at that point since the umpires likely would call the contest due to darkness. Such a scenario was acceptable to Pittsburgh since a doubleheader the following day would be tough for Chicago's decimated pitching staff.[61]

Before Brown tossed the first pitch to Gabby, he pulled his cap down, hitched his belt and wound up. He threw a curve ball that Hartnett took for strike one. On the next pitch, Mace tossed another curve that was low and outside. As Gabby swung at this pitch and missed, the crowd moaned, sensing that the inning was about to end. Brown wound up one final time and threw a third consecutive curve ball but this one stayed up in the zone and split the heart of the plate. Hartnett swung with all his might and sent the ball soaring to deep left field. Pirates left fielder Johnny Rizzo could only watch helplessly as Hartnett's blast dropped into a maze of hands in the left-field bleachers.[62]

Bedlam immediately broke loose as Cubs fans celebrated Hartnett's "Homer in the Gloamin" that had given their team a 6–5 victory. Newspapers, score cards, straw hats, felt hats and women's hats sailed onto the playing field as jubilant fans celebrated one of the most dramatic moments in baseball history. Many fans rushed onto the darkening field to greet Hartnett when he reached home plate. His teammates dashed to the plate first and used a flying wedge football formation to rescue their manager from the crowd and carry him away on their shoulders as soon as his foot touched the dish. On the mound, Mace Brown brushed his hand over his eyes and walked through the shadows to Pittsburgh's clubhouse. Pittsburgh's infielders and outfielders remained glued to the field for a few minutes, too stunned or shocked to move. In the Cubs locker room, players hugged and kissed Hartnett. An hour and a half after hitting his monumental home run, Hartnett finally peeled off his uniform and talked to the press. "That was the greatest thrill of my life," he announced. "I figured Brown for a curve on that 2–0 pitch and I got set. I sort of felt it was a home run when I hit it. The ball 'felt' good and I just gambled on a home run or nothing."[63]

The mood was somber and reserved in Pittsburgh's clubhouse. Pie Traynor's players were having a tough time coming to grips with the reality they no longer occupied first place. Pittsburgh had held down the National League's top spot continuously for 11 weeks since moving ahead of New York on July 12.[64] When someone in the locker room went up to Bob Klinger to congratulate him on pitching a fine game, the rookie hurler gruffly asked what was nice about it since the Pirates had lost. Pie Traynor and Jewel Ens sat in front of their lockers, chins on their chests, trying to recreate the game's dreadful details in their mind. After a few minutes, Traynor forced

11. Pittsburgh's Final Collapse and the Homer in the Gloamin'

a smile and asked for a cigarette. Mace Brown sat motionless, unable to get over the shock of watching Hartnett possibly yank the pennant right from his team's grasp. Brown finally broke his silence by standing up, tossing his sweatshirt into a corner and trampling on it. "Had him in the hole, too," he moaned. "Two strikes, no balls. Why couldn't that curve ball break for me instead of him?"[65]

Paul Waner stayed with Brown all night in an effort to console him and to make sure that he did not do anything drastic in his despair.[66] Bill Benswanger had actually collapsed and passed out in his box seat when Hartnett hit the homer.[67] Back in Pittsburgh, diehard baseball fans were having a difficult time dealing with the Pirates' defeat. Kaspar Monahan, a drama critic for *The Pittsburgh Press,* started for the kitchen and accidentally walked into a clothes closet after listening to the deciding home run on his radio. An Edgewood housewife reported that her 13-year-old son had been listening to the game in the living room when the calamity occurred. When the boy informed her that he was not hungry for dinner and was going to his room to do homework instead of eating, she knew something was wrong. The worst case of withdrawal occurred in Carrick, where a father threw his radio out the window after Hartnett hit the homer and pinched his 11-year-old son until he cried. The man then told his wife that he would never work again and proceeded to walk out of the house.[68]

Even though it was bright and sunny in Pittsburgh on September 29, the day was black as night to devoted Pirates fans who now realized that the trip to the World Series that had seemed guaranteed only days ago was now in jeopardy. In addition to the disappointment for everyone connected with the fortunes of Pittsburgh's baseball squad, Pirates management stood to lose a lot of money if Chicago beat them out for the pennant. The front office had spent nearly $30,000 to construct a new press box at Forbes Field, while shelling out an additional $5,000 for the construction of temporary bleachers. Several more thousands of dollars had been spent on such incidentals as clerical help in handling World Series ticket applications, painting, ground repair, maintenance and additional preparations. The Pirates would have spent $40,000 in vain if they could not cop the National League flag.[69]

Although the Pirates were still mathematically in the hunt to claim a pennant, Gabby Hartnett's extraordinary feat the previous afternoon had left them devastated, demoralized and unable to mount any kind of counterattack. Chicago made it a three-game sweep on Thursday, September 29 by decimating the Pirates, 10–1. Bill Lee was brilliant as he pitched for the fourth consecutive day and tossed a complete game. A crowd of 42,628 ecstatic fans watched the Cubs claim their tenth straight victory and twentieth out of the past 23 contests, thereby increasing their National League lead over Pittsburgh to one-and-a-half games. Lee got all the runs he needed in the first inning when his teammates sent Pirates starter Russ Bauers to an early shower by scoring three runs on a hit, three walks and a sacrifice. The Cubs continued their assault against Ed Brandt, Cy Blanton and Mace Brown. Hero Gabby Hartnett was injured in the ninth frame when a foul tip off the bat of Johnny Rizzo struck him on the third finger of his right hand.[70]

Prior to the final game against Chicago, Benswanger gave Traynor a pep talk and told him that he would be back as Pittsburgh's manager in 1939 regardless of the season's final outcome. Benswanger also informed Pie that he could write his own terms into the contract.[71] Despite Benswanger's words of encouragement, things did not get much better for Traynor's troops when they arrived in Cincinnati for the final series of the season. Pittsburgh was shellacked for the second day in a row as the Reds won the first game of a doubleheader on Friday, September 30, by a score of 7–1. Paul Derringer picked up his twenty-first victory of the season as his teammates assaulted pitchers Jim Tobin, Bill Swift and Mace Brown for 12 hits. Cincinnati's cause was also aided by home runs from Wally Berger and Ernie Lombardi.[72] Pittsburgh's Russ Bauers finally stopped the bleeding during the afternoon's second game as he tossed a complete game and claimed a 4–2 victory that improved his record to 13–14.

The big Wisconsin lad possessed control, speed, curves, poise, and had so much confidence that he belted a triple and a double during his final two trips to the plate. A single, an infield out and another single gave Cincinnati a run in the second inning. Heading into the eighth frame, Bauers still had only allowed those two hits.[73] Pittsburgh broke a 1–1 deadlock in the fourth inning when Arky Vaughan drilled his seventh home run of the season. Vaughan scored again in the sixth frame when he walked, reached third after Gus Suhr rapped out his third straight hit by banging a single, and then scored on Billy Myers' error. The Pirates scored their final run in the seventh inning on Bauers' triple and Lloyd Waner's fly ball.[74] Second baseman Pep Young, who had been suffering from spike wounds on both his legs, rested during the second game and was replaced by Tommy Thevenow.[75]

Pittsburgh did not gain or lose any ground due to their doubleheader split with Cincinnati since the game between Chicago and St. Louis at Sportsman's Park was declared a 7–7 tie by umpires, making it necessary

11. Pittsburgh's Final Collapse and the Homer in the Gloamin'   205

for the two teams to play a doubleheader on Saturday, October 1.[76] Pie Traynor called on Reds-killer Red Lucas to oppose Cincinnati's Bucky Walters on the same day as Chicago's double tango with St. Louis. The Pirates still had a slim chance of capturing the National League pennant if they could win their remaining two games and Chicago lost two out of three against the Cardinals. If this occurred, the Pirates would win the flag by one mere percentage point, .587 to .586.[77]

The Pirates did plenty of scoreboard watching during their Saturday afternoon game at Crosley Field and their hopes were buoyed when St. Louis defeated Chicago, 4–3 in the first game of their doubleheader. Optimism did not prevail very long in Pittsburgh's dugout, however, as Bill McKechnie exercised a demon of sorts with a 9–6 victory. When the Cubs claimed the second game of their doubleheader against St. Louis by a score of 10–3, Pittsburgh's pennant hopes officially died and Chicago claimed the National League flag. Winning the game that knocked Pittsburgh out of the race was sweet vindication for McKechnie, who had been fired as the Pirates skipper 12 years ago after team dissension derailed a pennant repeat in 1926. Pitcher Jim Weaver also extracted some revenge against his former teammates as he was credited with the victory. Fireman Mace Brown could not hold a 5–4 lead after entering the fray in the fourth inning and watched his record drop to 15–9.[78]

In an odd coincidence, October 1 was the 11-year anniversary of Pittsburgh clinching the National League pennant in Cincinnati when Pie Traynor singled home the winning run.[79] While Traynor's heroics in 1927 had allowed the Pirates to face the Yankees in that World Series, there would be no rematch in 1938. Pie's troops finished up the 1938 campaign with a meaningless game against Cincinnati on Sunday, October 2. The Reds threw even more dirt on the corpse as McKechnie's boys prevailed in the finale, 5–4. Jim Tobin went the route for Pittsburgh and saw his record drop to 14–12 as Cincinnati's Wally Berger was destructive at the plate, going 3-for-4 with a home run. Berger's round-tripper over the left-field wall in the eighth inning settled the outcome by breaking a 4–4 tie. Johnny Rizzo was an absolute beast for Pittsburgh as he rapped out two singles, a double, and blasted his twenty-third home run of the season. Johnny also knocked in the Pirates' first three runs.[80]

Rizzo's great hitting surge during the season's final two days helped push his average over the .300 mark. He antagonized Cincinnati's pitchers to the tune of two singles, a double, a triple and two home runs on Saturday and Sunday. He also set an all-time team record for home runs in a season with 23 while driving in 111 runs, more than 25 ahead of his nearest teammate. Rizzo finished the season fifth in the National League in home runs and third in RBIs.[81] Pittsburgh's 1–6 record during the final road trip, combined with the Cubs' extraordinary hot streak, had sealed the team's fate. Final National League standings showed that Chicago finished the season with a record of 89–63, while Pittsburgh stood two games back at 86–64.

Possibly just as disturbing as choking during the season's final week was the fact that crucial games on the schedule were never played due to postponements: Pittsburgh only played 150 games, while Chicago participated in 152. Two of Pittsburgh's canceled contests were against the last-place Phillies. However, the Pirates only went 12–8 against Philadelphia in 1938, so there was no guarantee that those two games would have gone into the win column if they had been played. When breaking down the statistics, the pennant basically was lost because Pittsburgh went 10–12 against Chicago and posted a 12–10 record over a Cincinnati squad they had thoroughly dominated in 1937.

There was no welcoming party nor any victory celebration awaiting the Pirates when they returned to the Smoky City after one of the most disappointing road trips in club history. Pittsburgh's players were a downtrodden lot following the shocking events in Chicago.[82] When the Pirates had left Pittsburgh to journey west a week earlier, baseball fans throughout the city were talking about the upcoming World Series against New York. After the season ended on October 2, these same rooters were shaking their heads in despair, wondering what had happened. In 1927, a batting practice home run show by the New York Yankees supposedly had inflicted psychological damage on the Pirates before they were swept in that World Series. In 1938, it was a home run by Chicago's Gabby Hartnett that left the Pirates distraught and deprived them of the opportunity to oppose New York in the Fall Classic.

Veteran sportswriter Charles "Chilly" Doyle did not let the setbacks which plagued Pittsburgh during the season's final week deter him from going about the business of covering these Pirates for the *Pittsburgh-Sun Telegraph*. Through it all, Chilly still laughed and joked with those around him in the press box. There was no sense getting worked up since such things sometimes happened in baseball. "That's life," remarked Doyle. "Guess it just wasn't Pittsburgh's year."[83]

12

Disastrous Season and a Second-Division Finish in 1939

As the Pirates players started to disperse about the country, Pittsburgh's Chamber of Commerce officially announced that there would be no celebratory breakfast honoring the team. The Chamber acknowledged that a serious mistake had been made by prematurely inviting the Pirates to a pennant celebration.[1] After the team's final game on October 2, some players left directly for their homes in towns like Elmira, New York, and Allenton, Missouri. A train carrying the remainder — Paul Waner, Mace Brown, Cy Blanton, Arky Vaughan, Jim Tobin, Bill Brubaker, Johnny Gooch, Pie Traynor, Honus Wagner, Gus Suhr, Lee Handley, Lloyd Waner, Johnny Rizzo, Bill Swift, Rip Sewell and Joe Bowman — arrived in Pittsburgh on the evening of October 3. These men came back the Steel City to pack up family and personal belongings before embarking to their homes for a long, rough winter.[2]

Many Pittsburgh businessmen had reason to feel especially downcast over the fact that there would be no World Series appearance in 1938. The head of a chain store system in the Smoky City who had counted on Pittsburgh opposing New York in the World Series was stuck holding 50,000 live turtles with the names of Pirate players printed on their shells. The concessionaire at Forbes Field found himself with 100,000 hot dogs on hand which he had purchased in anticipation of the World Series. A large downtown store had bought 75,000 postcard photos of Pittsburgh's players that it now could not sell. The Pirates organization also took a huge financial hit as they had to return $3 million in checks for World Series tickets while also spending an additional $6,000 for postage and clerical assistance.[3] The Pittsburgh Base Ball Writers of America Chapter, which had paid to have 750 World Series press buttons made, sent them to baseball scribes throughout the country despite the Pirates' final failure.[4]

Had Pittsburgh hung on and claimed the National League pennant, manager Pie Traynor likely would have received dozens of telegrams offering congratulations and wishes of good luck in the upcoming World Series. When the Pirates were mathematically eliminated on October 1, Traynor only received one telegram offering condolences. The correspondence came from New York Giants manager Bill Terry, who weeks earlier had said the Pirates should quit playing baseball if they did not win the 1938 pennant. When that indeed happened, Terry proved himself to be a true sportsman by congratulating Traynor for having a successful season in spite of how the final week played out. "Naturally, you would have received hundreds of wires had you won," wrote Terry in his telegram. "But not from me because I think I should win every year. I have been through what you are going through now. I think you did a great job. Regards. Bill Terry."[5]

While Terry's initial comments weeks ago about the Pirates had been met with much resentment by Pittsburgh players and fans, this message of sympathy seemed to soothe some of the ill feelings toward New York's manager.[6] Pittsburgh's management team was particularly touched by Terry's remarks following the turbulent final days of the 1938 campaign, during which Traynor had lost ten pounds.[7] "That's one of the nicest things that ever happened to me," Traynor declared. "That's very big of Terry," added Bill Benswanger after he read Bill's wire. "I heartily agree with that last sentence. I think you did a great job."[8]

Traynor also showed good sportsmanship and his total dedication to helping even a National League rival against New York in the upcoming World Series. When it had seemed apparent that Pittsburgh would play the Yankees in the Fall Classic, Traynor sent Joe Schultz, Sr. to scout Joe McCarthy's powerhouse unit. Pie decided to turn over Schultz's notes to Chicago's Gabby Hartnett on the eve of the series. Ford Frick, Schultz and Hartnett also held a meeting before Game One to assimilate the entire information.[9] Traynor's act was honorable considering that the Pirates were afforded one final indignity by Chicago's players the day before the Series opener. When Chicago had met the Corsairs during that climactic series at Wrigley Field, Hartnett's troops supposedly lulled Pittsburgh's players into believing they had the pennant all wrapped up.[10] Various members of the Cubs had asked Traynor's players to autograph a dozen baseballs inscribed with "National League Champions—1938," as personal keepsakes.[11] During

12. Disastrous Season and a Second-Division Finish in 1939

batting practice on October 4, Chicago's players hammered those autographed baseballs all over Wrigley Field.[12]

Scouting reports and special baseballs proved to be of no help to Chicago in the 1938 World Series. The Yankees pulled off a four-game sweep and claimed their third consecutive world championship as Chicago's late-season magic finally ended. Once the Fall Classic was over, shock and disappointment over the Pirates' monumental collapse slowly began to wane. As Pittsburgh's loyal rooters composed themselves once again, some started to take a more analytical approach.

One glaring difference between Pittsburgh and Chicago that became evident to those dissecting season statistics surrounded the two squads' pitching staffs. While Chicago's Gabby Hartnett had two hammers at the top of the rotation in Bill Lee (22–9, 2.66 ERA) and Clay Bryant (19–11, 3.10 ERA), Pie Traynor had been without a true ace. Traynor had envisioned Russ Bauers as his big gun, but the youngster needed a late-season surge to compile a mediocre 13–14 record, supported by a 3.07 ERA. The remainder of Pie's rotation was a bit enigmatic as Jim Tobin (14–12, 3.47 ERA), Bob Klinger (12–5, 2.99 ERA) and Cy Blanton (11–7, 3.70 ERA) had both good and bad moments. Traynor was left to lament over what Klinger might have accomplished during his rookie campaign if he had not been plagued by arm problems throughout most of the 1938 season.

Fireman Mace Brown was Traynor's top winner with a 15–9 record, coupled with an ERA of 3.80. Brown's season was a bit of a mixed bag, however, as he was absolutely brilliant before the All-Star break but seemed to run out of gas during the stretch drive. Mace went 3–7 during the season's final two-and-a-half months, while his ERA shot up from 3.18 on July 11 to its final mark. While the Cubs definitely had an advantage over Pittsburgh in pitching, Traynor's squad edged out Hartnett's troops in the batting department. The big story in Pittsburgh regarding work at the plate revolved around Johnny Rizzo's splendid rookie campaign. Rizzo had company in the .300 circle as Arky Vaughan led the Pirates in hitting with a .322 average, while Lloyd Waner was close behind at .313. The other starters, Gus Suhr (.294), Paul Waner (.280), Pep Young (.278), Jeep Handley (.268) and Al Todd (.265) did solid work at the plate. Heinie Manush also supplied Traynor with the pinch-hitting pop that had been lacking for much of the season, batting .308 while appearing in 15 September games.

Paul Waner's failure to reach the .300 mark for the first time during his 13 major league seasons was the result of a horrible batting slump in

April and May. What many Pirates fans did not know was that Traynor had asked Paul to curtail his drinking escapades when the Pirates got off to a blazing start. Traynor reasoned that Paul would be more valuable to the team sober as they battled to claim a National League pennant. Instead the outfielder's average began to plummet and Traynor eventually took him out for a drink to try to get him turned around. The results suggest that alcohol, which usually ruined the careers of baseball players, actually was of benefit to Paul Waner.[13] Some fans pondered whether things could have been different if Waner had been hitting with his usual vigor in May when Pittsburgh posted a 9–15 record.

While there may have been fans who were willing to use underachievers like Paul Waner as scapegoats for the team's failure to win a National League title, Arky Vaughan was not subjected to such scrutiny. Vaughan, who had been solid in all phases of the game for Pittsburgh in 1938, finished third in the voting for the National League's Most Valuable Player Award. Cincinnati's Ernie Lombardi walked away with the hardware with 229 points, while Chicago's Bill Lee finished second with 166 points and Vaughan tallied 163 points. Rookie outfielder Johnny Rizzo finished in sixth place with 96 points.[14] Rizzo and teammate Bob Klinger were also named to *The Sporting News*' 1938 All-Rookie Team.[15]

One day after the November 1 announcement that Lombardi had been named the league's Most Valuable Player, Pirates beat writer Lester Biederman of *The Pittsburgh Press* broke a major story about Arky Vaughan:

> You can label 1938 as the year of the biggest disappointment for Vaughan. He wanted to make it his biggest season and if there was one Pirate who hustled and gave everything, it was Vaughan.
>
> Arky had been called on the carpet several times by the front office and once or twice early this spring because — it was charged — he wasn't hustling. He didn't sign his 1938 contract until he arrived at spring training camp and when he talked matters over with President Bill Benswanger at that time, he was told he'd have to show more hustle.
>
> Vaughan is a peculiar player. He's quiet and doesn't show off, but goes about his work in his own way. You don't hear him shouting and yammering out there at shortstop but there isn't a pitcher on the team who would trade him for any other shortstop in either league.
>
> Arky was a little hurt at the insinuation that he didn't hustle. So he dedicated the 1938 season to the idea that he'd show his bosses a thing or two. Never known as a "pop-off" guy, he got into arguments galore this year. His fielding was spectacular all season long. Vaughan teamed up with Pep Young to land the Pirates the double play championship of the league. His batting was steady and he finished third, behind Lombardi and Mize.
>
> I remember one game in St. Louis this summer when I rode out to the ball-

12. Disastrous Season and a Second-Division Finish in 1939

park with Vaughan in a cab. Arky collected four hits that afternoon, but the Pirates lost the game.

Next day I told Vaughan he'd better ride out to the park with me again, because he got four hits the day before and the superstition might work that afternoon. He refused.

"We lost, didn't we? I'm going in a cab by myself," Vaughan replied.

Vaughan gave everything he had in an effort to swing the pennant to the Pirates. He wanted to be a member of a pennant-winning team before his career came to an end and he figured this was the year. He didn't especially care about leading the league in batting, except that if he could help the team to the pennant by doing so, that was okay with him.

On the day the Pirates finally lost the pennant, when they dropped that Saturday game to the Reds as the Cubs beat the Cards, Vaughan was the picture of dejection. His dream had gone."[16]

It was now time for the front office to begin making changes to the Pirates roster in preparation for the 1939 campaign. One thing that wouldn't change was the manager: a few weeks after the season concluded, Benswanger received Pie Traynor's 1939 signed contract in the mail. A significant salary increase was Pie's reward for almost leading Pittsburgh to the National League pennant in 1938. After doing some hunting in the Wisconsin woods with Burleigh Grimes and spending time at his home in Brookville, Indiana, Traynor had put the heartbreak of the 1938 campaign behind him. The receipt of this document was deemed a formality by Benswanger, who had told Traynor during the final series in Cincinnati that he would be back as Pittsburgh's manager in 1939. "We are more than satisfied with Pie's direction of the team," Benswanger said, "and do not blame him in the slightest for the loss of the pennant."[17]

It was believed that Traynor's salary had been bumped up to around $18,000 for the 1939 season, although Pittsburgh's front office did not release the contract details as per team policy.[18] With Traynor now in the fold for another year, attention turned to the roster. Partway through the 1938 season, Traynor had been convinced that it was time for a rebuilding project. Then the club had begun winning and the plans had changed, but nevertheless Traynor was not in control of a team with young talent whose better days were ahead. What would he decide to do?

Prior to the minor league meetings in New Orleans, Traynor and Benswanger held a conference together in Pittsburgh to map out strategy for addressing the team's most glaring needs. Traynor then expressed confidence that they had identified Pittsburgh's shortcomings and had a plan in place to put the Pirates one step closer to a National League pennant.[19] "I know that the fans here won't support the same team that faded in 1938 and

I'm going to do everything possible to remedy the situation," Traynor declared. "Our biggest need right now is a slugging outfielder and two pitchers. There are several fellows on the team who appear to be through in Pittsburgh and we will try to supply the new faces. A change would be better for all concerned. A couple of our pitchers went 'blooie' in the final weeks. I don't think they'll be back. I think our infield is in good shape. In fact, name me a team that has a better trio than Young, Vaughan and Handley? And speaking of first basemen, the National League hasn't had a standout first-sacker since Bill Terry quit playing. There are first basemen who are good, but none who can approach Terry. I'd like to add another catcher. We could have used a third backstop during that stretch drive and resting Al Todd more would have helped us. But we had no real replacements we could have banked on. We have several deals on the fire but none of them that we can mention at this time. They'll probably be completed or turned down at the minor league meeting in December at New Orleans. We're prepared to spend a little money and trade some of our talent to strengthen this club. But after all, we're not as bad off as some of these other clubs."[20]

The Pirates were represented in New Orleans by Traynor, Benswanger, vice-president Sam Watters, coach Jewel Ens and farm director Joe Schultz, Sr.[21] During their stay, the team was linked to many trade rumors, with the most credible one having Pittsburgh as the frontrunner to acquire 19-year-old Pacific Coast League sensation Fred Hutchinson from the Seattle Rainiers.[22]

In the end, however, Seattle president Emil Sick decided to deal Hutchinson to the Detroit Tigers. An angry Traynor complained about the Hutchinson situation to anybody who cared to listen. "Why does the American League have to get all of the promising young ball players?" Traynor asked. "Our offer was big enough and I thought we had him."[23]

Just when it seemed that Pirates officials would leave the meeting without making any changes to their roster, Traynor finally pulled off a deal on December 16 when he shipped Al Todd, outfielder Johnny Dickshot and cash to the Bees for backup catcher Ray Mueller.[24] Pie insisted Pittsburgh got the better of this deal with Boston as he cautioned Pirate fans that only time would tell how this transaction played out. "Why, I had to talk myself blue in the face to the Bees," Traynor said, "before they'd go through with this deal. I had to throw in Dickshot and then add some money. I realize Mueller only batted .237 last year and only drove in 35 runs. But he played most of his 83 games in that Boston park, where good hitters go daffy. I feel like he'll be a better hitter with us and naturally, I like his work behind the

12. Disastrous Season and a Second-Division Finish in 1939

plate. I went after Lopez first but didn't get very far. In Boston, Mueller didn't get very much work. Lopez broke his thumb last year and that gave Mueller a chance to play for awhile. But when Lopez was ready to go again, Mueller went back to the bench. He'll be our first string catcher this year."[25]

Even though Traynor was excited about acquiring Mueller, the sentiment of casual baseball observers across America was that the Pirates now had several reserve catchers and no regular. The transaction was so puzzling to some that reporters in Salt Lake City questioned the accuracy of the report from the United Press' Pittsburgh office. "Question Pirate-Bee trade of second-stringer for first-stringer, outfielder and cash. Please recheck," read the wire they sent in response. Pittsburgh's bureau manager assured the journalists in Salt Lake City that the original wire was accurate.[26]

Although baseball fans in Pittsburgh were scratching their heads over Mueller's acquisition, they were less surprised that Al Todd had been sent packing. For some time, there had been reports in Pittsburgh that Pirates management believed that Todd's poor hitting and handling of the pitching staff had been one of the biggest reasons for the late-season slide. Weeks before he was traded to Boston, Todd felt the need to defend himself. "I am convinced that it wasn't poor catching that cost the Pirates the pennant in 1938," Todd declared. "The records will show that our failure to cop the flag last season was not the fault of the catching department. The fact that I happened to strike out in a tight spot during the Chicago series doesn't mean that a change in the catching staff would make the club a pennant-winner in 1939, either."[27] But the trade of Todd suggested that his superiors felt otherwise.

On December 19, 1938, the Pirates were chosen as the biggest disappointment of the sports year by the Associated Press in its eighth annual poll on the subject. Fourteen of the 70 sports editors who participated in the voting selected the Pirates, who barely nosed out the runners-up, Rice Institute's football team. Boxer Max Schmeling finished third, followed by Dizzy Dean, who did little for Chicago until the end of the 1938 season.[28]

With 1938 now in the rear view mirror, Pie Traynor's players started making preparations for the 1939 season. Fireman Mace Brown signed his 1939 contract on January 3 and informed a Pittsburgh sportswriter that he had fully recovered from the shock of serving up Gabby Hartnett's home run in late September. "I'd like to forget about it, but gosh it was a nightmare," commented Brown while discussing that episode. "The pitch that Hartnett hit into the stands was a curve. He had twice missed a curve to set the count at 2–0. The third time I tried to slip it by him, but the ball didn't break as well as I hoped it would and when I saw Johnny Rizzo back up toward the wall, then stop, I knew it was all over. I guess it just wasn't in the books for us to win that pennant. There's only one thing to do now. That's to forget all that's happened and start in fresh next spring."[29]

But others would not be returning. On January 14, 1939, Benswanger announced that veteran pitcher Red Lucas had been given his unconditional release. It was a tough decision for Benswanger, who was very fond of the veteran hurler and appreciated his years of dedicated service. The letter notifying Lucas of his release was a fitting tribute to a great competitor who never got a chance to partake in a World Series during his 14-year career. "One of the hardest jobs a fellow in my position has to do is to write a letter like this," wrote Benswanger. "For several years we have thoroughly enjoyed our association with you and it has been a real pleasure to have you on our club. I think you are aware of this, and it always has been mutually pleasant, I am sure. But the life of a ball player is such that all things come to an end, and it is with keen and extreme regret that we enclose here with the official notice of your unconditional release. I mean it most sincerely when I say it is with the utmost regret. You have been faithful, a good worker, and a ball player a club can be proud of."[30]

Much of the responsibility for Pittsburgh's failures during the final week of the 1938 season was unjustly placed on the shoulders of catcher Al Todd. On December 16, 1938, Todd and outfielder Johnny Dickshot were traded to the Boston Bees for catcher Ray Mueller as Pie Traynor and William Benswanger started reshaping Pittsburgh's roster (National Baseball Hall of Fame Library, Cooperstown, New York).

During his time with the Pirates, Red Lucas had been the consummate team player. Known for keeping teammates loose with his engaging stories and wisecracks, Red would sit on the

12. Disastrous Season and a Second-Division Finish in 1939 215

bench and listen to some of Honus Wagner's "whoppers" and then tell a tale that was just a little more unbelievable. His usual greeting when he arrived at training camp was: "What's Honus been lying about all winter?"[31] Because Lucas had been so popular and dedicated during his five seasons with Pittsburgh, it came as a shock to Benswanger when Lucas blasted Pirates management after his release. "I'm 37 years old," said Lucas. "Been pitching in the majors for 14 years. Never felt better in five years. I'm ready to go. No job, though. Never had a sore arm. If I could work regularly some place, I'd still win ball games. Pie Traynor kept me on the bench for 54 consecutive days last summer. I needed work then. Would have helped the Pirates. If Pie had given me and one other pitcher regular turns we'd have breezed into the pennant. Then they hand me my release in January. If they knew they were going to release me, why didn't they do it in December? I could have caught on with somebody else then. Now the jobs are all filled. Had a chance to manage a Double-A team, now somebody else got the job. I don't like that."[32]

Benswanger wasted no time rebutting Lucas's claim that the Pirates had treated him unfairly.[33] "I don't want to get into an argument with Red, but I think we treated him fair," declared Benswanger. "He was a high salaried man, had been ever since he joined our club. He drew big money last year, but he wasn't very active. Red said he never had a sore arm. I know one time last summer he complained of a sore elbow and couldn't pitch for quite a few days. He gave us all he had while he was a member of the Pirates and I liked Red personally. Still do. I'm hoping the story is an exaggeration. I can believe Red is disappointed and I feel if Pie could have used Red during those 54 days he claims he was on the bench, I know Pie would have done it. After all, Pie wanted to win that pennant, too. Red might have been a little more gracious about the matter, though. That's one of the hardest things in baseball, to tell a fellow he's through. I remember when I was first made president of the club, I had to hand Remy Kremer his release. I called him into the office and told him. I hated to do it, but Remy was past his prime and was of little use to the club. Yet Remy was grateful. Know what he told me? 'Bill. I've been expecting this. I should have got my release a year ago. Thanks for keeping me on the payroll this long.' You know, you just can't figure out some ball players."[34]

All in all, however, there were very few changes that winter. By the time the Pirates returned to San Bernardino, California, for spring training, the team had only added catcher Ray Mueller, while subtracting catcher Al Todd, outfielder Johnny Dickshot and pitcher Red Lucas. There were a few prospects in camp, of course, but none of them projected as regulars. Cincinnati Reds general manager Larry MacPhail was blunt when he stated that Traynor had done nothing to improve a squad that had been overtaken by Chicago during the 1938 season's final week. "The Pirates blew the pennant last year when they should have won it," stated MacPhail. "If they couldn't win then, how can they do it this year? I see no improvement in Traynor's club."[35] MacPhail's assessment was a common one among baseball experts. On a positive note, the Pirates squad had all of their players under contract for the 1939 season except for Paul Waner, who was a holdout once again. Waner had expected to see his pay cut after batting a disappointing .280 in 1938, but he balked when the Pirates front office elected to chop 45 percent of his salary. When Paul was tendered a second contract with 20 percent of the original reduction restored, he also rejected that proposal. Benswanger then firmly declared that this was the club's final offer, while Waner replied that he preferred to remain in Florida playing golf.[36]

Pittsburgh's chances in the fight for the 1939 National League pennant were further damaged by two events that happened during spring training and the team's exhibition tour. One of the issues involved young pitcher Russ Bauers, whose childish behavior during spring training in 1938 had led to a knee injury that put him behind getting into shape. In 1939, Bauers showed up at camp 20 pounds overweight and was battered by opposing hitters during his first few spring appearances. While Bauers claimed he could carry the extra pounds because he was big and strong enough to do so, Traynor believed that the pitcher's weight gain was hindering his delivery and that Russ' effectiveness would return once he worked off the excess weight. Bauers was one of the hardest working players on the team, but he also owned one of the largest appetites when the dinner bell rang.[37]

Alas, Bauers' appetite for food was only surpassed by his desire to have a good time, get into trouble and exhibit the kind of behavior that ordained him as Traynor's problem child. On March 22, after a series of exhibition games in Los Angeles, most of the players arrived at the team hotel around dinner time and placed bags carrying their belongings in the hotel lobby before going into the dining room. The handbags belonging to Bauers and Ed Brandt were still in the lobby at 3:00 in the morning when Traynor finally gave up on waiting for the two players. When Pie arrived at the ballpark the following day, he handed Brandt his unconditional release and told Bauers he would talk to him that evening.[38]

Traynor and Bauers huddled after dinner and Bauers was severely admonished for his latest lapse in judgment. Though he was not fined on this occasion, Traynor warned the pitcher that the next violation of team rules would result in a sizable chunk of money being taken out of his first paycheck. Bauers promised to behave in the future.[39] Following the disciplinary action, Traynor stated that this incident was not Brandt's first violation of training rules in the past two years. Pie decided to cut the southpaw pitcher loose only after numerous warnings. Traynor also mentioned that he might be ready to crack the whip with one or two other offenders on the squad. "I'm sick and tired of these playboys and I'm going to have discipline if I have to run one or two more players off the squad," growled the usually mild-mannered manager.[40]

The second ominous event occurred during an exhibition game against Cleveland in New Orleans on April 9. The game should have been remembered for the pitching of Cy Blanton, who tossed a no-hitter against the Indians and allowed one runner to reach base.[41] The Pirates cruised to an easy 6–0 victory that was highlighted by a five-run eighth inning against Cleveland pitcher Johnny Allen. After Pep Young slammed a two-run homer that gave Pittsburgh a 5–0 lead, Jeep Handley stepped to the plate to face Allen. One of the Pirates players remarked in the dugout that Allen would probably try to knock Handley down following Young's homer.[42]

Allen's first pitch came screaming toward Handley's head and struck him on the mastoid bone, with his left ear acting as a cushion. Jeep dropped to the ground as the baseball rolled to Honus Wagner coaching at first base. All of the Pirates players jumped from the bench as their teammate lay motionless at the plate. Allen, who was the first person to reach Handley after the incident, was berated by the Pirates. One player screamed: "You've been doing that all of your life, Allen," while others demanded that retribution be extracted immediately. Jeep was unconscious as he was carried from the field and taken by ambulance to Hotel Dieu Hospital. After the ballgame ended, Allen expressed shock over the near tragedy. "I threw Handley a side-arm fast ball," said Allen, "trying for the outside corner of the plate. I could see the ball was going straight for Handley's head but I was surprised when he didn't make an attempt to avoid the ball."[43]

Handley regained consciousness at the hospital and was able to speak to his wife in Peoria via telephone. One day later, he was reported to be in good spirits, though still in pain, and X-rays showed that no fracture had occurred.[44] Doctors performed minor surgery to remove a clot near his left ear that was expected to keep Lee in the hospital for about a week.[45] President Bill Benswanger remained with Handley during his stay in the New Orleans hospital as rest and quiet was prescribed, while visitors were not permitted.⁴⁶ On the eve of Pittsburgh's opener in Cincinnati, Benswanger updated Handley's condition.⁴⁷

"Handley is coming along fine now," Benswanger said, "and will leave for his home in Peoria, Illinois, either tomorrow night or Monday. His physician in New Orleans advised him to remain at home about 10 days. Lee is quite a remarkable little fellow. All he wanted to talk about in the hospital was baseball. They operated Monday to remove a blood clot from his left ear, and the first question he asked after the operation was: 'Did the boys win today?' Handley told me that when he stepped up to the plate against Allen that day, just after 'Pep' Young had hit the home run, he knew he was going to have a pitch thrown at his head, but he just couldn't get out of the way of the ball. As far as I know, neither Allen nor any member or official of the Cleveland club has contacted Handley since the accident. They may have done so, without my knowledge, but I believe if they had Handley would have said something to me. The doctor also told me if Handley's ear hadn't cushioned the force of the ball the blow might have killed him."⁴⁸

While the Pirates lost a player in Handley whose energetic and peppery style of play would be sorely missed, there was also an important addition to the roster. Paul Waner met with Benswanger in New Orleans and accepted the club's second offer of $12,000, plus a bonus of $1,000 based on attendance figures.⁴⁹ This was a sizable cut from his $17,500 salary in 1938, but it would still make Waner one of the highest paid utility players in the National League, since Traynor was planning to platoon him in right field with veteran Heinie Manush and rookie Fern Bell.

Pittsburgh came out of the gate in fine fashion on opening day against Cincinnati at Crosley Field on April 17 as Cy Blanton and Mace Brown hurled the Pirates to a 7–5 victory. Unfortunately for Traynor, this was the only game his team won during the month of April — the Pirates proceeded to lose eight consecutive contests. Jeep Handley's return to the lineup on May 2 seemed to energize the Pirates and on May 27 they finally pushed their record above .500 with a 9–1 victory against Chicago. But another slump followed and it was beginning to look as though 1939 would not be Pittsburgh's year.

Prior to spring training, Traynor had expressed concern about the fragile psyches of his players. "What the Pirates will need," Traynor stated prior to spring training, "is a good course in psychology. I'll have to keep drumming into them that we must look ahead, forget the past and start in fresh. For all but five days, the Pirates were the best in the league. What's gone is

12. Disastrous Season and a Second-Division Finish in 1939

gone. We can't look over our shoulders and think what might have been. During a regular season, we try to leave every game in the clubhouse, win or lose, especially when we lose. We'll begin that way this spring and hope for the best."[50] As the 1939 season progressed, it was looking more and more as though the players had not recovered from the heartbreak of the previous September.

There were also physical obstacles to overcome. Russ Bauers was basically useless to Traynor during the season's first few months as a sore back, sore shoulder and sore arm prevented him from appearing in more than four games through the end of May.[51] Hurler Cy Blanton was forced to the sidelines on April 26 with torn ligaments above the elbow of his right arm. He missed nearly three months before finally returning to action on August 16. Pep Young suffered a wrenched knee in early May that sidelined him for a month and a half.[52]

On April 9, 1939, pitcher Cy Blanton tossed a no-hitter during an exhibition game against the Cleveland Indians in New Orleans. Earl Averill was the only Indians player who reached base when he walked in the sixth inning. This turned out to be the high point of Blanton's year, as he missed most of the 1939 campaign with an elbow injury (National Baseball Hall of Fame Library, Cooperstown, New York).

Healthy players were also struggling. Johnny Rizzo was suffering through a sophomore jinx, while new catcher Ray Mueller was benched at the end of April due to a hitting slump and replaced behind the plate by Ray Berres.[53]

While Pittsburgh stumbled through June with an 8–13 record, the team made a series of moves suggesting that a youth movement was underway. Veteran outfielders Woody Jensen and Heinie Manush were let go, while

23-year-old first baseman Elbie Fletcher was acquired. The Pirates rebounded by posting a 19–11 record in July, but the deals continued. Fletcher's play at first base pushed Gus Suhr to the bench and on July 28 he was shipped to Philadelphia.

But the injury jinx reared its ugly head again and Johnny Rizzo's slump deepened. Never known as a patient group of people, Pittsburgh's fans heckled and razzed Rizzo and the constant abuse seemed to crush the spirit of the struggling ball player. The consensus among some baseball followers in Pittsburgh was that Rizzo was a one-year wonder who would be placed on the trading block after the season.[54] In mid–August, the Pirates lost 12 straight games and hope of salvaging the season was abandoned. A bunch of youngsters were given playing time in September and the team lurched to a sixth-place finish with a record of 68–85.

At the conclusion of the 12-game losing streak, president Bill Benswanger had claimed that he did not blame Traynor for either Pittsburgh's collapse in September of 1938 or the disappointing 1939 season. "Naturally I've given some thought to the possibility of changing managers," stated Benswanger. "Every person in charge of a business would have to do the same thing. But if a few of our high priced men had delivered for us, we wouldn't be worrying about these things. We've got some exceptional talent in the minors — Outfielders Van Robays and Elliott and Pitcher Gee — and you can be certain they'll be ready for next season. I don't want to come out in the open and say we're going to do a general house-cleaning job. Then if we don't, we'll be accused of failure to keep our promises. We do want to make trades this winter and we're going to do all within our power to put them through. We could stand some new faces and we're going to try and get them. Yes, it's noticeable that losing the pennant to the Cubs in the final days of the race last year, took something out of some of our players. They still haven't got over it. We want to eliminate that mental hazard. The fans in Pittsburgh have been most loyal and we want to do our utmost to please them. And, another thing, this race still has a little more than five weeks to go and a lot of things can happen."[55]

Yet rumors of a managerial change continued, accompanied by whispers that opposing managers considered Traynor a difficult man when dickering over trade considerations. Brooklyn Dodgers manager Leo Durocher made that point very clear when he talked to Pittsburgh sportswriters about his desire to acquire Pirates outfielder Johnny Rizzo.[56] "Why, the Pirates should have changed 90 percent of the faces on that team after what happened last year," said Durocher. "They should make it about 95 percent for

12. Disastrous Season and a Second-Division Finish in 1939

next year, but they won't. The same faces every year and no wonder the fans in Pittsburgh get tired of watching them. I tried to make a deal with you fellows last winter but I got disgusted. I won't chase them again. If they want to trade with me this winter, Traynor will have to do the chasing this time. I've a better team than he does."[57]

A rumor surfaced during the season's final week that Traynor would be replaced as manager for the 1940 campaign by Frankie Frisch. It was said that Frisch had resigned his post as a baseball announcer who covered Boston Red Sox and Bees games so he could take a big league managerial post.[58] There even were claims that Frisch had already signed a three-year contract to be Pittsburgh's manager at an annual salary of $27,000 per year.[59] When Bill Benswanger was asked to comment on this rumor, he denied that a decision had been made. "I don't know anything about it," responded Benswanger. "Naturally, the way the Pirates have been going, I don't blame the rumors for hitting us. But to tell the truth, I haven't even talked to Pie Traynor about next year's contract. We can settle that matter after the season closes."[60]

However, everyone close to Traynor was aware that the manager had worked himself into a nervous wreck trying to salvage something from the wreckage of a squad that had crashed and burned during the latter stages of the 1938 campaign. While Pittsburgh fans were extremely disappointed by the way the team had played in 1939, Traynor was even more discouraged by the events of the past 13 months.[61] With rumors abounding that Frankie Frisch was going to take over the managerial reins in 1940, Pie made an important decision that spelled the end of a glorious 19-year relationship between one of baseball's greatest third basemen and the Pittsburgh Pirates.

13

The End of an Era

Longtime Pittsburgh baseball fans who had passionately rooted for the Pirates since Barney Dreyfuss took control of the franchise in 1899 could not fathom the possibility that Bill Benswanger planned on relieving Pie Traynor of his managerial duties. As they saw it, Traynor had always been such a favorite of Dreyfuss and his widow Florence, who was still chairman of the board of directors, that he would never be fired. Yet a source close to the situation believed a managerial change was a distinct possibility because Mrs. Dreyfuss was in declining health and thus was open to the possibility of selling the franchise. The anonymous informant also lent credence to the rumors that Frankie Frisch would be managing the Pirates in 1940.[1]

"When Barney Dreyfuss, late owner of the Pirates died, he said that Traynor could have a job with the Pittsburgh club as long as he wanted it," claimed the anonymous insider. "Mrs. Barney Dreyfuss, the widow, has tried to carry out Barney's wishes. She admires Traynor, as do Bill Benswanger and other club executives. Now, I happen to know that Benswanger would do nothing to hurt Traynor, but down in his heart he realizes that a change might be for the better of the team, at the same time feeling that Pie is the victim of a bad ball club. I take it that if Frisch goes to the Pirates, and it's my belief that he will, that Traynor will be given an opportunity to become a member of the official family of the club. This would be carrying out the wishes of Dreyfuss and at the same time be giving the Pirates a man who would prove valuable as a general overseer."[2]

All of these rumors were finally put to rest during a news conference on September 28. Fifteen minutes after having denied that Traynor had decided to resign, Benswanger announced that Pittsburgh's manager had indeed tendered his resignation. With Traynor by his side, Benswanger discussed the decision which ended Traynor's 19-year stint in a Pirates uniform.[3] While Pie was stepping down as manager, however, he would remain connected to the franchise as an assistant to farm system director Joe Schultz, Sr.[4] Traynor's resignation was effective at the end of the season after Pittsburgh played their final three games of the campaign against Cincinnati at Forbes Field.[5]

Pie Traynor pulled on his uniform one last time to manage the Pirates during a doubleheader against the Reds on October 1 at Forbes Field. Pie, who always told reporters and fans to give credit to the players after a victory and to blame him after a loss, exhibited no sentimental feelings prior to his final day at the helm. When a reporter asked Traynor if he planned on taking his uniform with him to keep as a memento, he shrugged his shoulders as he answered the question. "I don't think so," Traynor responded. "But there's one uniform I'll always save. That's the one they gave us in the first All-Star Game in Chicago in 1933. I consider being picked on that team an honor."[6]

A small crowd of about 3,500 fans turned out to watch Traynor manage the final two games of his career as Pittsburgh gained a split in the doubleheader against Cincinnati. Traynor occupied the first-base coaching box throughout the first contest and up until the third inning of the nightcap. Pie then rushed to the locker room, dressed and left Forbes Field before the game concluded.[7] Always a low-key player and manager, Traynor wanted to make his last exit without any fanfare.

While baseball fans throughout Pittsburgh always loved Pie Traynor the player, many never warmed up to his style as a manager. Scores of patrons who were inclined to believe that Traynor was too lenient toward his troops would have been shocked to know that Pie fined more players during his managerial tenure than most pilots in the National League. Pie detested the idea of publicizing these fines out of respect for the feelings of his players. Even though the general consensus seemed to be that Traynor should have gotten better results during his time as Pittsburgh's skipper, one fan who attended Pie's final effort on October 1 seemed to have changed his opinion. "I always thought Traynor was a poor manager until he took a terrible club and almost ran it into a pennant last year," claimed this Pirate fan. "He really had a poor team this year."[8]

Traynor's resignation closed an era in Pirates baseball history and it did not take long for a new one to begin. As had been rumored for several weeks, Frankie Frisch was introduced as Pittsburgh's new manager at a press conference on September 30, 1939. Frisch signed a two-year deal to manage Pittsburgh in 1940 and 1941 for an estimated salary of between $17,500 and $20,000 per year. Frankie initially requested a three-year deal, while Benswanger wanted to follow normal course and sign him for only one season. The two-year pact was thus a logical compromise.[9] When Frisch spoke to the press after Benswanger's announcement, he left no doubt that he planned on modeling the Pirates after his 1934 world championship Cardinals and that that would require an infusion of youth.

"I don't have very many set rules," Frisch declared, "but No. 1 players must go from first to third on singles. I like a running ball club and so do the fans. The Cardinals won the 1934 pennant and the World Series against Detroit on speed and I've never heard of a slow-footed team getting anywhere. I'm going to build my outfield around [Bob] Elliott and [Maurice] Van Robays. They're both young, and I understand they're both real major leaguers. I've had great reports on Elliott. [Johnny] Gee should fit in nicely and [Oad] Swigart may come through as a starter. I don't know much about [Frankie] Gustine but I do know about this kid, Joe Schultz [Jr.]. I had him at one of the Cardinals' training camps and he showed me plenty of power at the plate. I think the Pirates have the foundation for a good team. I was glad that Paul Waner finished up in great style. He still has a few good seasons left. I plan to take some of the younger fellows such as Elliott, Van Robays and Gustine, to camp with the battery men and get a line on them before the infielders and outfielders arrive."[10]

Frisch's planned rebuilding process meant that some veteran performers had played their last game as a member of the Pirates. Within weeks, he began to jettison key members of the team that had blown the 1938 National League pennant during the season's final week. On October 14, Frisch announced that Jewel Ens would not be retained as a coach for the 1940 campaign and that Mike Kelly of the Boston Bees would join his coaching staff.[11] Three days later, he announced that Johnny Gooch would not be back as a coach in 1940 but instead would be assigned to scouting duties in the south. The purge continued when Frisch fired Pirates batboy Porky Cohen and longtime Forbes Field clubhouse attendant Caleb "Socko" McCarey.[12] He did, however, announce that 65-year-old Honus Wagner would be back for an eighth season as a team coach. This decision seemed logical given Wagner's dedicated service to the Pirates organization for 25 years.[13] "He belongs to the Dreyfuss estate," stated Frisch in explaining his decision to keep Wagner on his coaching staff.[14]

Frisch next got down to the task of upgrading his roster. Many expected that outfielder Johnny Rizzo would be the first player out the door, but Frisch claimed he was not anxious to trade the youngster because of his ability as a long distance hitter. Instead, his first two deals involved members of the pitching staff. On December 6, 1939, Jim Tobin was traded to Boston for pitcher Johnny Lanning. Two days later, Frisch shipped veteran hurler Bill Swift to the Bees for twirler Danny MacFayden.[15] The trade of Tobin came as a surprise to some, but the pitcher had fallen into Pie Traynor's doghouse the previous summer and Frisch was intent on ridding the team of potential troublemakers.[16] On December 23, he eliminated another hurler from the staff when "Cy" Blanton was sent to Syracuse of the International League.

Outfielder Johnny Rizzo began the 1940 season in a Pirates uniform but his struggles continued and on May 8, 1940, he was shipped to the Cincinnati Reds in exchange for outfielder Vince DiMaggio. Two more Pirates players followed Rizzo out the door before the 1940 season ended. After courting Al Lopez for several years, Pittsburgh finally acquired the veteran catcher on June 14 by shipping backstop Ray Berres and $40,000 to Boston for his services. On September 30, second baseman Pep Young was traded to the Southern Association's Atlanta Crackers squad for infielder Alf Anderson.

The roles of Lloyd and Paul Waner also decreased in 1940 because Frankie Frisch was anxious to find playing time for Bob Elliott, Maurice Van Robays and Vince DiMaggio. Lloyd only appeared in 72 games and batted .259 while Paul saw action in 89 contests and hit .290. Paul Waner's days with the Pirates officially came to an end when he was released on December 5, 1940. Bill Benswanger informed Waner of the front office's intentions before the minor league meetings commenced and gave him permission to broker a deal with another team on his own. When Paul failed to find any interested parties, the Pirates gave him his unconditional release. The man who batted .340 over 15 seasons playing for Pittsburgh took his release graciously. "When a young fellow comes along, somebody has to move over and now it's me," said Paul Waner. "I have no regrets."[17]

Frisch's housecleaning continued on January 2, 1941, when third baseman Bill Brubaker was sold to the St. Louis Cardinals. Then Mace Brown was sold to the Brooklyn Dodgers on April 22. While the purchase price was not revealed, it was believed that Brooklyn had paid between $20,000 and $25,000 to acquire the man who had surrendered Gabby Hartnett's famous "Homer in the Gloamin'." Brown's fellow members of Pittsburgh's pitching staff were stunned by the deal, while team officials claimed that the money was going to be used to upgrade the infield and add another quality hurler. Frisch stated that Brown had been sent packing because he did not believe he could win for the Pirates.[18] Two weeks later, Lloyd Waner was traded to the Boston Braves for pitcher Nick Strincevich on May 7, 1941.

Lloyd had started one game for Frankie Frisch during the season's early weeks, so the trade should not have come as a shock. Nonetheless, he seemed a bit taken aback when he discussed his departure with sportswriter Les Biederman:

After starring for 14 seasons together in Pittsburgh, the Waner brothers saw their time as members of the Pirates end during a five-month span. On December 5, 1940, Paul Waner was handed his unconditional release. Lloyd soon followed his brother out of the Steel City when he was traded to the Boston Braves for pitcher Nick Strincevich on May 7, 1941 (National Baseball Hall of Fame Library, Cooperstown, New York).

> Naturally, I was surprised when they told me after the game yesterday that I had been traded for pitcher Nick Strincevich, but I knew something was in the wind.
>
> I wasn't used very much in spring training and hardly at all since the season started but somehow, even when you expect to be traded and finally are, it still comes as a bit of a shock.
>
> This afternoon I was a Pirate. This evening, I'm a Bostonian. But that's baseball. It happens every day and I have no regrets. Maybe it'll be a break for me, at that. I'll probably get a chance to play regularly in Boston and that's what I need. I can't stand sitting on the bench.
>
> I'm not downhearted, except that I'm leaving a city that's been pretty good to me. The Pittsburgh Baseball Club has always treated me fine, given me every break in the world and I know I've given the team 100 percent effort in every game. Say, do you know I was rooting for the wrong team during that game this afternoon.
>
> I batted against Strincevich last year and he looked pretty good. He has a sidearm sinker that's effective and maybe we'll both get going and make this trade stand out.
>
> I just wired my wife in Oklahoma City and am going to talk to her tonight. Instead of meeting me in Pittsburgh as we planned, she'll have to come all the way to Boston now.

I wish you'd thank all the fans in Pittsburgh for being so nice to me in my 14 years there and I'll always have a soft spot in my heart for them.

But, say, you'd better watch who you invite to your Baseball Writer's Dinner next winter as honor guests. See what happened to Paul and me?[19]

Veteran pitcher Joe Bowman joined the exodus when he was traded to the St. Paul Saints of the American Association in exchange for pitcher Oral Hildebrand on August 8, 1941. Up to this point, much of the major housecleaning had involved either players who were no longer seen as being viable contributors or veterans past their prime, but that changed after the 1941 campaign. Five days after the United States was ushered into World War II when Japan attacked Pearl Harbor on December 7, 29-year-old shortstop Arky Vaughan was traded to Brooklyn for infielder Pete Coscarart, catcher Babe Phelps, outfielder Jimmy Wasdell and pitcher Luke Hamlin.

Arky Vaughan had remained one of the National League's top players in 1940 by batting .300 and leading the circuit in games played (156), plate appearances (689), runs scored (113) and triples (15). Vaughan again led the club in hitting during the 1941 campaign despite the fact that he only appeared in 106 games due to injuries and Frisch souring on his ability.[20] Frisch had concluded that Vaughan was expendable because shortstop prospects Alf Anderson and Billy Cox were waiting in the wings. He agreed to the deal since it gave Pittsburgh four players who could plug potential gaps that might occur due to players entering the military service.[21] While this explanation seemed plausible, many local baseball fans felt the Pirates received quantity rather than quality in a deal they believed had been made because Vaughan was not a favorite of Frisch. Team president Bill Benswanger experienced mixed feelings about the trade. "Arky's been here a long time and I'm genuinely sorry to see him go," Benswanger stated. "But baseball is baseball. We didn't set out to get rid of Vaughan. And as long as Arky is going, he can't kick about the team he's headed for. Due to the uncertainty of war conditions, we felt we had to strengthen certain positions on the team and we had to pay to do that. We feel we're getting some good players who will help us and I wish Arky all the luck in the world."[22]

Besides considering Anderson and Cox as replacements for Vaughan, Frankie Frisch also planned on giving Lee Handley a look at shortstop during spring training. The fact that Handley would be joining his teammates seemed miraculous because he had been involved in a serious car accident in his hometown of Peoria on November 29, 1941. Pittsburgh's peppery little infielder was speeding along the highway when his vehicle hit a patch of slippery pavement and landed in a culvert.[23] Even though Handley was ejected through the top of the machine, he suffered nothing more than severe cuts to his face and head. Lee made a quick recovery and informed Pirates management that he would be present when spring training began.[24]

Handley was told to take it easy during the squad's first few workouts at San Bernardino, California. When he finally decided to cut loose and throw a baseball in his normal fashion, he discovered that his right arm was basically useless. Pittsburgh trainer Dr. Charles A. Jorgensen ordered Handley to desist at once. After a thorough examination, it was discovered that Handley had damaged the muscles and ligaments in his right shoulder. Frisch sent Handley to Los Angeles to see a specialist who had worked on pitchers Johnny Gee and Russ Bauers the previous year.[25] Once Handley was cleared to return to baseball, he was farmed out to the Toronto Maple Leafs of the International League. He remained with Toronto for the 1942 and 1943 seasons before making a triumphant return to the major leagues with Pittsburgh in 1944. The man known affectionately as Jeep played three more seasons in Pittsburgh before finishing his big league career in 1947 with the Philadelphia Phillies.

Bob Klinger and fellow hurler Russ Bauers both saw their baseball careers interrupted by World War II. After going 11–8 for the Pirates in 1943, Klinger joined the Navy. Bauers opted to enlist in the Army after pitching minor league baseball for Jersey City in 1941 and Albany in 1942. While Klinger was engaged in the Pacific theater for two years, he continued to play quite a bit of baseball.[26] Both pitchers hoped to return to Pittsburgh to resume their baseball careers after the war, but those aspirations were dashed. Bauers was released by the Pirates on March 22, 1946, while Klinger was cut loose on May 7, 1946.

By the summer of 1946, Jeep Handley, plus pitchers Rip Sewell and Kenny Heintzelman were the only players remaining who had appeared in at least one game for the 1938 Pirates. When Handley and Heintzelman moved to the Phillies in 1947, that left Sewell as the only player left from the squad which blew the pennant during the season's final week. Sewell remained a Pirate until he retired from baseball in 1950. By that time, the Dreyfuss family had severed its ties with the baseball franchise they had owned since 1900.

Two events occurred in 1946 which convinced Florence Dreyfuss that the time had come to sell the franchise. The first was that Boston attorney Robert Murphy, who had organized The American Baseball Guild, decided to focus on the Pittsburgh Pirates in his effort to unionize baseball. Murphy saw Pittsburgh as the best place to make his stand due to the city's rich industrial heritage. On June 7, the Pirates players voted 20–16 to strike, but the measure was defeated since a three-quarters vote was necessary for it to take effect.[27]

A second unfortunate situation surrounded a special day that the *Pitts-*

burgh Post-Gazette had for its 500 newsboys at Forbes Field. When that game was postponed due to rain, the paperboys returned on the following day, only to be turned away under direct orders from team vice-president Sam Watters. Pittsburgh management was excoriated in the local newspapers for not allowing these lads to use their rain checks. The *Pittsburgh Post-Gazette* ran a scathing editorial that upset Mrs. Dreyfuss. There had been numerous inquiries during the previous few years about whether the team was for sale. After those unfortunate incidents and a bad season on the field, Mrs. Dreyfuss told her son-in-law that the time was right to make a move. "Bill, I guess we better sell," Mrs. Dreyfuss told Benswanger.[28]

On August 8, 1946, the Dreyfuss family sold the team to a consortium that included singer Harry "Bing" Crosby, Indianapolis banker Frank McKinney, Columbus realtor John W. Galbreath and Tom Johnson, vice-president of the Standard Steel Spring Company.[29] While the Pittsburgh Pirates had claimed six National League pennants during Barney Dreyfuss' tenure as the team owner, Bill Benswanger had been unable to achieve similar glory as president of the franchise. The 1938 season was the closest Benswanger ever came to a World Series.

Ten years after the Pirates blew the 1938 pennant, a spring training no-hitter by St. Louis Cardinals pitcher Murry Dickson led Pie Traynor to reminisce about Cy Blanton's exhibition no-hitter against the Cleveland Indians nine years earlier on Easter Sunday, April 9, 1939. Traynor explained to writer Les Biederman how that game set in motion a devastating chain of events:

> I had intended to allow Blanton to go about six or seven innings that day in New Orleans against the Indians. I never saw Cy look as good as he did that spring. He was in great shape and his arm was loose and strong that year.
>
> Blanton walked through the first five innings. No hits. Not even a man on base. In the sixth inning, Earl Averill came up in a pinch and walked with two out. But Cy got out of the hole.
>
> I remember talking to a friend of mine and telling him I hoped the Indians would get a hit and break the spell. I didn't want Cy to go the full nine innings, yet I couldn't take him out with a no-hitter coming up.
>
> We had a 1 to 0 lead until the seventh, when Pep Young hit a homer with two aboard off Johnny Allen, who had just come into the game.
>
> When Blanton went out for the seventh, I could see him bearing down all the harder. He actually forced himself in those late innings—and that isn't any good for a pitcher in the spring.
>
> Well, we won the game, 6 to 0, Blanton had his no-hitter and then our troubles started. Allen was so upset over Young poking that homer that he beaned Lee Handley, who followed Young in the Pittsburgh batting order.
>
> Handley was in a hospital in New Orleans for weeks and never fully recovered from the effects of that beaning.

That no-hitter took so much out of Blanton's right arm that he was a total loss to us that season [1939].

He won the first game for us against the Reds, 7 to 5, but we had to take him out for Mace Brown, who saved the victory. He was knocked out of his next two starts for us.

I remember when he tried to go against the Cubs in his third start, he complained of his right elbow. X-rays showed torn ligaments above the elbow.

All season long, Cy appeared in only 42 innings for us, gave up 45 hits, 23 runs and won two and lost three. He was only 30 years old at the time and four years before he led the National League in earned-run allowance.

That no-hitter finished Cy. We shipped him to Syracuse in 1940, then the Phils took him on. But he didn't last. He died a few years ago.[30]

While Cy Blanton passed away on September 13, 1945, in Norman, Oklahoma, Pie Traynor's managerial career had experienced a slow death during his final season running the Pittsburgh Pirates in 1939. The former great third baseman, who was a fan favorite in the Steel City during his long tenure with Pittsburgh, could pinpoint the events which led to his resignation. While Traynor had no problem explaining the incidents that had ruined the 1939 season, the theories surrounding Pittsburgh's collapse in 1938 were varied. In Pie's defense, he actually did not expect his team to compete for a title in 1938 and had planned on starting a rebuilding project after the team played horrible baseball in May. Some people believed the Pirates wilted during the stretch drive because Traynor did not give his starters enough rest throughout the long campaign. Considering his bench options, it was no wonder Pie relied exclusively on his regulars to win baseball games.

However, Traynor could have fielded a unit in 1938 that would have run roughshod over the competition if he had responded to a telegram sent to him by *Pittsburgh Courier* sports editor Chester Washington. During the winter prior to the 1938 campaign, Washington offered to sell Traynor a group of star Negro League players at a minimal cost to the Pittsburgh Pirates. Included in this collection of star-studded performers who would have made the Pirates an unbeatable dynasty were Josh Gibson, Buck Leonard, Ray Brown, Satchel Paige and Cool Papa Bell. Washington's telegram went unanswered and the Pirates missed out on an opportunity to add some of the greatest players in baseball history to their roster. In fairness to Traynor, such an undertaking was not likely to be initiated while Judge Kenesaw Landis was baseball's commissioner.[31]

A majority of baseball fans in Pittsburgh believed the psychological damage that Gabby Hartnett's famous home run inflicted upon the Pirate players prevented them from regrouping and fighting for the pennant during the 1938 season's final five games. While team president Bill Benswanger understood the importance of Hartnett's home run in sealing Pittsburgh's fate, he blamed something much different and less sinister for the pennant being lost in September.[32]

"In my mind, the pennant was lost before that Cub series started," said Benswanger. "It is my firm belief that the hurricane that swept through the East prevented us from winning. We went East on the final trip, good and hot. Everybody knows that when a club is hot, it can make wrong plays and win; when it is cold, nothing turns out right. Well, we were winning game after game, close ones and easy ones. For example in Boston we defeated Tom Zachary, the left-hander who always had been a nemesis to us. And how did we do it? Hits by Gus Suhr and Lloyd Waner, both left-handed hitters against a southpaw, which gave us a 2-to-1 victory in the ninth. That's the way things were going when the hurricane struck.

"We were unable to play in Brooklyn and Philadelphia just when we needed every game, even with the odds in our favor. I wanted to play. Ford Frick, John Kiernan and other newspapermen told me not to worry, as we had the pennant sewed up. To my way of thinking, pennants are won only by winning ball games, and ball games can only be won if you play them. To lose by losing games is one thing; to lose by idleness is another.

"If we had played all those games in the East we would have gone to Chicago with such a lead that we could have lost all three games and still have won the flag. But as we sat around in hotel lobbies during the storm, a hot team cooled off and never regained its winning momentum. The Hartnett home run was an anticlimax, not the cause of our defeat."[33]

Gabby Hartnett's famous home run was the climactic event that prevented the Pittsburgh Pirates from returning to the World Series for the first time since 1927. An opportunity to oppose the New York Yankees once again in the Fall Classic seemed to evaporate as the result of one swing of the bat during a 154-game season. Even though Pittsburgh did fail in the end, they were the toast of baseball for more than two months of the 1938 season. This squad, which came very close to achieving the ultimate goal of winning a pennant, had been slowly cultivated through player procurement over a span of 13 years. After their failure in 1938, it only took Pirates management a few seasons to dismantle a team that came so close to claiming an unlikely pennant. Many possibilities have been offered as to why the 1938 Pittsburgh Pirates failed to win the National League pennant. Perhaps it was just a case of the season being one week too long.

Appendix A:
1938 Pittsburgh Pirates Roster

Pitchers

#51 Russ Bauers ("Big Boy") b. May 10, 1914, Townsend, Wisconsin — 6 feet 3 — 195 lbs

#46 Darrell Blanton ("Cy") b. July 6, 1908, Waurika, Oklahoma — 5 feet 11½ — 180 lbs

#48 Joe Bowman ("Showman") b. June 17, 1910, Argentine, Kansas — 6 feet 2 — 190 lbs

#49 Ed Brandt ("Big Ed") b. February 17, 1905, Spokane, Washington — 6 feet 1 — 190 lbs

#47 Mace Brown ("Fireman") b. May 21, 1909, North English, Iowa — 6 feet 1 — 190 lbs

#53 Kenneth Heintzelman ("Kenny") b. October 14, 1915, Peruque, Missouri — 5 feet 11½ — 185 lbs

#41 Bob Klinger ("Laughing Boy") b. June 4, 1908, Allenton, Missouri — 6 feet — 180 lbs

#40 Charles Lucas ("Red" — "The Nashville Narcissus" — "Old Rosebud") b. April 28, 1902, Columbia, Tennessee — 5 feet 9½ — 170 lbs

#44 Truett Sewell ("Rip") b. May 11, 1907, Decatur, Alabama — 6 feet 1 — 180 lbs

#45 William Swift ("Bill") b. June 19, 1908, Elmira, New York — 6 feet 1½ — 192 lbs

#50 Jim Tobin ("Abba Dabba") b. December 27, 1912, Oakland, California — 6 feet 0 — 185 lbs

Catchers

#32 Ray Berres ("Nippy") b. August 31, 1907, Kenosha, Wisconsin — 5 feet 9 — 170 lbs

#30 Alfred Todd ("Al") b. January 7, 1902, Troy, New York — 6 feet 1 — 198 lbs

Infielders

#25 Wilbur Brubaker ("Bill") b. November 7, 1910, Cleveland, Ohio — 6 feet 2 — 185 lbs

#20 Lee Handley ("Jeep") b. July 13, 1913, Clarion, Iowa — 5 feet 7 inches — 160 lbs

#24 August Suhr ("Gus" — "Goose") b. January 3, 1906, San Francisco, California — 6 feet — 180 lbs

#22, #52 Thomas Thevenow ("Tommy") b. September 6, 1903, Madison, Indiana — 5 feet 10 — 155 lbs

#21 Joseph Vaughan ("Arky" — "Floyd") b. March 9, 1912, Clifty, Arkansas — 5 feet 10½ — 175 lbs

#26 Lemuel Young ("Pep" — "Floyd") b. August 29, 1907, Jamestown, North Carolina — 5 feet 9 — 162 lbs

Outfielders

#17 Johnny Dickshot ("Ugly") b. January 24, 1910, Waukegan, Illinois — 6 feet — 195 lbs

#16 Forrest Jensen ("Woody") b. August 11, 1907, Bremerton, Washington — 5 feet 10½ — 160 lbs

#36 Henry Manush ("Heinie") b. July 20, 1901, Tuscumbia, Alabama — 6 feet 1 — 200 lbs

#12 Johnny Rizzo ("Blackie" — "Banjo Eyes" — "Cisco Kid") b. July 30, 1912, Houston, Texas — 6 feet — 190 lbs

#10 Lloyd Waner ("Little Poison" — "Muscles" — "Mousie") b. March 16, 1906, Harrah, Oklahoma — 5 feet 9 — 150 lbs

#11 Paul Waner ("Big Poison") b. April 16, 1903, Harrah, Oklahoma — 5 feet 8½ — 153 lbs

Manager

#35 Harold Traynor ("Pie") b. November 11, 1898, Framingham, Massachusetts — 6 feet 0 — 170 lbs

Coaches

#33 John Wagner ("Honus" — "The Flying Dutchman") b. February 24, 1874, Chartiers, Pennsylvania — 5 feet 11 — 200 lbs

John Gooch ("Johnny") b. November 9, 1897, Smyrna, Tennessee — 5 feet 11 — 175 lbs

Jewel Ens ("Uncle" — "Mutt") b. August 24, 1889, St. Louis, Missouri — 5 feet 10½ — 165 lbs

Appendix B: 1938 Statistics

Batting Statistics—Team Batting Average .279

	G	AB	R	H	2B	3B	HR	RBI	BB	SO	SB	AVG	SLG
Joe Bowman	18	21	5	7	0	1	0	1	1	3	0	.333	.429
Arky Vaughan	148	541	88	174	35	5	7	68	104	21	14	.322	.444
Lloyd Waner	147	619	79	194	25	7	5	57	28	11	5	.313	.401
Heinie Manush	15	13	2	4	1	1	0	4	2	0	0	.308	.538
Johnny Rizzo	143	555	97	167	31	9	23	111	54	61	1	.301	.514
Ed Brandt	24	37	5	11	2	0	0	3	1	9	0	.297	.351
Bill Brubaker	45	112	18	33	5	0	3	19	9	14	2	.295	.420
Gus Suhr	145	530	82	156	35	14	3	64	87	37	4	.294	.430
Paul Waner	148	625	77	175	31	6	6	69	47	28	2	.280	.378
Pep Young	149	562	58	156	36	5	4	79	40	64	7	.278	.381
Lee Handley	139	570	91	153	25	8	6	51	53	31	7	.268	.372
Al Todd	133	491	52	130	19	7	7	75	18	31	2	.265	.375
Jim Tobin	56	103	8	25	6	1	0	11	9	12	0	.243	.320
Russ Bauers	40	88	7	21	3	2	0	2	3	18	0	.239	.318
Ray Berres	40	100	7	23	2	0	0	6	8	10	0	.230	.250
Johnny Dickshot	29	35	3	8	0	0	0	4	8	5	3	.229	.229
Cy Blanton	29	64	4	13	0	0	0	7	1	17	0	.203	.203
Tommy Thevenow	15	25	2	5	0	0	0	2	4	0	0	.200	.200
Woody Jensen	68	125	12	25	4	0	0	10	1	3	0	.200	.232
Bill Swift	36	50	3	10	3	0	1	6	2	10	0	.200	.320
Bob Klinger	28	60	5	10	0	0	0	3	2	13	0	.167	.167
Mace Brown	51	38	1	5	2	0	0	5	0	8	0	.132	.184
Red Lucas	33	46	1	5	0	0	0	2	3	2	0	.109	.109
Rip Sewell	17	12	0	1	0	0	0	0	0	1	0	.083	.083
Ken Heintzelman	1	0	0	0	0	0	0	0	0	0	0	.000	.000

Pitching Statistics—Team ERA 3.46

	W	L	ERA	G	GS	CG	SV	IP	H	R	ER	HR	BB	SO
Bob Klinger	12	5	2.99	28	21	10	1	159.1	152	63	53	7	42	58
Russ Bauers	13	14	3.07	40	34	12	3	243.0	207	102	83	7	99	117
Bill Swift	7	5	3.24	36	9	2	4	150.0	155	65	54	9	40	77
Ed Brandt	5	4	3.46	24	13	5	0	96.1	93	44	37	3	35	38
Jim Tobin	14	12	3.47	40	33	14	0	241.1	254	109	93	17	66	70
Red Lucas	6	3	3.54	13	13	4	0	84.0	90	33	33	5	16	19
Cy Blanton	11	7	3.70	29	26	10	0	172.2	190	84	71	13	46	80
Mace Brown	15	9	3.80	51	2	0	5	132.2	155	68	56	5	44	55
Rip Sewell	0	1	4.23	17	0	0	1	38.1	41	27	18	3	21	17
Joe Bowman	3	4	4.65	17	1	0	1	60.0	68	33	31	2	20	25
Ken Heintzelman	0	0	9.00	1	0	0	0	2.0	1	2	2	0	3	1

Chapter Notes

Chapter 1

1. Lyle C. Wilson, "Roosevelt Warns War Nations: President Urges All Belligerents Be 'Quarantined,'" *The Pittsburgh Press*, October 5, 1937, page 1.
2. "Roosevelt Talk Stirs World: League Assembly Approves Resolution Calling for Far Eastern Conference," *The Pittsburgh Press*, October 6, 1937, page 1.
3. "Scribbled by Scribes: Ruppert Calls '27 Team the Best," *The Sporting News*, November 4, 1937, page 4.
4. *Ibid.*
5. Charles J. Doyle, "Bucs Would Equal the Best Farmers: Benswanger Moves to Get on Par with Yankees and Cards," *The Sporting News*, November 4, 1937, page 2.
6. Ford C. Frick, "Psychology the Hidden Factor of the Pirates Surprising Defeat," *Baseball Magazine*, December 1927, page 303.
7. *Ibid.*
8. Frick, "Psychology the Hidden Factor of the Pirates Surprising Defeat," page 304.
9. *Ibid.*
10. *Ibid.*
11. *Ibid.*
12. *Ibid.*
13. Frederick G. Lieb, *The Pittsburgh Pirates* (1948: reprint Carbondale: Southern Illinois University Press, 2003), page 230.
14. Frick, "Psychology the Hidden Factor of the Pirates Surprising Defeat," page 303.
15. *Ibid.*
16. "Babe Features Workout with Long Drives: Ruth, Huggins Confident of Defeating Pirates," *Pittsburgh Post-Gazette*, October 4, 1927, page 14.
17. Frick, "Psychology the Hidden Factor of the Pirates Surprising Defeat," page 303.
18. Richard Peterson, ed. *The Pirates Reader* (Pittsburgh: University of Pittsburgh Press, 2003), page 117.
19. Nick Robertson, "Hall of Famer Paul Waner Recalls 1927 Series: Tells About Getting Nicknames," *Sarasota Herald-Tribune*, October 4, 1960, page 11.
20. J.G. Taylor Spink, "Three and One: Looking Them over with J.G. Taylor Spink," *The Sporting News*, September 29, 1938, page 4.
21. "Shortstop Traynor Recalled by Pirates," *The Lewiston Daily Sun*, August 30, 1921, page 6.
22. "Sport Comment," *The Providence News*, November 2, 1923, page 28.
23. Ralph S. Davis, "Only One Part of It in Minds of Pirates: No Member of Pittsburg Team at World's Series," *The Sporting News*, October 25, 1923, page 3.
24. "Pie Traynor Says Maranville Trade Would Hurt Pirates' Pennant Chances," *The Pittsburgh Gazette Times*, January 22, 1924, page 11.
25. "Dreyfuss Says Traynor Was Approached: Pirates' Owner Demands World Series Be Called Off," *The Pittsburgh Gazette Times*, October 3, 1924, page 1.
26. *Ibid.*, page 5.
27. Honus Wagner, "Wagner Says Carey was Best in Series," *The Pittsburgh Press*, October 18, 1925, page 6.
28. *Ibid.*
29. "Pirate Squad in First Hard Practice Skit," *Milwaukee Sentinel*, March 6, 1926, page 10.
30. Lou Gehrig, "Yankee Defence Accords Pennock Steady Support," *The Ottawa Evening Citizen*, October 8, 1927, page 12.
31. Miller Huggins, "Huggins Praises Pirates: Mite Manager of World Champs Says Buccaneers Were Hard Fighters," *The Pittsburgh Press*, October 9, 1927, page 1.
32. Edward J. Neil, "Lloyd and Paul Won't Be Heroes, Says Pa Waner," *The Milwaukee Journal*, October 5, 1927, page 20.
33. Clifton Blue Parker, *Big and Little Poison: Paul and Lloyd Waner, Baseball Brothers* (Jefferson, NC: McFarland, 2003), page 25.
34. Lieb, *The Pittsburgh Pirates*, page 229.

35. George Chadwick, "Waner's Younger Brother Is Coming Batting Champ," *Youngstown Vindicator,* January 16, 1927, page 3C.
36. *Ibid.*
37. "Waner Boys, Pirate Heroes, Here Again," *The Pittsburgh Press,* November 7, 1927, page 27.
38. "Waners in Fold for 1928," *The Pittsburgh Press,* November 10, 1927, page 32.
39. Lou Wollen, "No Offer Made for Waners: No Club Bidding for Pirates Stars, Say Club Officials," *The Pittsburgh Press,* February 16, 1929, page 13.
40. *Ibid.*
41. "Waner Brothers to Stand Firm in Salary Demands: Poison Twins to Be Absent from Lineup Unless Given Increases," *The Pittsburgh Press,* February 26, 1929, page 33.
42. "Waners Firm in Demands: Three Contracts Returned to Bucs by Elder Waner," *Pittsburgh Post-Gazette,* February 26, 1929, page 18.
43. *Ibid.*
44. *Ibid.*
45. "Half of Waner Gang Signs with Pirates," *Prescott Evening Courier,* March 19, 1929, page 4.
46. Lou Wollen, "Paul Waner Will Not Lessen Salary Demands: Still Asks Top Figure," *The Pittsburgh Press,* March 23, 1929, page 1.
47. *Ibid.*
48. Lou Wollen, "Dreyfuss to Remain Firm in Stand with Paul Waner: Paul Must Make First Overtures," *The Pittsburgh Press,* March 29, 1929, page 42.
49. "'You Had Bad Year in 1929'— Dreyfuss; 'Big Poison' Smiles" *The Palm Beach Post,* March 31, 1929, page 6.
50. "Paul Waner Puts Name on Contract: Neither He Nor Dreyfuss Would Tell Final Terms of Compromise," *The Telegraph-Herald and Times Journal,* April 5, 1929, page 11.
51. Joe Williams, "Interference Caused Bush to Quit, Claimed: Frequent Suggestions by Magnate Arouses Ire of Buc Pilot," *The Pittsburgh Press,* August 29, 1929, page 32.
52. *Ibid.*
53. "Waners Sign for Next Ball Season," *The Toledo News-Bee,* October 19, 1929, page 12.
54. Fred Wertenbach, "Bartell Joins Grimes as Buccaneer Holdout: Dick's Demands Absurd — Dreyfuss," *The Pittsburgh Press,* February 28, 1930, page 21.
55. *Ibid.*
56. Ralph S. Davis, "Pittsburg Leaves Paso Robles Camp: Pirates Pull Up Stakes to Play Series of Exhibitions," *The Sporting News,* March 20, 1930, page 5.
57. *Ibid.*
58. "Grimes' Trip 'Down River' Penalty for Salary Tiff: Pirate Fans Await Results Before Condemning Trade," *The Pittsburgh Press,* April 10, 1930, page 34.
59. Edward F. Balinger, "Pirates Break Camp at Paso Robles: Open Three-Game Series in Frisco Against Missions," *Pittsburgh Post-Gazette,* March 18, 1930, page 18.
60. Ralph S. Davis, "Traynor Confident of Quick Return to Lineup: 'Pie's' Affliction Hits Pirates Hard," *The Pittsburgh Press,* March 20, 1930, page 61.
61. "Three Pittsburgh Regulars Are Out," *Milwaukee Sentinel,* April 15, 1930, page 13.
62. "Waner Going to Hospital: Lloyd to Enter Johns Hopkins in Baltimore to Have Case Diagnosed," *The Pittsburgh Press,* May 3, 1930, page 12.
63. "Waner May Retire from Pirate Team," *Berkeley Daily Gazette,* May 10, 1930, page 11.
64. "Reports Have Bartell Due to Be Traded," *The Pittsburgh Press,* September 25, 1930, page 34.
65. Ralph S. Davis, "Pirates Make Room to Add New Catcher: Bool's Release Regarded as Move Toward Another Trade," *The Sporting News,* November 20, 1930, page 3.
66. Edward F. Balinger, "Pirates Trade Bartell to the Phillies: Bucs Get Thevenow, Willoughby in Deal for Young Shortstop," *Pittsburgh Post-Gazette,* November 7, 1930, page 18.
67. "Sam Dreyfuss Dies Here of Pneumonia: Bucs' Vice President Losses Fight for Life," *The Pittsburgh Press,* February 23, 1931, page 1.

Chapter 2

1. Frederick G. Lieb, *The Pittsburgh Pirates* (1948: Reprint Carbondale: Southern Illinois University Press, 2003), page 242.
2. *Ibid.,* page 243.
3. *Ibid.*
4. *Ibid.*
5. "'Pie' Traynor Weds Cincy Girl: Pirate Captain, Eva Helmer Married Saturday," *The Pittsburgh Press,* January 4, 1931, page 1.
6. Ralph Davis, "Ralph Davis Says: Rumors About Paul Waner Enliven Off-Season for Bucco Fans," *The Pittsburgh Press,* December 4, 1930, page 32.
7. *Ibid.*
8. "Second Bucco Party Leaves: Adam Comorosky Expected to Sign Contract Before Departure Saturday," *The Pittsburgh Press,* February 25, 1931, page 27.
9. "Giants Learn About Sliding," *Rochester Evening Journal and The Post Express,* March 16, 1931, page 18.
10. Lieb, *The Pittsburgh Pirates,* page 247.
11. *Ibid.*
12. *Ibid.,* page 248.
13. *Ibid.*
14. L.W. Sheridan, "New Faces Will Bolster Pirate Team: Gibson out of Retirement to Manage," *Nashua Telegraph,* December 30, 1931, page 8.
15. Ralph Davis, "Ralph Davis Says: Barney

Dreyfuss Expects to Die in Diamond Harness," *The Pittsburgh Press*, February 28, 1931, page 9.

16. "Dreyfuss Ill, Stays at Home: Pirate President Foregoes Trip to West Baden," *The Pittsburgh Press*, December 2, 1931, page 29.

17. "Dreyfuss' Body Being Brought to Home Here: Family Is at Side as Pirate Owner Dies in New York." *Pittsburgh Post-Gazette*, February 6, 1932, page 1.

18. "Baseball Leaders, Friends Pay Tribute to Dreyfuss," *Pittsburgh Post-Gazette*, February 6, 1932, page 14.

19. *Ibid.*

20. Edward F. Balinger, "Baseball Gossip," *Pittsburgh Post-Gazette*, February 8, 1932, page 15.

21. "Rookie Quartet Makes Good in Majors: Early Campaign Finds Four Newcomers Cinch to Stick in Big Time," *The Ludington Daily News*, May 3, 1932, page 6.

22. "Bucs' Losing Streak Blamed on Vaughan," *The Milwaukee Journal*, August 29, 1932, page 2.

23. Lieb, *The Pittsburgh Pirates*, page 252.

24. "Two Pirate Stars Ordered to Rest," *The Milwaukee Journal*, April 23, 1934, page 2.

25. *Ibid.*

26. Edward F. Balinger, "Pie Traynor Takes over Pirate Reins: Succeeds Gibson in Sudden Change by Pirate Heads," *Pittsburgh Post-Gazette*, June 20, 1934, page 16.

27. Chester L. Smith, "The Village Smithy: Problem of Etiquet at Giants' Camp," *The Pittsburgh Press*, February 26, 1938, page 9.

28. *Ibid.*

29. *Ibid.*

30. Al Abrams, "Fans Favor Move Making Pie Traynor Pirate Pilot," *Pittsburgh Post-Gazette*, June 20, 1934, page 16.

31. *Ibid.*

32. Jeff Moshier, "Playing Square," *The Independent*, September 13, 1934, page 4A.

33. Edward F. Balinger, "Buccos Are Idle in East Again: Blaze Near Hostelry Provides Thrill for Players," *Pittsburgh Post-Gazette*, September 18, 1934, page 14.

34. Lieb, *The Pittsburgh Pirates*, pages 250–251.

35. Balinger, "Buccos Are Idle in East Again: Blaze Near Hostelry Provides Thrill for Players," page 14.

36. "Dizzy Dean Named Most Valuable Player: Cards' Ace Dethrones Carl Hubbell," *The Pittsburgh Press*, October 17, 1934, page 25.

37. "Traynor to Lead Pirate Club Again," *Milwaukee Sentinel*, October 31, 1934, page 13.

38. "Cubs Await Pirate Decision on Big Trade: Chicago Seeks Lindstrom and French, Offers Bush and Babe Herman in Deal," *The Pittsburgh Press*, November 22, 1934, page 27.

39. Herbert W. Barker, "Cubs and Pirates Furnish First Baseball 'Riot': Bush Sails into Joiner Following Verbal Exchange," *The Calgary Daily Herald*, April 30, 1935, page 7.

40. *Ibid.*

41. "Young Stars with Pirates," *The Milwaukee Journal*, May 30, 1935, page 2.

42. *Ibid.*

43. Havey J. Boyle, "Mirrors of Sport: Hans Lobert," *Pittsburgh Post-Gazette*, May 30, 1935, page 20.

44. *Ibid.*

45. *Ibid.*

46. Volney Walsh, "Pirates Count on Al Todd for Many Years of Service," *The Pittsburgh Press*, November 30, 1935, page 8.

47. "Traynor Sees 'Quarterback' Todd Big Help: Figures New Catcher to Protect Leads in Close Games," *Pittsburgh Post-Gazette*, March 13, 1936, page 20.

48. *Ibid.*

49. "'Little Poison' Returns to Bucs After Illness," *The Independent*, April 2, 1936, page 5A.

50. Al Abrams, "Sidelights on Sports," *Pittsburgh Post-Gazette*, April 14, 1936, page 20.

51. "Waner Says He Is No Holdout," *Sarasota Herald*, January 31, 1936, page 1.

52. "Paul Waner Signs," *The Windsor Daily Star*, March 10, 1936, page 2.

53. Jack Cuddy, "Vaughan Isn't Hitting — Looking for Luck Charms," *The Pittsburgh Press*, June 28, 1936, page 3.

54. *Ibid.*

55. "Four Managers May Lose Jobs: Bleacher Wolves Scrap in Major Leagues — Leaders Safe Enough," *The Spokesman-Review*, August 18, 1936, page 12.

Chapter 3

1. "Pie Traynor Signed: Will Manage Pittsburgh Club During 1937 Campaign," *The St. Joseph News*, October 30, 1936, page 18.

2. Edward F. Balinger, "Series to Break Money Records: Intake for Five Games is $1,035,186," *Pittsburgh Post-Gazette*, October 6, 1936, page 20.

3. Chester L. Smith, "The Village Smithy: Traynor Just Laughs at Giant Trade Rumor," *The Pittsburgh Press*, October 6, 1936, page 31.

4. Chester L. Smith, "Pirates Ready to Talk Trade for Dean: Cards' First Demand out of Reason," *The Pittsburgh Press*, November 29, 1936, page 3.

5. George Kirksey, "Bucs' Deal for Dizzy Dean Not Probable: Traynor and Company Trim Down Original Offer; Vaughan Not Included," *Greensburg Daily Tribune*, December 9, 1936, page 12.

6. *Ibid.*

7. Ralph Davis, "Schumacher Trade Kept Alive by Bucs: Traynor Believes Giants Haven't Closed Door on His Bid," *The Sporting News*, January 7, 1937, page 2.

8. Lyle C. Wilson, "Roosevelt Hits Courts

for Periling New Deal: Asks Congress for Wide Power to Deal with Spanish War; Admits NRA's Flaws— Court Flayed by President," *The Pittsburgh Press*, January 6, 1937, page 1.

9. Irving B. Pflaum, "500,000 Flee Homes in Madrid: Pilots Say 'Adios' by Dumping More Bombs on Capital," *The Pittsburgh Press*, January 10, 1937, page 1.

10. Claire M. Burcky, "100,000 Fans Jam Station for Ovation: Mayor Scully, Dr. Bowman Officially Great Rose Bowl Victors," *The Pittsburgh Press*, January 7, 1937, page 1.

11. Claire M. Burcky, "First Buc Squad Goes West Thursday: Will Reach Coast Camp on March 8," *The Pittsburgh Press*, February 28, 1937, page 3.

12. "Weaver Signs Buc Contract: P. Waner, Suhr, Brubaker Only Ones Outside Pirate Fold," *The Pittsburgh Press*, February 24, 1937, page 29.

13. "'Let Him Sit,' Says Benswanger of Waner: Outfielder Spurns New Contract," *The Pittsburgh Press*, March 4, 1937, page 27.

14. *Ibid*.

15. Ralph Davis, "Paul Waner Runs $500 Issue into a $15,000 Controversy," *The Sporting News*, March 11, 1937, page 1.

16. "'They'll Pay Me What I Want Or Here I Stay!' Waner: Bucs in the Wrong Holdout Star Says," *The Pittsburgh Press*, March 16, 1937, pages 26 & 28.

17. Chester L. Smith, "The Village Smithy: Pie Traynor Angry at Paul Waner," *The Pittsburgh Press*, March 28, 1937, page 3.

18. Chester L. Smith, "The Village Smithy: Boss Benswanger Plenty Peeved!" *The Pittsburgh Press*, March 30, 1937, page 22.

19. Chester L. Smith, "Waner Signs Contract: Holdout Ends After Session with Traynor," *The Pittsburgh Press*, April 9, 1937, page 1.

20. Chester L. Smith, "Remember That Right Fielder? His Name's Waner!: Sure, Paul's Back to Help Win Pennant," *The Pittsburgh Press*, April 10, 1937, page 8.

21. "Big Poison Is Confident Despite His Ragged Start," *Pittsburgh Post-Gazette*, April 12, 1937, page 16.

22. C.L. Smith, "Pirates Sign Coast Hurler," *The Pittsburgh Press*, April 15, 1937, page 30.

23. Chester L. Smith, "Traynor's Prayer for Pitchers Answered: Bowman, Tobin Ease Serious Situation," *The Pittsburgh Press*, April 16, 1937, page 48.

24. "Tough Luck! Death of Suhr's Mother Ends Streak," *The Pittsburgh Press*, June 6, 1937, page 1.

25. Charles J. Doyle, "Bucs Can't Elude Polo Grounds Hex: Lose First Place, Schulte Beaned and Suhr's String Broken," *The Sporting News*, June 10, 1937, page 2.

26. "Unlucky Pirates Lose to Giants, 7 to 5: Schulte Is Beaned; Suhr Misses Game," *The Pittsburgh Press*, June 6, 1937, page 1.

27. Fred W. Tuerk, "Lee Handley, Hero of House That Buc 'Jack' Built, Made Way Against Hardships as Boy," *The Sporting News*, February 25, 1937, page 10.

28. *Ibid*.

29. Carl T. Felker, "Lumberjack Bauers Unlimbers New Delivery Under Gooch's Tutelage to Win Job on Bucs," *The Sporting News*, May 6, 1937, page 3.

30. *Ibid*.

31. *Ibid*.

32. *Ibid*.

33. *Ibid*.

34. Charles J. Doyle, "Gossip Naming Mancuso as Buc Pilot, Fouls Out," *The Sporting News*, October 14, 1937, page 1.

35. "National League Standing on Tuesday Morning," *The Sporting News*, September 30, 1937, page 8.

36. *Ibid*.

37. Doyle, "Gossip Naming Mancuso as Buc Pilot, Fouls Out," *The Sporting News*, October 14, 1937, page 1.

38. "Traynor Back with Buccaneers," *Nashua Telegraph*, October 14, 1937, page 14.

39. Chester L. Smith, "The Village Smithy: Traynor Regards Dizzy Dean as Poor Risk No. 1," *The Pittsburgh Press*, November 2, 1937, page 25.

40. Smith, "The Village Smithy: Traynor Regards Dizzy Dean as Poor Risk No. 1," page 25.

41. Lester Biederman, "P. Waner, Swift, Young Bucs' Bait for Mungo," *The Pittsburgh Press*, December 5, 1937, page 1.

42. *Ibid*.

43. *Ibid*.

44. Lester Biederman, "Grimes, Awaiting 'Best' Deal, Hangs on to Mungo: Bucs, Cubs, Giants Balk at Demands," *The Pittsburgh Press*, December 6, 1937, page 28.

45. Lester Biederman, "Dullest Major League Confab Ended: Senior Loop Heads Panned for Failures," *The Pittsburgh Press*, December 8, 1937, page 34.

46. "Caught on the Fly," *The Sporting News*, November 25, 1937, page 9.

47. "Caught on the Fly," *The Sporting News*, December 9, 1937, page 9.

48. Charles J. Doyle, "Pirates to Benefit from New '38 Ball: Heavier Stitches Expected to Aid Their Curve Ball Artists," *The Sporting News*, October 7, 1937, page 7.

49. "New National Ball to Cut Averages: Waner Claims Dead Sphere Will Not Get Rid of 'Fluke' Hits," *The Spartanburg Herald*, December 26, 1937, page 8.

50. Lester Biederman, "Bucs Card 30 Games for Spring Training," *The Pittsburgh Press*, December 19, 1937, page 1.

51. *Ibid.*
52. "Scribbled by Scribes: Hoyt Dissects Pittsburgh Pirates," *The Sporting News*, December 23, 1937, page 4.
53. *Ibid.*

Chapter 4

1. "Traynor Here, Still Seeks Mungo," *The Pittsburgh Press*, December 21, 1937, page 32.
2. *Ibid.*
3. Charles J. Doyle, "Pie Keeps Plugging on Trade for Bucs: Hunt for Pitchers Spurred by Study of Official Averages," *The Sporting News*, December 30, 1937, page 3.
4. Charles J. Doyle, "New Stream-Lined Lee Handley to Pace Pirate Running Attack," *The Sporting News*, January 6, 1938, page 1.
5. "Traynor Here, Still Seeks Mungo," *The Pittsburgh Press*, December 21, 1937, page 32.
6. "7 to 10 Million Without Jobs, Unemployment Census Shows: Doubt Placed on Accuracy of U.S. Check," *The Pittsburgh Press*, January 2, 1938, page 1.
7. "Tarzan Can't Have Knotty Knees—Lou Turns Cowboy," *The Pittsburgh Press*, January 4, 1938, page 20.
8. Chester L. Smith, "The Village Smithy: Hoyt Forgets Doings of Yankees of His Day," *The Pittsburgh Press*, January 5, 1938, page 21.
9. *Ibid.*
10. "Pirates Deny Mungo Deal," *The Pittsburgh Press*, January 6, 1938, page 24.
11. "Waners Blast Benswanger," *The Pittsburgh Press*, January 7, 1937, page 33.
12. Charles J. Doyle, "P. Waner's Pop-Off Fizzles with Fans: 'Cheap Faces' Crack of Buc Star Meets Chilly Reception," *The Sporting News*, January 13, 1938, page 9.
13. *Ibid.*
14. Lester Biederman, "P. Waner 'Holditis' Not Annoying Bucs," *The Pittsburgh Press*, January 8, 1938, page 7.
15. "Jensen Joins Waners in Blast on Bucs, Calls 'Em 'Nickel Nursers'" *The Pittsburgh Press*, January 9, 1938, page 1.
16. *Ibid.*
17. *Ibid.*
18. Lester Biederman, "Bucs Spend $75,000; It Goes for New Players: Rizzo Highest Praised Purchase; Costs $25,000, Three Players," *The Pittsburgh Press*, January 9, 1938, page 3.
19. Lester Biederman, "Jensen's Blast 'Heats Stove League': 'Popping Off' Branded as Ridiculous," *The Pittsburgh Press*, January 10, 1938, page 22.
20. *Ibid.*
21. Chester L. Smith, "The Village Smithy: Pirates Not as Penurious as People Think," *The Pittsburgh Press*, January 11, 1938, page 22.
22. Lester Biederman, "Manager Traynor Hits at Pirate Outfielder," *The Pittsburgh Press*, January 11, 1938, page 22.
23. Lester Biederman, "'I Was Misquoted,' Woody Jensen Claims: Writer's Imagination Ran Away, He Says," *The Pittsburgh Press*, January 14, 1938, page 31.
24. Charles J. Doyle, "Jensen 'Tirade' Due to Turn into Trade: Buc Fly-Hawk Recants, But Swap Is Regarded as Likely," *The Sporting News*, January 20, 1938, page 10.
25. "Scribe Denies Jensen Charge," *The Pittsburgh Press*, January 15, 1938, page 7.
26. "'Need Slugger,' P. Waner's Opinion," *The Pittsburgh Press*, January 27, 1938, page 23.
27. *Ibid.*
28. Charles J. Doyle, "Bucs' Musical Boss Still Hears Discord: Cy Blanton Signs, But Gus Suhr Adds Another Sour Note," *The Sporting News*, February 3, 1938, page 5.
29. Biederman, "Buc Bosses Hope for Trades at New York Meeting: Mungo Swap Effort Will Be Renewed," page 3.
30. Lester Biederman, "Benswanger Keeps His Word with Jensen—Woody Signs Contract," *The Pittsburgh Press*, February 16, 1938, page 26.
31. Lester Biederman, "Pirates, with P. Waner in the Fold, Anticipate Little Holdout Trouble," *The Pittsburgh Press*, February 19, 1938, page 9.
32. Charles J. Doyle, "P. Waner's Signing Eases Buc 'Mutiny': Big Poison Quickly Accepts Terms in Benswanger Confab," *The Sporting News*, February 24, 1938, page 1.
33. Lester Biederman, "Lloyd Waner Accepts Terms; Only Three Bucs Unsigned," *The Pittsburgh Press*, February 25, 1938, page 37.
34. "'Bucs' Spirit O.K.—We Need Long Hitter,' Says L. Waner," *The Pittsburgh Press*, February 4, 1938, page 37.
35. Lester Biederman, "Suhr Accepts Bucs' Terms," *The Pittsburgh Press*, February 24, 1938, page 25.
36. "Vaughan, Brubaker Only Pirate Players Unsigned," *The Pittsburgh Press*, February 26, 1938, page 9.
37. Lester Biederman, "Benswanger Talks Trade with Cubs: 'Making Progress,' Says Pirate Prexy," *The Pittsburgh Press*, February 1, 1938, page 23.
38. *Ibid.*
39. Lester Biederman, "Sports Stew—Served Hot," *The Pittsburgh Press*, February 4, 1938, page 38.
40. *Ibid.*
41. Lester Biederman, "Insurance! Bucs Sign Thevenow for Infield Service," *The Pittsburgh Press*, February 23, 1938, page 24.
42. "Training Camp Notes: National League," *The Sporting News*, March 10, 1938, page 8.
43. Biederman, "'Off Season' Duties Keep Pirates Busy," page 20.
44. Doyle, "Pirate Boss Invites P. Waner to

Parley: Long-Distance Dickering Found to Be Unsatisfactory," page 2.
45. Lester Biederman, "Pirates' First Squad Heads West: Battery Men Begin Jaunt to San Berdoo," *The Pittsburgh Press*, March 2, 1938, page 25.
46. Lester Biederman, "Pirate Party Grows to Eighteen at Omaha: Heintzelman, Ens, Bowman Join Squad," *The Pittsburgh Press*, March 3, 1938, page 25.
47. Lester Biederman, "Coast Flood Delays Bucs' Arrival: Damage to Training Field Upsets Plans," *The Pittsburgh Press*, March 4, 1938, page 43.
48. "Training Camp Notes: National League," *The Sporting News*, March 10, 1938, page 8.
49. *Ibid.*
50. Biederman, "Coast Flood Delays Bucs' Arrival: Damage to Training Field Upsets Plans," page 43.
51. Lester Biederman, "Pirates May Reach Camp Tonight: Bucs Are Detoured by Way of Oakland," *The Pittsburgh Press*, March 5, 1938, page 7.
52. Lester Biederman, "Pirate Batterymen in First Workout: Pitchers, Catchers Eager for Action," *The Pittsburgh Press*, March 7, 1938, page 21.
53. Lester Biederman, "Pirates Expect to Reach San Berdoo Camp Today," *The Pittsburgh Press*, March 6, 1938, page 1.
54. Biederman, "Pirate Batterymen in First Workout: Pitchers, Catchers Eager for Action," page 21.
55. *Ibid.*
56. "Pirate Patter: Baseball Fever," *The Pittsburgh Press*, March 9, 1938, page 26.
57. "Training Camp Notes: National League," *The Sporting News*, March 17, 1938, page 6.
58. Lester Biederman, "Bad Weather Hampers Bucs' Early Workouts: Rain, Cold Impede Battery Conditioning," *The Pittsburgh Press*, March 10, 1938, page 24.
59. "Detoured: Bucs' Second Squad to Arrive Tomorrow," *The Pittsburgh Press*, March 11, 1938, page 38.
60. *Ibid.*
61. "Pirate Patter," *The Pittsburgh Press*, March 12, 1938, page 7.
62. Charles J. Doyle, "Jensen Jolted out of Pirate Outfield: Rizzo Is Given Call over Veteran, Who Irked Club Officials," *The Sporting News*, March 17, 1938, page 2.
63. Lester Biederman, "Ed Brandt Unsigned, Asks Parley with Benswanger," *The Pittsburgh Press*, March 1, 1938, page 23.
64. Doyle, "Jensen Jolted out of Pirate Outfield: Rizzo Is Given Call over Veteran, Who Irked Club Officials," page 2.
65. "Pirate Patter," *The Pittsburgh Press*, March 13, 1938, page 1.
66. Lester Biederman, "'I'll Stick,' Rizzo Promises Pie Traynor: 'Left Field Is Your's,' Pirate Skipper Tells New Recruit," *The Pittsburgh Press*, March 15, 1938, page 23.
67. Charles J. Doyle, "Pie's Counter Puts Hill Rookies High: Early Notices Give Bob Klinger Especially Strong Rating," *The Sporting News*, March 3, 1938, page 3.
68. *Ibid.*
69. Lester Biederman, "Bucs' Gain, Cubs' Loss: Pirates Best Bruins in Signing Bauers by Two Hours; Now He's Rated Best Buc Hurler," *The Pittsburgh Press*, March 13, 1938, page 6.
70. Lester Biederman, "Brown Stars as Bucs Beat White Sox, 4–2: Vaughan Tops Attack with Four Blows," *The Pittsburgh Press*, March 20, 1938, page 1.
71. "Pirate Patter: Pitchers Hit," *The Pittsburgh Press*, March 21, 1938, page 21.
72. Lester Biederman, "Pirates Open Series with San Francisco: Duke, Heintzelman Shine Against Cubs," *The Pittsburgh Press*, March 22, 1938, page 23.
73. "Pirate Patter: Visitor," *The Pittsburgh Press*, March 28, 1938, page 21.
74. "Suhr Day: 'Frisco Fans to Honor Buc Star Sunday," *The Pittsburgh Press*, March 23, 1938, page 24.
75. "Honors! Home Town Fans Honor Tobin and Suhr," *The Pittsburgh Press*, March 27, 1938, page 1.
76. *Ibid.*
77. Lester Biederman, "Rizzo Bucs' Hope of 'Fence Buster': Slugging Outfielder Adds Needed Punch," *The Pittsburgh Press*, March 28, 1938, page 21.
78. Lester Biederman, "Pirates Play Final Game in California: Seek 11th in Row Against Barstow," *The Pittsburgh Press*, April 4, 1938, page 23.
79. *Ibid.*

Chapter 5

1. "Pirate Patter: Banquet!" *The Pittsburgh Press*, March 30, 1938, page 25.
2. Lester Biederman, "Bucs Poison with Tobin on Staff," *The Pittsburgh Press*, February 8, 1938, page 25.
3. Lester Biederman, "Cubs Nominate Bucs as Toughest to Beat," *The Pittsburgh Press*, March 31, 1938, page 28.
4. "Pirate Patter: Banquet!" page 25.
5. Lester Biederman, "Bucs Await First Test with 'Angels': 'Big Three' to Get Hurling Assignment," *The Pittsburgh Press*, March 17, 1938, page 25.
6. Lester Biederman, "Small Town Exhibitions Irk Pirates: Corsairs 'Fed Up'; Await Sox Series," *The Pittsburgh Press*, April 5, 1938, page 22.
7. *Ibid.*
8. Charles J. Doyle, "Pirates' Pipes Dry, So

They Dusted Off: Injury to Bauers Dampers Fun and Traynor's Outlook," *The Sporting News,* April 14, 1938, page 2.

9. "Pirate Patter: Victim!" *The Pittsburgh Press,* April 4, 1938, page 23.

10. "'Non-Producers Have to Go'—Traynor: Train Brawl Brings Drastic Reaction," *The Pittsburgh Press,* April 7, 1938, page 28.

11. Lester Biederman, "'Clowning' Injury Puts Russ Bauers Out: Big Pitcher Injured Wrestling on Train," *The Pittsburgh Press,* April 6, 1938, page 18.

12. Doyle, "Pirates' Pipes Dry: So They Dusted Off: Injury to Bauers Dampers Fun and Traynor's Outlook," page 2.

13. Biederman, "'Clowning' Injury Puts Russ Bauers Out: Big Pitcher Injured Wrestling on Train," page 18.

14. "'Non-Producers Have to Go'—Traynor: Train Brawl Brings Drastic Reaction," page 29.

15. Doyle, "Pirates' Pipes Dry: So They Dusted Off: Injury to Bauers Dampers Fun and Traynor's Outlook," page 2.

16. Biederman, "'Clowning' Injury Puts Russ Bauers Out: Big Pitcher Injured Wrestling on Train," page 18.

17. "'Non-Producers Have to Go'—Traynor: Train Brawl Brings Drastic Reaction," page 29.

18. "Bauers May Rejoin Pirates Before Opener: St. Louis Physician Finds Ligament Torn," *The Pittsburgh Press,* April 8, 1938, page 50.

19. "Major League Notes," *The Sporting News,* April 14, 1938, page 7.

20. Lester Biederman, "Bucs Cool Off! Greeted by Snowstorm in Texas," *The Pittsburgh Press,* April 7, 1938, page 28.

21. "Chisox Beat Bucs, in Rabbits, Not Runs," *The Pittsburgh Press,* April 8, 1938, page 50.

22. Lester Biederman, "Bad Weather Keeps Pace with Pirates," *The Pittsburgh Press,* April 8, 1938, page 52.

23. Biederman, "'Clowning' Injury Puts Russ Bauers Out: Big Pitcher Injured Wrestling on Train," page 18.

24. "Pirates May Try to Land Whitney," *The Pittsburgh Press,* March 28, 1938, page 21.

25. "Rizzo's Hitting Cheers Bucs," *The Pittsburgh Press,* April 10, 1938, page 1.

26. Lester Biederman, "Bucs Show Plenty of Class, Sox Admit: 'They've Got Stuff,' Says Jimmy Dykes," *The Pittsburgh Press,* April 11, 1938, page 23.

27. Lester Biederman, "Four Buc Pitchers Ready for Opener: Bill Swift's Stint Shows He's All Set," *The Pittsburgh Press,* April 12, 1938, page 28.

28. "Pirate Patter: All Hands on Deck!" *The Pittsburgh Press,* April 13, 1938, page 27.

29. "Major League Notes," *The Sporting News,* April 21, 1938, page 7.

30. Lester Biederman, "Blanton to Pitch Season's Opener: Effective Work Earns Him Honor," *The Pittsburgh Press,* April 13, 1938, page 26.

31. "Major League Notes," *The Sporting News,* April 21, 1938, page 7.

32. "Pirate Patter: P. Waner Stopped," *The Pittsburgh Press,* April 14, 1938, page 30.

33. Lester Biederman, "Montreal May Get Three Pirate Rookies: Traynor Undecided on Duke and Sewell," *The Pittsburgh Press,* April 15, 1938, page 33.

34. "Pirate Patter: Vaughan Paces Bucs," *The Pittsburgh Press,* April 15, 1938, page 33.

35. Lester Biederman, "Pirates Give Young Talent Once-over: Hutchinson Infielder Draws High Praise," *The Pittsburgh Press,* April 16, 1938, page 9.

36. Lester Biederman, "Pirates Rained Out; Await Opening Game," *The Pittsburgh Press,* April 17, 1938, page 3.

37. "Pirate Patter: Traynor on Radio," *The Pittsburgh Press,* April 16, 1938, page 9.

38. Biederman, "Pirates Give Young Talent Once-over: Hutchinson Infielder Draws High Praise," page 9.

39. Biederman, "Pirates Rained Out: Await Opening Game," page 3.

40. Ibid.

41. Lester Biederman, "Bauers Cheers Bucs on Eve of Opener," *The Pittsburgh Press,* April 18, 1938, page 23.

42. Ibid.

43. Joe Williams, "Bucs Runners-Up! Picked to Finish Second to Giants—Rizzo, Waners Figured to Supply Punch," *The Pittsburgh Press,* April 15, 1938, page 35.

44. Chester L. Smith, "The Village Smithy: Bucs Have Stuff to Win Flag This Year, Says Pie," *The Pittsburgh Press,* April 19, 1938, page 26.

45. Ibid.

46. "'Diz' Can't Help Cubs Much, 'Pie' Infers," *The Pittsburgh Press,* April 17, 1938, page 1.

47. Ed Burns, "'Died on Bases' Called Knell of Pirates' Past Flag Hopes: Plenty of Hitting Power, Traynor Concedes, But Pay-Off Punch Is Lacking," *The Sporting News,* April 7, 1938, page 3.

48. Ibid.

49. "Shakeup! Even Pirate Uniforms Undergo Change in Getting Club Ready," *The Pittsburgh Press,* January 26, 1938, page 22.

50. "National League Standing on Tuesday Morning," *The Sporting News,* April 28, 1938, page 8.

51. Lester Biederman, "Bucs' Opening Form Shows Balanced Power: Pitchers, Hitters, Defense Start Well," *The Pittsburgh Press,* April 20, 1938, page 26.

52. Ibid.

53. "Pirate Patter: Brandt Gets Starting Job," *The Pittsburgh Press,* April 20, 1938, page 26.

54. Ibid.

55. Ibid.

56. "Pirate Patter: Fielding Counts Too!" *The Pittsburgh Press,* April 22, 1938, page 41.
57. George Kirksey, "Bucs and Senators Take Early Honors," *The Pittsburgh Press,* April 22, 1938, page 41.
58. "National League Standing on Tuesday Morning," *The Sporting News,* April 28, 1938, page 8.
59. "Celebration: C. of C. Honors Pirates Tomorrow," *The Pittsburgh Press,* April 21, 1938, page 28.
60. Chester L. Smith, "Traynor's 'Strongest Pirate Outfit' Makes Debut: 20,000 Fans Welcome Bucs Against Reds," *The Pittsburgh Press,* April 22, 1938, page 41.
61. "National League Standing on Tuesday Morning," *The Sporting News,* April 28, 1938, page 8.
62. Smith, "Traynor's 'Strongest Pirate Outfit' Makes Debut: 20,000 Fans Welcome Bucs Against Reds," page 41.
63. *Ibid.*
64. Lester Biederman, "Bauers, Fully Recovered, Earns Starting Role: Will Take Regular Turn Against Cubs," *The Pittsburgh Press,* April 23, 1938, page 8.
65. "National League Standing on Tuesday Morning," *The Sporting News,* April 28, 1938, page 8.
66. Lester Biederman, "Pirate Patter: Blanton-Schott," *The Pittsburgh Press,* April 23, 1938, page 8.
67. Chester L. Smith, "The Village Smithy: Rizzo One of Majors' Three Outstanding Rookies," *The Pittsburgh Press,* April 23, 1938, page 8.
68. "National League Standing on Tuesday Morning," *The Sporting News,* April 28, 1938, page 8.
69. Lester Biederman, "Rizzo's Loud Bat Helps Bucs Down Red, 6–2: Rookie Smashes Two Triples, Single as Pirates Win Fifth," *The Pittsburgh Press,* April 24, 1938, page 1.
70. "Tobin Goes After No. 2: Hard-Hitting Righthander May Oppose Southpaw Hollingsworth in Series Final with Reds Today," *The Pittsburgh Press,* April 24, 1938, page 1.
71. "National League Standing on Tuesday Morning," *The Sporting News,* April 28, 1938, page 8.
72. Charles J. Doyle, "Bucs Put on Spot by Flashy Getaway: Reverse Likely to Bring Blasts from Steamed-Up Fans," *The Sporting News,* April 28, 1938, page 5.
73. "Tobin Goes After No. 2: Hard-Hitting Righthander May Oppose Southpaw Hollingsworth in Series Final with Reds Today," page 1.
74. "Rizzo Day: Pirate Rookie to Be Honored June 4," *The Pittsburgh Press,* April 25, 1938, page 23.
75. Lester Biederman, "Strategy Helps Pirates Keep Unbeaten Record: 'Smart' Move Nets Victory in Eighth," *The Pittsburgh Press,* April 26, 1938, page 24.
76. *Ibid.*
77. *Ibid.*
78. "Pirate Patter: Bowman Ready," *The Pittsburgh Press,* April 27, 1938, page 24.
79. Lester Biederman, "Swift Pitches Way into Starting Role: Classy Relief Work Aids Hurling Staff," *The Pittsburgh Press,* April 27, 1938, page 24.
80. "Floyd Vaughan Has Big Day as Bucs Beat Cubs," *Sarasota Herald,* April 28, 1938, page 3.
81. *Ibid.*
82. "Pirate Patter: All in a Day's Work!" *The Pittsburgh Press,* April 28, 1938, page 28.
83. "Pirate Patter: What! Lloyd Waner Squawks!" *The Pittsburgh Press,* April 29, 1938, page 37.
84. Chester L. Smith, "The Village Smithy: Sarazan Passes Up PGA for British Open," *The Pittsburgh Press,* April 30, 1938, page 7.
85. "Pirate Patter: What! Lloyd Waner Squawks!" page 37.
86. Lester Biederman, "Bucs After 21st Win in a Row over Reds: Russ Bauers Will Pitch First Game," *The Pittsburgh Press,* April 30, 1938, page 7.
87. Lester Biederman, "Cold, Wet Grounds Postpones Cards' Finale: Bucs Leave Tonight for Series with Reds," *The Pittsburgh Press,* April 29, 1938, page 37.
88. Charles J. Doyle, "Traynor's Pirate Craft Far from Shell-Proof," *The Sporting News,* May 5, 1938, page 3.
89. *Ibid.*

Chapter 6

1. "Pirate Patter: Reds Prove Jinx to Todd," *The Pittsburgh Press,* May 2, 1938, page 27.
2. Sid Feder, "Pirates Begin Annual Fadeout Earlier Than Usual as Cubs Move Up in Race," *Prescott Evening Courier,* May 2, 1938, page 5.
3. Lester Biederman, "Lost — Or Mislaid — Bucs' Batting Punch!: Handley Replaces Brubaker at Third," *The Pittsburgh Press,* May 2, 1938, page 27.
4. Chester L. Smith, "The Village Smithy: East, West to 'Mix It' if Burleigh's in Form," *The Pittsburgh Press,* May 3, 1938, page 26.
5. Charles J. Doyle, "Rookie Johnny Rizzo Rises to Answer 'Here' to Pirates' Long Search for Pay-Off Punch," *The Sporting News,* May 5, 1938, page 3.
6. *Ibid.*
7. *Ibid.*
8. *Ibid.*
9. *Ibid.*
10. *Ibid.*
11. *Ibid.*

12. Fred Landucci, "Sports Stew — Served Hot," *The Pittsburgh Press*, May 4, 1938, page 30.
13. *Ibid*.
14. Lester Biederman, "Tighten Up, Bucs! Slump's Getting Serious!: Defense Weakness Proving Too Costly," *The Pittsburgh Press*, May 4, 1938, page 28.
15. *Ibid*.
16. "Pirate Patter: Waner Act Revived!" *The Pittsburgh Press*, May 5, 1938, page 28.
17. *Ibid*.
18. "National League Standing on Tuesday Morning," *The Sporting News*, May 12, 1938, page 8.
19. "Pirate Patter: Waner Act Revived!" page 28.
20. *Ibid*.
21. Lester Biederman, "Pirate Patter: Robbery!" *The Pittsburgh Press*, May 6, 1938, page 46.
22. Lester Biederman, "Pirate Patter: And He Laughed!" *The Pittsburgh Press*, May 7, 1938, page 7.
23. "National League Standing on Tuesday Morning," *The Sporting News*, May 12, 1938, page 8.
24. "Pirates Will Play at McKeesport Park," *The Pittsburgh Press*, May 5, 1938, page 28.
25. Biederman, "Pirate Patter: Robbery!" page 46.
26. Biederman, "Pirate Patter: And He Laughed!" page 7.
27. *Ibid*.
28. Charles J. Doyle, "Pirates Still Being Terrified by Terry: Buccos Roll Over in Two Games When Memphis Bill Scowls," *The Sporting News*, May 12, 1938, page 1.
29. Biederman, "Pirate Patter: And He Laughed!" page 7.
30. "National League Standing on Tuesday Morning," *The Sporting News*, May 12, 1938, page 8.
31. Lester Biederman, "Ott's Bat Brings Terrys from Behind in Eighth," *The Pittsburgh Press*, May 8, 1938, page 3.
32. Lester Biederman, "Pirate Triumph Postpones Shakeup: Paul, Suhr Get Respite from Bench," *The Pittsburgh Press*, May 9, 1938, page 23.
33. Lester Biederman, "Pirate Patter: Handley's Guilty!" *The Pittsburgh Press*, May 9, 1938, page 23.
34. *Ibid*.
35. "Pirate Patter: Casey Walks out on Win," *The Pittsburgh Press*, May 10, 1938, page 26.
36. Lester Biederman, "Cold Cancels Final Bees-Pirates Game: Handley Lone Bright Spot in Bucs' Slump," *The Pittsburgh Press*, May 10, 1938, page 26.
37. Lester Biederman, "Cold Keeps Pirates Idle Again: Phils Play Single Game Tomorrow," *The Pittsburgh Press*, May 11, 1938, page 24.
38. Biederman, "Cold Cancels Final Bees-Pirates Game: Handley Lone Bright Spot in Bucs' Slump," page 26.
39. Lester Biederman, "Boos Will Soon Turn to Cheers, Paul Says," *The Pittsburgh Press*, May 11, 1938, page 24.
40. *Ibid*.
41. *Ibid*.
42. *Ibid*.
43. *Ibid*.
44. Lester Biederman, "Cold Ruins Phil Finale; Bucs Go West Tonight," *The Pittsburgh Press*, May 12, 1938, page 26.
45. Chester L. Smith, "The Village Smithy: Traynor Ready to Roll Up Sleeves and Wade in," *The Pittsburgh Press*, May 13, 1938, page 41.
46. Biederman, "Cold Keeps Pirates Idle Again: Phils Play Single Game Tomorrow," page 24.
47. Charles J. Doyle, "Pie Turns Crusty, Gives Pirates Jolt: Benches Paul Waner and Suhr, When Two Vets Slump," *The Sporting News*, May 19, 1938, page 6.
48. Lester Biederman, "Want Game Saved? Call Mace Brown: Pirate Star Tops in Relief Hurling," *The Pittsburgh Press*, May 14, 1938, page 7.
49. Lester Biederman, "Traynor Curtails Pitching Squad as Rain Halts Pirates: Heintzelman, Duke Shipped to Montreal," *The Pittsburgh Press*, May 15, 1938, page 1.
50. "Pirates Down Chicago Team in 11th Round," *Schenectady Gazette*, May 16, 1938, page 16.
51. Biederman, "Traynor Curtails Pitching Squad as Rain Halts Pirates: Heintzelman, Duke Shipped to Montreal," page 1.
52. "National League Standing on Tuesday," *The Sporting News*, May 19, 1938, page 8.
53. Biederman, "Traynor Curtails Pitching Squad as Rain Halts Pirates: Heintzelman, Duke Shipped to Montreal," page 1.
54. Chester L. Smith, "The Village Smithy: Duke Puzzled as to Why He Never Got Chance," *The Pittsburgh Press*, May 16, 1938, page 21.
55. Charles J. Doyle, "Pirates' Big Shots Still So Many Duds: Three Games Dropped in Boston, All by One-Run Margin," *The Sporting News*, May 26, 1938, page 3.
56. Lester Biederman, "Bauers' Jinx Newest Pirate Problem: P. Waner, Suhr Back for Needed Punch," *The Pittsburgh Press*, May 18, 1938, page 26.
57. "Pirate Patter: Klinger Gets Chance Today," *The Pittsburgh Press*, May 18, 1938, page 26.
58. *Ibid*.
59. "National League Standing on Tuesday Morning," *The Sporting News*, May 26, 1938, page 8.
60. Lester Biederman, "Where's That Buc Power? Hurlers Ask: Pitching Brilliant, But

Mates Fold Up," *The Pittsburgh Press,* May 19, 1938, page 25.
  61. "Pirate Patter: Double Pay for Overtime?" *The Pittsburgh Press,* May 20, 1938, page 35.
  62. *Ibid.*
  63. Fred Landucci, "Sports Stew—Served Hot," *The Pittsburgh Press,* May 20, 1938, page 36.
  64. Lester Biederman, "P. Waner's Hitting .207! That's What's Wrong!: Rizzo, Vaughan, Todd Away Below Form," *The Pittsburgh Press,* May 21, 1938, page 7.
  65. *Ibid.*
  66. "Pirate Patter: Brandt Against Hubbell!" *The Pittsburgh Press,* May 22, 1938, page 1.
  67. "Bucs, Phils, Dodgers in Trade Rumors," *The Pittsburgh Press,* May 22, 1938, page 1.
  68. *Ibid.*
  69. "Pirate Patter: Slump-Checkers!" *The Pittsburgh Press,* May 23, 1938, page 22.
  70. "Swift a Father," *The Pittsburgh Press,* May 23, 1938, page 22.
  71. "Bucs Plan to Rebuild—But It Will Be Piece-by-Piece," *The Pittsburgh Press,* May 24, 1938, page 23.
  72. *Ibid.*
  73. Chester L. Smith, "The Village Smithy: Pirates' Head Man Explains Rebuilding Plans," *The Pittsburgh Press,* May 25, 1938, page 26.
  74. Lester Biederman, "Lloyd Now 'Big Poison' of Waners: First Pirate-Phil Battle Rained Out," *The Pittsburgh Press,* May 24, 1938, page 25.
  75. Lester Biederman, "Rizzo's Recovery Hope of Bucs: Phils 'Band Box' May Revive Slugger," *The Pittsburgh Press,* May 25, 1938, page 26.
  76. Biederman. "Lloyd Now 'Big Poison' of Waners: First Pirate-Phil Battle Rained Out," page 25.
  77. *Ibid.*
  78. Biederman, "Rizzo's Recovery Hope of Bucs: Phils 'Band Box' May Revive Slugger," page 26.
  79. "Pirates Rained Out; Play Here Tomorrow," *The Pittsburgh Press,* May 26, 1938, page 26.
  80. Lester Biederman, "Pirates Open Home Stay with Cubs: Klinger Gets Chance; May Alter Lineup," *The Pittsburgh Press,* May 27, 1938, page 34.
  81. Lester Biederman, "Pirate Patter: Bucs Need Starter!" *The Pittsburgh Press,* May 28, 1938, page 6.
  82. *Ibid.*
  83. *Ibid.*
  84. Lester Biederman, "Cubs Pound Bauers and Sewell, Win 9 to 3: Bruins Score Nine Runs in 7th-Inning," *The Pittsburgh Press,* May 29, 1938, page 1.
  85. "National League Standing on Tuesday Morning," *The Sporting News,* June 2, 1938, page 8.

Chapter 7

  1. Charles J. Doyle, "Traynor Reaches Show-Down Stage on Bucs; Ready to Drop Vets in Rebuilding Program: P. Waner Included on Doubtful List," *The Sporting News,* June 2, 1938, page 1.
  2. *Ibid.*
  3. *Ibid.*
  4. "National League Standing on Tuesday Morning," *The Sporting News,* June 2, 1938, page 8.
  5. *Ibid.*
  6. Lester Biederman, "Pirate Patter: Next Come Giants," *The Pittsburgh Press,* May 31, 1938, page 24.
  7. *Ibid.*
  8. *Ibid.*
  9. Lester Biederman, "Bauers' Form Revives Pirates Hopes: Recovery of Hurling Ace Aids Morale," *The Pittsburgh Press,* June 2, 1938, page 27.
  10. "Suhr Honored," *The Pittsburgh Press,* June 1, 1938, page 25.
  11. Lester Biederman, "Pirate Patter: Pirate Injuries," *The Pittsburgh Press,* June 2, 1938, page 27.
  12. "Bucs May Swap Young for Berger, Chiozza: Traynor Expected to Decide Today," *The Pittsburgh Press,* June 3, 1938, page 39.
  13. Lester Biederman, "'Let's Talk Trade,' Says Traynor to Bill Terry: Buc Pilot Seeks Real 'Fence-Buster,'" *The Pittsburgh Press,* June 1, 1938, page 25.
  14. "Bucs May Swap Young for Berger, Chiozza: Traynor Expected to Decide Today," page 39.
  15. *Ibid.*
  16. "Bill Terry Trying to Get Pep Young from Pittsburgh: Giants Offer Berger and Chiozza for Pirate Second-Sacker," *The Free Lance-Star,* June 3, 1938, page 3.
  17. *Ibid.*
  18. "Pirate Patter: Why He's 'Big Poison,'" *The Pittsburgh Press,* June 4, 1938, page 7.
  19. "In 2500-Hit Club: Paul Waner," *The Sporting News,* June 9, 1938, page 6.
  20. "Pirate Patter: Why He's 'Big Poison,'" page 7.
  21. "National League Standing on Tuesday Morning," *The Sporting News,* June 9, 1938, page 8.
  22. Lester Biederman, "Pirate Front Office Blocks Trade: Traynor Anxious to Complete Deal," *The Pittsburgh Press,* June 4, 1938, page 7.
  23. *Ibid.*
  24. Bucco, "Pirates Keep Young, Also Old Tradition: Spurn Terry's Second Sacker Bid for Fear of Helping Giants," *The Sporting News,* June 9, 1938, page 14.
  25. *Ibid.*
  26. Lester Biederman, "Pirates Best Brooklyn Dodgers, 4 to 3: Pepper Young Tops Attack as

Buccos Triumph in 11th," *The Pittsburgh Press,* June 5, 1938, page 1.

27. "Pirate Patter: Todd Hits," *The Pittsburgh Press,* June 5, 1938, page 1.

28. "Dodgers Wallop Bucs for 15 Hits, 10–5 Win," *The Gazette,* June 6, 1938, page 17.

29. Lester Biederman, "Pirate Patter: Young Strews His Pepper," *The Pittsburgh Press,* June 7, 1938, page 24.

30. "Fette Tagged for Seventh Loss of Year," *The Lewiston Daily Sun,* June 9, 1938, page 9.

31. Lester Biederman, "'It's Tough-But I Love It' Says Klinger, of Big League," *The Pittsburgh Press,* June 9, 1938, page 27.

32. Lester Biederman, "Pirate Patter: Suhr on Rampage!" *The Pittsburgh Press,* June 10, 1938, page 31.

33. "Pirates Win Over Boston, 5 to 3," *The Daily Times,* June 10, 1938, page 13.

34. Lester Biederman, "'Fireman' Brown Puts out Fire in Bee Hive," *The Pittsburgh Press,* June 10, 1938, page 31.

35. Lester Biederman, "Buc Errors Make Phils Look Good: Four Miscues Enable Wilson's Men to Win, 3–2," *The Pittsburgh Press,* June 11, 1938, page 11.

36. Charles J. Doyle, "Dinner-Bucket Play of Pirates Jars Pie: Buc Leader Comes to Conclusion Spirit Is Inborn-Asset," *The Sporting News,* June 16, 1938, page 14.

37. "Pirate Patter: National League's Loss!" *The Pittsburgh Press,* June 11, 1938, page 11.

38. "Klinger, Brandt to Hurl," *The Pittsburgh Press,* June 12, 1938, page 1.

39. Lester Biederman, "Pirates Defeat Phils, 4 to 3; Swift's Homer Scores Three: Rizzo and Young on Base When Bill Makes Hit," *The Pittsburgh Press,* June 12, 1938, page 1.

40. "Klinger, Brandt to Hurl," page 1.

41. Lester Biederman, "Another Pirate Trading Effort Fails: Phils Ignore Bid of Dickshot Or Jensen for Klein," *The Pittsburgh Press,* June 13, 1938, page 20.

42. Lester Biederman, "Pirate Patter: P. Waner, Suhr Hit Hard," *The Pittsburgh Press,* June 13, 1938, page 20.

43. Lester Biederman, "Pirates, Phillies Reopen Negotiations: Bucs Offer Dickshot, Or Jensen, Pitcher, and Cash for Klein," *The Pittsburgh Press,* June 14, 1938, page 23.

44. Lester Biederman, "Pirate Patter: Paul Waner, Suhr Keep Hitting Streaks Intact," *The Pittsburgh Press,* June 15, 1938, page 21.

45. *Ibid.*

46. Charles J. Doyle, "Buc Bids to Cards and Phils Revealed: Effort to Get Chuck Klein Balked by Demand of Quakers," *The Sporting News,* June 23, 1938, page 3.

47. Lester Biederman, "Trade Deadline Finds Buc Roster Unchanged," *The Pittsburgh Press,* June 16, 1938, page 25.

48. Sid Feder, "Reds, Pirates Look Dangerous to the Leaders," *The Gettysburg Times,* June 17, 1938, page 3.

49. "National League Standing on Tuesday Morning," *The Sporting News,* June 23, 1938, page 8.

50. *Ibid.*

51. "Pirates Wreck Phillies Twice: Take Opening Game, 14 to 4, and Capture Nightcap by 16 to 3 Tally," *St. Joseph Gazette,* June 20, 1938, page 5.

52. "National League Standing on Tuesday Morning," *The Sporting News,* June 30, 1938, page 8.

53. *Ibid.*

54. *Ibid.*

55. *Ibid.*

56. Lester Biederman, "Pirate Patter: Whipping Willows," *The Pittsburgh Press,* June 27, 1938, page 20.

57. "L. Waner, Vaughan, Brown, Pie's Pick for All-Stars," *The Pittsburgh Press,* June 26, 1938, page 1.

58. "Bucs at McKeesport for Game Tomorrow," *The Pittsburgh Press,* June 26, 1938, page 1.

59. Lester Biederman, "Reds Earn Rating as Pennant Threat: McKechnie's Club Gets Fine Hitting and Good Pitching," *The Pittsburgh Press,* June 28, 1938, page 21.

60. Lester Biederman, "Bauers' Fielding Latest Pirate Worry: Youngster's Pitching Good But Marred by Lack of Experience," *The Pittsburgh Press,* June 29, 1938, page 22.

61. *Ibid.*

62. "Pirate Patter: Bucs Hit Merry Clip," *The Pittsburgh Press,* June 30, 1938, page 30.

63. Lester Biederman, "Swift Puts Hold to Reds' Forward Surge: Vet Hurler Stars in Relief Job; Aids in Corsair Attack," *The Pittsburgh Press,* June 30, 1938, page 30.

64. "National League Standing on Tuesday Morning," *The Sporting News,* July 7, 1938, page 8.

65. Lester Biederman, "Rain Halts Opening of Buc-Cards Series," *The Pittsburgh Press,* July 1, 1938, page 27.

66. "Pirate Patter: A Swell Anniversary," *The Pittsburgh Press,* July 1, 1938, page 27.

Chapter 8

1. "Castleman Twirls New York to 14–1 Rout Over Phils: Hank Leiber's Big Bat Paces Giants—Bucs Beat Reds, 3–1," *Meriden Record,* July 1, 1938, page 12.

2. Lester Biederman, "Rain Halts Opening of Buc-Cards Series," *The Pittsburgh Press,* July 1, 1938, page 27.

3. Lester Biederman, "Klinger in Form, Bucs Beat Cards, 5–1: Young's Extra-Base Hit Brings Rookie Hurler Sixth Win," *The Pittsburgh Press,* July 3, 1938, page 1.

Notes — Chapter 8

4. "Pirate Patter: Frankie's Getting Childish," *The Pittsburgh Press,* July 3, 1938, page 1.
5. Biederman, "Klinger in Form, Bucs Beat Cards, 5–1: Young's Extra-Base Hit Brings Rookie Hurler Sixth Win," page 1.
6. "Pirate Patter: Frankie's Getting Childish," page 1.
7. "National League Standing on Tuesday Morning," *The Sporting News,* July 7, 1938, page 8.
8. *Ibid.*
9. Lester Biederman, "Pirate Trio Will Play for National Against American," *The Pittsburgh Press,* July 3, 1938, page 3.
10. Lester Biederman, "Pirates Hot After Pace-Setting Giants: Current Gait Best in Majors to Date; Win 23 out of 31 Games," *The Pittsburgh Press,* July 5, 1938, page 22.
11. *Ibid.*
12. "700 Join Baseball School, Buccos to Admit Only 400," *The Pittsburgh Press,* July 3, 1938, page 1.
13. "Schultz to Trim Pirate Baseball School Squad," *The Pittsburgh Press,* July 6, 1938, page 18.
14. Charles J. Doyle, "Mace Brown, All-Star Hero, 'Doesn't Feel at Home Without a Few Runners on the Bases,'" *The Sporting News,* July 14, 1938, page 3.
15. *Ibid.*
16. *Ibid.*
17. *Ibid.*
18. *Ibid.*
19. *Ibid.*
20. J.G. Taylor Spink, "Three and One: Looking Them Over with J.G. Taylor Spink," *The Sporting News,* July 14, 1938, page 4.
21. "Ban on All-Star Broadcast News to Pirate President," *The Pittsburgh Press,* July 9, 1938, page 7.
22. *Ibid.*
23. "Bucs Now 5 to 2 in Title Chase," *The Pittsburgh Press,* July 6, 1938, page 18.
24. "Pirates Continue to Burn Up Circuit: Klinger and Rizzo Big Guns in 8th Straight Triumph," *The Pittsburgh Press,* July 9, 1938, page 5.
25. "National League Standing on Tuesday Morning," *The Sporting News,* July 14, 1938, page 8.
26. *Ibid.*
27. "Blanton and Bauers! Cy and Russ Go After 10th and 11th in Row Today, Opposed to Weiland and Macon," *The Pittsburgh Press,* July 10, 1938, page 1.
28. "Pirates Win 9th in a Row, Beat Cards, 8–7: Rizzo Clouts Pair of Homers; Brown Captures No. 12," *The Pittsburgh Press,* July 10, 1938, page 1.
29. "Blanton and Bauers!: Cy and Russ Go After 10th and 11th in Row Today, Opposed to Weiland and Macon," page 1.

30. "Pirate Win 9th in a Row, Beat Cards, 8–7: Rizzo Clouts Pair of Homers; Brown Captures No. 12," page 1.
31. "National League Standing on Tuesday Morning," *The Sporting News,* July 14, 1938, page 8.
32. "Pirate Patter," *The Pittsburgh Press,* July 11, 1938, page 20.
33. *Ibid.*
34. Charles J. Doyle, "All Hands Helping Bucs Get Up Steam: Hitting, Fielding, Pitching Click in Sustained Victory Drive," *The Sporting News,* July 14, 1938, page 2.
35. "National League Standing on Tuesday Morning," *The Sporting News,* July 14, 1938, page 8.
36. "Who Says Pirates 'Too Proud to Fight?': Ens, Todd Banished in Seventh-Inning Brawl with Umpire," *The Pittsburgh Press,* July 12, 1938, page 19.
37. *Ibid.*
38. *Ibid.*, page 20.
39. Lester Biederman, "Pirates Open Home Stand with Dodgers: Bucs in Position to Pad Lead in Next Two Weeks," *The Pittsburgh Press,* July 13, 1938, page 19.
40. *Ibid.*
41. "National League Standing on Tuesday Morning," *The Sporting News,* July 21, 1938, page 8.
42. "Buc Heads Prepare for Sellout on Sunday," *The Pittsburgh Press,* July 13, 1938, page 19.
43. Chester L. Smith, "The Village Smithy: Pirates Are Awake to Their Opportunities," *The Pittsburgh Press,* July 14, 1938, page 25.
44. "Vaughan Nears .300 Circle: Buc Shortstop Clouting Ball in Lusty Fashion-Camilli's Homer Really Takes Off," *The Pittsburgh Press,* July 14, 1938, page 25.
45. "National League Standing on Tuesday Morning," *The Sporting News,* July 21, 1938, page 8.
46. Lester Biederman, "Dodgers Are Generosity Personified: Fitzsimmons' Wild Pitch in Ninth Keeps Bucs in Game," *The Pittsburgh Press,* July 15, 1938, page 27.
47. "National League Standing on Tuesday Morning," *The Sporting News,* July 21, 1938, page 8.
48. Lester Biederman, "Bucs Battle Giants; First Place at Stake: Corsairs Lead Over Terrymen Cut by Dodgers," *The Pittsburgh Press,* July 16, 1938, page 7.
49. "Pirate Patter: Babe Still Idol!" *The Pittsburgh Press,* July 16, 1938, page 7.
50. Charles J. Doyle, "Silent Waner Makes Flag Noise: 'I Don't See Any Club with Better Chance Than Bucs,' He Says," *The Sporting News,* July 21, 1938, page 2.
51. Chester L. Smith, "The Village Smithy: Always a Field Day with Giants in Town," *The Pittsburgh Press,* July 18, 1938, page 18.

52. "National League Standing on Tuesday Morning," *The Sporting News*, July 21, 1938, page 8.
53. "Expect 40,000 Crowd: Pirate-Giant Double-Header to Draw Capacity Throng; Tobin, Bauers Buc Hurlers," *The Pittsburgh Press*, July 17, 1938, page 4.
54. *Ibid.*, page 1 and 4.
55. Lester Biederman, "'Fireman' Brown Started out as a Catcher," *The Pittsburgh Press*, July 17, 1938, page 3.
56. "Come Early for Double-Header," *The Pittsburgh Press*, July 16, 1938, page 7.
57. Smith, "The Village Smithy: Always a Field Day with Giants in Town," page 18.
58. "Pirate Patter: A $20,000 Smack!" *The Pittsburgh Press*, July 18, 1938, page 18.
59. Smith, "The Village Smithy: Always a Field Day with Giants in Town," page 18.
60. *Ibid.*
61. Lester Biederman, "Pirates Still Can Win Edge in Series with New York: Bucs' Fighting Spirit Thrills Record Crowd," *The Pittsburgh Press*, July 18, 1938, page 18.
62. "Rizzo Fined $25," *The Pittsburgh Press*, July 18, 1938, page 18.
63. *Ibid.*
64. Lester Biederman, "Pirate Patter: Bucco King of Swat," *The Pittsburgh Press*, July 19, 1938, page 18.
65. Lester Biederman, "Bucs Best When Going Is Toughest: Club Shows Fight in Last Three Tilts with Giants," *The Pittsburgh Press*, July 19, 1938, page 18.
66. Chester L. Smith, "The Village Smithy: Traynor's Revitalized Forces Satisfy All," *The Pittsburgh Press*, July 19, 1938, page 18.
67. *Ibid.*
68. "National League Standing on Tuesday Morning," *The Sporting News*, July 28, 1938, page 8.
69. "Pirate Patter: Arky Pulls Ahead," *The Pittsburgh Press*, July 21, 1938, page 21.
70. "National League Standing on Tuesday Morning," *The Sporting News*, July 28, 1938, page 8.
71. "Pirate Patter: Arky Pulls Ahead," page 21.
72. Lester Biederman, "'You're Driving Me Crazy,' Pie Chants: Hairline Decisions Bring Worries and Cheer to Traynor," *The Pittsburgh Press*, July 22, 1938, page 25.
73. *Ibid.*
74. "Hartnett Figured to Put Cubs in Race: Managerial Shift, Although Rumored, Comes as Surprise," by Steve Snider, *The Pittsburgh Press*, July 21, 1938, page 21.
75. *Ibid.*
76. Chester L. Smith, "The Village Smithy: Clubowners' Moves Not Easily Fathomed," *The Pittsburgh Press*, July 22, 1938, page 25.
77. Lester Biederman, "Pirate Patter: Wanerville!" *The Pittsburgh Press*, July 23, 1938, page 13.
78. Lester Biederman, "Pirates Practice Doctrines of McGraw: Buccos Take Advantage of Every Break," *The Pittsburgh Press*, July 23, 1938, page 13.
79. "National League Standing on Tuesday Morning," *The Sporting News*, July 28, 1938, page 8.
80. "National League Standing on Tuesday Morning," *The Sporting News*, July 28, 1938, page 8.
81. Lester Biederman, "Eastern Trip to Test Pirates' Flag Drive," *The Pittsburgh Press*, July 25, 1938, page 20.
82. *Ibid.*
83. *Ibid.*

Chapter 9

1. "Tobin's Hard Luck Ends in Brilliant Exhibition," *The Pittsburgh Press*, July 25, 1938, page 21.
2. Lester Biederman, "Pirate Patter: Wanerville!" *The Pittsburgh Press*, July 23, 1938, page 13.
3. "Tobin's Hard Luck Ends in Brilliant Exhibition," page 21.
4. "National League Standing on Tuesday Morning," *The Sporting News*, August 4, 1938, page 8.
5. "Tobin's Hard Luck Ends in Brilliant Exhibition," page 21.
6. Charles J. Doyle, "Pirates, Though Cruising Boldly Ahead, Keeping Wary Eye Astern," *The Sporting News*, July 28, 1938, page 1.
7. Lester Biederman, "Pirates Jittery of Jinx on Eastern Trip: Shaky Philly Start Conjures Memories of Other Failures," *The Pittsburgh Press*, July 27, 1938, page 20.
8. *Ibid.*
9. "Pirate Patter: Arky's Speed Wins," *The Pittsburgh Press*, July 28, 1938, page 20.
10. Lester Biederman, "Sprained Muscle Puts Klinger on Shelf: Doctor Prescribes Rest Cure for Buc Hurler's Sore Arm," *The Pittsburgh Press*, July 28, 1938, page 20.
11. "National League Standing on Tuesday Morning," *The Sporting News*, August 4, 1938, page 8.
12. "Pirate Patter: Named After Waners," *The Pittsburgh Press*, July 29, 1938, page 29.
13. Lester Biederman, "Bucs Give Answer to Fighting Qualities: Pitching, Slugging Improves to Hold Big Lead in Race," *The Pittsburgh Press*, July 29, 1938, page 29.
14. Chester L. Smith, "The Village Smithy: Had It Not Been for Guglielmo Marconi," *The Pittsburgh Press*, July 28, 1938, page 20.
15. Charles J. Doyle, "Silent Paul Waner Makes Flag Noise: 'I Don't See Any Club with

Better Chance Than Bucs,'" He Says," *The Sporting News,* July 21, 1938, page 2.
16. *Ibid.*
17. Smith, "The Village Smithy: Had It Not Been for Guglielmo Marconi," page 20.
18. Lester Biederman, "All-Star Jinx Gets Mace Brown: Bucs' Star Relief Hurler Lacks Old 'Zip' Since Dream," *The Pittsburgh Press,* July 30, 1938, page 13.
19. *Ibid.*
20. *Ibid.*
21. Lester Biederman, "Bucs Continue Pace, Beat Dodgers, 9–2: Waner 'Act' Paves Way for Blanton," *The Pittsburgh Press,* July 31, 1938, page 1.
22. "National League Standing on Tuesday Morning," *The Sporting News,* August 4, 1938, page 8.
23. "National League Standing on Tuesday Morning," *The Sporting News,* August 4, 1938, page 8.
24. Lester Biederman, "Pirate Patter: Home Run Johnny!" *The Pittsburgh Press,* August 1, 1938, page 22.
25. "Pirate Patter: Wotta Month! Eh! Boys!" *The Pittsburgh Press,* July 31, 1938, page 4.
26. "Pirates Defeat Springfield," *The Pittsburgh Press,* August 2, 1938, page 19.
27. Lester Biederman, "Bucs Show Signs of Sizzling Pace: Handley and Young Begin 'Cracking Up' Under Heavy Strain," *The Pittsburgh Press,* August 3, 1938, page 18.
28. *Ibid.*
29. "Pittsburgh Takes Two from Boston; Yanks Beat Detroit in Eleventh: Blanton Takes Eighth in Row; Halted by Heat," *St. Joseph Gazette,* August 4, 1938, page 6.
30. "Pirate Patter: Todd Adds Winning Punch," *The Pittsburgh Press,* August 4, 1938, page 19.
31. *Ibid.*
32. *Ibid.*
33. Lester Biederman, "Bowman Aids in Bucs' Drive to Pad Lead: Brilliant Relief Work Takes Strain Off Hurling Staff," *The Pittsburgh Press,* August 4, 1938, page 19.
34. *Ibid.*
35. "National League Standing on Tuesday Morning," *The Sporting News,* August 11, 1938, page 8.
36. Charles J. Doyle, "Bucs' Backs Are Up Over Rizzo 'Dusting': Threaten Reprisals When Melton Pitch Flattens Rookie," *The Sporting News,* August 11, 1938, page 1.
37. Lester Biederman, "Pirates Need Left-Handed Pinch-Hitter: Red Lucas, Jensen Fail in Clutches," *The Pittsburgh Press,* August 6, 1938, page 7.
38. Jack Cuddy, "Rizzo Slaps 'Chain Gang,'" *The Pittsburgh Press,* August 7, 1938, page 1.
39. *Ibid.*
40. Lester Biederman, "50,000 May See Pirate-Giant Twin Bill: Saturday Contest Rained Out; Bucs Welcome Day's Rest," *The Pittsburgh Press,* August 7, 1938, page 1.
41. Biederman, "Pirates Need Left-Handed Pinch-Hitter: Red Lucas, Jensen Fail in Clutches," page 7.
42. Lester Biederman, "Pirate Patter: Mr. Mancuso Regrets," *The Pittsburgh Press,* August 8, 1938, page 20.
43. *Ibid.*
44. Lester Biederman, "Bowman Gives Bucs Much Needed 'Lift,'" *The Pittsburgh Press,* August 7, 1938, page 5.
45. Lester Biederman, "Pirate Patter: 'Porky' Works Magic," *The Pittsburgh Press,* August 9, 1938, page 22.
46. *Ibid.*
47. *Ibid.*
48. "National League Standing on Tuesday Morning," *The Sporting News,* August 11, 1938, page 8.
49. Lester Biederman, "Six and One-Half in Front! That's Bucs!: Hubbell Jinx, Giant Complex Shattered in Wild Flag Dash," *The Pittsburgh Press,* August 8, 1938, page 20.
50. Biederman, "Pirate Patter: Mr. Mancuso Regrets," page 20.
51. Biederman, "Six and One-Half in Front! That's Bucs! Hubbell Jinx, Giant Complex Shattered in Wild Flag Dash," page 20.
52. "National League Standing on Tuesday Morning," *The Sporting News,* August 11, 1938, page 8.
53. Biederman, "Six and One-Half in Front! That's Bucs! Hubbell Jinx, Giant Complex Shattered in Wild Flag Dash," page 20.
54. Lester Biederman, "Pirates Set for Stretch Drive in Race: Exhibitions Over, Battle to Hold Lead," *The Pittsburgh Press,* August 9, 1938, page 22.
55. "National League Standing on Tuesday Morning," *The Sporting News,* August 18, 1938, page 8.
56. *Ibid.*
57. Charles J. Doyle, "Enjoins Station KQV," *The Sporting News,* August 11, 1938, page 10.
58. *Ibid.*
59. Lester Biederman, "Bauers' Recovery Bolsters Buc Hopes: Klinger, Blanton Seek Double Win Over Cards Today," *The Pittsburgh Press,* August 10, 1938, page 20.
60. Lester Biederman, "Pirate Patter: Ducky Duck-Soup," *The Pittsburgh Press,* August 10, 1938, page 20.
61. Lester Biederman, "Bucs Get 'Break' as Giants Fold Up: Maintain 6 1/2 Game Lead; 'Gabby's' Cubs Come Tomorrow," *The Pittsburgh Press,* August 11, 1938, page 21.
62. Lester Biederman, "Pirate Patter: No Need to Worry!" *The Pittsburgh Press,* August 11, 1938, page 21.

63. "National League Standing on Tuesday Morning," *The Sporting News,* August 18, 1938, page 8.
64. Lester Biederman, "Pirate Patter: Same Old Gabby!" *The Pittsburgh Press,* August 13, 1938, page 7.
65. "Rizzo Honored, Gets Gun: Admirers Present Outfielder with Gift; Bauers Faces French Today," *The Pittsburgh Press,* August 14, 1938, page 1.
66. *Ibid.*
67. *Ibid.*
68. "Cubs Again Bombard Pirates as Giants Split with Phillies: Dizzy Dean Fails to Last in Victory," *Reading Eagle,* August 14, 1938, page 11.
69. "National League Standing on Tuesday Morning," *The Sporting News,* August 18, 1938, page 8.
70. Lester Biederman, "Pirate Patter: Sore Arm Balks Klinger," *The Pittsburgh Press,* August 15, 1938, page 19.
71. Lester Biederman, "McKechnie Fights to Keep Reds in Race: Last Eastern Trip to Tell Tale for Western Contenders," *The Pittsburgh Press,* August 15, 1938, page 18.
72. Biederman, "Pirate Patter: Sore Arm Balks Klinger," page 19.
73. *Ibid.*
74. Lester Biederman, "Pirate Patter: He's Valuable," *The Pittsburgh Press,* August 16, 1938, page 18.
75. Lester Biederman, "Traynor Benches Suhr, Todd in Shake-Up: Brubaker Takes Over First; Berres Works Behind Bat," *The Pittsburgh Press,* August 16, 1938, page 18.
76. Lester Biederman, "Pirates Take Five-Game Lead into West: Brandt Or Lucas to Face Cardinals in First Meeting," *The Pittsburgh Press,* August 17, 1938, page 18.
77. "National League Standing on Tuesday Morning," *The Sporting News,* August 25, 1938, page 8.
78. Lester Biederman, "Bucs in Chicago for Important Series: Bruins Prime Dean, Lee to Get Jump in Four-Game Stand," *The Pittsburgh Press,* August 19, 1938, page 25.
79. "Pirate Patter: 'Luckless' Bauers!" *The Pittsburgh Press,* August 19, 1938, page 27.
80. Lester Biederman, "Pirates Rout Dean, Defeat Cubs, 5 to 2: Dizzy Chased in 6th; Corsairs Increase Lead to 5 1/2 Games," *The Pittsburgh Press,* August 21, 1938, page 1.
81. "National League Standing on Tuesday Morning," *The Sporting News,* September 1, 1938, page 8.
82. Lester Biederman, "Pirate Patter: 'Jeep' Shows Fight," *The Pittsburgh Press,* August 22, 1938, page 18.
83. *Ibid.*
84. "Pirate Patter: Money Pitcher!" *The Pittsburgh Press,* August 23, 1938, page 18.
85. Biederman, "Pirate Patter: 'Jeep' Shows Fight," page 18.
86. *Ibid.*
87. Hugh S. Fullerton, Jr. "Yanks Down A's Twice; Bucs Drop Doubleheader to Cubs," *The Meriden Daily Journal,* August 22, 1938, page 4.
88. "Arky Tells Secret of What's Making Pirates Click," *The Pittsburgh Press,* August 22, 1938, page 18.
89. "Pirate Patter: Money Pitcher!" page 18.
90. *Ibid.*

Chapter 10

1. Lester Biederman, "Fans' Tactics Bewilder Pace-Setting Bucs: Traynor, Players Mystified by 'Bird' as Club Still Wins," *The Pittsburgh Press,* August 24, 1938, page 20.
2. "National League Standing on Tuesday Morning," *The Sporting News,* September 1, 1938, page 8.
3. Biederman, "Fans' Tactics Bewilder Pace-Setting Bucs: Traynor, Players Mystified by 'Bird' as Club Still Wins," page 20.
4. Lester Biederman, "Pirate Patter: They Came to Boo!" *The Pittsburgh Press,* August 24, 1938, page 20.
5. Biederman, "Fans' Tactics Bewilder Pace-Setting Bucs: Traynor, Players Mystified by 'Bird' as Club Still Wins," page 20.
6. Lester Biederman, "Pirate Patter: Bucs Want to Fight!" *The Pittsburgh Press,* August 25, 1938, page 19.
7. Fred Landucci, "Sports Stew-Served Hot," *The Pittsburgh Press,* August 24, 1938, page 21.
8. Lester Biederman, "'Pep' Young Spark of Pirates' Drive: Flashy All-Around Work Furnishes Team's Inspiration," *The Pittsburgh Press,* August 25, 1938, page 19.
9. "National League Standing on Tuesday Morning," *The Sporting News,* September 1, 1938, page 8.
10. *Ibid.*
11. Lester Biederman, "Pirate Patter: Better Start Punching!" *The Pittsburgh Press,* August 26, 1938, page 28.
12. *Ibid.*
13. *Ibid.*
14. Lester Biederman, "Traynor Benches Rizzo and Handley: Dickshot; Brubaker Injected in Search for Hitting Strength," *The Pittsburgh Press,* August 26, 1938, page 28.
15. Lester Biederman, "Pirate Patter: Bubbling Water!" *The Pittsburgh Press,* August 27, 1938, page 7.
16. *Ibid.*
17. *Ibid.*
18. Lester Biederman, "Bucs End Losing Streak, Beat Phils, 6–1: Brandt's Masterful Hurling, Opportune Hitting Does Trick," *The Pittsburgh Press,* August 28, 1938, page 1.

Notes — Chapter 10

19. *Ibid.*
20. Lester Biederman, "Bucs Will Shake Slump Off, Wilson Says: Quakers' Manager Cautions Pirates Against Worrying," *The Pittsburgh Press*, August 27, 1938, page 7.
21. "National League Standing on Tuesday Morning," *The Sporting News*, September 1, 1938, page 8.
22. Lester Biederman, "Pirate Patter: 'Oh, Give Me a Home,'" *The Pittsburgh Press*, August 29, 1938, page 20.
23. Lester Biederman, "Vaughan Takes Rank with Best Shortstops: Buc Star Has Become Polished Performer in Field-Overcomes Throwing Weakness," *The Pittsburgh Press*, August 28, 1938, page 3.
24. Lester Biederman, "Bucs' Bats Boom Basehits Again!: Giants Due to Run into Hot Blasts," *The Pittsburgh Press*, August 30, 1938, page 18.
25. Lester Biederman, "Pirate Patter: Pep Young Really Celebrates Birthday!" *The Pittsburgh Press*, August 30, 1938, page 18.
26. Biederman, "Bucs' Bats Boom Basehits Again!: Giants Due to Run into Hot Blasts," page 18.
27. "National League Standing on Tuesday Morning," *The Sporting News*, September 8, 1938, page 8.
28. "Signing of Manush Hailed by Buccos," *The Pittsburgh Press*, August 31, 1938, page 27.
29. Lester Biederman, "Relief Hurlers Keymen in Bucs Drive: Bowman and Swift Perform Brilliantly Against Cardinals," *The Pittsburgh Press*, August 18, 1938, page 20.
30. "40,000 Watch Giants and Pirates Battle: World Series Air Shown by Record Week-Day Throng," *The Pittsburgh Press*, August 31, 1938, page 27.
31. "Pittsburgh Pirates Protest Giant Game: Claim Umpire Sears Erred in Calling Two Men Out," *The Portsmouth Times*, September 1, 1938, page 5.
32. "Protest! Bucs Appeal to Frick on Sears' Ruling," *The Pittsburgh Press*, September 1, 1938, pages 23–24.
33. *Ibid.*
34. Lester Biederman, "Pirate Patter: Assist for Brubaker!" *The Pittsburgh Press*, September 1, 1938, page 23.
35. Lester Biederman, "'Clinch Flag Early,' Pirates Theme: Bucs Hope to Step Up Tempo Within Next Three Weeks," *The Pittsburgh Press*, September 1, 1938, page 23.
36. "National League Standing on Tuesday Morning," *The Sporting News*, September 8, 1938, page 8.
37. Lester Biederman, "Waners Add to Terry's Heavy Burden," *The Pittsburgh Press*, September 2, 1938, page 27.
38. "National League Standing on Tuesday Morning," *The Sporting News*, September 8, 1938, page 8.
39. Charles J. Doyle, "Ex-Movie Magnate to Bid for Pirates on Report Pittsburgh Club Is for Sale: Mrs. Dreyfuss Open to Adequate Offer," *The Sporting News*, September 8, 1938, page 1.
40. "Good News! Hubbell Thinks Bucs Can Beat Yankees," *The Pittsburgh Press*, September 2, 1938, page 27.
41. Chester L. Smith, "The Village Smithy: Daniel Sees Six-Game World Series," *The Pittsburgh Press*, September 2, 1938, page 27.
42. *Ibid.*
43. Daniel M. Daniel, "Terry Stings Traynor by Shot That 'Bucs Should Win Or Quit,'" *The Sporting News*, September 8, 1938, page 1.
44. *Ibid.*
45. Lester Biederman, "Pirates Miss Vaughan's Bat, Fielding: Infield Jittery with Shortstop out of Lineup," *The Pittsburgh Press*, September 3, 1938, page 7.
46. "National League Standing on Tuesday Morning," *The Sporting News*, September 8, 1938, page 8.
47. "Pirate Patter: Better Get Back, Arky!" *The Pittsburgh Press*, September 4, 1938, page 1.
48. Lester Biederman, "Pirates, Cubs in Holiday Double-Header: Stiff Fight to Hold Lead in Prospect," *The Pittsburgh Press*, September 5, 1938, page 13.
49. *Ibid.*
50. Lester Biederman, "Pirate Patter: Medwick Easy for Bauers," *The Pittsburgh Press*, September 5, 1938, page 13.
51. Doyle, "Ex-Movie Magnate to Bid for Pirates on Report Pittsburgh Club Is for Sale: Mrs. Dreyfuss Open to Adequate Offer," page 1.
52. Biederman, "Pirates, Cubs in Holiday Double-Header: Stiff Fight to Hold Lead in Prospect," page 13.
53. Lester Biederman, "Pirates Miss Vaughan's Booming Bat: Buccaneers Lack Punch with Arky out of Lineup," *The Pittsburgh Press*, September 6, 1938, page 20.
54. Lester Biederman, "Circus Catches? ... Rizzo Thrills Fans with Them," *The Pittsburgh Press*, September 6, 1938, page 20.
55. Biederman, "Pirates Miss Vaughan's Booming Bat: Buccaneers Lack Punch with Arky out of Lineup," page 20.
56. Lester Biederman, "Pirates, Reds Open Important Series: Bob Klinger, Derringer to Take Mound," *The Pittsburgh Press*, September 7, 1938, page 24.
57. "National League Standing on Tuesday Morning," *The Sporting News*, September 15, 1938, page 8.
58. *Ibid.*
59. Lester Biederman, "Thevenow Comes Through in Emergency: Veteran, Filling in for

Vaughan, Sparkles Afield," *The Pittsburgh Press*, September 8, 1938, page 21.
  60. Chester L. Smith, "The Village Smithy: Traynor's Answer," *The Pittsburgh Press*, September 9, 1938, page 39.
  61. Lester Biederman, "Bucs Feel 'Heat' of Three Contenders: Cubs, Reds, Giants Get Back in Race," *The Pittsburgh Press*, September 9, 1938, page 39.
  62. "National League Standing on Tuesday Morning," *The Sporting News*, September 15, 1938, page 8.
  63. Lester Biederman, "Pirates Battle Cards; Vaughan Back in Lineup: Bauers Nominated to Face Crippled Redbirds in Opener," *The Pittsburgh Press*, September 10, 1938, page 7.
  64. "The Army Wins!" *The Pittsburgh Press*, September 10, 1938, page 7.
  65. "Bucs Are in! Noted Bookie Can't See How They Can Lose," *The Pittsburgh Press*, September 10, 1938, page 7.
  66. "National League Standing on Tuesday Morning," *The Sporting News*, September 15, 1938, page 8.
  67. "Pirate Patter: Cards Ballyhoo 'Daffy,'" *The Pittsburgh Press*, September 11, 1938, page 3.
  68. *Ibid.*
  69. *Ibid.*
  70. Lester Biederman, "Pirates Headed for Last Trip East in Chase of Pennant," *The Pittsburgh Press*, September 12, 1938, page 23.
  71. *Ibid.*
  72. *Ibid.*
  73. "Frisch Third Pilot Fired This Season," *The Pittsburgh Press*, September 12, 1938, page 22.
  74. *Ibid.*
  75. Biederman, "Pirates Headed for Last Trip East in Chase of Pennant," page 23.
  76. "Traynor Confident Pirates Will Win Senior Loop Flag: Manager of Leaders Says 'Every Club Is One to Beat,'" *Meriden Record*, September 14, 1938, page 4.
  77. *Ibid.*
  78. "Pirate Patter: Traynor Stays!" *The Pittsburgh Press*, September 15, 1938, page 26.
  79. *Ibid.*
  80. *Ibid.*
  81. *Ibid.*
  82. "National League Standing on Tuesday Morning," *The Sporting News*, September 22, 1938, page 8.
  83. Eddie Beachler, "Sports Stew-Served Hot," *The Pittsburgh Press*, September 13, 1938, page 23.

Chapter 11

  1. "'Doubleheader D.T.'s' Make Wreck of Affable 'Pie,'" *The Pittsburgh Press*, September 16, 1938, page 44.
  2. "Scribbled by Scribes: The Pennant Jitters," *The Sporting News*, September 22, 1938, page 4.
  3. "Pirate Patter: Rizzo Prize Rookie!" *The Pittsburgh Press*, September 17, 1938, page 8.
  4. *Ibid.*
  5. Lester Biederman, "Double Bills Ahead; Bucs Shy on Hurlers," *The Pittsburgh Press*, September 17, 1938, page 7.
  6. "Pirate Patter: Rizzo Prize Rookie!" page 8.
  7. Biederman, "Double Bills Ahead; Bucs Shy on Hurlers," page 7.
  8. Lester Biederman, "Pirate Patter: Joy in the Clubhouse," *The Pittsburgh Press*, September 18, 1938, page 5.
  9. "National League Standing on Tuesday Morning," *The Sporting News*, September 22, 1938, page 8.
  10. Lester Biederman, "Pirates Beat Bees in Ninth, 2–1; Cubs Win Two: L. Waner's Single Scores Winning Run; Klinger Is Victor," *The Pittsburgh Press*, September 18, 1938, page 1.
  11. *Ibid.*
  12. Biederman, "Pirate Patter: Joy in the Clubhouse," page 1.
  13. *Ibid.*
  14. *Ibid.*
  15. Biederman, "Pirates Beat Bees in Ninth, 2–1; Cubs Win Two: L. Waner's Single Scores Winning Run; Klinger Is Victor," page 1.
  16. "National League Standing on Tuesday Morning," *The Sporting News*, September 22, 1938, page 8.
  17. Lester Biederman, "Rain Washes out Pirates in Philly: Move to Brooklyn for New Series of Doubleheaders," *The Pittsburgh Press*, September 19, 1938, page 19.
  18. "National League Standing on Tuesday Morning," *The Sporting News*, September 22, 1938, page 8.
  19. Biederman, "Rain Washes out Pirates in Philly: Move to Brooklyn for New Series of Doubleheaders," page 19.
  20. George Kirksey, "'Washed Out' Games Put Bucs Nearer to Pennant," *The Pittsburgh Press*, September 20, 1938, page 22.
  21. "Pirate Patter: Breaks of the Game," *The Pittsburgh Press*, September 20, 1938, page 22.
  22. "National League Standing on Tuesday Morning," *The Sporting News*, September 22, 1938, page 8.
  23. *Ibid.*
  24. Lester Biederman, "Rain Delays Pirate-Dodger Doubleheader: Washout Today Will Make Doubleheaders Two Straight Days," *The Pittsburgh Press*, September 20, 1938, page 22.
  25. Lester Biederman, "Rain Again Delays Pirates and Dodgers: Three-Day Loaf Aid in Flag Chase," *The Pittsburgh Press*, September 21, 1938, page 16.

Notes — Chapter 11

26. "296 Die in Hurricane: Many Missing, Damage Above 100 Millions," *The Pittsburgh Press*, September 22, 1938, page 1.
27. Sid Feder, "Rain Good Break for Pittsburgh," *The Ottawa Evening Citizen*, September 22, 1938, page 11.
28. Lester Biederman, "Pirates Resume Chase to Clinch Flag: Lee Handley Hurt When Hit by Flying Bat; Brubaker Plays," *The Pittsburgh Press*, September 22, 1938, page 21.
29. "National League Standing on Tuesday Morning," *The Sporting News*, September 29, 1938, page 9.
30. Biederman, "Pirates Resume Chase to Clinch Flag: Lee Handley Hurt When Hit by Flying Bat; Brubaker Plays," page 21.
31. "Pirate Patter: Arky Most Valuable!" *The Pittsburgh Press*, September 23, 1938, page 39.
32. "'I'll Show That McCarthy,' Tobin's War Cry for Series," *The Pittsburgh Press*, September 22, 1938, page 23.
33. *Ibid.*
34. Lester Biederman, "Bucs Home to Put 'Clincher' on Flag: Three Games with Reds Local Finale," *The Pittsburgh Press*, September 23, 1938, page 39.
35. Lester Biederman, "Pirate Patter: Dead Ball!" *The Pittsburgh Press*, September 24, 1938, page 7.
36. *Ibid.*
37. Chester L. Smith, "The Village Smithy: Bucs Will Argue," *The Pittsburgh Press*, September 24, 1938, page 7.
38. "National League Standing on Tuesday Morning," *The Sporting News*, September 29, 1938, page 9.
39. Biederman, "Pirate Patter: Dead Ball!" page 7.
40. Lester Biederman, "Pirate Patter: It's Up to Rosebud," *The Pittsburgh Press*, September 25, 1938, page 5.
41. Lester Biederman, "Bucs Beat Reds, Hold Two-Game Lead: Bauers' Slick Work on Mound Big Aid in 4 to 1 Decision," *The Pittsburgh Press*, September 25, 1938, page 1.
42. *Ibid.*
43. Biederman, "Pirate Patter: It's Up to Rosebud," page 5.
44. *Ibid.*
45. Chilly Doyle, "Pirate Attendance Near 700,000 Mark," *The Sporting News*, September 29, 1938, page 1.
46. "National League Standing on Tuesday Morning," *The Sporting News*, September 29, 1938, page 11.
47. "Have Another Egg, Pie?: C. of C. Hands Pirates Pennant-Schedules 'Victory Breakfast' Monday," *The Pittsburgh Press*, September 27, 1938, page 21.
48. "Traynor Says Bucs Will Triumph: Pittsburgh Club Heads for Chicago; Crucial Series Opens There Today," *The Spartanburg Herald*, September 27, 1938, page 9.
49. *Ibid.*
50. Chester L. Smith, "The Village Smithy: Hartnett Open For Lot of Back-Talk," *The Pittsburgh Press*, September 27, 1938, page 21.
51. Lester Biederman, "Bucs Bank on Klinger to Keep Them in First Place: Rampaging Bruins Count on Bryant," *The Pittsburgh Press*, September 28, 1938, page 24.
52. *Ibid.*
53. Lester Biederman, "Pirate Patter: Baseball-Mad City!" *The Pittsburgh Press*, September 28, 1938, page 25.
54. Claire M. Burcky, "Hard on Nerves!: Mrs. Dreyfuss Keeps Busy to Relieve Strain of Important Series in Bucs' Flag Dash," *The Pittsburgh Press*, September 28, 1938, page 24.
55. *Ibid.*
56. Lester Biederman, "Pirate Patter: Gloom in Clubhouse!" *The Pittsburgh Press*, September 29, 1938, page 29.
57. *Ibid.*, page 27.
58. *Ibid.*, page 29.
59. *Ibid.*
60. *Ibid.*
61. Lester Biederman, "Pirates Pin Pennant Aspirations on Russ Bauers: Hartnett Names Big Bill Lee, His Mound Ace, to Face Bucs," *The Pittsburgh Press*, September 29, 1938, page 27.
62. Lester Biederman, "A Homer ... Then Bedlam: Cubs Carry Hero Gabby to Clubhouse as Thousands Cheer His Dramatic Ninth-Inning Blow," *The Pittsburgh Press*, September 29, 1938, page 27.
63. *Ibid.*
64. Biederman, "Pirates Pin Pennant Aspirations on Bauers: Hartnett Names Bib Bill Lee, His Mound Ace to Face Bucs," page 27.
65. Biederman, "Pirates Patter: Gloom in Clubhouse!" page 27.
66. Clifton Blue Parker, *Big and Little Poison: Paul and Lloyd Waner, Baseball Brothers* (Jefferson, NC: McFarland, 2003), page 203.
67. Dick Farrington, "Fanning with Farrington," *The Sporting News*, October 6, 1938, page 4.
68. Chester L. Smith, "The Village Smithy: How Gabby's Hit Affected Your Neighbor," *The Pittsburgh Press*, September 30, 1938, page 43.
69. Chester L. Smith, "Pity Poor Pa Pitt ...... It's a World Series Hangover ...... And What a Pip!" *The Pittsburgh Press*, September 29, 1938, page 27.
70. "National League Standing on Tuesday Morning," *The Sporting News*, October 6, 1938, page 8.
71. "Pie's Safe!: Benswanger Emphasizes Retention as Manager," *The Pittsburgh Press*, September 30, 1938, page 43.

72. "National League Standing on Tuesday Morning," *The Sporting News,* October 6, 1938, page 8.
73. Lester Biederman, "Pirates Flag Hopes Hinge on Cardinals: Cubs Can Clinch Pennant Today by Sweeping Twin Bill," *The Pittsburgh Press,* October 1, 1938, page 7.
74. "National League Standing on Tuesday Morning," *The Sporting News,* October 6, 1938, page 8.
75. Biederman, "Pirate Flag Hopes Hinge on Cardinals: Cubs Can Clinch Pennant Today by Sweeping Twin Bill," page 7.
76. "Corsairs Split with Reds, Cubs Tie Cards, 7–7: Pirates Still in Running for Flag; Cubs and Cards Play Double Header Today," *The Daily Times,* October 1, 1938, page 7.
77. *Ibid.*
78. Lester Biederman, "Cubs Clinch Pennant as Pirates Lose to Reds: McKechnie, Weaver Gain Vengeance in Reds' 9–6 Win," *The Pittsburgh Press,* October 2, 1938, page 1.
79. "Does Anybody Care? If They Do, Johnny Vander Meer May Oppose Rip Sewell in Reds-Pirates' Final Game of Season Today," *The Pittsburgh Press,* October 2, 1938, page 3.
80. Lester Biederman, "Pirates Hobble Home to Face Trade Talk," *The Pittsburgh Press,* October 3, 1938, page 21.
81. *Ibid.*
82. *Ibid.*
83. "In the Press Box: Flash," *The Sporting News,* October 6, 1938, page 2.

Chapter 12

1. "No Breakfast!" *The Pittsburgh Press,* October 2, 1938, page 1.
2. "Does Anybody Care? If They Do, Johnny Vander Meer May Oppose Rip Sewell in Reds-Pirates' Final Game of Season Today," *The Pittsburgh Press,* October 2, 1938, page 3.
3. "Caught on the Fly," *The Sporting News,* October 13, 1938, page 8.
4. Dick Farrington, "Fanning with Farrington," *The Sporting News,* October 20, 1938, page 4.
5. "Pirate Patter: Thanks, Bill," *The Pittsburgh Press,* October 3, 1938, page 21.
6. "Caught on the Fly," *The Sporting News,* October 13, 1938, page 8.
7. Dick Farrington, "Fanning with Farrington," *The Sporting News,* October 6, 1938, page 4.
8. "Pirate Patter: Thanks, Bill," page 21.
9. Dan Daniel, "Over the Fence: Cubs Get Players' Dope," *The Sporting News,* October 13, 1938, page 4.
10. Dan Daniel, "Over the Fence: That Dull Thud Was the Cubs," *The Sporting News,* October 13, 1938, page 4.
11. "Treat 'Em Kindly!" *The Pittsburgh Press,* October 5, 1938, page 23.
12. Daniel, "Over the Fence: That Dull Thud Was the Cubs," page 4.
13. Clifton Blue Parker, *Big and Little Poison: Paul and Lloyd Waner, Baseball Brothers* (Jefferson, NC: McFarland, 2003), pages 197–198.
14. "Lombardi Wins No. 1 Honors: Cincinnati Catcher Named by Writers as Most Valuable," *The Tuscaloosa News,* November 1, 1938, page 7.
15. "Klinger, Rizzo, on Sporting News' All-Rookie Team," *The Pittsburgh Press,* October 20, 1938, page 27.
16. Chester L. Smith, "The Village Smithy: Pertinent Items Concerning Crowley, Vaughan," *The Pittsburgh Press,* November 2, 1938, page 25.
17. Lester Biederman, "Traynor Signs to Pilot Bucs in 1939: Pirate Manager Given Substantial Salary Increase," *The Pittsburgh Press,* October 18, 1938, page 24.
18. "Pie Traynor Signs to Manage Pittsburgh Pirates in 1939: Presented with Salary Increase as He Is Renamed for Fifth Year," *Meriden Record,* October 19, 1938, page 4.
19. Lester Biederman, "Pie Seeks Slugging Outfielder, Pitchers: Traynor Would Like to Add Catcher," *The Pittsburgh Press,* November 22, 1938, page 27.
20. *Ibid.*
21. Lester Biederman, "Pie Traynor Hopes for at Least One Deal at Meetings," *The Pittsburgh Press,* December 4, 1938, page 3.
22. "Pirates Buy Hutchinson, Is Report: Benswanger Refuses to Affirm Or Deny Paying $50,000 for Star," *The Pittsburgh Press,* December 10, 1938, page 7.
23 "Pirates Talk Trade with Four Club Heads: Detroit Outbids Buccaneers for Fred Hutchinson," *The Pittsburgh Press,* December 13, 1938, page 27.
24. Lester Biederman, "Bucs Get Mueller for Todd-Dickshot: Bees' Second-String Catcher Comes Here in First Shakeup," *The Pittsburgh Press,* December 16, 1938, page 51.
25. Lester Biederman, "Traynor Insists Bucs Got Better of Trade: Pie Claims Mueller Buried Under Lopez' Brilliance," *The Pittsburgh Press,* December 17, 1938, page 7.
26. Chester L. Smith, "The Village Smithy: Pirates Now Have Three Utility Catchers," *The Pittsburgh Press,* December 17, 1938, page 7.
27. "Caught on the Fly," *The Sporting News,* November 24, 1938, page 7.
28. "Flop of Pittsburgh Pirates Big Sports Disappointment of 1938," *Ellensburg Daily Record,* December 19, 1938, page 6.
29. Lester Biederman, "Brown Signs '39 Contract; Young Balks: 'I Think I'm Worth More Than Club Has Offered Me,' Pep Explains," *The Pittsburgh Press,* January 4, 1939, page 19.

30. Lester Biederman, "'Rosebud' Lucas Released by Pirates: Ancient Righthander Moundman Ends Big League Career," *The Pittsburgh Press,* January 16, 1939, page 18.
31. Ibid.
32. Lester Biederman, "Red Lucas' Blast Draws Buc Retort," *The Pittsburgh Press,* February 14, 1939, page 20.
33. Ibid.
34. Ibid.
35. George Kirksey, "MacPhail Blasts Bucs," *The Pittsburgh Press,* February 8, 1939, page 22.
36. Charles J. Doyle, "Buc Take-Off Finds P. Waner Teeing Off: Vet Who Slumped to .280 at Bat Spurns Compromise Offer," *The Sporting News,* March 2, 1939, page 6.
37. Lester Biederman, "Bauers Again Traynor's 'Problem Child': Big Lumberjack's Poor Showing Due to Excess Weight," *The Pittsburgh Press,* March 23, 1939, page 30.
38. Lester Biederman, "Traynor Reads 'Riot Act' to Squad: Bauers Cautioned, Brandt Fired for Rules Violations," *The Pittsburgh Press,* March 24, 1939, page 43.
39. Ibid.
40. Charles J. Doyle, "Traynor 'Sick and Tired of Playboys,' Warns Other Pirates to Toe Line After Firing Brandt: Strong Reprimand Given Russ Bauers," *The Sporting News,* March 30, 1939, page 1.
41. Lester Biederman, "Les Biederman's Scoreboard: Blanton's 'No-Hitter' Peps Bucs," *The Pittsburgh Press,* April 10, 1939, page 22.
42. Lester Biederman, "Handley's Injury Revamps Pirate Plans: Brubaker to Take over at Third Pending 'Jeep's' Recovery," *The Pittsburgh Press,* April 10, 1939, page 22.
43. Ibid.
44. Ibid.
45. Charles J. Doyle, "20 Victories Pinned on Cy Blanton Pins: Buc Right-Hander Rated as '39 Ace if His Legs Stay in Shape," *The Sporting News,* April 20, 1939, page 8.
46. Biederman, "Handleys' Injury Revamps Pirates Plans: Brubaker to Take over at Third pending 'Jeep's' Recovery," page 22.
47. "Handley to Be Sent Home, Return to Lineup Uncertain," *The Pittsburgh Press,* April 16, 1939, page 3.
48. Ibid.
49. Biederman, "Les Biederman's Scoreboard: Blanton's 'No Hitter' Peps Bucs," page 22.
50. Lester Biederman, "Bucs Need Good Course in Psychology ... Pie Traynor Contends," *The Pittsburgh Press,* January 10, 1939, page 21.
51. Lester Biederman, "Blanton to Face Reds Again Tomorrow: Redleg Officials Say Crosley Field Will Be in Shape," *The Pittsburgh Press,* April 21, 1939, page 41.
52. Lester Biederman, "The Score-Board," *The Pittsburgh Press,* May 22, 1939, page 19.
53. Lester Biederman, "Mueller Benched in Move to Check Slump: Corsairs in Last Place After Fifth Consecutive Loss," *The Pittsburgh Press,* April 26, 1939, page 22.
54. "National League Standing on Tuesday Morning," *The Sporting News,* August 10, 1939, page 8.
55. Lester Biederman, "Benswanger Hints Traynor Will Be Kept: Rain Postpones Second Clash of Bucs and Giants," *The Pittsburgh Press,* August 25, 1939, page 33.
56. Lester Biederman, "Dodgers Anxious to Get Rizzo: Rain Postpones Final Series' Game in Brooklyn," *The Pittsburgh Press,* August 29, 1939, page 20.
57. Ibid.
58. "Pirates, Cubs Deny Frisch Pilot Rumor," *The Pittsburgh Press,* September 24, 1939, page 1.
59. "Pirate Prexy Denies Frisch Will Become Pirate Manager: Benswanger Discounts Rumor Former St. Louis Pilot Coming Here-Cold Keeps Bucs-Cubs Idle," *The Pittsburgh Press,* September 26, 1939, page 24.
60. "Pirates, Cubs Deny Frisch Pilot Rumor," page 1.
61. Lester Biederman, "Frankie Frisch Named to Manage Pirates in '40: Ex-Card Pilot Quits Radio to Return as Pittsburgh Leader," *The Sporting News,* September 28, 1939, page 1.

Chapter 13

1. Lester Biederman, "Frankie Frisch Named to Manage Pirates in '40: Ex-Card Pilot Quits Radio to Return as Pittsburgh Leader," *The Sporting News,* September 28, 1939, page 1.
2. Ibid.
3. Lester Biederman, "Old Flash Hopeful of New Dash in Bucs: Promising Youngsters Available for Frisch Next Spring," *The Sporting News,* October 5, 1939, page 6.
4. Lester Biederman, "Bucs Give Frisch Two-Year Contract," *The Pittsburgh Press,* October 1, 1939, page 11.
5. Biederman, "Old Flash Hopeful of New Dash in Bucs: Promising Youngsters Available for Frisch Next Spring," page 6.
6. Lester Biederman, "The Score-Board," *The Pittsburgh Press,* October 1, 1939, page 13.
7. Lester Biederman, "Frisch Takes over Pirates Tomorrow: New Manager to Meet Benswanger, Traynor; Players Go Home," *The Pittsburgh Press,* October 2, 1939, page 25.
8. Lester Biederman, "The Score-Board," *The Pittsburgh Press,* October 1, 1939, page 13.
9. Biederman, "Old Flash Hopeful of New Dash in Bucs: Promising Youngsters Available for Frisch Next Spring," page 6.
10. Lester Biederman, "Frisch Will Demand Daring Baseball, Would Put 'Gas House' Spirit

in Bucs," *The Pittsburgh Press*, October 3, 1939, page 25.

11. Lester Biederman, "Frisch Not to Swap 'to Get New Faces': Believes He Can 'Do Something' with Bucs as They Stand," *The Sporting News*, October 19, 1939, page 1.

12. *Ibid.*

13. "Caught on the Fly," *The Sporting News*, October 19, 1939, page 11.

14. Dick Farrington, "Fanning with Farrington," *The Sporting News*, October 12, 1939, page 4.

15. Lester Biederman, "Pirate Bosses Dazed by Landis' Edict: Decree Seen Aiding Youngster; Hurting Big Farm Systems," *The Pittsburgh Press*, December 9, 1939, page 7.

16. Charles J. Doyle, "New Buc Hurlers Fail to Excite Fans: Pittsburgh Sorry to Lose Tobin, Sees No Gain in Trades," *The Sporting News*, December 14, 1939, page 1.

17. Lester Biederman, "Paul Waner Leaves Great Record Here," *The Pittsburgh Press*, December 6, 1940, page 46.

18. Lester Biederman, "Mace Brown Deal May Be Forerunner to Other Trades," *The Pittsburgh Press*, April 23, 1941, page 29.

19. Lester Biederman, "The Scoreboard: Lloyd Waner Had Hunch He Would Be Traded," *The Pittsburgh Press*, May 8, 1941, page 29.

20. Frederick G. Lieb, *The Pittsburgh Pirates* (1948; reprint Carbondale: Southern Illinois University Press, 2003), page 270.

21. Lester Biederman, "Pirates Trade Vaughan to Brooklyn: Dodgers Give Hamlin, Coscarart, Phelps and Wasdell for Star Shortstop," *The Pittsburgh Press*, December 13, 1941, page 7.

22. *Ibid.*

23. Fred W. Tuerk, "Handley, Bold Buc, Drowns Tough Luck with Pluck: Misfortunes Run All the Way from Beanballs to Auto Running Off Road," *The Sporting News*, February 5, 1942, page 3.

24. Charles J. Doyle, "'Dead Arm' Throws Handley for a Loss: December Auto Accident Found to Have Impaired Wing," *The Sporting News*, March 12, 1942, page 1.

25. *Ibid.*

26. Charles J. Doyle, "Buc War Vets to Start Early: They'll Leave February 11 for Camp at El Centro with Batterymen," *The Sporting News*, December 27, 1945, page 7.

27. Lieb, *The Pittsburgh Pirates*, pages 282–283.

28. *Ibid.*

29. *Ibid.*

30. Lester Biederman, "Blanton's '39 No-Hitter Ruined Career, Led to Traynor's Release," *The Sporting News*, April 14, 1948, page 6.

31. David Finoli and Bill Ranier, *The Pittsburgh Pirates Encyclopedia* (Champaign, IL: Sports Publishing, 2003), page 97.

32. Lieb, *The Pittsburgh Pirates*, page 263.

33. *Ibid.*

Bibliography

Books

Cook, William A. *Waite Hoyt: A Biography of the Yankees' Schoolboy Wonder.* Jefferson, NC: McFarland, 2004.

Finoli, David and Bill Ranier. *The Pittsburgh Pirates Encyclopedia.* Champaign, IL: Sports Publishing, 2003.

Fleitz, David. *More Ghosts in the Gallery: Another Sixteen Little-Known Greats at Cooperstown.* Jefferson, NC: McFarland, 2007.

Honig, Donald. *The October Heroes: Great World Series Games Remembered by the Men Who Played Them.* Lincoln, NE: University of Nebraska Press, 1979.

Lieb, Frederick G. *The Pittsburgh Pirates.* 1948. Reprint, Carbondale: Southern University Press, 2003.

McCollister, John. *Bucs: The Story of the Pittsburgh Pirates.* Lenexa, Kansas: Addax Publishing, 1998.

McNeil, William F. *Gabby Hartnett: The Life and Times of the Cubs' Greatest Catcher.* Jefferson, NC: McFarland, 2004.

Parker, Clifton Blue. *Big and Little Poison: Paul and Lloyd Waner, Baseball Brothers.* Jefferson, NC: McFarland, 2003.

Peterson, Richard, ed. *The Pirates Reader.* Pittsburgh, PA: University of Pittsburgh Press, 2003.

Purdy, Dennis. *The Team By Team Encyclopedia of Major League Baseball.* New York, NY: Workman Publishing, 2006.

Ritter, Lawrence S. *The Glory of Their Times: The Story of the Early Days of Baseball Told by the Men Who Played It.* 1966. Reprint, New York, NY: William Morrow, 1984.

Smizik, Bob. *The Pittsburgh Pirates: An Illustrated History.* New York, NY: Walker, 1990.

Stout, Glenn, *The Cubs: The Complete Story of Chicago Cubs Baseball.* New York, NY: Houghton Mifflin, 2007.

Waldo, Ronald T. *The Battling Bucs of 1925: How the Pittsburgh Pirates Pulled Off the Greatest Comeback in World Series History.* Jefferson, NC: McFarland, 2012.

Newspapers and Magazines

Baseball Magazine
The Bend Bulletin (Bend, Oregon)
Berkeley Daily Gazette
The Calgary Daily Herald
Daily Journal-World (Lawrence, Kansas)
The Daily Times (Beaver and Rochester, Pennsylvania)
The Day (New London, Connecticut)
Ellensburg Daily Record (Ellensburg, Washington)
The Evening Herald (Rock Hill, South Carolina)
The Free Lance-Star (Fredericksburg, Virginia)
The Gazette (Montreal, Quebec)
The Gettysburg Times
Greensburg Daily Tribune (Greensburg, Pennsylvania)
The Independent (St. Petersburg, Florida)
The Kentucky New Era (Hopkinsville, Kentucky)
The Lewiston Daily Sun (Lewiston, Maine)

Lodi News-Sentinel (Lodi, California)
The Ludington Daily News (Ludington, Michigan)
The Meriden Daily Journal (Meriden, Connecticut)
Meriden Record (Meriden, Connecticut)
The Milwaukee Journal
Milwaukee Sentinel
Nashua Telegraph (Nashua, New Hampshire)
The News and Courier (Charleston, South Carolina)
The Ottawa Evening Citizen
The Palm Beach Post
The Pittsburgh Gazette Times
Pittsburgh Post-Gazette
The Pittsburgh Press
The Portsmouth Times (Portsmouth, Ohio)
Prescott Evening Courier (Prescott, Arizona)
The Providence News
Reading Eagle
The Register-Guard (Eugene, Oregon)
Rochester Evening Journal and the Post Express
St. Joseph Gazette (St. Joseph, Missouri)
The St. Joseph News-Press (St. Joseph, Missouri)
St. Petersburg Times
Sarasota Herald
Sarasota Herald-Tribune
Schenectady Gazette
The Spartanburg Herald (Spartanburg, South Carolina)
The Spokesman-Review (Spokane, Washington)
The Sporting News
The Telegraph-Herald and Times Journal (Dubuque, Iowa)
The Toledo News-Bee
The Tuscaloosa News
The Vancouver Sun
The Washington Reporter (Washington, Pennsylvania)
The Windsor Daily Star
Youngstown Vindicator

Websites

books.google.com
news.google.com
www.baseball-almanac.com
www.baseballhall.org
www.baseball-reference,com
www.databaseball.com
www.paperofrecord.com
www.retrosheet.org
www.sabr.org

Index

Numbers in ***bold italics*** indicate pages with photographs

Adams, Babe 8
Adams, Sparky 8
Aldridge, Vic 18
Allen, Johnny 129, 150, 217–218, 229
Anderson, Alf 225, 227
Anderson, Sparky 1
Arke, Robert 110–111
Arnovich, Morris 119
Atlanta Crackers 225
Atwood, Bill 147
Averill, Earl 229

Baker Bowl 104, 119, 147
Balinger, Edward F. "Ed" 29–30, 83
Ballanfant, Lee 100, 174
Barr, George 108, 134–135, 137, 201
Barrow, Ed 28
Bartell, Dick 21–23, 27, 109
Bartlesville Broncos 89
Bauers, Russ 44–47, 63, 65–66, 69–71, ***72***, 73, 75–78, 82, 84, 86, 92, 95, 99, 101–102, 105, 108–109, 112, 115, 117–119, 121–124, 128, 132–134, 136, 141–142, 144, 147, 158, 160, 162–163, 168, 171, 173, 177–178, 181–182, 189–190, 195, 198, 204, 209, 216–217, 219, 228
Bell, Cool Papa 230
Bell, Fern 218
Benswanger, Eleanor Florence (Dreyfuss) 25, 29, 62
Benswanger, William "Bill" 7, 25–26, ***29***, 31–34, 37, 39–42, 47–50, 53, 55–63, 65, 73, 80–81, 84, 91, 93, 98, 102, 107, 109, 111, 117, 131, 149, 157, 185, 189, 194–195, 203–204, 208, 210–211, 214–218, 220–223, 225, 227, 229, 231
Benswanger, William "Billy," Jr. 62
Berger, Wally 41, 49, 109, 111, 181, 190, 194–196, 204–205
Berres, Ray 57, 63, 69, 78, 83–84, 89, 95, 135, 152, 161–163, 167, 178, 219, 225

Biederman, Lester "Les" 61–62, 97, 124, 210, 225
Bigbee, Carson 8
Biggers, John D. 54
Birkofer, Ralph 41
Birmingham Barons 12
Blanton, Cy 35, 37–38, 41, 43, 49, 51, 62–63, 70–71, 75, 78–79, 83, 85, 89, 95, 102, 115, 119, 121, 125, 128, 132–133, 141, 144, 150, 152, 154, 156, 159–160, 162, 168, 172, 177–178, 181, 184, 190–191, 194, 204, 207, 209, 217–218, ***219***, 225, 229–230
Blood, Johnny 159
Bongiovanni, Nino 83
Bordagaray, Frenchy 118, 183
Boston Bees 41, 77, 88, 94–96, 99–101, 112, 114–115, 122–123, 132, 144–145, 148, 151–153, 159, 166, 168, 171, 180, 185, 187–189, 212–213, 221, 224–225
Boston Braves 1–2, 11–12, 22, 88, 225–226
Boston Red Sox 129, 181, 221
Bottomley, Jim 90
Bowman, Joe 43, 63, 70, 76, 78, 85, 92–93, 102, 112, 132, 149, 152, 154, ***155***, 160, 171, 178, 187–188, 207, 227
Brabson, Col. Fay W. 181
Brack, Gil "Gibby" 92, 121, 143, 147
Branca, Ralph 2
Brandt, Ed 41, 63, 70, 78, 85, 92, 95, 112, 118, 135, 142, 145, 149, 156–157, 166–167, 170, 179, 184, 189, 204, 216–217
Brannick, Eddie 69–70
Braves Field 99, 151, 153, 187
Breadon, Sam 90, 183
Bridwell, Bud 128
Brooklyn Dodgers 2, 33, 39, 41, 43, 48–49, 53, 55, 61, 77, 84, 91–93, 101–102, 112, 117, 121–123, 127, 136–138, 141, 149–151, 154, 169, 171–172, 190–192, 194, 220, 225, 227
Brotzman, W.S. 81–82
Brown, Jimmy 132

259

Brown, Joe E. 69
Brown, Jumbo 118, 139
Brown, Mace 3, 37–38, 63, 66, 75, 78, 80–81, 84–85, 89, 94–95, 98, 100, 102, 104, 115–116, 118–119, 122, 125, 127–132, 134–136, 139, 142–143, 147, 149, *150*, 153, 158–161, 166–168, 182, 187, 192, 194, 201–205, 207, 209, 213, 218, 225, 230
Brown, Ray 230
Browne, Earl 43
Brubaker, Bill 38, 41, 59–60, 62, 65, 74, 78–79, 82–86, 88–89, 94–96, 98, 110, 112, 143, 146, 156–157, 161–162, 166–167, 169–171, 178, 192, 207, 225
Brubaker, Lloyd Robert 110
Bryant, Clay 49, 99, 179, 198, 200, 209
Buffalo Bisons 53, 57
Burcky, Claire M. 199
Burns, Ed 78
Bush, Donie 8, 11, 16, 20–21, 31, 134
Bush, Guy 34–35
Butcher, Max 122, 168–169

Camilli, Dolph 92, 136–137, 149, 151
Carey, Max 8
Castleman, Slick 40
Cavarretta, Phil 98, 164, 201
Chadwick, George 17
Chicago Cubs 1–2, 13, 18, 21, 28, 30, 34–35, 48–51, 59, 61, 66–67, 69, 74–75, 77–78, 84–85, 98–99, 101, 104–106, 108, 116, 118, 130, 134–137, 143–144, 148, 151, 159–161, 163–164, 167, 170, 172, 179, 183, 185–186, 189–192, 194–196, 198–206, 208–211, 213, 216, 218, 220, 230–231
Chicago Mills 46
Chicago White Sox 1, 17, 42, 50–51, 66, 73–75, 83
Chiozza, Lou 49, 109, 111
Cincinnati Reds 2, 8, 31, 34, 45, 48, 61, 77, 81–83, 86, 88–91, 101, 118, 122–126, 128, 161–162, 164, 166, 170, 179–181, 183–184, 189, 191–192, 194–196, 204–206, 210–211, 216, 218, 223, 225, 230
Clark, Sen. Bennett 79
Clark, Cap 147
Clarke, Fred 8, 75, 90–91, 138, 185
Clemensen, Bill 63
Cleveland Indians 69, 164, 217–218, 229
Cobb, Bernie 40, 48
Cobb, Ty 5, 17, 110
Coffman, Dick 156, 172
Cohen, Porky 155–156, 199, 224
Collier, Lawrence 71
Collins, Rip 49, 200–201
Columbia Comers 17
Columbus Red Birds 48, 69, 80, 90–91

Combs, Earle 9–10
Comorosky, Adam 28, 31
Cooke, Dusty 82
Cooney, Johnny 95, 153, 188
Cooper, Wilbur 128
Corpus Christi Seahawks 89
Coscarart, Pete 227
Cox, Billy 227
Craft, Harry 83, 88, 181, 194
Cronin, Joe 129
Crosby, Harry "Bing" 229
Crosetti, Frankie 6
Crosley Field 128–130, 150–151, 180, 205, 218
Cuccinello, Tony 91, 110, 188–189
Cuyler, Hazen "Kiki" 18, 112, 121
Cycler Park 157

Dallas Steers 182
Daniel, Dan 175, 177
Danning, Harry 104, 174
Davis, Curt 78
Davis, Peaches 83, 86, 162
Davis, Ralph 42
Davis, Spud 119
Dean, Dizzy 34, 40–41, 48, 70, 77–78, 148–149, 160, 163, 198–199, 213
Dean, Paul "Daffy" 70, 182–183
Decker, Dr. H.R. 22
Demaree, Frank 49, 61, 101, 160
Derringer, Paul 48, 61, 180, 198, 204
DeStio, Dr. D.S. 80, 84
Detroit Tigers 1, 8, 12, 17, 129, 212, 224
Devine, Joe 43
Dickey, Bill 6, 129
Dickmann, Mayor Bernard F. 79
Dickshot, Johnny 44, 78, 84–86, 95–96, 98, 105, 109, 111, 117, 121, 146, 162, 169, 190–191, 212, 215
Dickson, Murry 229
DiMaggio, Joe 5–6, 67, 91, 129, 131
DiMaggio, Vince 144, 153, 166, 168, 188, 225
Dolan, Cozy 13
Doyle, Charles "Chilly" 28, 48, 63, 134, 138, 206
Doyle, Jack 131, 181
Doyle, Margaret 63
Dreyfuss, Barney 8, 10–14, 17–30, 42, 57, 112, 179, 189, 222, 224, 229
Dreyfuss, Carolyn (Wolf) 29
Dreyfuss, Florence (Wolf) 29–30, 62, 179, 199–200, 222, 228–229
Dreyfuss, Samuel "Sam" 21–22, 24, 26
Dugan, Joe 6–7, 9, 12
Duke, Marvin 53, 58, 63, 65, 70, 78, 99
Durocher, Leo 91, 129, 220
Dykes, Jimmy 74–75

Index

Ebbets Field 117, 121, 149, 191
Elliott, Bob 220, 224–225
Elmira Red Wings 90
English, Woody 91
Ens, Jewel 21–22, 27–28, 48, 63, 76, 108, 128, 134, 137, 156, 190, 201–202, 212, 224
Errickson, Dick 166
Essick, Vinegar Bill 27–28
Exposition Park 138, 200

Feder, Sid 88, 106, 118, 191
Feller, Bob 130
Fette, Lou 95, 114, 144, 166
Fitzsimmons, Freddie 137, 141, 171
Fletcher, Elbie 99, 144, 153, 166, 188–189, 220
Fogarty, Jack 116
Forbes Field 2, 8, 10, 33, 35, 55, 82–85, 91–95, 97, 104, 108, 110, 112, 115–116, 123–124, 126–128, 131–132, 136–142, 144–145, 149, 156, 158–160, 162, 165–166, 169, 171, 173–175, 177–179, 190–191, 194, 196, 200, 203, 207, 223–224, 229
Forrest, Steve 115
Foxx, Jimmy 129, 131
French, Larry 27, 30–31, 33–34, 67, 85, 98, 108, 135
Frick, Ford 8–9, 123, 137, 141, 173, 180, 184, 201, 208, 231
Frisch, Frankie 80–81, 127–128, 183, 221–225, 227–228

Galan, Augie 159, 161
Galbreath, John W. 229
Galveston Buccaneers 89
Garms, Debs 99, 153
Gee, Johnny 220, 224, 228
Gehrig, Lou 5–10, 16, 54, 129, 131
Gibson, George 12, 28–33
Gibson, Josh 230
Goetz, Larry 101, 141
Gomez, Lefty 5–6, 70
Gonzalez, Mike 183
Gooch, Johnny 9, 46, 63, 66, 207, 224
Goodman, Ival 87, 130, 181
Grace, Earl 37
Greenberg, Hank 5
Griggs, Art 27
Grimes, Burleigh 18, 21–22, 48–49, 171, 191, 211
Grimm, Charley 2, 35, 48–50, 69–70, 74, 101, 143, 159
Grissom, Lee 161
Grove, Lefty 150
Gumbert, Harry 141, 184
Gustine, Frankie 76, 224

Hack, Stan 99, 106, 129, 135
Hafey, Bud 48
Hallahan, Wild Bill 119, 168–169
Hamlin, Luke 137, 227
Handley, Gene 44–45
Handley, Lee "Jeep" 3, 44, **45**, 47, 54, 62, 65, 74, 78, 89, 91, 94–96, 98, 100, 102–103, 105, 107–110, 112, 114–115, 118–119, 121, 132, **133**, 134–137, 139, 143, 147, 149–153, 156–157, 161–164, 166, 169–171, 173, 178, 182, 184, 188, 191–192, 195–196, 199–200, 207, 209, 212, 217–218, 227–229
Handley, Lulu 44–45
Handley, Judge William E. 91
Hartnett, Gabby 2, 69, 104–105, 143, 159, 179, 198–204, 206, 208–209, 213, 225, 230–231
Haslin, Mickey 104
Hassett, Buddy 91–92, 112, 136, 149
Hazleton Mountaineers 46
Heintzelman, Kenneth "Ken" 40, 62–63, 78, 228
Henshaw, Roy 127–128, 158, 178
Herman, Babe 34
Herman, Billy 129, 199
Hershberger, Willard 27–28
Heydler, John 25
Hildebrand, Oral 227
Hinchman, Bill 63, 128
Hollingsworth, Al 88, 119, 148, 170, 190
Hope, Bob 69
Horner, Gov. Henry 79
Hornsby, Rogers 5, 18, 39
Houston Buffaloes 90
Howley, Dan 31
Hoyt, Waite 31, 34, 43, 51–56, 59
Hubbell, Carl 6, 70, 140, 156, 170, 173, 175, 177, 184
Hudson, Johnny 91–92
Huggins, Miller 8–10, 16
Hutchinson, Fred 212
Hutchinson, Ira 101
Hutchinson Larks 50
Hutchinson Wheat Shockers 89
Huxman, Gov. Walter A. 75
Hyland, Dr. Robert F. 71, 73, 76

James, Bill 17
Jennings, Hughie 12
Jensen, Forrest "Woody" 26–27, 34, 37, 40, 49, 56, **57**, 58–60, 65, 78, 85–86, 89, 95, 117–118, 140, 143, 145–146, 154, 170–171, 173, 187, 199, 219
Jersey City Giants 228
Johnson, Bob 131
Johnson, Sylvester "Syl" 119, 148

Index

Johnson, Tom 229
Johnson, Walter 8
Joiner, Roy 34–35
Jones, Percy 22
Jordan, Buck 147
Jorgensen, Dr. Charles A. 63, 71, 104, 160–161, 228
Jurges, Billy 34–35, 48–49, 61, 200

Kampouris, Alex 111
Kansas City Blues 12–13, 30, 37, 130
Kehr, Jimmie 96–97
Kelly, Mike 224
Kiernan, John 231
Kimball, Newell 49
Kiner, Ralph 3
Klein, Chuck 39, 117–118, 147–148, 169
Klem, Bill 164, 174, 201
Klinger, Bob 3, 47–48, 53, 58, 63, 66–67, 70, 78, 80–81, 85, 89, 96, 100, 102, 110, 114, 116, 118, 121, 126–127, 132, 135, 139, 142, 144, 148, 153–154, 159, 161, 163, 166–168, 175, *176*, 180, 184, 188–189, 192, 198, 200–202, 209–210, 228
Knoxville Smokies 46, 50
Koenig, Mark 10
Koy, Ernie 92, 112, 121
Kremer, Remy 215

La Feria Nighthawks 89
LaMaster, Wayne 119
Landis, Commissioner Kenesaw 13, 45–46, 99, 131, 230
Lanning, Johnny 122, 151, 166, 224
Lavagetto, Cookie 34–35, 40–41, 93, 112, 149, 151, 171
Lazzeri, Tony 8–9, 84, 91
Lee, Bill 84, 99, 105, 159, 179, 198–199, 201, 203–204, 209–210
Leiber, Hank 40, 49, 101, 109, 139
Leonard, Buck 230
Lesser, Sol 54
Levy, Lenny 127
Lightner, Pete 59
Lindstrom, Fred 31, 34
Lipscomb, Andy 127, 146, 181
Lobert, John "Hans" 35, 37
Logan, Bob 84
Lohrman, Bill 139
Lombardi, Ernesto "Ernie" 91, 129–130, 181, 192, 194, 196, 204, 210
Lopez, Al 189, 213, 225
Los Angeles Angels 66
Louisville Colonels 57
Lucas, Red "Old Rosebud" 31, 38, 49, 63, 70, 78, 82, 92, 95, 98, 101, 108, 112, 151, 154, 163, 168, 173–174, 179, 181, 190, 196, *197*, 205, 214–215
Luque, Dolf 184

MacFayden, Danny 144, 153, 224
Mackey, Leo 128
Mackrell, Joseph N. 33
Macon, Max 133, 178
MacPhail, Larry 61, 102, 216
Magerkurth, George 117, 135, 182
Mancuso, Gus 47, 49, 62, 140, 154, 157
Manush, Heinie 154, 172, 209, 218–219
Maranville, Rabbit 12–13
Marks, Dr. W.L. 22
Marshall, Judge Elder W. 149
Martin, Pepper 81, 115
Martin, Stu 108, 158
Mathewson, Christy 5, 35
Mauch, Gene 2
McCarey, Caleb "Socko" 158–159, 199, 224
McCarthy, Joe 6, 129, 175, 192, 194, 208
McCormick, Frank "Moose" 83, 130, 181
McCreery, Tom 128
McGee, Bill 126
McGraw, John 9, 13, 138
McKechnie, Bill 7–8, 12, 14, 18, 83, 86, 88, 123, 194, 205
McKeesport Tubers 93
McKinney, Frank 229
Meadows, Lee 10
Medwick, Joe "Ducky" 5, 48, 127, 134, 158
Meine, Heinie 27
Melton, Cliff 44, 70, 94, 109, 139, 153, 173, 174
Meusel, Bob 9–10
Miljus, Johnny 9
Miller, Dots 17
Mize, John Robert "Johnny" 86, 109, 162, 210
Mize, Johnny 127
Monahan, Kasper 203
Montreal Royals 46, 53, 58, 99
Moore, Gene 100
Moore, Jo-Jo 109
Moore, Terry 158, 178
Mueller, Emmett 147
Mueller, Ray 100, 212–213, 215, 219
Mulcahy, Hugh 119, 147
Mulvey, James 48–49
Mungo, Van Lingle 48–50, 53, 55–56, 61
Murphy, Gov. Frank 75
Murphy, Robert 228
Muskogee Chiefs 89
Myatt, George 174, 178
Myers, Billy 48, 195, 204

New York Giants 1–2, 6, 8, 12–14, 18–19, 31–33, 38–41, 43–44, 47, 49, 56, 62, 69–70, 77–78, 87, 93–94, 98, 101–102, 104, 106, 108–111, 116–118, 122–123, 125–126, 128, 131–132, 134, 136–141, 144–145, 147–150, 152–157, 159, 162–165, 167, 170–175, 177–178, 180, 183–187, 189, 202, 208
New York Yankees 1–2, 6–12, 16–17, 27–28, 40, 43, 50, 54–55, 70, 131, 164, 175, 177, 181, 192, 194–195, 205–209, 231
Newark Bears 192, 194
Nirella, Danny 82
Nugent, Gerry 102, 117–118

Oakland Oaks 43, 51, 194
O'Brien, Pat 69
O'Connell, Jimmy 13
O'Doul, Lefty 67
Osborn, Bob 30
Ott, Mel 5, 56, 94, 129, 139, 141, 156–157, 185

Padden, Tom 37, 40, 48
Page, Vance 200–201
Paige, Satchel 230
Parker, Dan 52, 186
Parker, Tiny 117
Paschal, Ben 10
Passeau, Claude 37, 143
Pearson, Monte 6
Pennock, Herb 9–10
Perris Hill Ball Park 64
Phelps, Babe 122, 227
Philadelphia Athletics 1
Philadelphia Phillies 2, 12–13, 23, 27, 35, 37, 39, 43, 46, 74, 77, 96–97, 102, 104, 115–119, 121, 141–144, 147–148, 155, 168–171, 185–186, 189–190, 192, 194, 199, 206, 220, 228, 230
Phillips, Eddie 30
Phillips 66 Oilers 73
Piet, Tony 31
Pinelli, Babe 167
Pipgras, George 9
Pittsburgh Panthers 41
Pittsburgh Pirates 1–3, 7–14, 16–23, 25–35, 37–53, 55–112, 114–119, 121–128, 130–175, 177–192, 194–196, 198–231
Polo Grounds 2, 6, 56, 102, 117–118, 151, 153–156, 183–185, 187
Portsmouth Truckers 12
Powell, Dick 69
Pressnell, Tot 91, 112, 122, 171

Quinn, Bob 110

Reagan, Bob 159
Reardon, Beans 86
Reynolds, Carl 200–201
Rhyne, Hal 17
Rice Owls 213
Richards, Preston 40
Richardson, Nolen 195
Rickey, Branch 40, 90, 110, 118
Riggs, Lew 181, 196
Ring, Jimmy 12
Ripple, Jimmy 117, 139
Rizzo, Johnny 3, 48, 57, 59, 61–62, 65–67, 69, 74–75, 78–85, 89–92, 94, 98–100, 102–105, 107–109, 115–119, 121–122, 124–128, 132–137, 141, *142*, 143, 145, 147, 149–153, 156–157, 160–162, 164, 167–170, 172–175, 178–185, 187, 194–196, 200–202, 204–207, 209–210, 214, 219–220, 224–225
Rochester Red Wings 90
Roosevelt, Pres. Franklin Delano 5–6, 41, 54
Root, Charlie 98, 201
Rosen, Goody 121
Ruether, Dutch 8–9
Ruffing, Red 70
Ruppert, Jacob 6–7, 195
Ruth, Babe 5–8, 10, 16–17, 56, 138

Sacramento Salons 47, 51, 53, 58
St. Joseph Saints 130
St. Louis Browns 39
St. Louis Cardinals 2, 8, 18, 27, 33–34, 40, 48, 50, 70, 75, 77–81, 86, 88, 90, 108–109, 114, 117–118, 126–127, 130–134, 153, 158–159, 162, 170, 177–183, 196, 198, 204–205, 211, 224–225, 229
St. Paul Saints 227
Salvo, Manuel 177
Sand, Heinie 13
San Diego Padres 1, 177
San Francisco Seals 17, 23, 51, 67
Savannah Indians 50
Scharein, George 143, 147, 170
Schmeling, Max 213
Schoonmaker, Judge F.B. 149, 157–158
Schott, Gene 180
Schulte, Fred 44
Schultz, Joe, Jr. 224
Schultz, Joe, Sr. 50, 128, 208, 212, 223
Schumacher, Hal 41, 49, 94, 170, 184
Scott, Pete 18
Scully, Mayor Cornelius D. 82
Sears, Ziggy 163–164, 173–174, 180
Seattle Rainiers 212
Seeds, Bob 139
Sewell, Luke 74–75

Index

Sewell, Truett "Rip" 53, 58, 63, 70, 78, 86, 91, 96, 100, 112, 123, 132, 142, 146, 207, 228
Shawkey, Bob 9–10
Shawnee Park 75
Shawnee Robins 47
Shea, Merv 137
Shibe Park 147–148, 190, 194
Shocker, Urban 9
Shoffner, Milt 99
Shoun, Clyde 78
Sick, Emil 212
Simmons, Al 90
Sivess, Pete 119, 143
Slaughter, Enos 80–81, 86, 90, 127, 158
Smith, Al 116, 143, 148, 169
Smith, Chester L. 54–55, 58, 77–78, 81, 177
Spencer, Roy 91–92
Spink, J.G. Taylor 131
Sportsman's Park 79, 132, 181–182, 204
Stainback, Tuck 78
Stallings, George 11
Stark, Dolly 201
Stengel, Casey 39, 95
Strincevich, Nick 225–226
Stripp, Joe 153, 189
Suhr, Gus 23, 27, 33–34, 37–38, 41, 44, 54, 60–61, 65, 67, 76, 78–79, 82, 84, 89, 93–95, 98, 100–102, 104–105, 107–109, 112, 114–117, 119, *120*, 121, 124–127, *133*, 134–137, 143–145, 148–149, 156, 161, 163, 168, 171–172, 174, 178, 182, 188–189, 195, 199–200, 204, 207, 209, 220, 231
Sutherland, Jock 41
Swift, Bill 30–31, 35, 37–38, 48–49, 60–61, 63, 70, 75, 78, 85, 99, 102, 112, 115–116, 118–119, 122, 124, 128, 149, 151, 153, 161–163, 178, 181, 184, 187, 196, 201, 204, 207, 224
Swift, Bill Jr. 124
Swigart, Oad 224
Syracuse Chiefs 225, 230

Tamulis, Vito 121, 171
Terry, Bill 6, 33, 38–39, 56, 62, 77, 87, 93, 98, 101–102, 108–112, 116, 123, 126, 128–129, 132, 139, 144, 156, 159, 170–172, 174–175, 177, 184, 208, 212
Thevenow, Tommy 23, 27, 30–31, 62, 65, 78, 146, 160, 171, 180, 204
Thomson, Bobby 2
Tobin, Jim 43, 47, 63, 67, 69–70, 75, 77–78, 80, 83–84, 86, 91, 96, 101–102, 104, 115, 117–119, 122, 124, 127, 132–133, 135, 137, 140–141, 144, 148, 151, 154, 156–157, 159, 162, 164–165, 172, 179, 191–192, *193*, 194, 198, 204–205, 207, 209, 224
Todd, Al 37–38, 44, 64–65, 73, 78–80, 82–84, 88, 95, 98, 100, 102, 105, 107, 112, 117–118, 121, 125–126, 133–137, 140, 143, 146–147, 150–152, 156, 161, 163, 167, 171–172, 174, 178, 181–182, 185, 188–190, 192, 194–196, 199–200, 209, 212–213, *214*, 215
Toronto Maple Leafs 45, 154, 172, 228
Traynor, Eva L. (Helmer) 26
Traynor, Harold "Pie" 2–3, 7, 10–14, *15*, 16, 18, 21–23, 26–27, 30–35, 37–44, 46–48, 50, 53–56, 58–59, 61–62, 64–86, 88–91, 93–102, 104–105, 107–112, 114–119, 121–128, 130, 132, 134–135, 137, 139–141, 143–147, 151–152, 154, 156–164, 166–175, 177–192, 195–196, 198–202, 204–205, 207–213, 215–223, 225, 229–230
Trosky, Hal 69
Tuber Field 93
Tulsa Oilers 28, 30, 130
Turner, Jim 100, 114, 144

Vander Meer, Johnny 123, 130, 150, 181, 195
Van Robays, Maurice 220, 224–225
Vaughan, Floyd "Arky" 3, 27–28, 30–31, 33, 35, *36*, 37–40, 44, 46, 48–49, 51, 54, 59–62, 65–68, 71, 73–76, 78–81, 84–86, 89, 91–92, 94, 98, 100–102, 104–105, 107–108, 110–111, 114, 117–118, 121, 123–129, 132, *133*, 134–136, 142–144, 147, 149, 161–162, 164, 167–168, 172, 177–182, 187, 192, 195–196, 198–200, 204, 207, 209–212, 227
Vitt, Oscar 17
Vogel, Otto 130

Wagner, Honus 5, 9, 14, 33, 35, 46, 68, 102, 128, 146, 207, 215, 217, 224
Wagner, Dr. J. Huber 94
Walker, Mayor Jimmy 49
Walters, Bucky 104, 115–116, 125, 194, 205
Waner, Lloyd 3, 11, 16–23, 27–28, 30–31, 33–34, 37–38, 44, 47, 56, 60–61, 67–68, 75, 78–80, 84, 86, 92, 94–96, 98–100, 102, *103*, 104–105, 107, 110, 114–115, 117–119, 121, 123, 124–129, 132, 136–137, 139, 146, 148, 150, 152, 156, 158, 160, 162, 167, 171–173, 175, 178, 180, 182, 185, 188, 190–192, 195–196, 200–201, 204, 207, 209, 225, *226*, 231
Waner, Ora Lee 16
Waner, Paul 3, 11, 16–21, 23, 26–27, 30–32, 34–35, 37–38, 41–44, 47–50, 55–56, 58–61, 67–68, 75, 78–81, 83–84, 86, 89, 92–95, *96*, 97–98, 100–105, 107–108, 110, 112, 114–119, 121–122, 124–125, 132–139,

144–145, 148, 150, 158, 162, 166, 169, 172–175, 180–185, 189–190, 192, 194–196, 200–201, 203, 207, 209–210, 216, 218, 224–225, *226*, 227
Waner, Paul, Jr. 97
Waner, Ralph 16
Warneke, Lon 159
Warren Moose 146
Warstler, Rabbit 115, 188
Wasdell, Jimmy 227
Washington, Chester 230
Washington Huskies 41
Washington Senators 7–8, 13–14, 140
Watters, Sam 7, 26, 30, 32, 42, 48, 58, 111, 191, 212, 229
Weaver, Jim 34, 58, 162, 205
Weiland, Bob 79, 162, 178
Weintraub, Phil 119, 169
Wentz, Lew 75, 199
West, Max 144, 168
White, Whizzer 159
Whitehead, Burgess 110
Whitney, Arthur "Pinky" 74
Wichita Aviators 26, 28

Wilkinson, Bill 17
Williams, Joe 77
Willoughby, Claude 23
Wilson, Jimmy 39, 46, 74, 117–118, 143, 169–171
World War Memorial Field 123
Wright, Glenn 12–13, 16, 18, 21, 27, 67
Wrigley, Phil K. 143
Wrigley Field 34, 98, 163, 196, 198–199, 201, 208–209

Yankee Stadium 6, 9, 175, 187
Young, Cy 5
Young, Floyd "Pep" 3, 35, 49, 62, 65, 76, 78–79, 82–86, 89, 92–93, 100, 102, 105, 107–109, 111–112, *113*, 115–116, 121–122, 126–127, 132, *133*, 134–136, 140, 143, 146–149, 151, 156, 158, 160–162, 164, 168–169, 171–172, 174, 178, 185, 188, 192, 195, 204, 209–210, 212, 217–219, 225, 229
York, Rudy 129

Zachary, Tom 231